T0347497

John Milton
Twentieth-Century Perspectives

General Editor

J. Martin Evans
Stanford University

Routledge
Taylor & Francis Group

Contents of the Collection

Volume 1
The Man and the Author

Volume 2
The Early Poems

Volume 3
Prose

Volume 4
Paradise Lost

Volume 5
Paradise Regained and *Samson Agonistes*

John Milton

Twentieth-Century Perspectives

Volume 4
Paradise Lost

Edited with introductions by

J. Martin Evans
Stanford University

Published in 2003 by
Routledge
270 Madison Avenue,
New York, NY 10016

Published in Great Britain by
Routledge
2 Park Square, Milton Park,
Abingdon, Oxon OX14 4RN
www.routledge.com

Routledge is an imprint of the Taylor & Francis Group.
Copyright © 2003 by Taylor & Francis Books, Inc.

Transferred to digital printing 2010.

Library of Congress Cataloging-in-Publication Data

John Milton : twentieth century perspectives / edited with introductions by J. Martin Evans.
    v. cm.
    Includes bibliographical references.
    Contents: v. 1. The man and the author — v. 2. The early poems — v. 3. Prose — v. 4. Paradise lost — v. 5. Paradise regained and Samson Agonistes.
ISBN 0-415-94046-X (set: alk paper)—ISBN 0-415-94047-8 (vol. 1: alk. paper) — ISBN 0-415-94048-6 (vol. 2: alk. paper) — ISBN 0-415-94049-4 (vol. 3: alk. paper) — ISBN 0-415-94050-8 (vol. 4: alk. paper) — ISBN 0-415-94051-6 (vol. 5: alk. paper)
    1. Milton, John, 1608–1674—Criticism and interpretation. I. Evans, J. Martin (John Martin).
PR3588 .J66 2002
821'.4—dc21   2002006044

ISBN 978-0-415-88519-5 (POD set)
ISBN 978-0-415-94046-7 (set)
ISBN 978-0-415-94047-4 (v. 1)
ISBN 978-0-415-94048-1 (v. 2)
ISBN 978-0-415-94049-8 (v. 3)
ISBN 978-0-415-94050-4 (v. 4)
ISBN 978-0-415-94051-1 (v. 5)

Acknowledgments

I would like to express my gratitude to the Department of English and the Office of the Dean of Humanities and Sciences of Stanford University for making available the resources that permitted me to bring this project to a timely conclusion.

These volumes are dedicated to the more than five hundred students who have studied Milton with me over the past forty years, either as undergraduate or graduate students at Stanford University, or as students in Stanford's Master of Liberal Arts program, or as participants in my Milton seminars for teachers sponsored by the National Endowment for the Humanities.

Contents

Volume Introduction

Arguably the most influential book on *Paradise Lost* to be written during the past fifty years is Stanley Fish's *Surprised by Sin* (1967). Two years before it appeared in print, Fish published what appears as the opening essay of the current volume, in which he lays out the essential principles that were to inform his book—that Milton's aim was "to recreate in the mind of the reader (which is, finally, the poem's scene) the drama of the Fall, to make him fall again exactly as Adam did," and that in order to achieve this end the poet repeatedly persuades us to commit errors and distortions that are then corrected by "an imperious voice which says with no consideration of our feelings, . . . 'you have made a mistake, just as I knew you would.'" In this way, the reader is gradually educated "to an awareness of his position and responsibilities as a fallen man and to a sense of the distance which separates him from the innocence once his," with the result that the entire reading experience becomes "the felt measure of man's loss." For more than twenty years, this view of *Paradise Lost* dominated critical thinking about the poem; in 1990, however, in the second of the essays reprinted here, John Rumrich vigorously challenged Fish's interpretation on the grounds that it transformed the champion of free intellectual enquiry into "a dictatorial teacher" who deliberately lures his charges into error and then berates them for failing to conform to his "authoritative understanding." Moreover, the seventeenth-century writers whose beliefs Fish used to construct that "understanding" were men like Richard Baxter and other relatively conservative Presbyterians, men, in short, who approved of everything that Milton himself despised. According to Rumrich, then, the point of the disparities and contradictions noted by Fish is not to humiliate us but to keep us "off balance and free of entanglements," to inspire in us the Christian equivalent of Keats's "negative capability" so that we can freely pursue "the human struggle for knowledge" in a world of perpetual uncertainty.

After these fundamental arguments about how *Paradise Lost* should be read, the second section takes up the vexed question of the poem's genre and style. As Balachandra Rajan makes clear in the opening essay, the two issues are intricately bound up with each other. Basing his argument on a lucid review of critical responses to Milton's manipulation of the epic genre, Rajan characterizes *Paradise Lost* as a "mixed-genre poem of deep generic uncertainty" that includes not only epic but tragedy and pastoral as well. We are "looking at a poem that is endeavoring to achieve its identity," he suggests, "and which . . . will form itself among contesting generic possibilities." Small wonder, then, that its "style" is so "various."

Not everyone has been as sensitive to the variety of Milton's poetic voices, however. In the opening salvo of what proved to be a long and fiercely fought campaign to dislodge Milton from his position as England's preeminent nondramatic poet, T. S. Eliot claimed in an essay first published in 1936 that Milton's style is "artificial and conventional" and that the author of *Paradise Lost* "writes English like a dead language." When Satan addresses his followers in Book V, for instance, he "is not thinking or conversing, but making a speech carefully prepared for him," a speech in which the words are arranged "for the sake of musical value, not for significance." Milton's poetry, Eliot thus concluded, "could only be an influence for the worse" upon his successors; indeed, he did "damage to the English language from which it has not wholly recovered."

Needless to say, numerous critics soon sprang to Milton's defense, but the most comprehensive and effective appreciation of his style did not appear until 1963 when Christopher Ricks published his definitive analysis of *Milton's Grand Style*, from which the next essay is excerpted. In passage after passage, Ricks showed, Milton's deviations from normal English word order "have a dynamic force of the astonishing kind which one finds almost everywhere in Dickens," the complications of the poem's syntax consistently reinforce or enact the meaning his words express, and Milton "achieves the elevated dignity of his Grand Style" without sacrificing either sense or sensitivity.

In the following articles, Linda Gregerson and Douglas Bush explore two additional features of Milton's epic style, his similes and his allusions. Gregerson's study of the poem's similes takes issue with Fish's observation in *Surprised by Sin* that the similes in *Paradise Lost* are superfluous as "an instrument of perception" because the faithful Christian requires no such assistance in discerning "the unity in diversity." On the contrary, Gregerson insists, although the similes portray knowledge as problematic, "they do not suggest that we throw away the tools we have and wait for grace as for rain." In the fallen world, we can only recognize what we do not know by what we know, and this is precisely the operation that the similes perform. In short, Milton's similes inculcate the "agility of mind" necessary for our pursuit of truth. According to Bush, the recurrent allusions to classical and biblical sources in *Paradise Lost* are very often ironic in the sense that they remind us of the characters' "ignorance of the future and of what is at stake" in the choices they make. To take just one of many possible examples, Adam's confident statement in Book VIII that "[I] approve the best, and follow what I approve" is undercut by the reader's awareness that he is twisting a famous phrase of Ovid's Medea: "video meliora proboque / deteriora sequor." Adam, too, the allusion predicts, will follow the worst, not the best, when the crucial moment comes in Book IX.

The remaining articles in this volume are concerned with the poem's substance rather than its style, with the theological and political ideologies it projects and with the principal characters it portrays. The section on theology opens with Dennis Danielson's detailed study of "Milton's Arminianism and *Paradise Lost.*" Focusing on the poet's representation of Adam and Eve's repentance at the end of Book X and the beginning of Book XI, he argues that Thomas Greene was quite wrong to suggest that Adam and Eve's contrition "occurred only by divine fiat." In fact, the episode illustrates the Arminian doctrine that God's "prevenient grace" restored to Man the free will he enjoyed before the Fall. Milton's portrayal of Adam and Eve's regeneration, Danielson believes, clearly demonstrates "the manner of God's gracious cultivation of the fruits of repentance" while at the same time affirming "both God's sovereign purpose and man's genuine creaturely freedom."

Whereas Milton's Arminian leanings have been widely recognized, his alleged Arianism has been bitterly debated since the late seventeenth century. Besides providing a comprehensive overview of the controversy, John Rumrich's recent contribution to the argument, "Milton's Arianism: why it matters," makes a powerful case for acknowledging the Arianism implicit in *Paradise Lost* and openly embraced in *De Doctrina.* The Son might be God's instrument in the poem, Rumrich argues, but his knowledge and position "derive from the Father and are contingent on the Son's voluntary, and therefore meritorious obedience. . . which entitles him to divine honors and worship, but not to the status of true divinity." In his study of the mortalist heresy in Milton's writings, Gordon Campbell, too, focuses on the relationship between *Paradise Lost* and *De Doctrina.* Adam's acceptance of the heresy in Book X of the epic, Campbell claims, "is nothing more than an attempt to deny the consequences of his fall." His echo of the Son's description of his own death in Book III is intended to warn us "that Adam is being incautiously dogmatic" when he declares that "all of me then shall die." Indeed, only a few lines later, as he approaches repentance, he "casts off the mortalism which had given false security" against the nightmare of a living death.

The doctrine of the *felix culpa*, the subject of the remaining two articles in this section, is not in itself a heresy—indeed, as A. O. Lovejoy showed in a seminal essay published in 1937, the belief that the Fall was in some sense "fortunate" has a long and distinguished history in orthodox Christian theology—but it can lead to some rather startling conclusions. According to Millicent Bell, for example, the notion that Adam and Eve "fell" from a state of original perfection is a "fallacy." In reality, they were fallen from the very beginning, as their narcissistic, intemperate, and lustful behavior in Books IV, V, and VIII demonstrate, so the act of eating the forbidden fruit simply confronted them with their own sinfulness and thus made possible the redemption. The so-called Fall, then, was "only the climax of self-realization reached by humankind already fallen," and as such it was not only necessary but fortunate. Virginia Mollenkott, on the contrary, insists that "contrary to widespread opinion since Lovejoy, Milton does not espouse the doctrine of the Fortunate Fall." Redemption is the remedy, not the result, of Adam and Eve's disobedience, and the idea that their life in the fallen world will be happier than their unfallen life in Eden is flatly contradicted by God's words in Book XI: "Happier had it suffic'd him to have known / Good by itself, and Evil not at all" (88–89).

Thanks partly to the emergence of new historicism and partly to the influence of feminist criticism, the past twenty years have seen a dramatic upsurge of interest in the revolutionary and sexual politics of Milton's epic. In the first article in this next section, Paul Stevens investigates the extent to which *Paradise Lost* "authorizes colonial activity even while it satirizes the abuses of early modern colonialism." Far from being "a poet against empire," as David Quint maintained in *Epic and Empire*, Milton embodied in his description of paradise the mentality "responsible for the building of European colonial empires." Barbara Lewalski, on the other hand, relates the poem to England's domestic politics during the 1650s and 1660s, showing how such features as the ten-book format, the use of blank verse, and the representations of hell, heaven, and Eden all serve to convey the poet's militant ideology by prompting his readers "to think again, and think rightly, about monarchy, tyranny, rebellion, liberty, hierarchy, and republicanism."

The last two essays in this section take up the contentious issue of Milton's sexual politics. In the first, Christine Froula focuses on the autobiographical narratives of Adam and Eve and the poet's invocations of the Muse in order to demonstrate that the repression of female creativity lies at the heart of *Paradise Lost*. Just as Milton trans-sexualizes the source of his inspiration by transforming the female Urania into the male principle that impregnates the vast abyss at the beginning of the creation, so he silences Eve by equating her desire for autonomy with narcissism, thereby turning her into a mere mirror of "patriarchal authority." William Shullenberger's spirited defence of *Paradise Lost* addresses not only Froula's critique but also several other feminist responses to the poem as well, including those of Sandra Gilbert, Marcia Landy, and Jackie DiSalvo. Despite the explicit declarations of female subordination throughout the text, he argues, "we need to proceed very carefully in assessing Milton's description of gender differences." And if we do, we will discover that Adam's "contemplation" and "valor" and Eve's "softness" and "sweet attractive grace" are "essentially inadequate in the absence of the other." In practice, if not in theory, the relationship between the two characters is reciprocal and interdependent rather than hierarchical. The dynamics of sexual identity in the poem, Shullenberger suggests, "are considerably more complicated than feminist criticism has yet acknowledged."

The final section of this volume contains a series of essays on the poem's major characters: Satan, Sin, Death, the Father, the Son, Adam, Eve, and the poet himself. Of all these characters none has provoked more controversy than the first. Is Satan a hero, as John Dryden, Percy Bysshe Shelley, Robert Lowell, and many others have declared, or is he a fool, as C. S. Lewis proposed? After a brief review of several important contributions to the debate, Balachandra Rajan develops a skillfully nuanced account of the complex impression the Devil makes on the reader during the course of the narrative. The traditional alternatives "hero" or "fool" are entirely inadequate to describe him, Rajan asserts. The heroic figure we encounter at the beginning of the poem taken together with his inexorable decline in Books IV through X is a sermon on both the weakness and the strength of evil. Milton's Satan is "a poetic synthesis" of two apparently incompatible phenomena. William Riggs takes the argument a step further by claiming that Milton was acutely sensitive "to both the appeals and the dangers of Satanism" and "knew exactly to what extent he was 'of the Devil's party'" as William Blake had put it. Indeed, Milton actually anticipated the Satanist response "by repeatedly asking us to compare his portrait of the poet with his portrait of Satan." The remarkable analogies between the two figures, Riggs goes on to show, are intended "to demonstrate an undeluded recognition of the satanic potential of his poetic act" while at the same time insisting on the crucial distinction between true and false heroism, divine and diabolic inspiration. Stephen Fallon's essay investigates the nature of the remaining two members of the infernal trinity, Sin and Death. Its springboard is Dr. Samuel Johnson's famous objection to the introduction of allegorical figures into a literal narrative. Basing his argument on Milton's Augustinian ontology of evil, according to which evil is a privation of good, the genealogy of allegory from Plato to Descartes, and a close reading of Books II, III, and X, Fallon shows that the poet's treatment of Satan's progeny not only illustrates his doctrinal beliefs but comments on the fate of allegory itself.

Milton's God has attracted far less commentary than his Devil, and most of that commentary has been negative. By making him a character in the story, critics complain, Milton traps him in chronology and thus gives the impression that the Fall is foreordained; by making him speak in his own defence, Milton implies that the Almighty feels somewhat uneasy about the degree to which he is or is not responsible for the Fall; and by making him demand his pound of flesh from fallen humanity, Milton turns him into a bloodthirsty Shylock. Gary Hamilton's article counters these objections by suggesting that "Milton reflects in God's defense of himself the restlessness of an age that had come to have doubts about the goodness of its Calvinist God." The presiding deity of *Paradise Lost*, Hamilton argues, is conceived in essentially Arminian terms, and the speeches that Milton puts into God's mouth in Book III are designed to fend off Calvinist teachings concerning divine foreknowledge, divine grace, and the nature of election. "If we can hear in this defense the words of the Divine Teacher, proclaiming truths that needed to be proclaimed, the voice may sound more like the voice of authority which Milton intended it to be."

Finally, in an essay that looks back to Millicent Bell's discussion of the fallacy of the Fall, Thomas Blackburn points out that in the state of innocence Adam and Eve may be sinless but they are not ignorant of the difference between right and wrong. Experientially they live in a world of pure goodness, but conceptually they are well aware of the existence and nature of evil and consequently they are free and responsible moral agents. When they eat the forbidden fruit, however, evil becomes "actualized as part of their direct personal experience," while good becomes a mere conceptual memory. The only knowledge Adam and Eve acquire thereby is of "good lost and evil got" as Milton put it. The Fall, then, is neither a transition from ignorance to enlightenment nor an inevitable consequence of inherent imperfection, as Bell proposed, but a moral degeneration from innocence to guilt. The "felt measure of man's loss" that Fish ascribed to the poem's narrative strategy is thus validated by Milton's account of paradise itself.

John Milton

Volume 4

Paradise Lost

Stanley Fish

The Harassed Reader in
Paradise Lost

I

I WOULD like to suggest something about *Paradise Lost* that is not new except for the literalness with which the point will be made: (1) the poem's centre of reference is its reader who is also its subject; (2) Milton's purpose is to educate the reader to an awareness of his position and responsibilities as a fallen man, and to a sense of the distance which separates him from the innocence once his; (3) Milton's method is to recreate in the mind of the reader (which is, finally, the poem's scene) the drama of the Fall, to make him fall again exactly as Adam did, and with Adam's troubled clarity, that is to say, "not deceived". In a limited sense few would deny the truth of my first two statements; Milton's concern with the ethical imperatives of political and social behavior would hardly allow him to write an epic which did not attempt to give his audience a basis for moral action; but I do not think the third has been accepted in the way that I intend it.

A. J. Waldock, one of many sensitive readers who have confronted the poem since 1940, writes that "*Paradise Lost* is an epic poem of singularly hard and definite outline, expressing itself (or so at least would be our first impressions) with unmistakable clarity and point".[1] In the course of his book, Waldock expands the reservation indicated by his parentheses into a reading which predicates a disparity between Milton's intention and his performance:

> In a sense Milton's central theme denied him the full expression of his deepest interests. It was likely, then, that as his really deep interests could not find outlet in his poem in the right way they might find outlet in the wrong way. And to a certain extent they do; they find vents and safety-valves often in inopportune places. Adam cannot give Milton much scope to express what he really feels about life: but Satan is there, Satan gives him scope. And the result is that the balance is somewhat disturbed; pressures are set up that are at times disquieting, that seem to threaten more than once, indeed, the equilibrium of the poem.[2]

The "unconscious meaning" portion of Waldock's thesis is, I think, as wrong as his description of the reading experience as "disquieting" is right. If we transfer the emphasis from Milton's interests

2

and intentions which are available to us only from a distance, to our responses which are available directly, the disparity between intention and execution becomes a disparity between reader expectation and reading experience; and the resulting "pressures" can be seen as part of an intelligible pattern. In this way we are led to consider our own experience as a part of the poem's subject.

By "hard and definite outline" I take Waldock to mean the sense of continuity and direction evoked by the simultaneous introduction of the epic tradition and Christian myth. The "definiteness" of a genre classification leads the reader to expect a series of formal stimuli—martial encounters, complex similes, an epic voice—to which his response is more or less automatic; the hardness of the Christian myth predetermines his sympathies; the union of the two allows the assumption of a comfortable reading experience in which conveniently labelled protagonists act out rather simple roles in a succession of familiar situations. The reader is prepared to hiss the devil off the stage and applaud the pronouncements of a partisan and somewhat human deity who is not unlike Tasso's "il Padre eterno". But of course this is not the case; no sensitive reading of *Paradise Lost* tallies with these expectations, and it is my contention that Milton ostentatiously calls them up in order to provide his reader with the shock of their disappointment. This is not to say merely that Milton communicates a part of his meaning by a caculated departure from convention; every poet does that; but that Milton consciously wants to worry his reader, to force him to doubt the correctness of his responses, and to bring him to the realization that his inability to read the poem with any confidence in his own perception is its focus.

Milton's programme of reader harassment begins in the opening lines; the reader, however, may not be aware of it until line 84 when Satan speaks for the first time. The speech is a powerful one, moving smoothly from the *exclamatio* of "But O how fall'n" (84) to the regret and apparent logic of "till then who knew/The force of those dire Arms" (93-4), the determination of "courage never to submit or yield" (108) and the grand defiance of "Irreconcilable to our grand Foe,/Who now triumphs, and in th' excess of joy/Sole reigning holds the Tyrrany of Heav'n" (122-24). This is our first view of Satan and the impression given, reinforced by a succession of speeches in Book I, is described by Waldock: "fortitude in adversity, enormous endurance, a certain splendid recklessness, remarkable powers of rising to an occasion, extraordinary qualities of leadership (shown not least in his salutary taunts)".[3] But in each case Milton follows the voice of Satan with a comment which complicates, and according to some, falsifies, our reaction to it:

> So spake th' Apostate Angel, though in pain,
> Vaunting aloud, but rackt with deep despair. (125-26)

3

Waldock's indignation at this authorial intrusion is instructive:

> If one observes what is happening one sees that there is hardly a great speech of Satan's that Milton is not at pains to correct, to damp down and neutralize. He will put some glorious thing in Satan's mouth, then anxious about the effect of it, will pull us gently by the sleeve, saying (for this is what it amounts to): 'Do not be carried away by this fellow: he *sounds* splendid, but take my word for it . . .' Has there been much despair in what we have just been listening to? The speech would almost seem to be incompatible with that. To accept Milton's comment here . . . as if it had a validity equal to that of the speech itself is surely very naive critical procedure . . . in any work of imaginative literature at all it is the demonstration, by the very nature of the case, that has the higher validity; an allegation can possess no comparable authority. Of course they should agree; but if they do not then the demonstration must carry the day. (Pp 77-78.)

There are several assumptions here:

(1) There is a disparity between our response to the speech and the epic voice's evaluation of it.
(2) Ideally, there should be no disparity.
(3) Milton's intention is to correct *his* error.
(4) He wants us to discount the effect of the speech through a kind of mathematical cancellation.
(5) The question of relative authority is purely an aesthetic one. That is, the reader is obliged to harken to the most dramatically persuasive of any conflicting voices.

Of these I can assent only to the first. The comment of the epic voice comes as a shock to the reader who at once realizes that it does not tally with his experience. It is not enough to analyze, as Lewis and others have, the speciousness of Satan's rhetoric. It is the nature of sophistory to lull the reasoning process; logic is a safeguard against a rhetorical effect only after the effect has been noted. The deep distrust, even fear, of verbal manipulation in the seventeenth century is a recognition of the fact that there is no adequate defense against eloquence at the moment of impact. (Thus the insistence in the latter half of the century on the complete absence of rhetoric. The Royal Society, Sprat promises, will "separate the knowledge of Nature from the colours of Rhetorick, the devices of Fancy, or the delightful deceit of Fables.")[1] In other words one can analyze the process of deception only after it is successful. The reader who is stopped short by Milton's rebuke (for so it is) will, perhaps, retrace his steps and note more carefully the inconsistency of a Tyranny that involves an excess of joy, the perversity of "study of revenge, immortal hate" (a line that had slipped past him sandwiched respectably, between will and courage), the sophistry of the transfer of power from the Potent Victor of 95 to the Fate of 116, and the irony, in the larger picture, of "that were *low* indeed" and "in *foresight* more advanc't". The fit reader Milton has in mind would go further and recognize in Satan's finest moment—"And courage never to submit or yield"—an almost literal translation of *Georgic IV*, 84, "usque adeo obnixi non cedere". Virgil's "praise" is for his bees whose heroic posturing is presented in terms that are at least ambiguous:

> ipsi per medias acies insignibus alis
> ingentis animos angusto in pectore versant,
> usque adeo obnixi non cedere, dum gravis aut hos
> aut hos versa fuga victor dare terga subegit.
> hi motus animorum atque haec certamina tanta
> pulveris exigui iactu compressa quiescunt. (82-87)[5]

If we apply these verses to Satan, the line in question mocks him and in the unique time scheme of *Paradise Lost* looks both backward (the Victor has already driven the rebel host to flight) and forward (in terms of the reading experience, the event is yet to come). I believe that all this and more is there, but that the complexities of the passage will be apparent only when the reader has been led to them by the necessity of accounting for the distance between his initial response and the *obiter dictum* of the epic voice. When he is so led, the reader is made aware that Milton is correcting not a mistake of composition, but the weakness all men evince in the face of eloquence. The error is his not Milton's; and when Waldock invokes some unidentified critical principle ("they should agree") he objects to an effect Milton anticipates and desires.

But this is more than a stylistic trick to assure the perception of irony. For, as Waldock points out, this first epic interjection introduces a pattern that is operative throughout. In Books I and II these "correctives" are particularly numerous and, if the word can be used here, tactless. Waldock falsifies his experience of the poem I think, when he characterizes Milton's countermands as gentle; we are not warned ("Do not be carried away by this fellow"), but accused, taunted by an imperious voice which says with no consideration of our feelings, "I know that you *have been* carried away by what you have just heard; you should not have been; you have made a mistake, just as I knew you would"; and we resent this rebuke, not, as Waldock suggests, because our aesthetic sense balks at a clumsy attempt to neutralize an unintentional effect, but because a failing has been exposed in a context that forces us to acknowledge it. We are angry at the epic voice, not for fudging, but for being right, for insisting that we become our own critics. There is little in the human situation more humiliating in both senses of the word, than the public acceptance of a deserved rebuke. Arnold Stein writes, "the formal perspective does not force itself upon Satan's speech, does not label and editorialize the impressive willfulness out of existence; but rather sets up a dramatic conflict between the local context of the immediate utterance and the larger context of which the formal perspective is expression. This conflict marks

5

. . . the tormented relationship between the external boast and the internal despair".[6] Stein's comment is valuable, but it ignores the way the reader is drawn into the poem not as an observer who coolly notes the interaction of patterns (this is the mode of Jonsonian comedy and masque), but as a participant whose mind is the locus of that interaction. Milton insists on this since his concern with the reader is necessarily more direct than it might be in any other poem; and to grant the reader the status of the slightly arrogant perceiver-of-ironies Stein invents would be to deny him the full *benefit* (I use the word deliberately, confident that Milton would approve) of the reading experience. Stein's "dramatic conflict" is there as are his various perspectives, but they are actualized, that is translated into felt meaning, only through the more pervasive drama (between reader and poem) I hope to describe.

The result of such encounters is the adoption of a new way of reading. After I, 125-26 the reader proceeds determined not to be caught out again; but invariably he is. If Satanic pronouncements are now met with a certain caution, if there is a new willingness to search for complexities and ironies beneath simple surfaces, this mental armour is never quite strong enough to resist the insidious attack of verbal power; and always the irritatingly omniscient epic voice is there to point out a deception even as it succeeds. As the poem proceeds and this little drama is repeated, the reader's only gain is an awareness of what is happening to him; he understands that his responses are being controlled and mocked by the same authority, and realizes that while his efforts to free himself from this rhetorical bind are futile, that very futility becomes a way to self-knowledge. *Control* is the important concept here, for my claim is not merely that this pattern is in the poem (it would be difficult to find one that is not), but that Milton (*a*) consciously put it there and (*b*) expected his reader to notice it. Belial's speech in Book II is a case in point. It is the only speech that merits an introductory warning:

> On th' other side up rose
> *Belial*, in act more graceful and humane;
> A fairer person lost not Heav'n; he seem'd
> For dignity compos'd and high exploit:
> But all was false and hollow; though his Tongue
> Dropt Manna, and could make the worse appear
> The better reason to perplex and dash
> Maturest Counsels: for his thoughts were low;
> To vice industrious, but to Nobler deeds
> Timorous and slothful: yet he pleas'd the ear,
> And with persuasive accent thus began.   (II, 108-18)

The intensity of the warning indicates the extent of the danger: Belial's apparent solidity, which is visible, must be contrasted to his hollowness, which is not, the manna of his tongue to the lowness of mind it obscures; and the "yet" in "yet he Pleas'd the ear", more than a final admonition before the reader is to be left to his own resources, is an admission of wonder by the epic voice itself (*yet*, he pleased . . .) and one of the early cracks in its facade of omniscience. Belial's appeal is a skilful union of logical machinery ("*First*, what Revenge?") and rhetorical insinuation. The easy roll of his periods literally cuts through the contortions of Moloch's bluster, and the series of *traductio*-s around the word "worse" are an indirect comment on the "what can be worse" of the "Sceptr'd King's" desperation. The ploys are effective, and since in the attempt to measure the relative merits of the two devils we forget that their entire counsel is baseless, the return of the epic voice yields one more slight shock at the inevitability of our susceptibility:

> Thus *Belial* with words cloth'd in reason's garb
> Counsell'd ignoble ease, and peaceful sloth,
> Not Peace: (226-28)

Waldock complains, "Belial's words are not only 'cloath'd in reason's garb': they *are* reasonable".[7] Belial's words are *not* reasonable, although a single uncritical reading will yield the appearance of reason rather than the reality of his ignoble ease. Again the flaw in the speech is to be located precisely at its strongest point. Belial cries at line 146: "for who would lose,/Though full of pain, this intellectual being,/Those thoughts that wander through Eternity,/To perish rather, swallow'd up and lost/In the wide womb of uncreated night". In other words, do we wish to give up our nature, our sense of identity? The rhetorical question evokes an emphatic "no" from the assembled devils and the reader. Yet at line 215 Belial offers his final argument, the possibility of adapting to their now noxious environment: "Our purer essence then will overcome/Thir noxious vapor, or enur'd not feel,/Or chang'd at length, and to the place conform'd/In temper and in nature, will receive/Familiar the fierce heat, and void of pain". If this is less spectacular than the question posed at 146, it is still a direct answer to that question, Belial *is* willing to lose "this intellectual being". The choice is not, as he suggests, between annihilation and continued existence, but between different kinds of annihilation—Moloch's suicidal thrust at the Almighty or his own gradual surrender of identity, no less suicidal, much less honest. This will be obvious on a second reading. My intention is not to refute Waldock, but to suggest that while his reaction to the epic voice ("they *are* reasonable") is the correct one, Milton expects his reader to go beyond it, to see in the explicitness of the before and after warnings an immediate challenge to his own assessment of the speech.

It is almost a laboratory demonstration, especially since the case is an easy one; Belial's rhetoric calls attention to itself and is thus less dangerous than other lures the reader has met and will continue ιο meet throughout the poem. The whole is reminiscent of Spenser's technique in the *Faerie Queene*, I.9. There the approach to Despair's cave is pointedly detailed and the detail is calculated to repel; the man himself is more terrible than the Blatant Beast or the dragon of I.12, for his ugliness is something we recognize. Spenser's test of his reader is less stringent than Milton's; he makes his warning the experience of this description rather than an abstract statement of disapproval. It is, of course, not enough. Despair's adaptation of Christian rhetoric (guilt, grace) is masterful and the Redcross Knight (along with the reader) allows the impression of one set of appearances (the old man's ugliness) to be effaced by another`(the Circean lure of his rhetoric): "Sleepe after toyle, port after stormie seas,/Ease after warre, death after life does greatly please" (40). Spenser eases us along by making it impossible to assign stanza 42 to either the knight or Despair. At that point the syntactical ambiguity is telling; the dialogue is over, and we have joined them both in a three part unanimity that leads inexorably to the decision of 51:

> At last, resolv'd to worke his finall smart
> He lifted up his hand that backe again did start.

Una's exhortation and accusation—"Come, come away, fraile, feeble, fleshly wight"—is for us as well as her St. George, and we need the reminder that she brings to us from a context *outside* the experience of the poem: "In heavenly mercies has thou not a part?" Without this *deus ex machina* we could not escape; without Milton's "snubs" we could not be jolted out of a perspective that is after all *ours*. The lesson in both poems is that the only defense against verbal manipulation (or appearances) is a commitment that stands above the evidence of things that are seen, and the method of both poems is to lead us beyond our perspective by making us feel its inadequacies and the necessity of accepting something which baldly contradicts it. The result is instruction, and instruction is possible only because the reader is asked to observe, analyze, and *place* his experience, that is to think about it.

II

The wariness these encounters with demonic attraction make us feel is part of a larger pattern in which we are taught the hardest of all lessons, distrust of our own abilities and perceptions. This distrust extends to all the conventional ways of knowing that might enable a reader to locate himself in the world of any poem. The questions we ask of our reading experience are in large part the questions we ask of our day to day experience. Where are we, what are the physical components of our surroundings, what time is it? And while the hard and clear outline of *Paradise Lost* suggests that the answers to these questions are readily available to us, immediate contexts repeatedly tell us that they are not. Consider, for example, the case of Satan's spear. I have seen responsible critics affirm, casually, that Satan's spear is as large as the mast of a ship; the poem of course affirms nothing of the kind, but, more important, it deliberately encourages such an affirmation, at least temporarily:

> His spear, to equal which the tallest Pine
> Hewn on *Norwegian* Hills to be the Mast
> Of some great Ammiral, were but a wand. (I, 292-94)

Throughout *Paradise Lost*, Milton relies on the operation of three truths so obvious that many critics fail to take them into account: (1) the reading experience takes place in time, that is, we necessarily read one word after another; (2) the childish habit of moving the eyes along a page and back again is never really abandoned although in maturity the movement is more mental than physical, and defies measurement; therefore the line as a unit is a resting place even when rhyme is absent; (3) a mind asked to order a succession of rapidly given bits of detail (mental or physical) seizes on the simplest scheme of organization which offers itself. In this simile, the first line supplies that scheme in the overt comparison between the spear and the tallest pine, and the impression given is one of equality. This is not necessarily so, since logically the following lines could assert any number of things about the relationship between the two objects; but because they are objects, offering the mind the convenience of focal points that are concrete, and because they are linked in the reading sequence by an abstract term of relationship (equal), the reader is encouraged to take from the line an image, however faint and wavering, of the two side by side. As he proceeds that image will be reinforced, since Milton demands that he attach to it the information given in 293 and the first half of 294; that is, in order to maintain the control over the text that a long syntactical unit tends to diminish, the reader will accept "hewn on Norwegian hills" as an adjunct of the tallest pine in a very real way. By providing a scene or background (*memoria*) the phrase allows him to strengthen his hold on what now promises to be an increasingly complex statement of relationships. And in the construction of that background the pine frees itself from the hypothetical blur of the first line; it is now real, and through an unavoidable process of association the spear which stood in an undefined relationship to an undefined pine is seen (and I mean the word literally) in a kind of apposition to a conveniently visual pine. (This all happens very quickly in the mind of the reader who does not have time to analyze the cerebreal adjustments forced upon him by the simile.) In short the equation (in size) of the two objects, in 292 only a possibility, is posited by the reader in 292-294 because it simplifies his task; and this movement towards simplification will be encouraged, for Milton's fit reader, by the obvious reference in "to be the Mast/Of some Great Ammiral" to the staff of the Cyclops Polyphemus, identified in the *Aeneid* as a lopped pine[8]

9

and likened in the *Odyssey* to "the mast of some black ship of twenty oars".[9]

The construction of the image and the formulation of the relationship between its components are blocked by the second half of line 294, "were but a wand". This does several things, and I must resort to the mechanical aid of enumeration: (1) in the confusion that follows this rupture of the reading sequence, the reader loses his hold on the visual focal points, and is unable to associate firmly the wand with either of them. The result is the momentary diminution of Satan's spear as well as the pine, although a second, and more wary reading, will correct this; but, corrected, the impression remains (in line 295 a miniature Satan supports himself on a wand-like spear) and in the larger perspective, this aspect of the simile is one of many instances in the poem where Milton's praise of Satan is qualified even as it is bestowed.

(2) The simile illustrates Milton's solution of an apparently insoluble problem. How does a poet provide for his audience a perspective that is beyond the field of its perception? To put the case in terms of *Paradise Lost*, the simile as it functions in other poems will not do here. A simile, especially an epic simile, is an attempt to place persons and/or things, perceived in *a* time and *a* space, in the larger perspective from which their significance must finally be determined. This is possible because the components of the simile have a point of contact—their existence in the larger perspective—which allows the poem to yoke them together without identifying them. Often, part of the statement a simile makes concerns the relationship between the components and the larger perspective in addition to the more obvious relationship between the components themselves; poets suggest this perspective with words like smaller and greater. Thus a trapped hero is at once like and unlike a trapped wolf, and the difference involves their respective positions in a hierarchy that includes more than the physical comparison. A complex and "tight" simile then can be an almost scientific description of a bit of the world in which for "the immediate relations of the crude data of experience" are substituted "more refined logical entities, such as relations between relations, or classes of relations, or classes of classes of relations".[10] In Milton's poem, however, the components of a simile often do not have a point of contact that makes their comparison possible in a meaningful (i.e., relatable or comprehensible) way. A man exists and a wolf exists and if categories are enlarged sufficiently it can be said without distortion that they exist on a comparable level; a man exists and Satan (or God) exists, but any statement that considers their respective existences from a human perspective, however inclusive, is necessarily reductive, and is liable to falsify rather than clarify; and of course the human perspective is the only one available. To return to Book I, had Milton asserted the identity of Satan's spear and the

tallest pine, he would not only have sacrificed the awe that attends incomprehensibility; he would also have lied, since clearly the personae of his extra-terestrial drama are not confined within the limitations of our time and space. On the other hand, had he said that the spear is larger than one can imagine, he would have sacrificed the concreteness so necessary to the formulation of an effective image. What he does instead is grant the reader the convenience of concreteness (indeed fill his mind with it) and then tell him that what he sees is not what is there ("there" is never located). The result is almost a feat of prestidigation: for the rhetorical negation of the scene so painstakingly constructed does not erase it; we are relieved of the necessity of believing the image true, but permitted to retain the solidity it offers our straining imaginations. Paradoxically, our awareness of the inadequacy of what is described and what we can apprehend provides, if only negatively, a sense of what cannot be described and what we cannot apprehend. Thus Milton is able to suggest a reality beyond this one by forcing us to feel, dramatically, its unavailability.

(3) Finally, the experience of reading the simile tells us a great deal about ourselves. How large is Satan's spear? The answer is, we don't know, although it is important that for a moment we think we do. Of course, one can construct, as James Whaler does, a statement of relative magnitudes (Spear is to pine as pine is to wand)[11] but while this may be logical, it is not encouraged by the logic of the reading experience which says to us: If one were to compare Satan's spear with the tallest pine the comparison would be inadequate. I submit that any attempt either to search out masts of Norwegian ships or determine the mean length of wands is irrelevant, however attractive the prospect to a certain kind of mind.

Another instance may make the case clearer. In Book III, Satan lands on the Sun:

> There lands the Fiend, a spot like which perhaps
> Astronomer in the Sun's lucent Orb
> Through his glaz'd optic Tube yet never saw. (588-90)

Again in the first line two focal points (spot and fiend) are offered the reader who sets them side by side in his mind; again the detail of the next one and one half lines is attached to the image, and a scene is formed, strengthening the implied equality of spot and fiend; indeed the physicality of the impression is so persuasive that the reader is led to join the astronomer and looks with him through a reassuringly specific telescope ("glaz'd optic Tube") to see—nothing at all ("yet never saw"). In both similes the reader is encouraged to assume that his perceptions extend to the object the poet would present, only to be informed that he is in error; and both similes are constructed in such a way that the error must be made before it can be acknowledged by a surprised reader. (The parallel to the rhetorical drama between

11

demonic attraction and authorial rebuke should be obvious.) For, however many times the simile is reread, the "yet never saw" is unexpected. The mind can not perform two operations at the same time, and one can either cling to the imminence of the disclaimer and repeat, silently, " 'yet never saw' is coming, 'yet never saw' is coming", or yield to the demands of the image and attend to its construction; and since the choice is really no choice at all—after each reading the negative is only a memory and cannot complete with the immediacy of the sensory evocation—the tail-like half line always surprises.

Of course Milton wants the reader to pull himself up and reread, for this provides a controlled framework within which he is able to realize the extent and implication of his difficulty, much like the framework provided by the before and after warnings surrounding Belial's speech. The implication is personal; the similes and many other effects, say to the reader: "I know that you rely upon your senses for your apprehension of reality, but they are unreliable and hopelessly limited". Significantly, Galileo is introduced in both similes; the Tuscan artist's glass represents the furthest extension of human perception, and that is not enough. The entire pattern, of which the instances I analyze here are the smallest part, is, among other things, a preparation for the moment in Book VIII when Adam responds to Raphel's astronomical dissertation: "To whom thus Adam clear'd of doubt". Reader reaction is involuntary: cleared of doubt? by that impossibly tortuous and equivocal description of two all too probable universes?[12] By this point, however, we are able to place our reaction, since Adam's experience here parallels ours in so many places (and a large part of the poem's meaning is communicated by our awareness of the relationship between Adam and ourselves). He *is* cleared of doubt, not because he now knows how the universe is constructed, but because he knows that he can not know; what clears him of doubt is the certainty of self-doubt, and as with us this certainty is the result of a superior's willingness to grant him, momentarily, the security of his perspective. Milton's lesson is one that twentieth century science is just now beginning to learn:

> Finally, I come to what it seems to me may well be from the long range point of view the most revolutionary of the insights to be derived from our recent experiences in physics, more revolutionary than the insights afforded by the discoveries of Galileo and Newton. or of Darwin. This is the insight that it is impossible to transcend the human reference point . . . The new insight comes from a realization that the structure of nature may eventually be such that our processes of thought do not correspond to it sufficiently to permit us to think about it at all.[13]

In *Paradise Lost*, our sense of time proves as illusory as our sense of space and physicality. Jackson Cope quotes with approval

12

Sigfried Giedion and Joseph Frank who find in modern literature a new way of thinking about time:

> The flow of time which has its literary reflection in the Aristotelian development of an action having beginning, middle and end is . . . frozen into the labyrinthine planes of a spatial block which . . . can only be perceived by travelling both temporally and physically from point to point, but whose form has neither beginning, middle, end nor center, and must be effectively conceived as a simultaneity of multiple views.[14]

And Mrs. Isabel MacCaffrey identifies the "simultaneity of multiple views" with the eternal moment of God, a moment she argues that Milton makes ours:

> The long view of time as illusory, telescoped into a single vision, had been adopted in fancy by Christian writers . . . Writing of Heaven and the little heaven of Paradise, Milton by a powerful releasing act of the imagination transposed the intuitive single glance of God into the poem's mythical structure. Our vision of history becomes for the time being that of the Creator 'whose eye Views all things at one view' (ii., 189-90); like him, we are stationed on a 'prospect high Wherin past, present, future he beholds'.   (iii.77-78).[15]

The experience of every reader, I think, affirms the truth of these statements; Milton does convince us that the world of his poem is a static one which "slights chronology in favor of a folded structure which continually returns upon itself, or a spiral that circles about a single center".[16] The question I would ask is how does he so convince us? His insistence on simultaneity is easily documented. How many times do we see Christ ascend, after the war in Heaven, after the passion, after Harrowing Hell, after giving Satan his death wound, after the creation, after the final conflagration, at the day of final judgment? How many times do our first parents fall, and how many times are they accorded grace? The answer to all these questions is, "many times" or is it all the time (at each point of time) or perhaps at one, and the same, time. My difficulty with the preceding sentence is a part of my point: I cannot let go of the word "time" and the idea of sequence; timelessness (I am forced to resort to a question-begging negative) is an interesting concept, but we are all of us trapped in the necessity of experiencing in time, and the attempt even to conceive of a state where words like day and evening measure space rather than duration is a difficult one; Chaucer's Troilus, among others, is defeated by it. Mrs. MacCaffrey asserts that "spatial imagining" is part of Milton's "mental climate" and the researches of Walter Ong, among others, support her; but if Milton has implanted the eternal moment "into the poem's mythical structure", how does the reader, who, in Cope's words, must travel "temporally and physically from point to point", root it out? Obviously many readers do not; witness the critics who are troubled

13

by contradictory or "impossible" sequences and inartistic repetitions. Again the reactions of these anti-Miltonists are the surest guide to the poet's method; for it is only by encouraging and then "breaking" conventional responses and expectations that Milton can point his reader beyond them. To return to Waldock, part of the poem's apparently "hard and definite" outline is the easy chronology it seems to offer; but the pressures of innumerable local contexts demand adjustments that give the lie to the illusion of sequence and reveal in still another way the inability of the reader to consider this poem as he would any other.

In the opening lines of Book I, chronology and sequence are suggested at once in what is almost a plot line: man disobeys, eats fruit, suffers woe and awaits rescue. It is a very old and simple story, one that promises a comfortable correlation of plot station and emotional response: horror and fear at the act, sorrow at the result, joy at the happy ending, the whole bound up in the certain knowledge of cause and effect. As Milton crowds more history into his invocation the reader, who likes to know what time it is, will attempt to locate each detail on the continuum of his story line. The inspiration of the shepherd, Moses, is easily placed between the fall and the restoration; at this point many readers will feel the first twinge of complication, for Moses is a type of Christ who as the second Adam restores the first by persevering when he could not; as one begins to construct statements of relationship between the three, the clarity of lines 1-3 fade. Of course there is nothing to force the construction of such statements, and Milton thoughtfully provides in the very next line the sequence establishing phrase, "In the Beginning". Reassured both by the ordering power of "beginning" and by the allusion to Genesis (which is, after all, the original of all once-upon-a-times), the reader proceeds with the invocation, noting no doubt, all the riches unearthed by generations of critical exegesis, but still firmly in control of chronology; and that sense of control is reinforced by the two-word introduction to the story proper: "Say first", for with the first we automatically posit a second and then a third, and in sum, a neat row of causal statements leading all the way to an end already known.

The security of sequence, however, is soon taken away. I have for some time conducted a private poll with a single question. "What is your reaction when the second half of line 54—'for *now* the thought' —tells you that you are *now* with Satan, in Hell?" The unanimous reply is, "surprise", and an involuntary question: how did I come to be here? Upon re-reading, the descent to Hell is again easy and again unchartable. At line 26 the time scheme is still manageable: there is (*a*) poem time, the *now* in which the reader sits in his chair and listens, with Milton, to the muse, and (*b*) the named point in the past when the story ("our Grand Parents . . . so highly to fall off") and our understanding of it ("say first what cause") is assumed to

14

begin. At 33, the "first" is set back to the act of Satan, now suggested but not firmly identified as the cause of 27, and a third time (*c*) is introduced, further from (*a*) than (*b*), yet still manageable; but Satan's act also has its antecedent: "what time his Pride/Had cast him out from Heav'n (36-7); by this point, "what time" is both an assertion and a question as the reader struggles to maintain an awkward, backward-moving perspective. There is now a time (*d*) and after (that is, before) that an (*e*) "aspiring . . . He trusted to have equalled the most High" (38,40). Time (*f*) breaks the pattern, returning to (*d*) and providing, in the extended description of 44-53, a respite from sudden shifts. To summarize: the reader has been asked repeatedly to readjust his idea of "in the beginning" while holding in suspension two plot lines (Adam and Eve's and Satan's) that are eventually, he knows, to be connected. The effort strains the mind to its capacity, and the relief offered by the vivid and easy picture of Satan falling is more than welcome.[17] It is at this time, when the reader's attention has relaxed, that Milton slips by him the "now" of 54 and the present tense of "torments", the first present in the passage. The effect is to alert the reader both to his location (Hell) and to his inability to retrace the journey that brought him there. Re-reading leads him only to repeat the mental operations the passage demands, and while the arrival in Hell is anticipated, it is always a surprise. The technique is of course the technique of the spot and spear similes, and of the clash between involuntary response and authorial rebuke, and again Milton's intention is to strip from us another of the natural aids we bring to the task of reading. The passage itself tells us this in lines 50-51, although the message may pass unnoted at first: "Nine times the Space that measures Day and Night". Does space measure day and night? Are day and night space? The line raises these questions, and the half-line that follows answers them, not "to mortal men" who think in terms of duration and sequence, not to us. In this poem we must, we will, learn a new time.

The learning process is slow at first; the reader does not necessarily draw the inferences I do from this early passage; but again it is the frequency of such instances, that makes my case. In Book II, when the fallen Angels disperse, some of them explore "on bold adventure" their new home. One of the landmarks they pass is "Lethe the River of Oblivion", and Milton pauses to describe its part in God's future plans: "At certain revolutions all the damn'd/ . . . They ferry over this *Lethean* Sound/Both to and fro, their sorrow to augment,/And wish and struggle, as they pass to reach/The tempting stream, with one small drop to lose/In sweet forgetfulness all pain and woe,/All in one moment and so near the brink;/But Fate withstands" (597-98, 604-10). At 614 the poet continues with "Thus roving on/In confused march forlorn", and only the phrase "adventurous bands" in 615 tells the reader that the poet has returned to the fallen angels.

15

The mistake is a natural one: "forlorn" describes perfectly the state of the damned, as does "Confused march" their movements "to and fro": indeed a second reflection suggests no mistake at all; the fallen angels *are* the damned, and one drop of Lethe would allow them to lose their woe in the oblivion Moloch would welcome. Fate *does* withstand. What Milton has done by allowing this momentary confusion is point to the identity of these damned and all damned. As they fly past Lethe the fallen angels are all those who will become them; they do not stand for their successors (the word defeats me), they *state* them. In *Paradise Lost*, history and the historical sense are denied and the reader is forced to see events he necessarily perceives in sequence as time identities. Milton cannot recreate the eternal moment, but by encouraging and then blocking the construction of sequential relationships he can lead the reader to accept the necessity of, and perhaps even apprehend, negatively, a time that is ultimately unavailable to him because of his limitations.

This translation of felt ambiguities, confusions, and tautologies into a conviction of timelessness in the narrative is assured partially by the uniqueness of Milton's "fable". "For the Renaissance", notes Mrs. MacCaffrey, "all myths are reflections, distorted or mutilated though they may be, of the one true myth".[18] For Milton all history is a replay of the history he is telling, all rebellions, one rebellion, all falls, one fall, all heroism the heroism of Christ. And his readers who share this Christian view of history will be prepared to make the connection that exists potentially in the detail of the narrative. The similes are particularly relevant here. The first of these compares Satan to Leviathan, but the comparison, to the informed reader, is a tautology; Satan *is* Leviathan and the simile presents two aspects of one, rather than the juxtaposition of two, components. This implies that Satan is, at the moment of the simile, already deceiving "The Pilot of some small night-founder'd Skiff"; and if the reader has attended to the lesson of his recent encounter with the epic voice he recognizes himself as that pilot, moored during the speech of I, 84-126 by the side of Leviathan. The contests between Satan and Adam, Leviathan and the pilot, rhetoric and the reader—the simile compresses them, and all deceptions, into a single instant, forever recurring. The celebrated falling-leaves simile moves from angel form to leaves to sedge to Busiris and his Memphian Chivalry, or in typological terms (Pharoah and Herod are the most common types of Satan) from fallen angels to fallen angels. The compression here is so complex that it defies analysis: the fallen angels as they *lie* on the burning lake (the Red Sea) are already *pursuing* the Sojourners of Goshen (Adam and Eve, the Israelites, the reader) who are for the moment on the safe shore (Paradise, the reader's chair). In Book XII, 191, Pharoah becomes the River-Dragon or Leviathan (*Isaiah* 27.1), pointing to the ultimate unity of the Leviathan and falling leaves similes themselves. As similes they are uninformative; how numberless are the falling angels? they are as numberless as Pharaoh's host, that is, as fallen angels, and Pharaoh's host encompasses all the damned who have been, are, and will be, all the damned who will fly longingly above Lethe. As vehicles of perception they tell us a great deal, about the cosmos as it is in a reality we necessarily distort, about the ultimate subjectivity of sequential time, about ourselves.

There are many such instances in the early books and together they create a sensitivity to the difficulties of writing and reading this particular poem. When Milton's epic voice remarks that pagan fablers err relating the story of Mulciber's ejection from Heaven (I, 747), he does not mean to say that the story is not true, but that it is a distorted version of the story he is telling, and that any attempt to apprehend the nature of the angels' fall by comparing it to the fall of Mulciber or of Hesiod's giants involves another distortion that can not be allowed if *Paradise Lost* is to be read correctly. On the other hand the attempt is hazarded (the reader cannot help it), the distortion is acknowledged along with the unavailability of the correct reading, and Milton's point is made despite, or rather because of, the intractability, of his material. When Satan's flight from the judgment of God's scales (IV, 1015) is presented in a line that paraphrases the last line of the *Aeneid*, the first impulse is to translate the allusion into a comparison that might begin, "Satan is like Turnus in that . . ."; but of course, the relationship as it exists in a reality beyond that formed by our sense of literary history, is quite the opposite. Turnus' defiance of the fates and his inevitable defeat are significant and comprehensible only in the light of what Satan did in a past that our time signatures can not name and is about to do in a present (poem time) that is increasingly difficult to identify. Whatever the allusion adds to the richness of the poem's texture or to Milton's case for superiority in the epic genre, it is also one more assault on the confidence of a reader who is met at every turn with demands his intellect cannot even consider.

III

Most poets write for an audience assumed fit. Why is the fitness of Milton's audience a concern of the poem itself? One answer to this question has been given in the preceding pages: only by forcing upon his reader an awareness of his limited perspective can Milton provide even a negative intuition of what another would be like; it is a brilliant solution to the impossible demands of his subject, enabling him to avoid the falsification of anthropomorphism and the ineffectiveness of abstraction. Another answer follows from this one: the reader who fails repeatedly before the pressures of the poem soon realizes that his difficulty proves its major assertions— the fact of the fall, and his own (that is Adam's) responsibility for it,

17

and the subsequent woes of the human situation. The reasoning is circular, but the circularity is appropriate to the uniqueness of the poem's subject matter; for while in most poems effects are achieved through the manipulation of reader response, this poet is telling the story that *created* and still creates the responses of its reader and of all readers. The reader who falls before the lures of Satanic rhetoric displays again the weakness of Adam, and his inability to avoid repeating that fall throughout indicates the extent to which Adam's lapse has made the reassertion of right reason impossible. In short, the reader's difficulty is the result of the act that is the poem's subject. The reading experience becomes the felt measure of man's loss, and since Milton always supplies a corrective to the reader's errors and distortions, what other critics have seen as the "disquieting" aspect of that experience can be placed in a context that makes sense of it.

The ultimate assault is on the reader's values. The fifth inference I drew from Waldock's criticism of the intrusive epic voice was that for him the question of relative authority is a purely aesthetic one. "Milton's allegations clash with his demonstrations . . . in any work of imaginative literature at all it is the demonstration . . . that has the higher validity: an allegation can possess no comparable authority". In his brilliantly perverse *Milton's God* William Empson asserts "all the characters are on trial in any civilized narrative"[19] and Waldock would, I think, include the epic voice in this statement. The insistence on the superiority of showing as opposed to telling is, as Wayne Booth has shown, a modern one, and particularly unfortunate in this case since it ignores the historical reality of the genre.[20] When Homer names Achilles wrathful, do we search the narrative for proof he is not; is Odysseus' craft on trial or do we accept it because we accept the authority of the epic voice? Do we attempt to make a case for Aeneas' *im*piety? There is an obvious retort to all this: the authority of epic voices in other epics is accepted because their comments either confirm or anticipate the reading experience; Milton invites us to put his epic voice on trial by allowing the reading experience to contradict it. (Waldock: "Of course they should agree."). I agree that the reader can not help but notice the clash of authorities; his familiarity with the genre would lead him to look to the epic voice for guidance and clarification. But I do not think that any fit reader would resolve the problem, as Waldock does, and decide immediately and happily for the poem (and for himself) and against the prescience of its narrator. Milton assumes a predisposition in favour of the epic voice rather than a modern eagerness to put that voice on trial; he expects his reader to worry about the clash, to place it in a context that would resolve a troublesome contradiction and allow him to reunite with an authority who is a natural ally against the difficulties of the poem. The reader who does this gains more than a clarification of perspective. Although re-reading does reveal the inconsistencies and sophistries of the Satanic party line, it does not deny the reality of the values inherent in the Satanic stance. Waldock's summary of these values will serve again: "fortitude in adversity, enormous endurance, a certain splendid recklessness". In a word, heroism, or at least a form of heroism most of us find easy to admire because it is visible and flamboyant. Satan's initial attractiveness owes as much to a traditional and accepted idea of what is heroic as it does to our weakness before the rhetorical lure. Waldock complains there is not "much despair in what we have just been listening to". Just so! Despair and courage are sometimes indistinguishable, and the example of Moloch will suggest that one can shade into the other. True courage or heroism is often physically unimpressive and as beings who operate on the basis of appearances we require special instruction before we can recognize it. The lesson Milton would teach us here is a subtle one, and we have learned it when we see that Satan is indeed heroic and that heroism, or what we are taught to recognize as heroism, is on trial. If this poem does anything to its reader it forces him to make finer and finer discriminations. Perhaps the most important aspect of the process I have been describing—the creation of a reader who is fit because he knows and understands his limitations— begins here at I, 125 when Milton's authorial corrective casts the first stone at the concept of epic heroism, and begins to educate us toward the meaningful acceptance of something better.

That something is, of course, Christian heroism; and as it emerges from *Comus, Lycidas, Samson Agonistes,* and ultimately in *Paradise Regained* Christian heroism is more an attitude than an abstraction, more a stance than a program for action. The attitude is called faith, and the stance is characterised by provisionality. The sign of Christian heroism is a willingness to move in a world where moral decision is imperative, but where moral guidelines are obscure. It is the heroism of Abraham who "when he was called . . . obeyed; *and he went out, not knowing whither he went*" (*Hebrews,* 11.8). This is a difficult heroism for its tentativeness involves a burden the conventional hero could not bear, the burden enjoined by the simultaneous awareness of uncertainty and the necessity of action. The explanation of this "unfair" situation lies of course in the fact of original sin; what makes the situation tolerable and finally joyful for the Christian hero is his belief (which is itself an act of faith) in the benignanty of the prime mover.[21] Abraham and the other heroes of faith in *Hebrews,* 11 go out because they trust in an all-seeing deity who observes their blindness with compassion. "These all died in faith, not having received the promises, but having seen them afar off, and were persuaded of them, and embraced them, and confessed that they were strangers and pilgrims on the earth" (*Hebrews,* 11.13). In *Paradise Lost* the definition of Christian heroism is still another aspect of the relationship between

19

the poem and a reader who must move between his immediate experience of a poetic effect and the authority of a "hard and definite outline". He must remain open to the first and await (not demand) the guidance of the second. He must, in other words, attune the operations of his mind (and of his eyes) to the demands of the poem's universe, and forge for himself a *modus vivendi* that will allow him to proceed, however uncertainly. When he does this successfully (tentatively), that is when he learns how to read the poem, he will himself become the Christian hero who is, after all, the only fit reader. In the end, the education of Milton's reader, the identification of his hero, and the description of his style, are one.[22]

NOTES

1. *Paradise Lost And Its Critics* (Cambridge, 1961), p. 15. I consider Waldock's book, first published in 1947, to be the most forthright statement of an anti-Miltonism that can be found in the criticism of Leavis and Eliot, and more recently of Empson and John Peter. Indeed, Mr. Peter, in his *A Critique of Paradise Lost* (Columbia, 1960), says of Waldock's essay, "I have wondered whether the agreements between it and some of my own chapters might not have passed the point where such things cease to be comforting", and Empson records his agreement with Waldock at several points. Bernard Bergonzi concludes his analysis of Waldock with this statement: "no attempt has been made to defend the poem in the same detailed and specific manner in which it has been attacked" (*The Living Milton*, ed. Frank Kermode, London, 1960, p. 171). This essay is such an attempt. Bergonzi goes on to assert that "a successful answer to Waldock would have to show that narrative structure of *Paradise Lost does* possess the kind of coherence and psychological plausibility that we have come to expect from the novel. Again, there can be no doubt that it does not" (p. 174). I shall argue that the coherence and psychological plausibility of the poem are to be found in the relationship between its effects and the mind of its reader. To some extent my reading has been anticipated by Joseph Summers in his brilliant study, *The Muse's Method* (Harvard, 1962). See especially pp. 30-31: "Milton anticipated . . . the technique of the 'guilty reader' . . . The readers as well as the characters have been involved in the evil and have been forced to recognize and to judge their involvement." See also Anne Ferry's *Milton's Epic Voice: The Narrator in Paradise Lost* (Harvard, 1963), pp. 44-66.
2. *Ibid.*, p. 24.
3. *Ibid.*, p. 77.
4. Quoted by Basil Willey in *The Seventeenth Century Background* (New York: Doubleday Anchor Books, 1955), p. 211.
5. As Davis Harding points out (*The Club of Hercules*, Urbana, 1962, p. 103-08), this passage is also the basis of the bee-simile at line 768. The reader who catches the allusion here at line 108 will carry it with him to the end of the book and to the simile.
6. *Answerable Style* (Minneapolis, 1953), p. 124.
7. *Op. cit.*, p. 79.
8. III. 659. Harding insists that "if this passage does not conjure up a mental picture of Polyphemus on the mountaintop, steadying his footsteps with a lopped pine . . . it has not communicated its full meaning to us" (*The Club of Hercules*, p. 63). In my reading the "full meaning" of the passage involves a recognition of the inadequacy of the mental picture so conjured up.
9. The translation is E. V. Rieu's in the Penguin Classic edition (Baltimore, 1946), p. 148.

20

10. A. N. Whitehead in *The Limits of Language* (New York, 1962), pp. 13-14. In classical theory metaphor is that figure of speech whose operation bears the closest resemblance to the operations of dialectic and logic. Aristotle defines it in the *Poetics* as "a transference either from genus to species or from species to genus, or from species to species".

11. See "The Miltonic Simile", *PMLA*, XLVI (1931), 1064.

12. Milton clearly anticipates this reaction when he describes the dialogue in the "argument"; "Adam inquires concerning celestial Motions, is *doubtfully* answer'd".

13. Percy Bridgeman, in *The Limits of Language*, p. 21.

14. *The Metaphoric Structure of Paradise Lost* (Baltimore, 1962), pp. 14-15.

15. *Op. cit.*, p. 53.

16. *Ibid.*, p. 45.

17. The technique is reminiscent of Virgil's "historical present", which is used by the Roman poet to bring the action of his epic before the reader's eyes.

18. *Op. cit.*, p. 14.

19. Norfolk, 1961, p. 94.

20. *The Rhetoric of Fiction* (Chicago, 1961), p. 4. ". . . even Homer writes scarcely a page without some kind of direct clarification of motives, of expectations, and of the relative importance of events. And though the gods themselves are often unreliable, Homer—the Homer we know—is not. What he tells us usually goes deeper and is more accurate than anything we are likely to learn about real people and events."

21. Faith can not help us make the decisions forced on us by a difficult and obscure universe; but it can make the necessity of deciding more bearable.

22. An obvious objection to this way of resolving the contradictions so many have seen in *Paradise Lost* is the excessively self-conscious reader it posits, a reader who continually makes discriminations of incredible delicacy, a reader who is able to accept, even use, reproof and confusion, a reader who is, in sum, the detachedly involved observer of his own mental processes. Could Milton have assumed such a reader? I believe that he could have and did, and that my reading is true not only to the poem but to its historical context, although the remarks that follow are intended to be the barest outline of an argument that will be presented soon in book-length form. My argument is based on the opposition of rhetoric, the art of appearances, to dialectic, the pursuit of a scientific-mathematical truth. Aristotle locates the power of rhetoric in the "defects of our hearers" (*Rhetoric*, 3.1); the pressures of Christianity transforms the vagueness of the "defects of our hearers" into the precision of "original sin". Each text presents a problem for the Christian reader who must learn to resist the impulse to dwell on the niceties of rhetoric and attend only to the moral doctrine contained therein. Of course a rhetorical stimulus can be resisted if it is first recognized, that is felt. The crucial moment, in the reading experience then is the moment between the first response to the lure and its rejection or acceptance. That moment is analogous to the crucial stage in the progress of sin, that moment between the consideration of sin and assent or rejection. The three stages of sin—suggestion-delectation-consent find their analogies in the reading experience—response to the pull of the rhetorical, the moment of decision (whether or not to surrender to it), the abandonment of one's intellectual awareness to it. In practical terms this results in a program of Christian reading, one that involves referring all appeals to the repository of Christian morality a reader must bring to a poem if it is to be read "properly". Boccaccio writes: "But I repeat my advice to those who would appreciate poetry, and unwind its difficult involutions. You must read, you must persevere, you must sit up nights; you must inquire, and exert the utmost power of your mind" (*Boccaccio on Poetry*), ed. C. G. Osgood, Princeton, 1930, p. 62). In Milton's poem the epic voice acts as surrogate for the

"power of mind" that has defected to the lures the poem offers. What Milton does then is translate a philosophical-religious commonplace into a method of procedure. The method is possible and successful because the reader is taught by his theology to see in its operation the evidence of his own weakness or sin. In other words, rhetoric becomes the object attacked, and since rhetoric is firmly attached in the poem to the psychology of fallen man, the attack is finally on the reader who is forced by an inspired epic voice to acknowledge its success. The entire pattern is framed in the seventeenth century by an epistomology that stresses analysis and precision, and preaches a distrust of the rhetorical and emotional, and by an aesthetic that regards a poem as a potential instrument of conversion.

Uninventing Milton

John Peter Rumrich[1]

In 1961, William Empson in his controversial *Milton's God* challenged what he called the growing "neo-Christian" bias of Milton scholars, holding this responsible for tendentious overstatement of the orthodoxy of *Paradise Lost* and understatement of the sincerity and difficulty of its attempted theodicy. Empson claimed that, in fact, *Paradise Lost*'s "struggling" and "searching" outside the limits of "traditional Christianity" represent the "chief source of its fascination and poignancy."[2] Works like C. S. Lewis's *Preface to Paradise Lost*, according to Empson, misrepresent the epic by claiming it for Christianity's "great central tradition."[3] Contemporary Milton scholars have for the most part dismissed and even derided Empson's thesis, while Lewis's position—though with certain refinements—has, at least until recently, become increasingly dominant. This consolidation of the "neo-Christian" position owes much to the crystallizing impact of Stanley Fish's *Surprised by Sin*.

First published in 1967, Fish's work appealed to the more restless among its contemporary audience in part because it took a revolutionary theoretical stance—now referred to as reception aesthetics—that placed the reader in the center of the epic action or, rather, placed the center of the epic action in the reader. Milton scholarship has since become increasingly adventuresome and theoretically varied. Yet, as I have already implied, recent opinions of Milton and his epic are, historically speaking, more notable for their harmony than for their discord, and this harmony is traceable to Fish's theoretically sophisticated update of Lewis's orthodox model. Beyond its appeal to freethinkers appreciative of innovative critical methods, *Surprised by Sin* also pleased their natural opponents, those conservative scholars who saw Milton as a champion of traditional Christianity. In what is becoming a familiar irony, *Surprised by Sin* thus accomplished the theoretical liberation of Milton studies by placing a destabilizing hermeneutics in the service of conservative ideology.

The consensus that I am noting is relative and increasingly subject to at least tacit dissent.[4] Still, even the most recent and widely acclaimed scholarship—whatever its theoretical orientation—generally subscribes to the main points of

1/My thanks go to the University of Texas Research Institute for a grant that enabled me to write this essay. Wayne A. Rebhorn, of the University of Texas, read an early draft and suggested several helpful changes. I am also grateful to the Newberry Library's Milton Seminar, whose members, particularly Stephen M. Fallon and David Loewenstein, not only showed interest in the paper on which this essay was based but improved it with their insights and challenging questions.
2/William Empson, *Milton's God* (1961; reprint, Cambridge, 1981), pp. 10–11.
3/C. S. Lewis, *A Preface to Paradise Lost* (London, 1942), p. 92.
4/In his preface to the second edition of *Surprised by Sin* (1967; revised, Berkeley, 1971), Stanley Fish admitted that it is a "thesis book" and thus reductive (p. x). Until recently this frank admission anticipated most of the reservations that have been expressed about his work. Lately, however, the movement toward a broader view of *Paradise Lost* appears in an increasing emphasis on the poem's potential inconsistencies and duality. See, e.g., Sanford Budick, *The Dividing Muse* (New Haven, Conn., 1985), pp. 34–35, 98. As I later note, such scholars as William Kerrigan and Christopher Hill have challenged the reigning orthodoxy, as has Leopold Damrosch, Jr., in *God's Plot and Man's Stories* (Chicago, 1985). Current scholarship appears to be taking the dissent even farther, particularly Joseph

Fish's invention, treating them as fundamental to the contemporary understanding of *Paradise Lost* and its author. Nor do I use the term "invention" pejoratively. Fish himself suggests the term, and like him, I define "invention" to mean an adaptation to the features of an interpretive community that proves both rhetorically adept and politically viable (for Fish these modifiers are synonymous).[5] In this essay, however, I attempt to uninvent the contemporary Milton, arguing that, apart from the prejudice warping many particulars of his interpretation, Empson's general vision of Milton as a poet searching after divine justice makes better sense out of *Paradise Lost*.

What are the chief characteristics of Fish's version of the author of *Paradise Lost*? According to one recent, award-winning book, "Stanley Fish has shown how *Paradise Lost* is constructed for evangelical purposes so as to elicit a pattern of alternating identification with and rejection of the characters, in order to convict the reader of sin."[6] In other words, the poem's narrator manipulates the sympathy of his readers to make them blamable. Milton achieves this evangelical purpose by exploiting the disjunction between readers' fallen psyches and what a 1986 study calls the poet's "didactic theology": "Theological and psychological genres appear to conflict with one another, and the dominant genre of the hexameron overrules affective drama, didactic theology retroactively canceling profane psychological motivations. (This is to put into generic terms Stanley Fish's argument about the presentation of God.)"[7] Scholars have agreed that the epic simile—particularly as employed in the first two books—is Milton's most conspicuous device for eliciting and then correcting fallen response: "There can be little doubt," remarks another award-winning author, "that some of the similes have been designed as didactic redundancies."[8] However redundant the didacticism, Milton's strategic genius nevertheless is generally deemed to render it immediate and personal. "As Stanley Fish has emphasized," according to another 1986 book, Milton encourages readers to "effectively interiorize" the theological lessons contained within the epic's "catechetical formulations."[9] In sum, the contemporary generation of Milton scholars seems to agree that *Paradise Lost* instructs readers by convicting them of sin. Milton makes an affective appeal (e.g., in the similes) and then, having provoked fallen

---

Wittreich's *Interpreting "Samson Agonistes"* (Princeton, N.J., 1986); Michael Wilding's *Dragon's Teeth* (Oxford, 1987); and James G. Turner's *One Flesh: Paradisal Marriage in the Age of Milton* (Oxford, 1987). A recent essay by Fish, "Truth and Indeterminacy in *Areopagitica*," which appears in *Re-Membering Milton*, ed. Margaret W. Ferguson and Mary Nyquist (London, 1987), pp. 234–54, implies a change in his understanding of Milton's didacticism. According to Fish, the effect of *Areopagitica* is "disorienting, but it is also (or so Milton's claim would be) salutary, for in the process of being disoriented the reader is provoked to just the kind of labor and exercise that is necessary to the constitution of his or her own virtue" (p. 243). There is a clear difference here from the Milton who teaches by accusation and repetition of traditional doctrine. Of course, for Fish the change may be attributable to the difference between Milton's prose oration and his epic.

5/Stanley Fish, *Is There a Text in This Class?* (Cambridge, Mass., 1980), pp. 16, 335.

6/Georgia B. Christopher, *Milton and the Science of the Saints* (Princeton, N.J., 1982), p. 144. The award mentioned here and elsewhere in this essay is the Milton Society's annual Hanford Award for the outstanding contribution to Milton studies. This award may be taken to measure both the excellence of a work and its acceptance among the interpretive community of Milton scholars. I have deliberately chosen recent and acclaimed books (which for the most part I also admire) in order to emphasize the extent to which even now our Milton is Fish's Milton.

7/Christopher Kendrick, *Milton: A Study in Ideology and Form* (London, 1986), pp. 139, 201.

8/William Kerrigan, *The Sacred Complex* (Cambridge, Mass., 1983), p. 99. In what appears to be a tactical concession, Kerrigan admits the didactic redundancy of the similes before diverging from the consensus.

9/Kathleen M. Swaim, *Before and After the Fall* (Amherst, Mass., 1986), p. 32.

engagement, masters it with redundant didacticism. This didacticism amounts to scripturally based Christianity discoverable in catechetical formulations. Armed with a theory that defined reading *Paradise Lost* as a process of ethical self-interpretation, Fish measured the potential complexity of a reader's moral consciousness by a voluntarist criterion of obedience to God. William Kerrigan identifies the psychological appeal of Fish's argument: "*Paradise Lost* combines mythopoeic narrative with rational theodicy. . . . In many readers the figure of Satan generates a tension between these two poles: his mythopoeic grandeur at the opening of the work opposes his discursive condemnation by the narrator and the heavenly characters. . . . In claiming that the tension was deliberate, Fish healed an old division in Milton studies. . . . The pious reader can entertain potentially rebellious attitudes knowing that, as signs of his fallenness, these attitudes already confirm the doctrinal content of the poem and therefore have a piety all their own."[10] It testifies to the sway of Fish's argument that even those scholars whose disagreement with it is rather striking—as Kerrigan's implicitly is—either maintain a tactful silence or open with a rhetorical gesture of submission.[11] Kerrigan thus evokes a wounded interpretive community healed by Fish's ministrations. Fish's therapy, however, can also be seen as an analogue of God's strategy for dealing with fallen angels, permitting their continued activity so that they might suffer repeated defeat and increasing frustration.

In *A Preface to Paradise Lost*, Lewis too rested his interpretation on Milton's supposed intentions toward his audience. According to Lewis, Milton wished to produce a particular effect "on the ordinary educated and Christian audience of his time."[12] Being relatively precise about Milton's beliefs, Lewis had to argue that the poet suppressed his differences from the intended audience so that he could represent Christianity's central tradition and satisfy decorum. For example, Milton's heresies were, in Lewis's phrase, "private theological whimsies" that he "laid aside" while composing his great public utterance (p. 92). Some of Milton's most painstakingly arrived at beliefs, the products of decades of study and contemplation, thus lost their status as carefully defined positions integral to a comprehensive religious philosophy and appeared instead as the amateurish musings of a dilettante. Lewis's tactic exemplifies a paradoxical inconsistency that has continued to plague the arguments of certain Miltonists: in order to make the poet appear more orthodox than he was, they implicitly or explicitly denigrate his acumen or seriousness as a theologian.[13]

10/Kerrigan, pp. 98-99.
11/In an otherwise highly laudatory review, the late Philip Gallagher complained of "an undercurrent of profound eccentricity in [*The Sacred Complex*'s] subtext . . . that would seek . . . to recapture Milton for the Saurats and Hills and—though Kerrigan would deny it—the Waldocks and Empsons of this world" (*Milton Quarterly* 18 [1984]: 87). Gallagher's figures, aside from provoking wonder at the prospect of a profound yet eccentric undercurrent, imply that Milton is a trophy in an intellectual war, an object secured only by removal to the camp of the victors. Inasmuch as *Milton Quarterly* is perhaps the most specific organ for communication among Milton scholars, Gallagher's sensitivity to Kerrigan's tactful, mild dissent from Fish's Milton is noteworthy. One expects controversy over Kerrigan's bold psychohistorical analysis, but Gallagher's response indicates that the key issue in Milton studies is not the critic's theoretical orientation but the poet's allegiance to traditional, mainstream Christianity. The theodicy must not be seen as seriously questioning or deviating from that orthodoxy.
12/Lewis, p. 91.
13/A notable instance of the willingness to ignore Milton's heresies on account of his alleged theological incompetence appears in the late C. A. Patrides' "Milton and the Arian Controversy," *Proceedings of the*

Ironically, Lewis saw Milton as having performed a religious role remarkably similar to the one that he himself would later perform—that of discounting sectarian diversity so as to identify and promote the essence of Christian belief. Lewis arrived at this assessment despite Milton's famous definition in *Areopagitica* of his own ecumenism as one of "dissimilitudes," brotherly or not.[14] Even if literature fails to hold a mirror up to nature, *Paradise Lost* apparently does hold one up to its interpreters: Lewis proposed a Milton who champions mainstream Christianity; Fish, one whose feistiness and tactical ingenuity resemble Fish's own. I am not arguing that interpretation is merely an exercise in narcissism. Both Lewis and Fish have taught readers of *Paradise Lost* much that is useful and apt, and they have done so in large part because they tempered the inescapable tendency to find oneself wherever one looks with a conscientious if selective regard for Milton's historical context. This historical foundation is as obvious in Lewis's appeal to Milton's "ordinary educated and Christian" reader as it is in Fish's historically based reconstruction of Milton's "reader whose education, opinions, concerns, linguistic competencies, and so on make him capable of having the experience the author wished to provide."[15] Fish's more recent theoretical pronouncements, practically speaking, do not affect his handling of historical evidence. We may agree that interpretations succeed or fail only by reference to the interpretive strategies of a given community of readers.[16] But if that community accepts an interpretation on the basis of strategies involving claims of historical accuracy and consistency, the interpretation may presumably be challenged on the basis of the same criteria.[17] My intention, then, is to propose a more consistent rendering of the historical context of John Milton and *Paradise Lost*.

I

Given what we do know about Milton's attitudes, Lewis's contention that Milton suppressed certain firmly held beliefs for reasons of decorum appears improbable. Milton frequently defied convention and reinvented decorum whenever he thought this was necessary for the expression of his highly original ideas and convictions. Still, Lewis's unlikely version of Milton is no less likely than the one that has developed over the last twenty years. Milton did at least place a high value on classical aesthetic canons, though his version of them is idiosyncratic and unpredictable. Unfortunately, Lewis's fiction of an "ordinary educated and Chris-

---

American Philosophical Society 120 (1976): 245–52. Patrides' claim seems odd, given his willingness in *Milton and the Christian Tradition* (Oxford, 1966) to identify Milton's beliefs with those of a variety of theological writers other than Milton.

14. *The Complete Prose Works of John Milton*, ed. Don M. Wolfe et al., 8 vols. (New Haven, Conn., 1953–82), 2:555. References to Milton's prose follow this edition and will be noted parenthetically in the text.

15. Fish, *Is There a Text in This Class?* p. 160.

16. Ibid., p. 174. See also the lucid presentation of Fish's position in Steven Mailloux, *Interpretive Conventions* (Ithaca, N.Y., 1982), p. 29.

17. Truly objective interpretation may well be an impossibility. Yet, given the context of a particular interpretive community, objectively correct interpretation is precisely what we attempt to achieve. In practice, Fish's hermeneutic assumptions do not differ from those E. D. Hirsch expresses in *Validity in Interpretation* (New Haven, Conn., 1967), pp. 1–67, 209–44. Hirsch attempts to define meaning by focusing on authorial intention as reconstructed through historically appropriate evidence. Fish wishes to achieve roughly the same end by reconstructing the historically appropriate reader. By focusing on the typical seventeenth-century reader, however, Fish neglects Milton's singularity and falls into the historicist trap of reducing the subject to his background.

tian audience," which for him vaguely approximated an almost Platonic ideal of essential Christian belief, has lately been particularized chiefly in terms of seventeenth-century English Puritanism.

The politico-religious groupings we use to categorize seventeenth-century England are slippery and invite caution and qualification. There were, for example, Arminians of the right (those accused of being crypto-Catholics), and Arminians of the left (those uncomfortable with Calvin's harsh deity); Independents who championed toleration in the interest of nonconformity, and Cavaliers who desired it because of Papist sympathies; Presbyterians who stood by the King, and Presbyterians who backed Parliament against him. These rather notorious historical complications of policy and faith scarcely begin to reflect the complex reality of a century lived by Muggletonians, Monarchists, Anabaptists, Antinomians, Quakers, Rosicrucians, Ranters, Republicans, Levellers, Rota-men, Diggers, and Seekers— to name but a few. When one gets down to specifics, the word "ordinary," even when qualified by "educated and Christian," becomes problematic. Nevertheless, for purposes of argument, the seventeenth-century English incarnation of Lewis's "ordinary" audience could be defined—by virtue of being a rough majority of the educated male minority—as mainly low church Anglican and Presbyterian, more or less convinced of the bondage of the will and imbued with attitudes and values appropriate to what we now call the nascent bourgeoisie. And no doubt Milton did share certain of this group's characteristics.[18] Undeniably, however, in his vernacular pamphlets and Latin treatises, when Milton does address this "ordinary" audience, he most often does so to oppose what they believed, did, or planned to do—in government, religion, and education. In other words, the odds are that if Milton composed his theodicy with such an audience in mind, his own opinion on the subject was distinct from theirs.

Indeed, the theodicy is the crucial test case; and for Fish, Milton fits in perfectly with mainstream Reformation opinion: "'That thou may'st believe and be confirm'd' would have been a more honest—literal is the better word—*propositio* than 'justify the ways of God to men.'"[19] Given that "ordinary" opinion in seventeenth-century England was deeply inimical to the assumptions underlying theodicy, the stated aim of *Paradise Lost* may well appear as ironic bait designed to bring out—so as to correct—the offensive presumption of fallen humankind. But Milton's view of the propriety of theodicy is characteristically opposed to that of the posited audience and in fact rests on premises more properly associated with the context of Christian humanism.[20] Though Reformation Christianity and Renaissance humanism agree at many points, on this crucial issue they are divided. In fact, the debates on free will between Luther and Erasmus repeatedly return to this fundamental difference in attitude.

18/ Christopher Hill, *Milton and the English Revolution* (New York, 1977), offers the most informed and thorough analysis of Milton's ideology in its contemporary context.
19/ Fish, *Surprised by Sin* (n. 4 above), p. 289.
20/ Miltonists of an earlier generation, led by Douglas Bush and James H. Hanford, were inclined to categorize Milton as a Christian humanist, even as the current generation emphasizes the poet's Puritanism instead. Unfortunately, neither group of Miltonists has fully articulated the distinction. Although I here identify Milton with the humanists, I refrain from placing him wholly or even primarily in either category. On the Puritans' debt to Christian humanism, especially in the realm of social reform, see Margo Todd, *Christian Humanism and the Puritan Social Order* (Cambridge, 1987).

Like the majority of Milton's Puritan contemporaries, Luther rejected freedom of the will. Yet he admits that "it gives the greatest possible offense to common sense or natural reason that God by his own sheer will should abandon, harden, and damn men as if he enjoyed the sins and the vast eternal torments of his wretched creatures."[21] Although Luther understands that the denial of free choice leads reason inevitably to this conclusion, for him this conclusion simply testifies to the character of reason as, in one of Luther's typically salty phrases, "the devil's whore" (p. 16). Hence, while Luther concedes that the assertion of free will is actually "sweating and toiling to excuse the goodness of God," he nevertheless insists that this primary gesture of theodicy only displays fallen humanity's arrogance all the more clearly: "Here they demand that God should act according to human justice, and do what seems right to them"; "he may damn none but those who in our judgment have deserved it" (pp. 244, 258). Insofar as Luther is concerned—and in this respect he exemplifies the attitude presumed in Fish's version of *Paradise Lost*—the whole idea of a theodicy appears grossly supercilious, an illusion of freedom and dignity inspired by the devil.

Erasmus, on the other hand, did not construe "sweating and toiling" on behalf of God's goodness as an offense. He insisted on the power of free choice, "which can do and does, in relation to God, whatever it pleases, uninhibited by any law or sovereign authority" (p. 170). Freedom of choice, for Erasmus as for Milton, applies to "the things which lead to eternal salvation . . . , the words and works of God which are presented to human will so that it may apply itself to them or turn away from them" (p. 172). Luther objected that no such autonomous power resides in the human psyche, that "no one has it in his own power to think a good or bad thought" (p. 64). The state described by Adam as characteristic of sleep (*Paradise Lost* 5.100–13) is in Luther's reckoning the inescapable psychological condition of humanity.[22]

Adam does admit that the content of human and even divine thought is to a certain degree involuntary—"Evil into the mind of God or Man / May come or go"—but insists on the ultimate authority of rational volition: "So unapprov'd," evil leaves "no spot or blame behind" (5.117–19). Adam's "so unapprov'd," nonsense to Luther, is an index to the distinction between the Arminian Milton and the majority of his Puritan contemporaries on the inextricably involved issues of free will and theodicy. As Dennis Danielson has convincingly demonstrated, Milton's identification with the Arminian dissent from orthodox Puritan determinism recapitulates Erasmus's humanist aversion to Lutheran bondage of the will.[23] For the Arminians as for Erasmus, humankind enjoys the freedom to reason and choose; and this freedom, while it imposes the heavy burden of responsibility, also entitles reason, if not fully to comprehend the ways of God, then at least to construct a case for continued patience and fortitude, even when faced with apparently senseless woe. In light of Milton's unwavering, foundational insistence on freedom of will, therefore, to portray his theodical intention as ironic implies uncharacteristic incon-

21. Desiderius Erasmus and Martin Luther, *Free Will and Salvation*, ed. E. Gordon Rupp and Phillip Watson (Philadelphia, 1979), p. 244. Textual references to Luther and Erasmus follow this edition.
22. References to Milton's poetry follow *John Milton: Complete Poems and Major Prose*, ed. Merritt Y. Hughes (Indianapolis, 1957).
23. Dennis Danielson, *Milton's Good God* (Cambridge, 1982), pp. 66–69, 75–82.

sistency in his thought. This inconsistency becomes even more palpable when we remember that Milton's practice as a poet and pamphleteer everywhere relies on theodicy as the motive for political principle and the cue for action.

II

It is similarly inconsistent to link Milton's didacticism with "a tradition of didacticism which finds expression in a distrust of the affective and an insistence on the intellectual involvement of the listener pupil"; yet Fish does make this connection, and it leads him to the extreme position that Milton shared Plato's hostility to the unreasonable appeal of poetry.[24] No doubt Milton prized reason and distrusted ungoverned passion, but his vocational commitment was to an Orphean art, which *Of Education* characterizes as "simple, sensuous, and passionate" (2.403) and whose magical power to move audiences he repeatedly celebrated (e.g., *Ad Patrem*, lines 21–22).

Of those characters in *Paradise Lost* customarily considered good, only Raphael appears to stand for the anticarnal bias with which Fish associates Milton. And the seraph does so explicitly only on the occasion when he scolds Adam for his passion for Eve (8.579–94). Raphael, who in this scene has rightly been described as boorish, generally suffers the complacency that can accompany the material privileges of angelic being.[25] Repeatedly, he stresses the inexpressible grandeur of heaven at the same time that he condescends to praise earthly life as comparable, if separate and unequal. More to the point, Raphael ventures forth to Earth from a realm where sexuality as an expression of love is, from what I can gather, monosexual, nonprocreative, relatively fleeting, and promiscuous.[26] Small wonder, then, that he should lack sympathy with the "sweet reluctant amorous delay" of more focused and unspectacular human sexuality (4.311).

Pierre Bourdieu has argued that the aesthetic distinction between spiritual and natural satisfaction correlates with the class distinction between the cultivated bourgeoisie and the lower orders.[27] Whether the limits imposed by an individual's material and cultural background can ever be transcended is a question fundamental to modern ideological controversy. Milton himself presents an interesting test case. Though we consider him a member of what we call the bourgeoisie by

---

24/ Fish, *Surprised by Sin*, pp. 7, 88–89.

25/ On Raphael's crudity, see Northrop Frye, *Five Essays on Milton's Epics* (London, 1966). Others have perceived Raphael's limitations. See, e.g., Peter Lindenbaum, "Lovemaking in Milton's Paradise," *Milton Studies* 6 (1974): 294–95.

26/ Although the narrator informs us that "Spirits . . . / Can either Sex assume," the power of assumption implies nothing definite about gender; the angels are not hermaphrodites, though they may be, at least when fallen, transvestites (1.423–24; but see 10.890). Admittedly, this distinction is not always a clear one; nevertheless, Milton consistently depicts angels as masculine. I use the word "fleeting" to characterize angelic sex because I wish to avoid the connotations of "easy" in describing the typical speed and immediacy with which angels' desires are gratified. In calling the angels promiscuous, I am building on Raphael's description of their effortless lovemaking in a kingdom of universal love and perfect communion. Neither Milton nor Raphael suggests that angels have particular lovers. (Indeed, Milton did not advocate monogamy even in human marriage.) Finally, by describing the angels as nonprocreative, I note the most significant sexual difference between angels and humans, one that Raphael neglects in expressing his contempt for human passion and preference for heavenly love—angels do not breed. Lewis addresses the issue of angelic lovemaking in comparable terms and, I think, rightly attributes the details of Milton's depiction to the influence of seventeenth-century science (pp. 112–15). But he also judges Milton imprudent—I think wrongly—for having raised the matter at all.

27/ Pierre Bourdieu, *Distinction*, trans. Richard Nice (Cambridge, Mass., 1984), p. 490.

way of economic background and formal education, Christopher Hill has convincingly argued that he went beyond its boundaries, or at least redefined them, in the formation of his political, theological, and aesthetic outlook.[28] This is not to deny that his attitudes and convictions can still be generally described, in Bourdieu's sense, as cultivated and bourgeois. Specifically, however, Milton's philosophy of material monism departs significantly from what would have to be considered the primary moral and aesthetic philosophy of the bourgeoisie—Neoplatonic Christianity opposing human carnality to the "godly instinct in man."[29] Actually, one might well argue that, in Milton's version of Paradise, human carnality *is* the "godly instinct in man." Certainly, *Paradise Lost* defies the conventional Christian dichotomy between body and soul as well as much of the prejudice against the body that historically accompanies this dichotomy.

The passages in the epic commonly allowed as evidence of Milton's unusual affirmation of the body and his material monism in general involve human sexuality and angelic digestion and lovemaking (4.739 ff.; 5.407 ff.; 8.620 ff.) But Milton's monism is more pervasive than these isolated passages suggest. For Milton, even God has a carnal side—though not, as orthodox opinion held, because of the incarnation of the Son. Milton did not consider the Son truly God.[30] Chaos and Night, however, do personify the material force essential to God's being—his flesh, so to speak.[31] Milton depicts Chaos and Night as eternal and infinite (*Paradise Lost* 2.891-96), and, as he repeatedly insists in *Christian Doctrine*, eternity and infinity belong to the essence of God and God alone. If the realm of Chaos is eternal and infinite, therefore, it must be a definitive attribute or dimension of God himself, a condition of his very being.

Unfortunately, the one scholar who recognized the compelling logic that supports an essential link between God and Chaos nevertheless rejected the identification.[32] Other scholars have either ignored the issue or gotten the facts wrong. Fish and Lewis virtually exclude Chaos and Night from their studies. A. B. Chambers, on the other hand, contended that "Chaos and Night are the enemies of God," a position that recently has been pushed to the extreme of depicting Chaos as the cosmic principle of evil.[33] Even the usually illuminating Isabel MacCaffrey insisted that Chaos constitutes no part of God because "God is pure actuality."[34]

Yet Milton claims in *Christian Doctrine* that "God cannot rightly be called *Actus Purus*, or pure actuality . . . for thus he could do nothing except what he does do, and he would do that of necessity, although in fact he is omnipotent and utterly free in his actions" (6:145-46). Logically, a God who creates *ex deo* must include potential if he is to act freely. Furthermore, if creatures are to enjoy free

---

28/ Hill, *Milton and the English Revolution* (n. 18 above), pp. 69-79.
29/ The phrase is Fish's, *Surprised by Sin*, p. 7.
30/ Michael Bauman, *Milton's Arianism* (Frankfurt am Main, 1987), argues the case for Milton's Arianism in definitive detail. The history of the controversy over Milton's rejection of Trinitarian thought is long and involved, particularly over the last quarter century. Without going into detail, I would suggest that the profound reluctance of Milton scholars to admit Milton's categorical Arianism is again symptomatic of the powerful desire to see him as orthodox on the essentials of Christianity.
31/ John Peter Rumrich, *Matter of Glory* (Pittsburgh, 1987), pp. 61-69.
32/ Walter Clyde Curry, *Milton's Ontology, Cosmogony, and Physics* (Lexington, Ky., 1957), p. 77.
33/ A. B. Chambers, "Chaos in *Paradise Lost*," *Journal of the History of Ideas* 24 (1963): 65; Regina Schwartz, "Milton's Hostile Chaos," *ELH* 52 (1985): 337-74.
34/ Isabel MacCaffrey, "*Paradise Lost*" *as* "*Myth*" (Cambridge, Mass., 1959), p. 164.

will, as Milton insists they do, and if God himself is to maintain perfect control, as by definition he does, then he must have access to and sole authority over the realm of infinite possibility. Such access and authority allow him ultimately to define and govern any conceivable situation that could arise from the freely willed actions of finite creatures in a finite creation. Far from being God's enemies, therefore, Chaos and Night allegorically represent the infinite and eternal realm of indeterminacy fundamental to divine sovereignty and omnipotence (*Paradise Lost* 2.910-16; 7.150- 73, 218-21). Even if, to the apparent confusion of the theodicy, Milton portrays Chaos and Night as acting in the interests of anarchy and aiding and abetting Satan (2.1007-09), logically we must accept them as representing an essential aspect of God himself. They stand for the material potency of his being—his flesh or, to use a more precise analogy, his womb. That the failure to draw this inevitable conclusion has plagued the work of otherwise reliable scholars indicates how strong the urge has been to see Milton as more orthodox than logic allows. Though scholars have been willing to admit that Milton was a materialist, that in *Paradise Lost* even angels eat and make love, they have not been willing to admit that the consequences of his monist philosophy apply also to the deity who governs the epic cosmos.

III

Fish's representation of *Paradise Lost* as an ironic theodicy informed by traditional anticarnal assumptions is symptomatic of an underlying error concerning Milton's epistemology. For an Independent like Milton, truth was a goal to be worked toward rather than an accomplished set of beliefs; and tradition at its best was only a partial record of an ongoing search, an untrustworthy record that preserved many errors. Yet Fish's Milton is supposed to have adopted the narrative persona of a dictatorial teacher who leads his charges into error and then reproaches them with a traditional, authoritative interpretation of the action. How should we reconcile this narrator with the authorial voice that, in *The Doctrine and Discipline of Divorce*, allegorized custom or tradition as the puffed-up countenance of monstrous error (2:223)? Milton's conviction that submission to external interpretive authority undermines true virtue (2:543) was fundamental to his disenchantment with the "ordinary" Christians of this time, particularly with those who in his opinion enslaved themselves to tradition and did not seek for themselves the truths of revelation. The sources that Fish cites as analogues for Milton's pedagogical method and message, however, tend to recommend an automatic, habitual, unreasoning response to trial and temptation. Merely voluntary behavior and avoidance of temptation, leading to what *Areopagitica* describes as "a fugitive and cloister'd virtue" (2:515), never found praise in Milton's work, nor does *Paradise Lost* use the force of epic to instill such habits in its readers.

For example, when the subject is the reader's tendency to fall under the spell of Satan's rhetoric, Richard Baxter appears in Fish as the corroborating authority for the narrator's supposed rebuke: "In this case, the failure (if we can call it that) involves the momentary relaxation of a vigilance that must indeed be eternal. Richard Baxter (*The Saints Everlasting Rest*, c. 1650) warns: 'Not only the open profane, the swearer, the drunkard, and the enemies of godliness, will prove hurtful companions to us, though these indeed are chiefly to be avoided: but too frequent society with persons merely civil and moral, whose conversation is empty and

31

unedifying, may much divert thoughts from heaven.'"[35] Baxter's teaching closely resembles that which Milton ridicules in *Areopagitica*: "'Tis next alleg'd we must not expose our selves to temptations without necessity, and next to that not imploy our time in vain things" (2.521). Milton's reply? "We must regulat all recreations and pastimes, all that is delightfull to man. No musick must be heard, no song be set or sung, but what is grave and *Dorick*"—and so on for several pages of mockery (2:523–56). Though he is difficult to categorize, Baxter may be viewed as a relatively conservative Presbyterian—one who argued that Christian citizens would owe obedience even to a Nero, thought that James I understated the divine right of kings, and once claimed that hell is paved with the skulls of unbaptized infants. He and Milton disagreed on nearly every political and ecclesiastical issue of their day, yet Fish uses his opinions to define the intended readership whose basic attitudes Milton shared.[36] Perhaps one could argue that the virginal Milton of the late 1630s and early 1640s would have supported Baxter's admonition to avoid "the enemies of godliness" and even the society of those "merely civil and moral." In the anti-episcopal tracts, written prior to his denunciation of the Presbyterians as the "New Forcers of Conscience," Milton attests to the purity of his youth and his abhorrence of pollution. But by the time he wrote *Areopagitica* and the divorce tracts, whatever sympathy he may have had with the notion of evil as an avoidable contaminant is gone.

One could overlook Fish's appeal to Baxter if it were an isolated slip or if Milton and Baxter at least agreed on the points for which Baxter is cited—a near impossibility given the ideological chasm that separated them. But, beginning in his preface with a citation of Richard Bernard, whose zeal and censoriousness were reportedly of the sort Jonson loved to satirize, Fish repeatedly appeals to Presbyterians and other relatively conservative Puritans to establish the "tradition of didacticism" within which Milton supposedly worked.[37] Milton would have thought them bad company: at best, hirelings; at worst, traitors. They were men who stood for religious conformity and tithes and often for ecclesiastical and political coercion

---

35/ Fish, *Surprised by Sin*, p. 12.

36/ Baxter was loyal to the monarchy, a supporter of episcopacy and liturgy and an opponent of the sects dividing English society, who was willing to risk his life to speak out against the regicides. He helped bring about the Restoration and was afterward offered a bishopric. Milton, on the other hand, denounced the Presbyterians, deplored professional clergy, defended the regicides, gloried in sectarian controversy, risked his life to propose alternatives to the Restoration, and afterward was persecuted, imprisoned, slandered, and in danger of execution. Christopher Hill, *The Experience of Defeat* (New York, 1984), notes that Baxter despised Milton's honored friend, the ardent republican Sir Henry Vane, and commented on his bravery in facing execution with words recalling the sentiments of those who in *Macbeth* report the execution of the rebellious Thane of Cawdor: "The manner of his death procured him more applause than all the actions of his life" (p. 73). David Masson, *Life of John Milton*, 6 vols. (1874–81; reprint, Gloucester, Mass., 1965), details Baxter's transition from conservative Presbyterianism to moderate Episcopalianism (6:99–105) and cites his discomfort with Cromwell's inclination to religious toleration (3:385–87, 525). William Lamont, *Richard Baxter and the Millennium* (London, 1979), depicts a Baxter almost Hobbesian in his deep pessimism over human nature and in his consequent advocacy of absolutist government. Even Baxter's discomfort with rigid determinism—mentioned by Danielson (n. 23 above), pp. 79–80; and Damrosch (n. 4 above), pp. 57–58—which appears to ally him with Milton on the key issue of free will, grew out of his horror at the antinomianism attendant on it. Indeed, Baxter was attracted to Presbyterianism primarily because of the articulate control it would allow (paid) clergy over the behavior and faith of individual parishioners.

37/ On Bernard, see *The Dictionary of National Biography*, ed. Leslie Stephen and Sidney Lee, 63 vols. (London, 1885–1900), 4:386–87.

in matters of interpretation and devotion. Aside from the seven citations of Baxter, mostly from *The Arrogancy of Reason against Divine Revelations Repressed* (1655), Fish cites Daniel Dyke's *The Mystery of Selfe-Deceiving* (1615) (five times), John Preston's *Sins Overthrow or a Godly and Learned Treatise of Mortification* (1633) (four times), and John Corbet's *Self-Imployment in Secret* (1681) (twice). Milton wrote in an astonishing variety of prose and verse forms but never published anything that remotely resembles these prescriptive treatises, whose self-righteous intentions to instruct others in holiness appear so obviously in their titles. Milton's great theological work *Christian Doctrine* differs from these fundamentally in tone, intention, and method. Even if Milton might admit that reason can exceed its limits, it defies credibility to imagine him writing a work designed to repress "the arrogancy of reason."

Certainly, Milton's aim in *Paradise Lost* is at least in part didactic. With his experience as a teacher and sense of prophetic mission, Milton was conditioned for and eager to perform a didactic role. I object only to the still current tendency to see Milton as a knuckle-rapping, peremptory prig—a teacher who already knows the truth of things, humiliates and berates his charges for their errors, and requires conformity to his authoritative understanding. "We are not warned," insists Fish, "but accused, taunted by an imperious voice," one which all but sneers in passing judgment: "You have made a mistake, just as I knew you would."[38] Because Fish argues his case so persuasively, and consequently has been so generally influential, a generation of students has been taught to hear Milton's epic narrator as a censorious preacher. Milton at his worst, a caricature drawn from the least admirable moments of the prose pamphlets, has become for many the voice heard in his most complex, splendidly varied, and sublime composition.

IV

The foregoing suggests some of the difficulties in specifically defining a fit, contemporary audience for *Paradise Lost*, especially when the orthodox opinions and attitudes supposed to characterize this hypothetical audience are also attributed to Milton himself and used to determine the epic's meaning. Once his attempt at historical reconstruction is rejected, Fish's argument then depends on the response of actual readers. His account of such responses can be summarized in three related propositions: (1) the disjunction between the grand portrayal of Satan and the narrator's corrective commentary is designed to warn readers of their sinful tendencies; (2) Eve's decision to eat the apple, precipitated by the failure of her will, is designed to warn readers of the culpability of the overweening, empirical intellect; and (3) Christian heroism consists in the will to obey divine commands regardless of other considerations.

Fish contends that the first two books of the epic elicit sympathy for Satan and even agreement with his cause.[39] Yet I think it clear that the early parts of the poem are in part designed to keep readers off balance and free from entanglements. However we define it, Milton's "ordinary" audience shared at least one characteristic with any audience of any epic that includes a trip to the underworld; they were

38/Fish, *Surprised by Sin*, p. 9.
39/Ibid., p. 12.

eager to know what hell is like. Theories about hell and fallen angels were matters of especially heated and popular speculation in the seventeenth century, and Milton counts on this morbid fascination. But his readers do not accompany the hero on an increasingly riveting journey to the underworld, where, typically, extraordinary knowledge is imparted both to the hero and the audience. Instead, Milton's readers start in hell, without any established narrative sympathies, and, having been plunged in confusion, they may quite possibly leave it in the same state. As opposed to Dante's gentler but analogous opening, the descent into Milton's hell is neither peripatetic nor gradual. One begins in the midst of hell as well as in the midst of things; and though such a beginning is not without precedent, surely one effect of initiating the action from the very pit of the inferno—at perhaps the most dramatic moment of its history—is to overwhelm readers, effectively stunning them into at least a partial suspension of both sympathy and judgment.

As if beginning with giant forms weltering on a burning lake were not enough to amaze readers, Milton's depiction of hell quickly focuses on the perplexing epistemological condition of the damned. The conditional addressee of Satan's first speech never receives a more definite salutation than "If thou beest hee," suggesting that the anxiety of perpetual uncertainty is fundamental to Miltonic damnation (1.84). Accordingly, interrogatives of description tend to translate into indefinite exclamations of dismay: "How unlike!" "how fall'n! how chang'd!" (1.75, 84). One cannot know what hell is like, just as one cannot know if Beelzebub is (will be? was?) still really Beelzebub; the hope abandoned at these infernal gates is that based on the law of identity, the hope of an answer.

The message of all the similes that appear in books 1 and 2 seems to be that hell and its inhabitants are "not like," "far . . . beyond / Compare," "far other once," so that a bewildered Satan in describing his companions finally resorts— with almost comical effect—to a lame non-simile, "like to what ye are, / Great things resolv'd" (1.296, 587–88, 607; 2.391–92). Contrary to what Fish argues concerning the similes of hell, their tendency to undermine points of reference even as they establish them need not be taken as a device to instill in alert readers distrust of *their* natural perceptions or moral values—as if the reader and not hell were the source of the confusion.[40] The narrator's self-consuming similes may simply be designed to express the shiftiness of a locale in which ambiguity is constitutional.

Aside from enduring the anguish of irremediable confusion, Satan does, as Fish claims, display an aristocratic temper. But Fish also claims that the narrator, through his commentary on Satan's fiery speech, rebukes readers for their inclination to side with the devil:

> So spake th' Apostate Angel, though in pain,
> Vaunting aloud, but rackt with deep despair.
> [1.125–26]

To gauge everyman's reaction to this passage, Fish cites—of all commentators—the notably extreme A. J. A. Waldock, who interpreted the narrator's comment as a gentle if intrusive qualification of Satan's speech. Fish then stakes Waldock to a

40/Ibid., p. 28.

34

more tenuous claim: "Waldock falsifies his experience of the poem, I think, when he characterizes Milton's countermands as gentle. . . . We resent this rebuke, not, as Waldock suggests, because our aesthetic sense balks at a clumsy attempt to neutralize an unintentional effect, but because a failing has been exposed in a context that forces us to acknowledge it. We are angry at the epic voice, not for fudging, but for being right, for insisting that we become our own critics. There is little in the human situation more humiliating in both senses of the word, than the public acceptance of a deserved rebuke."[41] Reflecting on the disjunction between Satan's speech and the narrator's comment, Fish supposes that Waldock, refusing to be properly humiliated, lies about his true emotional response—a secret anger that Fish supposes every reader shares and that actually involves resentment, fear of public shame, and guilt.

But why should Waldock "falsify" his reaction—particularly if it involves feelings so widely shared, some of which, at least, other readers have not hesitated to express concerning other passages? No doubt feelings such as Fish describes are easily triggered, but no matter how I read this passage I cannot take the narrator's comment as a humiliating "rebuke," and with the exception of Fish's invented Waldock, I do not know of any reader who ever has.

Without denying the Romantics' sympathy for Satan, we may still recognize an alternative and more feasible response to Satan's speech and the narrator's comment. First, readers innocent of the critical wars on this issue may actually reserve judgment on Satan and his claims, as they might regarding a loud, occasionally coherent man sprawled on the sidewalk outside some exclusive club, hurling imprecations at the (unseen) management within. At this point, at least, most would still cut Satan a wide berth even if, for whatever reason, they felt sympathy for his plight. In any case, the narrator's commentary on Satan's expressions of defiance should be understood as adding to the primary impression of confusion, astonishment, and absurdity. Confronted with the verbal fist-shaking of a supine speaker who can barely lift his head, one cannot help but notice the incongruity between his physical and rhetorical postures. The narrator's derisive use of "Apostate" etymologically underscores the incongruity, and his analysis of the emotional dissonance between heroic vaunting and internal misery confirms the paralyzing inconsistency of the spectacle, while establishing and immediately qualifying the pity of it also.

In beginning *Paradise Lost*, readers consistently find themselves surrounded by senselessness. If we sympathize with Satan, it is because he, like us, though for different reasons, is dazed and confused. Hence, against the contemporary understanding of Milton's poetry as prescriptive and authoritarian, I propose that the first books of *Paradise Lost* actually work to inspire in readers a Christian negative capability.[42] As a didact who espoused an Independent's epistemology, Milton consistently asked his contemporaries to tolerate uncertainty, doubt, and division in seeking truth. Evil and error, or the potential for them, he believed to be inextricably involved with human life, fallen or unfallen, and direct encounter with them the

---

41/Ibid., p. 9.
42/I am alluding to Keats's letter to his brother and sister-in-law where he defines negative capability as "when man is capable of being in uncertainties, Mysteries, doubts, without any irritable searching after fact and reason." John Keats, *Selected Poems and Letters*, ed. Douglas Bush (Boston, 1959), p. 261. To modify Keats's words to fit Milton's sentiments, substitute "didactic doctrine" for "fact and reason."

only path to virtue. Though Fish cites him as an ethical model, Bunyan's Christian, fleeing with his hands over his ears, "crying Life, Life, Eternal Life," adopts precisely the reverse of the warfaring attitude that Milton unswervingly connects with true virtue.[43]

In rejecting Fish's application of Bunyan, I do not wish to deny that in Milton's view wisdom is generally attended by wariness, just as in Spenser's *Faerie Queene* Una is attended by the dwarf. But as in Spenser, wisdom in Milton will sometimes venture where dwarfish prudence fears to tread. Thus, to move to the second point of contention, Fish's insistence in *Surprised by Sin* that Eve should respond to temptation with an automatic, purely volitional rejection belies Milton's insistent identification of reason and choice, from *Areopagitica* ("reason is but choosing"—2:527) to *Paradise Lost* ("Reason also is choice"—3.108).[44] Eve succumbs to temptation no_ because she is "won to reason," nor because the snake successfully initiates her "into the mysteries of empirical science," but because she fails to exercise her rational power against its sophistries.[45] Milton could not have praised a fugitive Eve, who, in effect, would have run from temptation with her hands over her ears.

In fact, Eve's only attempt to answer the serpent follows precisely the course recommended by Fish: she offers a dull recitation of the prohibition (9.651–54, 659–63). The budding empiricist whom Fish wishes to see in the disobedient Eve would surely raise objections to the serpent's story, or at least require experimental confirmation ("let us feed the elephant an apple and see if it will talk"). She could have asked questions or drawn distinctions that would establish rational grounds for resistance. But instead she appeals merely to the divine prohibition, and for Milton a simple "no," a "no" not actively supported by reason, was never enough. If he agreed with Spenser that prudence and wisdom will sometimes part company, he would prefer that reason and temperance never did. In *Areopagitica* Milton even misremembers Spenser by having the Palmer Reason accompany Guyon into the Cave of Mammon (2:516). Unfortunately, Eve lets the serpent do her thinking for her and allows his erection of a false tradition and false construction of the divine word to stand unopposed. As Milton's God comments in *Paradise Regain'd*, humanity is "by fallacy surpris'd," which suggests that the first sin may be considered at least as much a rational failure as a volitional one (1.155).

It would be foolish to argue that reason alone suffices to constitute Christian heroism. Fish rightly stresses obedience to God as the definitive mark of a Christian hero. In expanding the argument to include the third point of contention, I mean only to add that, for Milton, reason cannot be separated from or—as in Fish's discussion of Eve—opposed to obedience. Abdiel exemplifies true heroism, says Fish, insofar as he represents pure obedience: "Abdiel is a hero because he says

---

43/ Fish, *Surprised by Sin*, p. 48. The implied equation of didactic content between *Pilgrim's Progress* (eight citations in *Surprised by Sin*) and *Paradise Lost* is further evidence of Fish's historical misconstruction of Milton's epic horizon.

44/ Ibid., pp. 247–54. Much has been written on the applicability of Milton's arguments in *Areopagitica* to *Paradise Lost*. The scene in the epic that has caused dispute over the validity of these arguments for prelapsarian situations is the separation scene in book 9. In order to justify her departure from Adam, Eve draws heavily on the reasoning found in *Areopagitica*. For a summary of the relevant critical opinions and a careful analysis, see Diane Kelsey McColley, *Milton's Eve* (Urbana, Ill., 1983), pp. 141–45.

45/ Fish, *Surprised by Sin*, pp. 254, 250.

36

'Shalt Thou give Law to God?' (the declarative form would be 'Thy will be done').["46" But Abdiel is heroic not because his answer to Satan is a simple "no." His defiance of Satan's illegitimate authority rests instead on an alternative construction of the revelation of the Son as God's image (5.809-45). Abdiel himself describes his resistance as a triumph of reason:

> His puissance, trusting in th' Almighty's aid,
> I mean to try, whose Reason I have tri'd
> Unsound and false; nor is it aught but just,
> That he who in debate of Truth hath won,
> Should win in Arms, in both disputes alike
> Victor; though brutish that contest and foul,
> When Reason hath to deal with force, yet so
> Most reason is that Reason overcome.
>   [6.119-26]

Abdiel does not go to the extreme associated with the ancient Stoics—that one should not obey God so much as agree with him. Yet his refusal to follow Satan has a rational as well as a volitional basis; indeed, his punning judgment ("most reason is") that he *should* triumph in arms over Satan expresses a nearly syllogistic theodical expectation. In the voluntarist world that Fish imagines, however, there is no place for the subjunctive mood in contemplating God's ways—certainly not the hortatory *ought* or *should*. Yet I cannot help thinking that if Abdiel were to fail in his single combat, God would by rights have some explaining to do. Here, though, we double back toward the ground already covered by Luther and Erasmus.

V

Having begun with an examination of theoretical premises, and now ending with particular readings of various scenes in Milton's epic, I have attempted to establish a coherent opposition to what is still the most influential contemporary study of *Paradise Lost*. In so doing I have not relied chiefly on new evidence concerning Milton or his epic, nor have I proposed a new theory for reading *Paradise Lost*. Instead, I have simply recollected some of what is already understood about Milton and his poem and have attempted to show the inconsistency of Fish's Milton with what is generally admitted about him in other contexts. Some bits of this picture, itself a product of interpretation, are not so generally admitted as others—the place of Chaos in Milton's theology, for example. Yet, after all disclaimers are duly noted and weighed, jarring discrepancies remain in this invented Milton. The Milton in the midst of our interpretive community, or at least one widely accepted version of him, is an imposter.

Surprised by Sin is most clearly inaccurate in its vision of Milton and his epic when it diminishes the theodicy by describing it as a disingenuous ploy. Not only does this contention imply blatant theological inconsistency on Milton's part— particularly concerning the ramifications of his systematic and unswerving assertions of free will—but it also ignores the presence of theodicy almost everywhere in Milton's writing, from "On the Death of a Fair Infant" to *Samson Agonistes*. Did Milton always bait his traps the same way, encouraging theodical presumption only

---

46/ Ibid., p. 183.

to castigate it? One supposes that Milton's "ordinary" audience would eventually have tired of this one-trick Pegasus and its predictable and thus ineffective didactic subterfuge.

A subtler error in Fish's argument concerns the supposed origins of Milton's didacticism in a tradition of anticarnal dualism. Actually, within the context of heretical material monism, Milton consistently carnalizes spirituality and spiritualizes carnality, blurring the distinction between, and even identifying, creatures' carnal and divine instincts. Moreover, his God, in the allegorical personages of Chaos and Night, has his own fleshly side of material potency, which substantiates his infinite creative power and absolute freedom.

Concerning the tone of the didacticism in *Paradise Lost*, I have claimed that Fish attributes to Milton an unsuitable, offensive didactic persona, one that runs counter to his decisively Independent epistemological principles. To support this contention, my discussion turned finally to the poem itself and questioned Fish's interpretation on three key points, suggesting alternatives more appropriate to an author for whom a genuine theodicy was possible and whose confidence in human dignity and reason allowed for heroism beyond mere submission.

It may be objected that rather than uninvent Milton, this essay merely reinvents him or adds another to the crowd; the real John Milton cannot stand up. Admittedly, Fish's invention makes it difficult to view *Paradise Lost* in isolation from the subjectivity of its readers or its didactic effect on them. Nor do I suppose it desirable to do so; if Fish fails in his invention of Milton, he achieves a measure of success in his invention of the reader. Given the now unignorable presence of Milton's interpretive community, this essay has left an obvious question still unanswered. It is this: if Milton's attempt at theodicy is genuine, how can it be said to succeed when so many readers, even if they do not side with Satan, dislike his God and find his defense of providence unconvincing?

To discuss this question fully lies beyond my present scope, but in concluding I wish nevertheless to suggest that the problem lies in our understanding of the nature of theodicy and in our expectation of the kind of teaching that *Paradise Lost* should offer. The notion of a rational theodicy need not imply the comprehension and approval by reason of things as they are, nor even of divine providence as their author. What Jeffrey Barnouw has identified as the intention governing Leibniz's theodicy applies also to Milton's: "to justify the persistence of moral striving even in the face of apparent futility."[47] Milton's theodicy need not enable us to formulate an answer to the problem of evil in order to succeed. It works if it enables us to walk out of the poem with Adam and Eve, ready to encounter what the world has in store.[48] The literary didacticism of *Paradise Lost* is not built around the catechetical framework of doctrinal and moral lessons to be learned, but it instead concerns the human struggle for knowledge and our necessarily imperfect and subjective grasp of truth. Milton's epic encourages us to join with our first parents in inventing the theodicy—encourages us to seek an interpretive resolution that allows for negotiation between the extremes of suicidal despair and false dreams. Such a

47/ Jeffrey Barnouw, "The Separation of Reason and Faith in Bacon and Hobbes, and in Leibniz's Theodicy," *Journal of the History of Ideas* 42 (1981): 607-28.
48/ Kerrigan (n. 8 above), pp. 296-97.

resolution uncovers what the poem has to offer in the way of "equipment for living" or what Warwick Wadlington describes as "the reflection of and contribution to human being."[49] More to the point of this essay, such an approach concentrates not so much on the admonitory or doctrinal Milton as on his attempts to foster in his readers precisely the willingness to persevere in the field of this world that he believed essential to the constitution of human virtue.

University of Texas at Austin

49/Kenneth Burke, *The Philosophy of Literary Form* (1941, 1967; revised, Berkeley, 1973), pp. 293-304; Warwick Wadlington, *Reading Faulknerian Tragedy* (Ithaca, N.Y., 1987), p. 32.

PARADISE LOST:
THE UNCERTAIN EPIC

Balachandra Rajan

THE PROBLEM of the genre of *Paradise Lost* seems to have been a problem from the day the poem was published. Dryden may have said that "this man . . . cuts us all out and the ancients too,"[1] but it did not take long for the caution of the critic to make its inroads on the generosity of the poet. In the preface to *Sylvae* (1685) the objections are stylistic—to the "flats" among Milton's elevations, to his "antiquated words," and to the "perpetual harshness" of their sound. But eight years later, in the *Discourse Concerning the Original and Progress of Satire*, the qualifications become more substantial. The earlier objections are repeated, and Milton's lack of talent in rhyming is added to them. But we are also told that Milton's subject "is not that of an heroic poem properly so called. His design is the losing of our happiness; his event is not prosperous like that of all other epic works; his heavenly machines are many and his human persons are but two."[2] In the dedication to his translation of the *Aeneid* (1697) Dryden begins by saying that "a heroic poem, truly such, is undoubtedly the greatest work which the soul of man is capable to perform."[3] Homer and Virgil are sovereign in the genre. "The next, but the next with a long interval between was the *Jerusalem*."[4] Spenser would have had a better case than some continental claimants to the succession "had his action been finished, or had been one." Milton's title would have been less suspect "if the devil had not been his hero, instead of Adam; if the giant had not failed the knight, and driven him out of his stronghold, to wander through the world with his lady errant; and if there had not been more machining persons than human in his poem."[5] Dryden, it will be observed, gives his objections force by both repeating and extending them. To earlier statements about the unfortunate outcome and the excess of heavenly machinery in *Paradise Lost* he now adds the suggestion that the action, the epic propriety of which may be dubious, is in any case centered on the wrong hero. The persistence of crucial objections and the adding of related ones thus come to constitute a platform from which the genre of the poem can be interrogated.

41

Much can be discerned from Dryden's platform. The unfortunate outcome exposes Milton's poem to consideration as tragic rather than epic. If Satan is the hero, he is the hero within an antiquest that invites us to view *Paradise Lost* as anti-epic or parodic epic. Addison's response to Dryden argues that no hero was intended but suggests Christ, if need be, as the hero. This defense of the poem converts it into a providential epic, but one which engages the human only at its periphery.[6] It thus undermines one of Dryden's objections but only at the cost of underlining another. The Romantic reinstatement of Satan as the hero is, of course, not an endorsement of Dryden. It attacks the question of what the poem is by suggesting that there is a poem other than the official poem in which the real nature of Milton's accomplishment is to be found. Generic uncertainty is compounded by viewing *Paradise Lost* as an act of creative subversion in which the true poem overthrows the establishment exercise.

The two-poem theory, in turn, has ramifications which continue into the present. We can simply reverse the Romantic valuation and regard the true poem as the official one. The true poem can then stand in relation to the false as icon does to idol, or as reality to parody within an antithetical universe.[7] We can regard the two poems as confronting each other creatively or as A. J. A. Waldock would have it, locked in destructive conflict.[8] It can be argued that the two poems only appear to be two and that it is the purpose of reader education to bring them into concurrence.[9] Finally, like A. S. P. Woodhouse, we can think of the two poems as engaged with each other through a double protagonist, each functioning within a different genre.[10]

It may be that the course of criticism after Dryden is misguided and that, as John M. Steadman proposes, Milton is writing an "illustrious" epic fully compatible with Italian Neo-Aristotelianism, while Dryden's criticisms are made from the vantage point of a Neo-Aristotelianism that is distinctly French.[11] Certainly neither Aristotle nor the Italians prescribe a fortunate outcome for the epic. But Milton published *Paradise Lost* in 1667, when Italian Neo-Aristotelianism was hardly representative of current critical trends. We are accustomed to these gestures of obsolescence in Milton, which include the imaginative adoption of a slightly antiquated model of the universe. The voice of the outsider is also a voice from the past, a voice disowning if not excoriating the triviality of the present. Nevertheless, the history of reading *Paradise Lost* points to real difficulties which are not disposed of by a more accurate generic assignation. A poem which may be two poems initially or finally, in which there are three possible heroes and even the possibility of two heroes rather than one, is not a poem about which one can be certain.

Some of the problems of placing *Paradise Lost* are interestingly suggested by William Willkie in a preface (1757) to a heroic poem of his own. Willkie is writing about the difficulties of reconciling the untrue with the true, or historical, in an epic poem. Spenser accomplishes this reconciliation through the evasions of allegory. Willkie then notes (remembering Dryden) that in *Paradise Lost* "persons in machinery overshadow the human characters" and adds (remembering Addison) that "the heroes of the poem are all of them immortal." *Paradise Lost* escapes a requirement that looms over epic poetry by being "a work altogether irregular. . . . The subject of it is not epic, but tragic. . . . Adam and Eve are not designed to be objects of admiration, but of pity. . . . It is tragic in its plot but epic in its dress and machinery."[12]

Willkie may be the first critic to recognize that *Paradise Lost* is not only a mixed-genre poem but a mixed-genre poem with a different protagonist for each of its primary genres. It is true that given Aristotle's views of the importance of plot, the identification of the epic with "dress and machinery" relegates it to a status in *Paradise Lost* which is peripheral rather than central. It is also true that Willkie describes *Paradise Lost* as "altogether irregular," though he does so in an age which was beginning to admire irregularity; the observation does not mean that the poem is to be reproached for its generic lawlessness. Nevertheless, Willkie's remarks do broach the question of whether it is necessary or even desirable to locate *Paradise Lost* unambiguously within any single genre.

It may be argued that the difficulties surrounding the generic assignation of *Paradise Lost* are difficulties encountered by the reader rather than difficulties to which the author admits. That does not make the difficulties any less real, but it may be instructive to look at some of the ways in which the poem announces itself and at the related proposition that the poem always knows what kind of a poem it is. *Paradise Lost* treats itself as "adventurous Song" in the first book (13), as "sacred Song" in the third book (29), as "Song" of which the "copious matter" is the Son's name and arts (III, 412–13), as "Song" related to "celestial song" in the seventh book (12, 30), and as "Heroic Song" in the ninth book, but only after the audience has been advised that the forthcoming notes of the song will be "Tragic" (6, 25). These descriptions are not so divergent as to render reconciliation difficult, but they certainly do not suggest resolute consistency in the poem's classification of itself. They suggest rather the desire to have the best of several worlds, which is characteristic of a mixed-genre poet.

In the poems that precede *Paradise Lost,* Milton's attitude to inherited genres is powerfully revisionary. We console ourselves by describing it as a strong case of tradition and the individual talent or by saying, as John Reesing does, that Milton strains the mold but does not break it.[13] The *Ode on the Morning of Christ's Nativity,* in describing itself as both a hymn and an ode, may be initiating Milton's career with a mixed-genre announcement.[14] In *Comus* the poet makes use of the antithetical dispositions of a genre new enough to be open to experiment in order to construct a staging ground for issues and confrontations which we have come to call Miltonic. *Lycidas* directs the capacity of the pastoral for protest into a protest against the pastoral genre itself. In each case Milton identifies certain propensities of the genre as giving the genre its way of achieving understanding and then reorganizes the form around those propensities. In each case the ordering power of the genre is made to compass a higher degree of inclusiveness than the genre has hitherto accommodated. We can expect these creative habits to continue as Milton comes to his most inclusive undertaking.

A primary characteristic of the epic is inclusiveness. When Aristotle differentiates tragedy from epic, he does not do so on the basis of the outcome, the agent, or the emotion excited by the literary work. His concern is with the manner of presentation and the magnitude of the action.[15] The tragic action should confine itself as far as possible to a single circuit of the sun. The epic action can be longer, and a month is extended to a year by Italian critics. While the longer action can sustain itself by an adequate proliferation of incident, the epic, as it graduates from the tale of a tribe to the statement of a civilization, tends increasingly to sustain itself by cultural omnivorousness as much as by narrative complication. The epic and the encyclopedic are thus brought into convergence. In a late epic the encyclopedic interest will involve consideration of the uses of the past, including the past of the epic genre itself. When the generic inheritance is codified to the extent of seeming petrified, the consideration can be revisionary and can extend—as is arguable in Milton's case—into a revisionary treatment of the whole past. A genre can also be enlarged and thus freed from impending exhaustion of possibilities by incorporating into it the possibilities of another genre not hitherto digested. Mixed genres are thus a natural deliverance from the constraints of a genre which it is necessary to use and which has already been used too heavily. In an epic, such absorptiveness can be particularly felicitous since it is clearly the literary application of a principle on which the epic has increasingly been based. An encyclopedic epic should include a generic compendium.

Studies by Rosalie Colie and more recently by Barbara Lewalski have drawn attention tellingly to the generic inclusiveness of *Paradise Lost*.[16] Lewalski's suggestion that the various genres in the epic are means of accommodation to the reader, or of the narrator within the poem to the auditor, also responds to a problem that arises when we think of the epic as a generic compendium. The encyclopedic substance of an epic is a matter of what it contains; the generic variety is a matter of how what is contained is conveyed. Multeity of genres is most convincingly called for when the area of exploration is sufficiently inclusive to require more than one style of mediation or access. God's creation, as a fully comprehensive poem, is also a poem that engages us in an adequate variety of relationships. Any mimesis of the perfect original should be similarly rich in means of accommodation or opportunities for engagement.[17]

Nevertheless, it should not be assumed that the purpose, or even the designed purpose, of generic multeity is always to contribute to the overall harmony, to show how many styles of discourse lead us to the one Word, or to the unifying capability that is the "one word" of the poem. Multiple genres can provide the ingredients for subversion as well as for synthesis. Their purpose may be to show not the overall concord but the fragmentation of any single style of understanding that unavoidably comes about when the fictive is brought into engagement with the actual. I am not suggesting that Milton's use of mixed genres was governed by this principle or that it proceeded to this point irrespective of the original principle by which it was governed. But on the other hand it is not easy to argue that his poem is the unperturbed implementation of a "great idea" or "fore-conceit," as the Creation is in the seventh book of *Paradise Lost*. A blueprint for the epic must have existed in the author's mind, particularly if, as Allan H. Gilbert long ago argued,[18] the poem was not written in the order in which it unfolds. But the blueprint cannot have been unaffected by the stresses and strains within the poem and by the poem's reconsideration of itself during the deeply frustrating decade of its formation.

If many genres are to be fitted together harmoniously in a poem, they must be subject to a primary genre which is unambiguously proclaimed and clearly dominant. When a primary genre is subject to revisionary treatment and when its status is further undermined by another genre asserting a claim to primacy, the subordinate genres are as likely to reflect this central confrontation as to soothe it.

In *The Reason of Church-Government* (1642), Milton was asking himself "whether those dramatic constitutions wherein Sophocles and

Euripides raigne" were not "more doctrinal and exemplary to a nation"
(YP, I, 812–15) than the epic undertaking by which he was fascinated.[19]
We know from Edward Phillips that *Paradise Lost* began as a tragedy and
that Milton showed Phillips the first ten lines of Satan's address to the sun
as the planned beginning of the drama he intended to write.[20] The draft of
"Adam unparadiz'd" in the Trinity manuscript shows us the dramatic
nucleus in which *Paradise Lost* began. Even though the poem moved
away from the nucleus it continued to remain engaged to its origins.

The ten books of the first edition of *Paradise Lost*, read as five acts
of two books each, are tragic in several of their dispositons. In the fourth
act the Creation is undone by the Fall. The fifth act gives us the tragic
aftermath of the fourth, the expansion of evil into space and its extension
into history. The repentance of Adam and Eve, sandwiched between
two huge movements of destructiveness, simply does not have the importance which the twelve-book version succeeds in winning from it. It
is true that Christ's victory is the climax of the third act, but this matters
less when Satan's victory is so effectively dominant in the fifth.

If this reading of the tragic weight of the ten-book structure is not
erroneous, we can regard the twelve-book version as designed, among
other things, to take corrective action. The creative forces are underlined slightly in the poems contest of energies. Christ's presence in the
poem is strengthened by the division of the poem into three parts, each
consisting of four books, with Christ the protagonist of the four central
books. Two victories of light—the Battle in Heaven, and the Creation—
are juxtaposed at the center of this central part. The repentance of Adam
and Eve is given greater weight. Having said this much, it becomes
important to add that the degree of corrective action is slight. It may be
that no more could be done, since the poem had been in print for seven
years. It may also be that Milton did not wish to do more.

Arthur E. Barker rightly observes that the twelve-book version
does not supersede the ten-book one, that one must read both poems
and be aware of both patterns, and that the poem is suspended "between the horns of a paradox."[21] For such a paradox to exist, the poem's
primary genres must be in contest with, rather than concordant with,
each other. The poem does not seek the assimilation of one genre by
another or even, to quote Coleridge's famous phrase, "the balance or
reconciliation of opposite or discordant qualities."[22] Rather it seeks to
navigate between genres, remaining responsive to the current of each
without surrendering to the pull of either.

Such a hypothesis seems natural when we remind ourselves of the
poem's antithetical world, the embattled contraries between which the

choosing center is suspended, as the poem itself is suspended creatively between competing claims on its identity. It is not simply a mixed-genre poem but a poem of which generic uncertainty may be a keynote. Critics may be understandably reluctant to admit uncertainty at the heart of a poem. A work of art thus divided is considered to be in a state of civil war. But creative indeterminacy can also be read as a sign of the authentic rather than the chaotic. Two powerful patterns of possibility contest with each other, as they do in reality. The outcome will shift from moment to moment. The poem's obligation is to draw the field of force and not to delineate the local and interim settlement.

Against this hypothesis it can be argued that Aristotle treats tragedy and epic as concordant genres.[23] The manner of presentation and the magnitude of the action are important but not fundamental differences and certainly not differences that might place either genre in potential conflict with the other. When Thomas Hobbes tells us that "the heroic poem, dramatic, is tragedy," he is carrying convergence a step further. He does so in proceeding to the masterfully sterile conclusion that "there can be no more or less than six kinds of poetry."[24] The Italian critics avoid Hobbes's overwhelming simplicity, but, as Steadman shows, they do not on the whole regard tragedy and epic as divergent.[25]

This objection has force. It can be partially countered by arguing that even though the Italian critics may not have seen tragedy and epic as divergent, they did recognize the creative potentiality of divergent genres. If God's creation is the perfect poem, its mimesis may consist not only of simulating its variety (which includes generic variety) but also of simulating the manner in which the first poem triumphed over its own divisiveness. Creation, we must not forget, was won out of chaos, from equal energies implacably opposed. The best poem may be that in which the center succeeds in holding against the maximum of centrifugal force. Like Milton's universe, such a poem is continually threatened by its contents. Tasso seems to be advocating a poetics of contrariety on this model when he argues that "the art of composing a poem resembles the plan of the Universe which is composed of contraries." He goes on to maintain that "such a variety will be so much the more marvellous as it brings with it a measure of difficulty and almost impossibility."[26] Guarini is less given to the tour de force than Tasso. In defending tragicomedy, Guarini considers it as a third genre arising from two genres which are divergent, but not so divergent that they cannot be creatively mingled. Each genre tempers the other so that the overall composition corresponds more fully "to the mixture of the human body which consists entirely in the tempering of the four humors."[27]

There is thus some sanction in Renaissance criticism for divergent genres curbing each other's excesses, or divergent genres being made to submit to the cohesive force of the poem. Milton's poem can be viewed from both prospects, but like any deeply creative achievement it has to go beyond the gestures towards it that are made by critical theory.

As has been indicated, Milton equivocates mildly about the kind of song he is singing when he links *Paradise Lost* to that particular word. The varying epithets are not difficult to bring together, but the variations remind us to be cautious in our classification of the poem. No more than a reminder is needed, since the poem at its very outset, in announcing the compass of its subject, is also conveying that announcement through a vivid drama of contesting genres. The opening lines of *Paradise Lost* have been commented on in great detail and from what may seem every possible perspective,[28] but their status as a generic manifesto still remains to be examined. In attempting the unattempted Milton may have been attempting an unattempted mixture.

Milton's virtuosity in stating the subject of the whole poem before the predicate of its initial sentence isolates the first five lines spectacularly from the narrative flow. The minidrama of these lines is therefore all the more effective in counselling us not only on what the poem is to be about but also on how it is to be experienced. From the beginning the tragic weight accumulates, reinforced by the alliterative joinings and by the alternative scansions of the first line. If the dominant stress falls on "Mans," we are reading a poem somberly homocentric in its allocation of destructiveness. If it falls on "First" we are reading a poem of the gestation of evil, with the alliterative movement through "First," "Fruit," and "Forbidden" compounding the inexorable growth.[29] "Tree," "tast," and "mortal" are the origin of this growth, though dramatically they are arrived at as its climax, the tragic center of the darkening song. "World" and "woe" sound the dimensions of a universe of tragedy. Nothing so far has restrained the onward movement, the accumulation of sorrow. The prospective genre of the poem—tragedy—has been uncomprisingly and, it would seem, irrevocably stated. Yet on the basis of a text from the Book of Romans (v, 19) a countermovement launches itself, generating itself from the previous movements by virtue of the coupling between man and "greater Man." There is even a counter-alliteration, responding to the massed alliterative linkages of destructiveness, affirming the victory of the light in "Restore" and "regain." This is what one might say on a superficial reading. A reading more open to the poem's reality would recognize that the relationship between human tragedy and providential epic is more complex than the simple overcoming of one genre by another. It is possible to say, by adjusting one's mind slightly to the impact of the opening, that the epic retrieval stands at the horizon of the poem, while the tragic gestation (to which the bulk of the first five lines are given) unavoidably dominates its stage. It is possible to reflect on the distancing force of "till" and ask if the deliverance at the horizon is more than potential. How far does the tragic actuality frustrate and even nullify the epic promise? It is certainly true, as the mind moves with the poem in its unfolding, that we cannot avoid passing through the tragic proliferation before arriving at the genre that might contain it. The two genres are, in fact, inexorably entangled by the powerfully staged drama of the poem's syntax. The poem does not choose between affiliations. It forms itself out of the contest between them.

Paradise Lost presents itself not only as a mixed-genre poem but as a mixed-genre poem of deep generic uncertainty. It has to be uncertain because the very history that it seeks to understand has, perhaps fortunately, not yet found its genre. The poem seeks its identity between contesting possibilities, as does that human community which is both the poem's subject and its audience.

Though the contest of primary genres in the opening lines of *Paradise Lost* has been examined, not every genre in those first five lines has been identified. Between the accumulating onslaught of the tragic, "Under her own waight groaning" as the twelfth book says of history (539), and the restorative encirclement of the providential, there is the muted phrase "With loss of *Eden*." The residual alliteration with "World" and "woe" attaches this part of the line to the tragic momentum. The loss can be taken as the sum of our sadness, the distillation of everything that has gone before it in the sentence. But the half-line is also an entry into a possible triumphant future, that Ithaca which the highest of heroes may regain. The phrase stands between two worlds, distanced from itself by the poem's initial onslaught of destructiveness and distanced again from itself by the postponing force of "till." The curiously nondescript language suggests the absence, or rather the residual and unavoidably veiled presence, of what the phrase invokes. It can no longer be known in its own right but only through the genres of loss and seeking.

In the days when it was fashionable to distinguish between the real and the nominal subjects of *Paradise Lost*, Paul Elmer More observed that the real subject of the poem was Paradise.[30] The remark is neither naive nor tautological. The strong affinities of Eden with Arcadia, the Golden Age, and the pastoral strain in the Bible not only establish it in the landscape of memory, including literary memory, but also affiliate it to a third genre, the pastoral. The three genres, in turn, affiliate themselves to the three main locales of the poem, so that we can think with caution but without injustice of a tragic Hell (including human fallenness), an epic Heaven, and a pastoral Paradise. Since the forces in the universe of *Paradise Lost* converge so powerfully upon its choosing center, one can argue that the pastoral understanding plays a crucial part in the poem's declaration of itself.

John R. Knott, Jr., skillfully underlines the *otium* of Paradise, its "grateful vicissitude," the harmony of man with nature, and the harmony of nature with itself.[31] Cities in *Paradise Lost* are not statements of civilization. Babel and Pandemonium tell of their pride. The world is likened once to a metropolis "With glistering Spires and Pinnacles adorn'd" (III, 550), but it is viewed thus by Satan in the image of the desirable. Little is said of the metropolitan amenities of Heaven except that its shape is "undetermined," that it is adorned with opal towers and battlements of sapphire (II, 1047–50), and that the dust of its main road is gold (VII, 577). It is Satan, not God, who lives in what might metaphorically be called a palace, a superstructure built on a structure of pyramids and towers "From Diamond Quarries hew'n, and Rocks of Gold" (V, 754–61). Heaven is most frequently spoken of in pastoral language, possibly as an accommodation to Adam, who is unfamiliar with city life, but more probably to indicate the continuity between the celestial and the unfallen.

Yet though the ideal order of *Paradise Lost* has extensive pastoral elements and though the poem can be poignantly pastoral in its nostalgia, the "happy rural seat of various view" (IV, 247) does not always open out into pastoral prospects. The weeping trees that are spoken of in the next line suggest a place haunted by tragedy as well as by creative plenitude. There is much foreboding in the language of Paradise—in the wantonness of its energies, the "mazy error" of its brooks, and in its surpassing of that "fair field" where the "fairer flower," Proserpina, was gathered (V, 294–97; IV, 268–72; IV, 237–40). More important, Paradise is not a place of tranquility, of fragile but deep peace before the gathering storm. In its nature it is free from the burden of the past, but in its nature it is also singularly subject to the anxieties of the unprecedented. Nearly everything that happens in Paradise happens for the first time, so if one's response to life is not the result of a pre-existent, celestially implanted program, it can only come together and manifest a pattern through a series of related improvisations. Baffling dreams, angelic visitations, and discussions with the author of one's being on the need of the self for an otherness seem part of the normalities of Paradise.

"Is there no change of death in Paradise?" Wallace Stevens asks. "Does ripe fruit never fall? Or do the boughs / Hang always heavy in that perfect sky."[32] In the stasis of perfection, all change is the death of perfection. Yet not to change is to perpetuate the permanence of lifelessness. Milton provides for change in Paradise that is quite other than the "change of death," thereby adroitly satisfying the second of Stevens's desiderata for a supreme fiction: "It must change."[33] In his repeated use of the figure of the dance in describing ideal order, he advises us of a perfection consummated in motion rather than memorialized in stillness.[34] Motion must include alteration in one's state of being as well as alteration in one's place, and this alteration takes place, as Raphael suggests, by the working of a body up to spirit, "in bounds / Proportioned to each kind" (V, 478–79). Such evolution cannot take place by standing still on an ontological escalator. In a world in which the perfection of the human species includes the power of free choice—a power the importance of which is underlined by the enormous cosmic price which the divine is prepared to pay to keep it in being—there must be a steady succession of opportunities for self-formative choosing. It is hard to believe that Adam and Eve, if they had not eaten of the apple, would have lived happily ever after as creative gardeners.[35] The Appleton estate in Marvell's poem subversively mimeticizes the world from which it withdraws. Milton's Garden, in its crises, makes itself continuous with that future which is to become its tragic legacy. It is no accident that the images Michael uses to characterize progress in history correspond to the images Raphael uses to characterize upward evolution on the ontological scale (V, 996–98; V, 575–77; XII, 300–304). In the first place, the equivalence makes evident the restoration of the *status quo ante*. By making himself eligible for the continuing intervention of "supernal grace," man is able to stand as he once did "On even ground against his mortal foe" (III, 179). In the second place, the statement of equivalence, made through figures of progress with which we are not unfamiliar, joins the prelapsarian and postlapsarian worlds. The status of man is radically different, and his commitment to destructiveness requires the steady application of a counterforce that no longer lies within his natural capacity. But if the conditions for that counterforce are brought into being, the two worlds can reflect each other in their opportunities and challenges. The pastoral idyll never quite existed. The Garden was fully itself only in creative dependence on a shaping principle beyond itself. It was not a place of withdrawal but of change and growth built on evolving interrelationships with the entire structure of reality which surrounded it. What was lost was not the Garden but that creative possibility which the Garden embodied and promised.

This excursion into the poem suggests how it responds to those stresses and balances which the first five lines urge so compellingly on our reading of what follows. The pastoral statement does not exist by itself. It is annexed in the first place to a tragic unfolding through which we are obliged to make our way in order to measure what is meant by "loss of *Eden*." It is attached in the second place to a providential counter-poem through which the lost possibilities can be recovered and fulfilled. In fact, its location and attachments are suggestive of the created world in *Paradise Lost*, suspended from Heaven by a golden chain and connected to Hell by a causeway. What the pastoral center comes to mean depends on how it is oriented. As a generic claim, it must yield to those more powerful claimants which seek possession of the structure of things.[36] The drama of genres which the first five lines enact is thus singularly accurate in prefiguring not only the generic character of the poem but the disposition of real forces which that character represents.

One of the unusual strengths of *Paradise Lost* is the poem's capacity to reconsider itself. It can indulge in "tedious havoc" and then excoriate it (IX, 27–33). It can describe the fall of Mulciber in language of limpid beauty and then pull us back from our involvement with a "Thus they relate / Erring" (I, 738–48), leaving us to wonder whether the event is being questioned or whether language itself is being rebuked as falsification. It propounds huge structures of elaboration and ornament to arrive at the "upright heart" in its unadorned authenticity. It uses the past with lavish erudition and overgoes it with competitive zest, largely to underline the obsolescence of what it invokes. It appoints Michael, the leader of the angelic battalions, to preach the politics of nonviolence and the primacy of the interior victory. Some of these dismissals are designed to educate the reader and to instruct him in discriminating truth from its cunning resemblance (see YP, II, 154). Others arise because the poem, in charting the progress from shadowy types to truth, endows itself with a history that to some degree mirrors the history it interprets. But we are also looking at a poem that is endeavoring to achieve its identity and which, as the opening lines have promised, will form itself among contesting generic possibilities. It must not only make itself but justify what it makes against the challenges of an era of deep change. Since its attitude to the inheritance is so powerfully revisionary, honesty demands that it also be self-revising.

In the fifth book of *Paradise Lost* Adam and Eve, after a troubled night, do not simply address the Almighty in prayer. Rather they participate in a prayer which the whole creation offers to its maker out of the way in which it moves and lives. The prayer is Vaughan's "great hymn / And Symphony of nature," the ardent music of "the world in tune." It is also Herbert's "something understood," a structure of relationships which the mind experiences as the ground of its being.[37] "Firm peace" and "wonted calm" are its consequences (V, 209–10). We are told that Adam and Eve have previously made their "unisons" in "various style" (145–46). The plentitude of innocence offers more than one way of access and relationship. The "unmediated" art of the person praying (148–49)[38] may even find the opportunity to invent a genre.

At the end of the tenth book, Adam and Eve pray again. The first prayer preceded the descent of Raphael. The second precedes the descent of Michael. The world has changed, and a lost structure of possibility, borne away as in the real world on the flood of history's disappointments, has also taken with it its proper language. The new desolation calls for the unadorned, the concentration on what is primary. Many poems have an energy of destitution within them, waving their leaves and flowers in the sun so that they may wither into the truth of themselves.[39] In *Paradise Lost* that destitutive energy is launched by an immense act of original destructiveness. From the moment that Adam and Eve eat the apple, much in the poem is rendered obsolete, including some of its literary genres. In these stern dismissals lies a great deal of the poem's authenticity as well as its weight of sadness. But the world remains before us and remains capable of yielding us its language. If *Paradise Lost* is an uncertain epic, it is uncertain not because it is confused or vacillating, but because it is clear about how it must form itself.

University of Western Ontario

NOTES

1. *Early Lives of Milton*, ed. Helen Darbishire (London, 1932), p. 296.
2. *Of Dramatic Poetry and Other Critical Essays*, ed. George Watson (London, 1962), II, 32, 84–85.
3. Ibid., II, 223.
4. Ibid., II, 232. For futher statements on the sovereignty of Virgil and Homer in the genre, see II, 167; II, 195. Spenser (II, 150; II, 83–84) is Virgilian. But Milton, though Spenser's "poetical son" (II, 270), is Homeric rather than Virgilian (II, 150).

5. Ibid., II, 233.

6. *Milton, The Critical Heritage*, ed. John T. Shawcross (London, 1970), p. 166.

7. John M. Steadman, *Milton and the Renaissance Hero* (Oxford, 1967); Balachandra Rajan, "The Cunning Resemblance," in *Milton Studies*, VII, ed. Albert C. Labriola and Michael Lieb (Pittsburgh, 1975), pp. 29–48.

8. *"Paradise Lost" and Its Critics* (Cambridge, 1947).

9. Stanley Fish, *Surprised by Sin* (Berkeley and Los Angeles, 1971).

10. *The Heavenly Muse*, ed. Hugh MacCallum (Toronto, 1972), pp. 176–94.

11. *Epic and Tragic Structure in "Paradise Lost"* (Chicago, 1976).

12. William Willkie, "Preface to the *Epigoniad*," in *Milton 1732–1801, the Critical Heritage*, ed. John T. Shawcross (London, 1972), p. 240.

13. *Milton's Poetic Art* (Cambridge, Mass., 1969), p. 49. See also p. 135.

14. For the poem as a hymn see Philip Rollinson, "Milton's Nativity Poem and the Decorum of Genre," in *Milton Studies*, VII, pp. 165–88. For the poem as an ode, see David B. Morris, "Drama and Stasis in Milton's *Ode on the Morning of Christ's Nativity*," *SP*, LVII (1971), 207–22. For the poem as both, see Hugh MacCallum, "The Narrator of Milton's *On the Morning of Christ's Nativity*," in *Familiar Colloquy: Essays Presented to Arthur Edward Barker*, ed. Patricia Bruckmann (Salzburg, 1976), pp. 179–95. Milton's reference in *The Reason of Church-Government* to "magnifick Odes and Hymns" (YP, I, 815), suggests that he may have thought of the two genres as strongly related to each other. The relationship may well be in the manner envisaged by Nehemiah Rogers, who writes of hymns as "special songs of praise and thanksgiving" and of odes as containing "doctrine of the chiefe good, or mans eternall felicitie" and as being made "after a more majesticall forme, than ordinary" (*A Strange Vineyard in Palaestina: in an Exposition of Isaiahs Parabolical Song of the Beloved* [London, 1623], pp. 8–9).

15. *Poetics*, 1449b, 1459b.

16. Rosalie Colie, *The Resources of Kind: Genre Theory in the Renaissance*, ed. Barbara K. Lewalski (Berkeley and Los Angeles, 1973); Lewalski, "The Genres of *Paradise Lost*," paper read at the Modern Language Association Meeting, San Francisco, Dec. 28, 1979; cf. Lewalski's essay in this volume.

17. Tasso describes the writing of a poem as "a work almost godlike that seems to imitate the First Maker" (*Discourses on the Heroic Poem*, trans. Mariella Cavalchini and Irene Samuel [Oxford, 1971], p. 97). For the creation as the perfect poem see also S. K. Heninger, Jr., *Touches of Sweet Harmony* (San Marino, Calif., 1976), pp. 290–94.

18. *On the Composition of "Paradise Lost"* (Chapel Hill, N.C., 1947).

19. Milton's "whether" reflects the continuous controversy about the status of epic and tragedy relative to each other. The Renaissance and, more emphatically, Dryden found epic the higher of the two genres. But Aristotle (*Poetics*, 1402a) had declared in favor of tragedy.

20. "The Life of Mr. John Milton," in *Early Lives of Milton*, pp. 72–73.

21. "Structural Pattern in *Paradise Lost*," rpt. in *Milton: Modern Essays in Criticism*, ed. Arthur E. Barker (New York, 1965), p. 154.

22. *Biographia Literaria*, XIV.

23. *Poetics*, loc. cit.

24. "The Answer of Mr. Hobbes to Sr. Will. D'Avenant's Preface before *Gondibert*," in *Critical Essays of the Seventeenth Century*, ed. J. E. Spingarn, 3 vols. (Oxford, 1908), II, 54–55.

25. *Epic and Tragic Structure in "Paradise Lost."*

26. *Discourses on the Heroic Poem*, p. 78.

27. "The Compendium of Tragicomic Poetry," in *Literary Criticism: Plato to Dryden*, ed. Allan H. Gilbert (New York, 1940), p. 512.

28. Among the examinations are David Daiches, "The Opening of *Paradise Lost*," in *The Living Milton*, ed. Frank Kermode (London, 1960), pp. 55–69, and Joseph Summers, *The Muse's Method* (London, 1962), pp. 11–31. Book-length studies of the invocations include Anne D. Ferry, *Milton's Epic Voice* (Cambridge, Mass., 1963), and William Riggs, *The Christian Poet in "Paradise Lost"* (Berkeley and Los Angeles, 1972).

29. In asking some seventy students to read this line, I have found that 45 percent put the dominant stress on "Mans" and 45 percent put it on "First." The remainder put it on the third syllable of "disobedience." Of those stressing "Mans," the great majority were men. Of those stressing "First" the great majority were women.

30. *Shelburne Essays*, quoted by E. M. W. Tillyard, *Milton* (London, 1930), p. 283.

31. *Milton's Pastoral Vision* (Chicago, 1971). The phrase from PL "grateful vicissitude" (VI, 8), describes the alternation of light and darkness issuing from a cave within the mount of God. It is used by Summers (*Muse's Method*, pp. 71–86) as emblematic of Paradise.

32. "Sunday Morning," in *Harmonium* (New York, 1923), p. 92.

33. *Notes Toward a Supreme Fiction* (Cummington, Mass., 1942), p. 21.

34. Summers, *Muse's Method*, pp. 85–86.

35. See, for example, Barbara K. Lewalski, "Innocence and Experience in Milton's Eden," in *New Essays on "Paradise Lost,"* ed. Thomas Kranidas (Berkeley and Los Angeles, 1969), pp. 86–117.

36. Knott observes (*Milton's Pastoral Vision*, p. xiv) that "the very conflict of modes, epic against pastoral, seems to doom Eden in advance."

37. Vaughan, "The Morning-watch," in *The Complete Poetry of Henry Vaughan*, ed. French Fogle (New York, 1964), pp. 176–77. Herbert, "Prayer" (1), in *The Works of George Herbert*, ed. F. E. Hutchinson (Oxford, 1941), p. 51.

38. Since the poet cannot attain a prelapsarian oneness with creation, his verse in *PL*, IX, 24 is "unpremeditated" rather than "unmeditated." The word has specific and intriguing echoes in the "unpremeditated art" of Shelley's skylark and in the "unpremeditated, joyous energy" which Yeats finds in the statues of Mausolus and Artemisia at the British Museum (*Autobiographies* [London, 1955], p. 150).

39. The thought is from Yeats, "The Coming of Wisdom with Times," in *Collected Poems* (London, 1950), p. 105.

A NOTE ON THE VERSE OF JOHN MILTON

WHILE it must be admitted that Milton is a very great poet indeed, it is something of a puzzle to decide in what his greatness consists. On analysis, the marks against him appear both more numerous and more significant than the marks to his credit. As a man, he is antipathetic. Either from the moralist's point of view, or from the theologian's point of view, or from the psychologist's point of view, or from that of the political philosopher, or judging by the ordinary standards of likeableness in human beings, Milton is unsatisfactory. The doubts which I have to express about him are more serious than these. His greatness as a poet has been sufficiently celebrated, though I think largely for the wrong reasons, and without the proper reservations. His misdeeds as a poet have been called attention to, as by Mr. Ezra Pound, but usually in passing. What seems to me necessary is to assert at the same time his greatness—in that what he could do well he did better than any one else has ever done it—and the serious charges to be made against him, in respect of the deterioration—the peculiar kind of deterioration—to which he subjected the language.

Many people will agree that a man may be a great artist, and yet have a bad influence. There is more of Milton's influence in the badness of the bad verse of the eighteenth century than of anybody's else: he certainly did more harm than Dryden and Pope, and perhaps a good deal of the obloquy which has fallen on these two poets, especially the latter, because of their influence, ought to be transferred to Milton. But to put the matter simply in terms of 'bad influence' is not necessarily to bring a serious charge: because a good deal of the responsibility, when we state the problem in these terms, may devolve on the eighteenth-century poets themselves for being such bad poets that they were incapable of being influenced except for ill. There is a good deal more to the charge against Milton than this; and it appears a good deal more serious if we affirm that Milton's poetry could *only* be an influence for the worse, upon any poet whatever. It is more serious, also, if we affirm that Milton's bad influence may be traced much farther than the eighteenth century, and much farther than upon bad poets: if we say that it was an influence against which we still have to struggle.

There is a large class of persons, including some who appear in print as critics, who regard any censure upon a 'great' poet as a breach of the peace, as an act of wanton iconoclasm, or even hoodlumism. The kind of derogatory criticism that I have to make upon Milton is not intended for such persons, who cannot understand that it is more important, in some vital respects, to be a *good* poet than to be a *great* poet; and of what I have to say I consider that the only jury of judgement is that of the ablest poetical practitioners of my own time.

The most important fact about Milton, for my purposes, is his blindness. I do not mean that to go blind in middle life is itself enough to determine the whole nature of a man's poetry. Blindness must be considered in conjunction with Milton's personality and character, and the peculiar education which he received. It must also be considered in connexion with his devotion to, and expertness in, the art of music. Had Milton been a man of very keen senses—I mean of *all* the five senses—his blindness would not have mattered so much. But for a man whose sensuousness, such as it was, had been withered early by book-learning, and whose gifts were naturally aural, it mattered a great deal. It would seem, indeed, to have helped him to concentrate on what he could do best.

At no period is the visual imagination conspicuous in Milton's poetry. It would be as well to give a few illustrations of what I mean by visual imagination. From *Macbeth*:

> This guest of summer,
> The temple-haunting martlet, does approve
> By his loved mansionry that the heaven's breath
> Smells wooingly here: no jutty, frieze,
> Buttress, nor coign of vantage, but this bird

Hath made his pendant bed and procreant cradle:
Where they most breed and haunt, I have observed
The air is delicate.

It may be observed that such an image, as well as another
familiar quotation from a little later in the same play,

Light thickens, and the crow
Makes wing to the rooky wood

not only offer something to the eye, but, so to speak, to the
common sense. I mean that they convey the feeling of being
in a particular place at a particular time. The comparison
with Shakespeare offers another indication of the peculiarity
of Milton. With Shakespeare, far more than with any other
poet in English, the combinations of words offer perpetual
novelty; they enlarge the meaning of the individual words
joined: thus 'procreant cradle', 'rooky wood'. In comparison, Milton's images do not give this sense of particularity,
nor are the separate words developed in significance. His
language is, if one may use the term without disparagement,
artificial and *conventional*.

O'er the smooth *enamelled* green . . .

. . . paths of this drear wood
The nodding horror of whose shady brows
Threats the forlorn and wandering passenger.

('Shady brow' here is a diminution of the value of the two
words from their use in the line from *Dr. Faustus*

Shadowing more beauty in their airy brows.)

The imagery in *L'Allegro* and *Il Penseroso* is all general:

While the ploughman near at hand,
Whistles o'er the furrowed land,
And the milkmaid singeth blithe,
And the mower whets his scythe,
And every shepherd tells his tale
Under the hawthorn in the dale.

It is not a particular ploughman, milkmaid, and shepherd
that Milton sees (as Wordsworth might see them); the sensuous effect of these verses is entirely on the ear, and is joined
to the concepts of ploughman, milkmaid, and shepherd.

Even in his most mature work, Milton does not infuse new
life into the word, as Shakespeare does.

> The sun to me is dark
> And silent as the moon,
> When she deserts the night
> Hid in her vacant interlunar cave.

Here *interlunar* is certainly a stroke of genius, but is merely
combined with 'vacant' and 'cave', rather than giving and
receiving life from them. Thus it is not so unfair, as it might
at first appear, to say that Milton writes English like a dead
language. The criticism has been made with regard to his
involved syntax. But a tortuous style, when its peculiarity is
aimed at precision (as with Henry James), is not necessarily
a dead one; only when the complication is dictated by a
demand of verbal music, instead of by any demand of sense.

> Thrones, dominations, princedoms, virtues, powers,
> If these magnific titles yet remain
> Not merely titular, since by decree
> Another now hath to himself engrossed
> All power, and us eclipsed under the name
> Of King anointed, for whom all this haste
> Of midnight march, and hurried meeting here,
> This only to consult how we may best
> With what may be devised of honours new
> Receive him coming to receive from us
> Knee-tribute yet unpaid, prostration vile,
> Too much to one, but double how endured,
> To one and to his image now proclaimed?

With which compare:

> However, he didn't mind thinking that if Cissy should prove
> all that was likely enough their having a subject in common
> couldn't but practically conduce; though the moral of it all
> amounted rather to a portent, the one that Haughty, by the
> same token, had done least to reassure him against, of the extent
> to which the native jungle harboured the female specimen and
> to which its ostensible cover, the vast level of mixed growths
> stirred wavingly in whatever breeze, was apt to be identifiable
> but as an agitation of the latest redundant thing in ladies' hats.

This quotation, taken almost at random from *The Ivory*

Tower, is not intended to represent Henry James at any hypothetical 'best', any more than the noble passage from *Paradise Lost* is meant to be Milton's hypothetical worst. The question is the difference of intention, in the elaboration of styles both of which depart so far from lucid simplicity. The sound, of course, is never irrelevant, and the style of James certainly depends for its effect a good deal on the sound of a voice, James's own, painfully explaining. But the complication, with James, is due to a determination not to simplify, and in that simplification lose any of the real intricacies and by-paths of mental movement; whereas the complication of a Miltonic sentence is an active complication, a complication deliberately introduced into what was a previously simplified and abstract thought. The dark angel here is not *thinking* or conversing, but making a speech carefully prepared for him; and the arrangement is for the sake of musical value, not for significance. A straightforward utterance, as of a Homeric or Dantesque character, would make the speaker very much more real to us; but reality is no part of the intention. We have in fact to read such a passage not analytically, to get the poetic impression. I am not suggesting that Milton has no idea to convey, which he regards as important: only that the syntax is determined by the musical significance, by the auditory imagination, rather than by the attempt to follow actual speech or thought. It is at least more nearly possible to distinguish the pleasure which arises from the *noise*, from the pleasure due to other elements, than with the verse of Shakespeare, in which the auditory imagination and the imagination of the other senses are more nearly fused, and fused together with the thought. The result with Milton is, in one sense of the word, *rhetoric*. That term is not intended to be derogatory. This kind of 'rhetoric' is not necessarily bad in itself, though likely to be bad in its influence; and it may be considered bad in relation to the historical life of a language as a whole. I have said elsewhere that the living English which was Shakespeare's became split up into two components one of which was exploited by Milton and the other by Dryden. Of the two, I still think

Dryden's development the healthier, because it was Dryden who preserved, so far as it was preserved at all, the tradition of conversational language in poetry: and I might add that it seems to me easier to get back to healthy language from Dryden than it is to get back to it from Milton. For what such a generalization is worth, Milton's influence on the eighteenth century was much more deplorable than Dryden's.

If several very important reservations and exceptions are made, I think that it is not unprofitable to compare Milton's development with that of Mr. James Joyce. The initial similarities are strong musical tastes and abilities, followed by musical training, wide and curious knowledge, gift for acquiring languages, and remarkable powers of memory perhaps fortified by defective vision. The important difference is that Mr. Joyce's imagination is not naturally of so purely auditory a type as Milton's. In his early work, and at least in part of *Ulysses*, there is visual and other imagination of the highest kind; and I may be mistaken in thinking that the later part of *Ulysses* shows a turning from the visible world to draw rather on the resources of phantasmagoria. In any case, one may suppose that the replenishment of visual imagery during later years has been insufficient; so that what I find in *Work in Progress* is an auditory imagination abnormally sharpened at the expense of the visual. There is still a little to be seen, and what there is to see is worth looking at. And I would repeat that with Mr. Joyce this development seems to me largely due to circumstances: whereas Milton may be said never to have seen anything. For Milton, therefore, the concentration on sound was wholly a benefit. Indeed, I find, in reading *Paradise Lost*, that I am happiest where there is least to visualize. The eye is not shocked in his twilit Hell as it is in the Garden of Eden, where I for one can get pleasure from the verse only by the deliberate effort not to visualize Adam and Eve and their surroundings.

I am not suggesting any close parallel between the 'rhetoric' of Milton and the later style of Mr. Joyce. It is a different music; and Joyce always maintains some contact with the conversational tone. But it may prove to be equally a blind alley for the future development of the language: being preferable to Milton's, in the respect that it cannot be imitated.

A disadvantage of the rhetorical style appears to be, that a dislocation takes place, through the hypertrophy of the auditory imagination at the expense of the visual and tactile, so that the inner meaning is separated from the surface, and tends to become something occult, or at least without effect upon the reader until fully understood. To extract every-thing possible from *Paradise Lost*, it would seem necessary to read it in two different ways, first solely for the sound, and second for the sense. The full beauty of his long periods can hardly be enjoyed while we are wrestling with the meaning as well; and for the pleasure of the ear the meaning is hardly necessary, except in so far as certain key-words indicate the emotional tone of the passage.' Now Shakespeare, or Dante, will bear innumerable readings, but at each reading all the elements of appreciation can be present. There is no inter-ruption between the surface that these poets present to you and the core. While, therefore, I cannot pretend to have penetrated to any 'secret' of these poets, I feel that such appreciation of their work as I am capable of points in the right direction; whereas I cannot feel that my appreciation of Milton leads anywhere outside of the mazes of sound. That, I feel, would be the matter for a separate study, like that of Blake's prophetic books; it might be well worth the trouble, but would have little to do with my interest in the poetry. So far as I perceive anything, it is a glimpse of a theology that I find in large part repellent, expressed through a mythology which would have better been left in the Book of Genesis, upon which Milton has not improved. There seems to me to be a division, in Milton, between the philo-sopher or theologian and the poet; and, for the latter,. I suspect also that this concentration upon the auditory imagination leads to at least an occasional levity. I can enjoy the roll of

> . . . Cambalu, seat of Cathaian Can
> And Samarchand by Oxus, Temir's throne,

To Paquin of Sinaean kings, and thence
To Agra and Lahor of great Mogul
Down to the golden Chersonese, or where
The Persian in Ecbatan sate, or since
In Hispahan, or where the Russian Ksar
In Mosco, or the Sultan in Bizance,
Turchestan-born . . .

and the rest of it, but I feel that this is not serious poetry, not poetry fully occupied about its business, but rather a solemn game. More often, admittedly, Milton uses proper names in moderation, to obtain the same effect of magnificence with them as does Marlowe—nowhere perhaps better than in the passage from *Lycidas*:

Whether beyond the stormy Hebrides,
Where thou perhaps under the whelming tide
Visit'st the bottom of the monstrous world;
Or whether thou to our moist vows deny'd,
Sleep'st by the fable of Bellerus old,
Where the great vision of the guarded Mount
Looks toward Namancos and Bayona's hold . . .

than which, for the single effect of grandeur of sound, there is nothing finer in poetry.

I make no attempt to appraise the 'greatness' of Milton in relation to poets who seem to me more comprehensive and better balanced; it has seemed to me more fruitful for the present to press the parallel between *Paradise Lost* and *Work in Progress*; and both Milton and Mr. Joyce are so exalted in their own kinds, in the whole of literature, that the only writers with whom to compare them are writers who have attempted something very different. Our views about Mr. Joyce, in any case, must remain at the present time tentative. But there are two attitudes both of which are necessary and right to adopt in considering the work of any poet. One is when we isolate him, when we try to understand the rules of his own game, adopt his own point of view: the other, perhaps less usual, is when we measure him by outside standards, most pertinently by the standards of language and of something called Poetry, in our own language and in the whole history of European literature. It is from the second point of view that my objections to Milton are made: it is from this point of view that we can go so far as to say that, although his work realizes superbly one important element in poetry, he may still be considered as having done damage to the English language from which it has not wholly recovered.

T. S. ELIOT.

One of Dr. Johnson's most famous criticisms of Milton was prophetic of much of the twentieth-century dissatisfaction:

The truth is, that both in prose and verse, he had formed his style by a perverse and pedantick principle. He was desirous to use English words with a foreign idiom. This in all his prose is discovered and condemned, for there judgement operates freely, neither softened by the beauty nor awed by the dignity of his thoughts; but such is the power of his poetry that his call is obeyed without resistance, the reader feels himself in captivity to a higher and a nobler mind, and criticism sinks in admiration. . . . Of him, at last, may be said what Jonson says of Spenser, that 'he wrote no language', but has formed what Butler calls 'a Babylonish Dialect', in itself harsh and barbarous, but made by exalted genius and extensive learning the vehicle of so much instruction and so much pleasure that, like other lovers, we find grace in its deformity.[1]

This is not quite to say, with the sturdy frankness of Dr. Leavis, 'we dislike his verse'. But it is clear that, for Johnson, Milton's verse was good in spite of his deviation from normal English, not because of it. The reader willingly puts up with the deformity, but there is no doubt about its being a deformity.

Plainly there are times when Milton deviates from the usual word-order for the bad reason that he is in the habit of it. And there are times when he does so for the inadequate and well-known reason that the result sounds more magniloquent, or—in Addison's phrase—'to give his Verse the greater Sound, and throw it out of Prose'. Yet it is interesting that Addison went on to say, 'I must confess, that I think his Stile, tho' admirable in general, is in some Places too much stiffened and obscured by the frequent Use of those Methods, which *Aristotle* has prescribed for the raising of it'.[2] But this, as he saw, does not apply to the usual run of the verse, in which the syntax is meaningfully controlled with great success.

[1] *Lives of the Poets*, ed. Hill, i. 190–1.
[2] *The Spectator*, No. 285 (26 Jan. 1712).

Its first success is obvious enough: his natural port was gigantic loftiness. Milton achieves this loftiness as much by word-order as by the sonority, dignity or weight of the words themselves. Mr. Eliot has put the positive side excellently:

It is only in the period that the wave-length of Milton's verse is to be found: it is his ability to give a perfect and unique pattern to every paragraph, such that the full beauty of the line is found in its context, and his ability to work in larger musical units than any other poet— that is to me the most conclusive evidence of Milton's supreme mastery. The peculiar feeling, almost a physical sensation of a breathless leap, communicated by Milton's long periods, and by his alone, is impossible to procure from rhymed verse.[1]

The power and sublimity of a 'breathless leap' are there in the opening lines of the poem:

> Of Mans First Disobedience, and the Fruit
> Of that Forbidden Tree, whose mortal tast
> Brought Death into the World, and all our woe,
> With loss of Eden, till one greater Man
> Restore us, and regain the blissful Seat,
> Sing Heav'nly Muse . . .

Matthew Arnold[2] acutely commented: 'So chary of a sentence is he, so resolute not to let it escape him till he has crowded into it all he can, that it is not till the thirty-ninth word in the sentence that he will give us the key to it, the word of action, the verb.'

But such withholding of the verb 'sing' (*Of Mans First Disobedience . . . Sing*) might be no more than perverse. Its justification is in the heroic way that it states the magnitude of the poem's subject and so the magnitude of its task

(*Disobedience . . . Death . . . woe . . . loss of Eden . . . one greater Man*),

while still insisting that this vastness is within the poet's compass. The word-order quite literally encompasses the huge themes. 'Where couldst thou words of such a compass

---

[1] 'Milton II.' *On Poetry and Poets*, pp. 157-8.
[2] *On Translating Homer*, III (1861).

find?' asked Marvell, wondering at Milton's achievement of his *vast Design*: 'a Work so infinite he spann'd'.

A poet is always insisting, as if by magic, that his control of words is a control of experience; and here we are given a 'breathless' sense of Milton's *adventrous Song* with at the same time a reassuring sense of how firmly it is within his control. The curve of the sentence is not discursive—however wide the gyre, this falcon hears its falconer.

The verb is, as Arnold saw, the 'key' to the sentence—in the sense that it embodies Milton's power to open the subjects of his poem. Yet we would not be very interested in, or impressed by, a key unless we had first been given some idea of what riches we will be shown.

'So *resolute* not to let it escape him . . .', said Arnold, and the word may be used as a transition to a fine comment by Mr. Empson. He quotes Valdes's lines to Faustus, lines which deliberately hold back until the end the ominous condition *If learned Faustus will be resolute*:

Faustus,
These books, thy wit, and our experience,
Shall make all nations to canonise us.
As Indian moors obey their Spanish lords
So shall the spirits of every element
Be always serviceable to us three;
Like lions shall they guard us when we please,
Like Almain rutters, with their horsemen's staves,
Or Lapland giants, trotting by our sides,
Sometimes like women, or unwedded maids
Shadowing more beauty in their airy brows
Than have the white breasts of the queen of love:
From Venice shall they drag huge argosies,
And from America the golden fleece
That yearly stuffs old Philip's treasury;
If learned Faustus will be resolute.

'That a conditional clause should have been held back through all these successive lightnings of poetry, that after their achievement it should still be present with the same conviction and *resolution*, is itself a statement of heroic character.'[1] That is nobly said, and such heroism is one of Milton's glories too. He is even able to sustain such effects over vaster distances. Though his single lines may not be mightier than Marlowe's, his sentences often are.

Take Belial's reply to Moloch during the council in Hell. Moloch has asked rhetorically 'what can be worse than to dwell here,' and Belial seizes the phrase and holds it aloft:

> What can we suffer worse? is this then worst,
> Thus sitting, thus consulting, thus in Arms?

And at once he launches his argument, wheeling through six lines with a hawk's-eye view of their past torments, and plunging home with *that sure was worse*. But that telling reminder offers no pause, and Belial circles again, this time above their future torments. He drives relentlessly through 'what if . . . or . . . what if . . .', and then sweeps to his annihilating climax, foreseen and deliberately held back:

> What if the breath that kindl'd those grim fires
> Awak'd should blow them into sevenfold rage
> And plunge us in the Flames? or from above
> Should intermitted vengeance Arme again
> His red right hand to plague us? what if all
> Her stores were op'n'd, and this Firmament
> Of Hell should spout her Cataracts of Fire,
> Impendent horrors, threatning hideous fall
> One day upon our heads; while we perhaps
> Designing or exhorting glorious Warr,
> Caught in a fierie Tempest shall be hurl'd
> Each on his rock transfixt, the sport and prey
> Of racking whirlwinds, or for ever sunk
> Under yon boyling Ocean, wrapt in Chains;
> There to converse with everlasting groans,
> Unrespited, unpitied, unrepreevd,
> Ages of hopeless end; this would be worse.   (ii. 170–86)

When a sentence surges forward like that, the end of it seems less a destination than a destiny.

[1] *Seven Types of Ambiguity* (1930; 2nd ed., 1947), p. 32.

It is this ability to harness the thrust of his syntax which sustains Milton's great argument—even the smallest passages have a dynamic force of the astonishing kind which one finds almost everywhere in Dickens. And lines which one has long admired for their brilliant succinctness, lines like 'Better to reign in Hell, then serve in Heav'n' which from one point of view have the free-standing strength of proverbs —even such lines take on greater force when they come as the clinching of a surge of feeling:

> What matter where, if I be still the same,
> And what I should be, all but less then hee
> Whom Thunder hath made greater? Here at least
> We shall be free; th' Almighty hath not built
> Here for his envy, will not drive us hence:
> Here we may reign secure, and in my choyce
> To reign is worth ambition though in Hell:
> Better to reign in Hell, then serve in Heav'n. (1. 256–63)

It is easy to see how much the power of the last line is created by its context if we remember Dryden's setting in *The State of Innocence.* In Dryden the line is witty:

> Chang'd as we are, we'er yet from Homage free;
> We have, by Hell, at least, gain'd liberty:
> That's worth our fall; thus low tho' we are driven,
> Better to Rule in Hell, than serve in Heaven. (Act 1)

Yet in Milton the line was not the less witty for being heroic.

III. SYNTAX AND SENSE

For Milton, the stars in their dance were

> Eccentric, intervolv'd, yet regular
> Then most, when most irregular they seem. (v. 623–4)

For many of Milton's critics, his words are merely eccentric, intervolved and irregular. But just as it was useful to start by looking at the Milton controversy, so it is as well to study the specific criticisms of Milton's word-order that have been made by those who agree with Dr. Leavis. Do Milton's

syntactical effects make his style not grand but grandiose?
Mr. John Peter's examples must be considered, leading as
they naturally do to a discussion of tortuousness in the
Grand Style, and from there to Dr. Davie's important and—
I hope—mistaken analysis of Milton's syntax. Hostile criticism often deserves the compliment of rational opposition
—there is something Philistine about Mr. Douglas Bush's
manly view that 'As for his syntax, it never troubles those
who leave it alone'.[1] So now we know—but do we? It would
not really do, at any rate, to treat Mr. Peter and Dr. Davie
as if they were meddling children who won't leave well alone.

Mr. Peter's *Critique of Paradise Lost* is much less telling
in its criticism of the style than of the events in the poem. In
fact he seems to me altogether more successful when he
points out Milton's stylistic successes. He has, for example,
an excellent discussion of the many oxymorons in the early
books, and the way in which larger passages have 'the same
kind of vitality, on a diffuse scale, that an oxymoron has
succinctly'.[2] That is, a vibrancy which makes us struggle to
reconcile two views of the fallen angels, and which 'finally
leaves the verse with a special forcefulness, imparting to the
devils themselves a striking and enigmatic fascination'.

But when Mr. Peter gives a page of examples of Milton's
bad syntax, he unfortunately omits to say just what is wrong,
merely introducing them with: 'This readiness to assume
that certain ideas have been fully absorbed and integrated
into the poem when they have not is roughly analogous to
a common fault in the epic's style, a fault which is all too
easy to exemplify.'[3] That kind of brisk evasion Mr. Peter
learned from Dr. Leavis, who often practises a large economy
to save analysis: 'But a comparison will save analysis. . . .'

---

[1] *English Literature in the Earlier 17th Century* (1945), p. 389.
[2] p. 39. In *The French Biblical Epic in the 17th Century* (1955, pp. 159, 218)
Dr. R. A. Sayce shows how Saint-Amant and Coras use oxymoron (e.g. *douce
imposture*) to disguise moral uncertainties. Milton's use of what Dr. Sayce calls
'a figure which in its condensed violence is perhaps especially characteristic of
baroque poetry' is the more valid one that Mr. Peter sums up as 'enigmatic fascination'.   [3] p. 161.

Yet it is impossible to say that there is something wrong with the syntax of a few lines from Milton unless one first considers the context. And Milton deserves the compliment of clear rather than muttered complaint.

Nor can one even catch what complaint is being muttered when Mr. Peter offers as his first example that admirable line describing Satan's destination as 'His journies end and our beginning woe' (III. 633). What is wrong with it? It seems perfectly straightforward, memorable and succinct, so simple and clear as to withstand any charge of being un-English. The 'un-English' of *Scrutiny* critics is always in danger of turning into the vague and apoplectic splutter which goes with *un British*.

Mr. Peter's next example is a better one for his argument, Satan's angry jibe at Michael during the war:

> Hast thou turnd the least of these
> To flight, or if to fall, but that they rise
> Unvanquisht, easier to transact with mee
> That thou shouldst hope, imperious, & with threats
> To chase me hence? (VI. 284–8)

The opening and closing phrases strike with strong clarity; and the belated 'imperious' breaks out with an angry scorn that is dramatically apt. But it would be hard to defend the inversion in 'easier to transact with me that thou shouldst hope'. True, it thrusts the contempt of *easier* on us straightaway, but this is perhaps not enough recompense for what seems inappropriately circuitous, pedantry rather than oratory. The lines are not at all obscure, and so ought not to incur disproportionate censure; but they hardly show Miltonic inversion at its expressive best.

It is un-English tortuousness which Mr. Peter presumably dislikes in his next example, the lines describing the life on the Earth after the Creation:

> Aire, Water, Earth,
> By Fowl, Fish, Beast, was flown, was swum, was walkt
> Frequent. (VII. 502–4)

But are the lines bad? (One would first have to remember that 'frequent' here means 'crowded, full'.) The lines certainly are artificial and complicated, but why shouldn't they be? They are not wilfully so, but because Milton needs to suggest both the teeming activity of the Earth, and the fundamental order and harmony of it. So he presents an active throng of monosyllables while at the same time grouping them into a pattern of triplets. Landor elsewhere disliked such a use of passive verbs: 'This Latinism is inadmissible; there is no loophole in our language for its reception.'[1] But the point of the passive verbs is to insist, as Hopkins might, that at last the great elements of the Earth which God had earlier created are being used according to his plan. The Earth is there to be walked, and the water to be swum. The immediately preceding words bring this out:

> Earth in her rich attire
> Consummate lovly smil'd.

That is, rejoices and is beautiful in being consummated, completed and made use of. All that is still wanted is man,

> the Master work, the end
> Of all yet don.

Not that these lines show Milton at his best. But they do give a sense of the thronging life of the Earth which is yet, unlike that presented by Comus, ordered into the divine harmony of 'trinal triplicities'. Nor are the passive verbs merely clumsy. They are to bring out what the air, water, and earth are for—the purposeful magnanimity of the Creation. It is because the air was flown that God most deeply saw that it was good.

Still with disapproval, but still without comment, Mr. Peter then quotes the closing words of a speech when Eve argues with Adam about leaving him:

> Thoughts, which how found they harbour in thy brest,
> Adam, missthought of her to thee so dear?   (IX. 288–9)

---

[1] *Imaginary Conversations*: 'Southey and Landor'. *Works*, ed. T. E. Welby (1927–31), v. 259.

The lines are admittedly tortuous, and they may well use a foreign idiom. But perhaps they *use* it, rather than merely copy it. Is tortuousness out of keeping here? Eve is hurt by Adam's 'unkindness', and she is also keen to get her own way. She starts naturally enough with 'Thoughts, which . . .', and then breaks across with the indignation of a more direct syntax, a hurt question: 'how found they harbour in thy brest?' And then, with a fine austereness, she condemns the thoughts as *missthought*, and ends with the time-honoured appeal, 'how could you think such things of me?'—'missthought of her to thee so dear'. The word-order unfolds with admirable psychological truth, and it combines in exactly the right proportions the pathos, the indignation, and the tearfulness.[1] That such is the intention is plain from the line that follows: 'To whom with healing words Adam reply'd.'

If there is anything wrong with the syntax, it is the opposite of what would be suggested by Mr. Peter's disapproval: not that the word-order is meaninglessly contorted, but that it makes too thorough-going an effort to trace the contours of thought becoming speech—the sort of well-intentioned extremism which one finds in Hopkins or Joyce at their less successful.

The final example which Mr. Peter offers for our condemnation comes from the Son's intercession for Man to the Father:

> Let him live
> Before thee reconcil'd, at least his days
> Numberd, though sad. (XI. 38–40)

Certainly this is characteristically Miltonic—it exactly fits Mr. Empson's unforgettable account of 'the sliding, sideways, broadening movement, normal to Milton'.[2] But the lines are to me characteristically good rather than bad. They beautifully combine two kinds of movement, forward and spinning, like that triumphant line 'Erroneous, there to

[1] Richardson said: 'the Note of Interrogation at the end of the Sentence gives a Poignancy to it' (p. 405)—*poignancy* in 1734 meaning more 'piercing' than 'pathetic'. [2] *Some Versions*, p. 162.

wander and forlorne'. Raleigh reminded us that 'De Quincey speaks of the "slow planetary wheelings" of Milton's verse, and the metaphor is a happy one; the verse revolves on its axis at every line, but it always has another motion, and is related to a more distant centre'.[1]

It may seem strange that Matthew Arnold should have spoken of the 'self-retarding movement' of Milton's verse, for what verse has greater momentum? Yet Arnold was right. Though one of the movements drives forward, the other is circling on itself. The Grand Style has the energy of Satan, who 'Throws his steep flight in many an Aerie wheele'. Or the energy of the stars, with 'their various motions'. In serene lines like those of the interceding Son, the style even has the various motions of the Earth itself:

> Or Shee from West her silent course advance
> With inoffensive pace that spinning sleeps
> On her soft Axle, while she paces Eev'n,
> And bears thee soft with the smooth Air along.   (VIII. 163-6)

The Leavisite position assumes that Milton's style is continuously grand, and therefore continuously deviating from the usual spoken or written word-order. This is an odd idea to have about a poet who begins the most important book of his epic with the laconic audacity of

> No more of talk where God or Angel Guest . . .

That must be the least pompous opening anywhere in a sublime poem, and it is to that quiet brittleness that we owe the full power of the lines that follow, the lines that on an age-old anvil wince and sing:

> Anger and just rebuke, and judgement giv'n,
> That brought into this World a world of woe . . .

And many of the memorable lines in Milton have the directness of 'No more of talk . . .'. Satan asking 'What matter where, if I be still the same'. Belial broken in one descriptive

---

[1] *Milton* (1900), p. 192. F. T. Prince has an interesting account of the sources of this syntactical pattern (*The Italian Element in Milton's Verse*, 1954, pp. 112-19).

phrase, 'A fairer person lost not Heav'n'. Eve in love with Adam:

> from his Lip
> Not Words alone pleas'd her—

admirable in that it means exactly what it says, and is neither a high-minded 'Puritan' sneer at the Lip, nor a low-minded cynical sneer at the Words:

> O when meet now
> Such pairs, in Love and mutual Honour joyn'd?

Or Adam presumptuously thinking that God will look silly if now that they have fallen he destroys them:

> least the Adversary
> Triumph and say; Fickle their State whom God
> Most Favors, who can please him long? Mee first
> He ruind, now Mankind; whom will he next? (IX. 947–50)

The important thing about the syntax there is the way that the brusque simplicity of 'who can please him long?' and 'whom will he next?' is played against the grand inversions of 'Fickle their State . . .' and 'Mee first he ruind'. The laconic and the colloquial burst out all the more strongly.

Mr. Hallett Smith has pointed to this in Adam's words after his creation, where 'the Latinized elliptical construction' of the second line 'suddenly resolves itself with ease and grace' in the next:

> Tell'me, how may I know him, how adore,
> From whom I have that thus I move and live,
> And feel that I am happier then I know. (VIII. 280–2)

One might add that the unusual complication of the second line is in contrast with simplicity, not only externally, but also internally. Internally, in that the words themselves (as distinct from their order) are very uncomplicated and usual —they stand for the most basic of ideas. Externally, in that the complicated construction is immediately succeeded by straightforward simplicity. 'There could hardly be more natural and inevitable English than this', says Mr. Hallett

Smith.[1] And it is the natural last line that is the *raison d'être* of the sentence. The second line departs from English not because Milton has a 'callousness to the intrinsic nature of English' (Dr. Leavis), but because he values that intrinsic nature and wishes us to feel its power. It is not easy for a poet to put power behind such simplicity, especially in a poem the subject and genre of which forbid too colloquial a style. Mr. John Crowe Ransom has said that 'we should be so much in favor of tragedy and irony as not to think it good policy to require them in all our poems, for fear we might bring them into bad fame'.[2] In the same spirit, we might say that we should be so in favour of natural English as not to require it in all our poems, or throughout all our poems. At any rate, this seems less implausible than the view that the author of the closing lines of *Paradise Lost* was callous to the English language.

Often we find that the complication not only prepares the way for an energetic simplicity, but is also dramatically apt. The lines describing Satan's search for Eve build up through a pattern of repetitions that dramatically enacts Satan's repeated seeking and restless wishing, until Eve is spied— and at that point we break into a clearing, a line of verse which has neither the link of repetition which is in all the preceding lines, nor the endless spilling run-over into the next line: instead a simple single Marlovian line.

> He sought them both, but wish'd his hap might find
> Eve separate, he wish'd, but not with hope
> Of what so seldom chanc'd, when to his wish,
> Beyond his hope, Eve separate he spies,
> Veil'd in a Cloud of Fragrance, where she stood ... (IX. 421–5)[3]

In this patterning, sounds are as effective as meanings, so that *hap ... hope ... hope* weaves the same net as *wish'd ... wish'd ... wish*. That net is woven by Satan: Eve appears in the direct innocence of a veil.

[1] 'No Middle Flight', *Huntington Library Quarterly* (1951–2), xv. 162.

[2] Quoted by Arnold Stein for a different purpose, *E.L.H.* (1949), xvi. 133.

[3] R. M. Adams oddly calls the pattern here 'a kind of verbal frippery' (*Ikon*, 1955, p. 89).

Sometimes Milton uses this device almost to the point of self-parody, as when Satan meets Death. Milton's difficulty here is real enough. He has no wish at all to depart from the traditional representation of Death. He needs, in fact, to say what he does say: 'black it stood as night, fierce as ten furies, terrible as hell'. But how can he possibly put any grandeur into such conventional words? His method, which is here admittedly more expressive than subtle, is to work up to this traditional simplicity through an entanglement of philosophical doubts and difficulties—all until the point when we will realize the trenchancy of those traditional representations which can cut through the mesh:

> The other shape,
> If shape it might be call'd that shape had none
> Distinguishable in member, joynt, or limb,
> Or substance might be call'd that shadow seem'd,
> For each seem'd either; black it stood as Night,
> Fierce as ten Furies, terrible as Hell . . .   (ii. 666–71)

The power of this sort of syntax can be seen by comparing two similes in *Henry VI Part III*, where Richard is soliloquizing about his villainy. The first simile is straightforward; it proceeds through point by point correspondence, and has the clarity of an epic simile rather than the vigour of a dramatic one:

> Why then I do but dream on sovereignty,
> Like one that stands upon a promontory,
> And spies a far-off shore, where he would tread,
> Wishing his foot were equal with his eye,
> And chides the sea, that sunders him from thence,
> Saying, he'll lade it dry, to have his way;
> So do I wish the crown, being so far off . . .

But this same soliloquy includes a very different simile. As Richard tells how he is lost in a thorny wood, the clustering repetitions thicken around him until the climax cuts through them:

> And I, like one lost in a thorny wood,

That rents the thorns, and is rent with the thorns,
Seeking a way, and straying from the way,
Not knowing how to find the open air,
But toiling desperately to find it out,
Torment myself, to catch the English crown:
And from that torment I will free myself,
Or hew my way out with a bloody axe.   (Act III, scene ii)

The last line cuts through the thorns as if it were itself an axe—and 'bloody axe' reminds us savagely what the thorns really are. It is not necessary, because of this simile, to say that the other one is poor—but its success is a smaller achievement. Yet in spite of what Dr. Leavis says, Milton's syntax seems to me to be at least as often like the dramatic simile as it is like the epic one.

For Donald Davie, 'Dr. Leavis's account of this Miltonic music (there are other musics, in other poems) seems more clearly just on each new reading.'[1] Certainly one of the surprising things about Dr. Davie's excellent book *Articulate Energy* was that 'An Inquiry into the Syntax of English Poetry' should wish to say so very little about Milton. But in the course of the book it turned out that Dr. Davie doesn't really think of Milton as *English* poetry. 'In order to get syntactical closeness, Landor treats the English language as if it were Latin. And even if we make Milton himself a special case, it must be admitted as a rule that "strength" is not worth this sort of sacrifice.'[2]

Then in his later study (in *The Living Milton*) Dr. Davie lucidly deplored most of the syntax in *Paradise Lost*. The essay seems to me more successful on successes than on failures, but it certainly provides a useful critical foothold. Not only is it a very interesting piece of criticism in its own right, but it is also devoted to a subject where there is all too little useful criticism.[3]

[1] 'Syntax and Music in *P.L.*', *The Living Milton*, p. 83.
[2] *Articulate Energy* (1955), p. 62.
[3] J. B. Broadbent has some excellent local comments on syntax (*Some Graver*

Dr. Davie begins by discussing two syntactical successes.
First,

> Him the Almighty Power
> Hurld headlong flaming from th' Ethereal Skie
> With hideous ruine and combustion down
> To bottomless perdition, there to dwell
> In Adamantine Chains and penal Fire,
> Who durst defie th' Omnipotent to Arms. (I. 44–49)

The success here Dr. Davie described as *muscular*: 'The placing of "Him", "down" and "To", in particular, gives us the illusion as we read that our own muscles are tightening in panic as we experience in our own bodies a movement just as headlong and precipitate as the one described.' The second example presents Satan journeying through the mud of Chaos (II. 939–50): 'Milton crowds stressed syllables together so as to make the vocal exertion in reading image the physical exertion described. It is the reader, too, who flounders, stumbles, pushes doggedly on.'

Dr. Davie then turns from such 'muscular' or 'dramatic' effects to another kind of success where metre is played against syntax and word-order: *narrative* effects. By this, he means that 'the language is deployed, just as the episodes are in a story, so as always to provoke the question "And then?"—to provoke this question and to answer it in unexpected ways. If any arrangement of language is a sequence of verbal events, here syntax is employed so as to make the most of each word's eventfulness, so as to make each keyword, like each new episode in a well told story, at once surprising and just.' He quotes the invocation to Book III, pointing particularly to two effects. First,

> Then feed on thoughts, that voluntarie move
> Harmonious numbers . . .

'At the line-ending "move" seems intransitive, and as such wholly satisfying; until the swing on to the next line,

Subject, e.g. pp. 164, 184). So have the eighteenth-century editors (e.g. Richardson on 'If thou beest he . . .').

"Harmonious numbers", reveals it (a little surprise, but a wholly fair one) as transitive. This flicker of hesitation about whether the thoughts move only themselves, or something else, makes us see that the numbers aren't really "something else" but are the very thoughts themselves, seen under a new aspect; the placing of "move", which produces the momentary uncertainty about its grammar, ties together "thoughts" and "numbers" in a relation far closer than cause and effect'.

That is a very useful insight into Milton's style. And there follows a similarly acute and subtle commentary on the slight surprise in the word *Day*:

> Thus with the Year
> Seasons return, but not to me returns
> Day . . .

—where we would expect 'Spring'.

At which Dr. Davie makes his general point, that all such effects depend on the narrative question 'What happens next?', on the poet's realizing that language, unlike the pictorial arts, operates through time, 'in terms of successive events, each new sentence a new small action with its own sometimes complicated plot'. And this perception, as he rightly insists, is one 'which much of the most influential modern criticism—working as it does through spatial metaphors, talking of "the figure in the carpet", of tensions balanced and cancelling out inside structures—seems expressly designed to obscure'.

But at this point Dr. Davie enters the second section of his essay, and we meet the surprising statement that 'these effects are rather the exception than the rule. Neither kinetic and dramatic effect, as in the lines on Satan's fall, nor narrative and musical effect, as in the invocation to Light, are in evidence at all frequently as we read *Paradise Lost*.'

Surprising, in the first place, because the tone implies—and the later stages of the argument insist—that such effects ought to be the rule rather than the exception. Yet surely it is probable that most of the syntax used by any poet will be neither dramatic nor narrative, but simply expository and descriptive. Such effects are certainly an added beauty, as powerful in their way as metaphor. But no one demands that poetry should be all metaphor. Even if, as is so often done, we take Donne as the antithesis of Milton, such effects are still the exception rather than the rule. Dr. Davie is setting a mistaken standard here: he is asking for an all-pervasive syntactical density and activity that would be likely to produce too rich a style—an equivalent of *Finnegans Wake*, perhaps. And indeed Dr. Davie himself has elsewhere given a more realistic point of view: 'We may wonder whether the syntax of poetry can ever be aesthetically neutral, a matter of indifference. It can, however. It can be unremarkable, like a human frame that is neither close-knit nor loose-limbed, neither well- nor ill-proportioned, but just normal. Much syntax in poetry is of this kind, and is therefore not poetic syntax as I understand it'.[1]

Yet it would be a pity if there were very little 'poetic syntax' in Milton. At which, one comes to the second surprising point about the essay; that the examples are not so self-evidently bad as Dr. Davie assumes.

> Others with vast Typhoean rage more fell
> Rend up both Rocks and Hills, and ride the Air
> In whirlwind; Hell scarce holds the wilde uproar.
> As when Alcides from Oechalia Crown'd
> With conquest, felt th' envenom'd robe, and tore
> Through pain up by the roots Thessalian Pines,
> And Lichas from the top of Oeta threw
> Into th' Euboic Sea.   (II. 539–46)

Dr. Davie says that 'where the line is not end-stopped, the swing of the reading eye or voice around the line-ending is not turned to poetically expressive use'. But then he at once has to make an exception of the first two lines, 'where we swing around the line-ending to come hard upon the energetic verb, "Rend" '. He then objects that 'there is no expressive or dramatic reason why "Air" should be separated in this way from "In whirlwind"—a phrase which merely

[1] *Articulate Energy*, p. 67.

dangles limply into the next line'. Yet this is surely to miss the utter difference in tone between the two phrases, 'Ride the Air' and 'In whirlwind'—a difference which is successfully emphasized by the line-break. 'Ride the Air' gives a momentary suggestion of serenity, of strong and calm control. 'In whirlwind' shatters this into 'wild uproar'.

'So with thy whirlwind them pursue', Milton had written in his translation of Psalm lxxxiii. And in *Paradise Lost* whirlwinds are always one of the torments that pursue the fallen angels, who are 'orewhelm'd with Floods and Whirlwinds', 'the sport and prey of racking whirlwinds'—who are condemned to a land 'beat with perpetual storms of Whirlwind', and who are defeated by Christ's chariot which 'forth rush'd with whirl-wind sound'.[1]

The fallen angels have no control, no calm, and their strength is that of rage and pain. Elsewhere the divine calm, the divine control and strength, demand the serenity of 'Crystallin' rather than the uproar of 'whirlwind':

> Hee on the wings of Cherub rode sublime
> On the Crystallin Skie . . . (VI. 771–2)

The fact is that Milton often uses half-lines like 'In whirlwind' to jar against the previous line, as in the final phrase of

> and with ambitious aim
> Against the Throne and Monarchy of God
> Rais'd impious War in Heav'n and Battel proud
> With vain attempt. (I. 41–44)

That deflates. Dr. Davie might say it 'dangles limply', but the limpness is that of Satan. Dr. Broadbent commented crisply on these lines: 'The very heavy final stress on "proud" lengthens the pause before the next line, so that "With vain attempt" comes as a surprising snort of derision.'[2]

Dr. Davie's next point is even more arguable. He quotes

---

[1] I. 77; II. 182, 589; VI. 749. For the whirlwind of God see Ezek. i. 4; Isa. lxvi. 15; Jer. xxx. 23; Amos i. 14. It is relevant that the name *Typhon* means *whirlwind*, as M. Y. Hughes notes in his ed. (1957).

[2] 'Milton's Hell', *E.L.H.* (1954), xxi. 163.

Tore
Through pain up by the roots Thessalian Pines,

and says that 'the interposition of "Through pain" precludes both of two possible dramatic effects—either the violence of "Tore" at the beginning of the line, or the even more effective muscularity of having "tore" separated by the line-ending from "Up" '.

But surely the line as written has an 'even more effective muscularity', in separating *tore* and *up* even more violently. The agonized word-order presents the knotted effort of Hercules. The writhing of the strength and of the pain are almost those of Laocoön. In fact the line seems an outstanding example for the first, not the second, section of Dr. Davie's essay.

On the last two lines,

And Lichas from the top of Oeta threw
Into th' Euboic Sea,

he remarks: 'The Latinate inversion of word-order means that as we launch out from "threw" into the last line, we are asking not "*What* was thrown?" but only the much less interesting question "thrown where?" In fact, this question is so unexciting that we don't even ask it; so that "Into th' Euboic Sea" hangs superfluous—the sentence could just as well have ended where the line ends, after "threw".'

Again this seems wrong-headed. It is not self-evident that 'What was thrown?' is a more interesting question than 'thrown where?' The impressive thing is not that Hercules was able to throw a man—that is not a superhuman feat of strength—but that he was able to throw him such a long way. No doubt there are contexts in which 'What was thrown?' is a much more interesting question, but it is odd to suppose that there is a Platonic quality of 'Interest' to which that question is always much closer. In this case, it seems clear that 'thrown where?' is more interesting, and that the sentence could not 'just as well have ended where the line ends'.

All of Dr. Davie's objections to this passage are interesting, and they raise important points about Milton's Grand Style —but all are very vulnerable. Indeed, considering his charges, as so often in Milton criticism, brings out just how good the lines are. The same is true of another example:

> Th' undaunted Fiend what this might be admir'd,
> Admir'd, not fear'd; God and his Son except,
> Created thing naught vallu'd he nor shun'd;
> And with disdainful look thus first began. (ii. 677–80)

'The line-endings', says Dr. Davie, 'are so far from being dramatically significant that Milton seems to have gone perversely out of his way to eliminate all that might be suspenseful. Inversion of word-order answers the question of what the Fiend "admir'd", before we have the chance to ask it. If we had been made to wait for the object of "admir'd" until after admiration had been distinguished from fear and the distinction elaborated on, a powerful suspense would have been built up. Instead the narrative run is halted while the distinction is laboriously made in a parenthesis which has all the distracting inertness of a footnote.'

The vigour of Dr. Davie's style should not disguise the oddity of what he is saying. 'What this might be' does not really *answer* 'the question of what the Fiend "admir'd" before we have the chance to ask it', because it is not an answer—it deliberately withholds any reassuring identification of the terrible shape. Satan does not, any more than we, know what faces him; but, whatever it might be, his superb courage is such that he is struck only with wonder and not fear. The distinction which to Dr. Davie has the 'inertness of a footnote' has to me the calm of supreme courage. 'Inert' will of course do as a description, provided we find it heroic that at such a moment Satan is inert, unmoved, *undaunted*— that he can command the imperturbability of a 'disdainful look'. 'Hell trembled', but Satan did not.

Indeed, the suspense is maintained just because we *are* in a vital sense 'made to wait for the object of "admir'd" '. The developing syntax may offer 'what this might be', but that

only brings home how terrifyingly the 'object' remains undefined, and our feelings are hardly set at rest. Certainly the
lines have poise—the poise is that of Satan. This is clear
when these calm lines are set in their context, following
immediately on lines very different in style: the hectic,
elusive, spilling phantasmagoria that introduces Death.[1] To
come on this poise after what has just preceded it, is to feel
the full weight of 'what this might be', and the full weight of
Satan's courage. So perhaps the narrative run is not halted
but suspended—and creates suspense.

If Dr. Davie's examples fail to convince, then the third
part of his essay becomes an interesting irrelevance, since it
is concerned to explain how this weakness of syntax came
about, and to relate it to Milton's larger deficiency in narrative—his creation of an encyclopaedia instead of a poem.
But Dr. Davie very properly forces us to look closely at the
syntax. It seems to me that here Milton achieves the elevated
dignity of his Grand Style without sacrificing sense and
sensitivity.

IV. THE UNSUCCESSFUL METAPHOR

Milton's syntax can in most cases be defended—it is not
wilful or merely magniloquent. But when we turn to the
place of metaphor in the Grand Style, more has to be conceded to the anti-Miltonists. It seems true that Milton's
style is not very metaphorical, and that this is in some ways
a pity. 'The greatest thing by far is to be a master of metaphor', said Aristotle, and most critics have concurred. But
modern critics seem often to talk as if metaphor were the
only source of poetic power and beauty. Though Milton
certainly does not show Shakespearian fertility of metaphor,
he creates similar effects by other means. Perhaps the effects
that I am to consider as part of the Grand Style and of Milton's delicate subtlety could be called in some sense metaphorical. But it is wiser to grant the point.

[1] Quoted on p. 39 above.

THE LIMBS OF TRUTH: MILTON'S USE OF SIMILE IN *PARADISE LOST*

Linda Gregerson

M Y SPECIFIC topic is the Miltonic simile, the materials that compose it, the ends it serves. The figure of speech is a turn of the mind; the simile's ground is epistemology. The artist makes both an artifact and an instrument with which to see, like the Tuscan artist's glass. The figure made from the language of men goes into the making of an artifact called *Paradise Lost*. To know the function of figure and poem, we must know how Milton believes we come to know.

We and the poem and the author live after the Fall; that limits our means. Stanley Fish has written a book about reading after the Fall, and his point is, first, that reading is not an innocent act. This seems to me to be indisputable. The reader is not innocent of what he reads, but is implicated, called to judgment, to render and receive. Judgment is a placing of the self in relation to the thing seen. And where do we find ourselves while reading *Paradise Lost?* In sin, says Fish; and the way we know is one of our sins. So he posits the poem as a *via negativa*, provoking, one by one, our perceptual habits that we may regard them in the light of faith and discover them to be impasses, props that characterize and maintain us in the fallen state. The next step is presumably to cast them off.

Among the movements of mind that seem to us to render the world articulate is the drawing of likenesses, which give voice at once to division and to a unity of structure or plan. "The superfluousness of the simile as an instrument of perception is, I believe, part of Milton's point. . . . those who walk with faith . . . are able, *immediately*, to discern the unity in diversity."[1] In this portion of his thesis, Fish seems to ignore a great deal of Milton's poem. God, it is our premise, sees everything as one and at once. But the angels, for example, cannot discern hypocrisy; their unity of vision, if such it be, fails to admit such doubleness and is therefore incomplete. Man, even before the Fall, is further still from divine omniscience; Adam's "sudden apprehension" (VIII, 354) of the animals he names is exceptional:

Immediate are the Acts of God, more swift
Than time or motion, but to human ears
Cannot without procéss of speech be told,
So told as earthly notion can receive.   (VII, 176–79)[2]

The discrepancy need not be mere impediment: "what surmounts the reach / Of human sense, I shall delineate so, / By lik'ning spiritual to corporal forms" (V, 571–73). Raphael's analogical method of instruction is presumably endorsed by the underlying coherence and continuity of creation. The forms of understanding itself are potentially part of a gradual, uninterrupted sequence: "In contemplation of created things / By steps we may ascend to God" (V, 511–12). The angel's expressed uncertainties about relation simply underscore its potency. On the one hand, the tale related may "unfold / The secrets of another World, perhaps / Not lawful to reveal" (V, 568–70); the story of understanding may be wrongfully abridged. On the other hand, relations drawn by the narrator may have a fuller ontological warrant than we yet divine: "though what if Earth / Be but the shadow of Heav'n, and things therein / Each to other like more than on Earth is thought?" (V, 574–76).

The Fall, in any case, is not an utter corruption of God-like apprehension. For man, understanding has always proceeded in time: before the Fall, the requisite time is that of discourse, and of perfection in obedience; after the Fall, time is invaded by death and becomes the time of history. When Satan rebels, he receives a "discontinuous wound" (VI, 329); when man rebels, his progress toward God becomes discontinuous, at least as perceived by human sense. In Michael's narration, the divine pattern must now be fulfilled by death and rebirth; Adam, too, must repeatedly die to one form of consciousness and awake to another. His senses are scattered by Michael's tidings (XI, 294) and restored by the angel's mild words to Eve; he sinks into a trance on the Hill of Paradise (XI, 420) and is then recalled; his mortal sight begins to fail (XII, 9), and henceforth pictures are made with words. The path has been broken at intervals but exists after as before the Fall. "Those who walk with faith" do not reach God at once, but must journey to him.

Raphael advises Adam to "be lowly wise" (VIII, 173) but does his best to "lift / Human imagination" to the "highth / Of Godlike Power" (VI, 299–301). Adam is to curb his inquiry into the motions of the stars, but only that he may better address his steps to the course which will lead him by degrees to God. He is warned against eating the fruit, but is encouraged to know himself (VIII, 437ff.), having known the beasts. The boundaries he discovers are the boundaries of ordered progress, not the pattern of stasis. When Adam reiterates to Michael the limits "Of knowledge, what this Vessel can contain; / Beyond which was my folly to aspire" (XII, 559–60), he repents, not of inquiry in general, but of the sin of disobedience and the pride of the "worldly wise" (XII, 568). Man's longing may be for immediate apprehension, but his sinning lies in false abbreviation: by plucking the fruit, to take the walls of heaven by storm; by worldly wisdom, to erect the walls where he stands.

Raphael expounds the angelic and human modes of understanding:

> Fancy and understanding, whence the Soul
> Reason receives, and reason is her being,
> Discursive, or Intuitive; discourse
> Is oftest yours, the latter most is ours,
> Differing but in degree, of kind the same.   (V, 486–90)

The Latin root *discurrere* means to run to and fro. The similes in *Paradise Lost* have been characterized as errant, wanderings off the path. But discourse, even before the Fall, goes to and fro. Nor does the eye go straight down the page, but back and forth, like Spenser's plowman, who is also the penman.

The Miltonic similes portray knowledge as problematic; they do not suggest we throw away the tools we have and wait for grace as for rain. The rain does no good if the field or the page is not plowed. "To be still searching for what we know not by what we know . . . this is the golden rule"(*Areopagitica*, p. 742). This calls for motion in two respects: first, because the truth historical man achieves is by nature incomplete. To rest in the accomplished truth is to be guilty of pride or even of heresy, for we pretend to be as God:

Our faith and knowledge thrives by exercise, as well as our limbs and complexion. Truth is compared in scripture to a streaming fountain; if her waters flow not in a perpetual progression, they sicken into a muddy pool of conformity and tradition. A man may be a heretic in the truth. (*Areopagitica*, p. 739)

Secondly, what we must know is precisely what we do not know. Our course, since the Fall, is discontinous. We must step beyond the confines of our understanding, and must do so continually, for the point is neither to domesticate otherness nor to resolve it into terms we already know. Malvolio reads according to an error of this kind ("If I could make that resemble something in me!") and is trapped. In *Paradise Lost*, we proceed by perceived alliance (with a Pilot, with a peasant, with Adam and Eve), but not by assimilation. If we seek to place ourselves in the poem, it is not to eradicate what is elsewhere, but precisely to engage it. The fallen angels are trapped in the limits of the conceivable ("For who can yet believe, though after loss . . ." I, 631) and thus compound their sin. There is more in this world than we may conceive, and that we may not forget it we must tackle the limit repeatedly. The figures in the poem are markedly anachronistic, oxymoronic, and this is to bring us to a verge. As we get in place, the sands shift. Only in movement can we be oriented toward God, who is with us but is not assimilable.[3]

The figures from which my examples are drawn are primarily those of Book I, where they fall as thick as autumnal leaves. Though similes are unevenly distributed in *Paradise Lost*,[4] I do not believe they alter in kind as the poem proceeds. They develop in relation to one another, as well as to the surrounding text, so the first book, with its impacted figurative language, is simply a convenient source. The work the similes do is of five kinds.

I. On the simplest level, the vehicle conveys real information about the tenor, or locates it in an experiential realm.

a. It may do this by stimulating the sensual memory: "As when the Sun new ris'n / Looks through the Horizontal misty Air / Shorn of his Beams" (I, 594–96). T. S. Eliot says that the visual imagination is "at no period . . . conspicuous in Milton's poetry."[5] The generalization has its point, but sacrifices certain detail. The image above is not, like the light from Eden, vision remembered and generalized. The phenomenon is particular and rendered with such accuracy as to invent for the community of readers a shared remembrance. Lucifer's radiance, diminished, has a body by which we may know it.

b. A subject may be modified by means of its analogue; the attributes of the latter attach to the former. Thus Satan is like a vulture on Immaus bred because he too is after prey (III, 431 ff.). The fallen angels are like locusts, not simply because of their number, but because they threaten to plague the earth as locusts once plagued Egypt (I, 338 ff.).

c. And similes may be mimetic; they may induce in the reader an experience which characterizes the subject. The vulture's flight begins a sentence which extends for forty-five lines, proceeds across lands we know by hearsay alone to light on an oxymoron, a windy Sea of Land (III, 431 ff.). And twenty lines of a second sentence pass before the place is named. The grammatical suspension gives the reader a little sampling of Limbo itself.

II. The simile may be proleptic.[6] Those in *Paradise Lost* are anachronistic by nature, appealing as they do to the myths and experience of men not yet created at the time of the Fall. They often prefigure subsequent events in the story. Thus Satan is compared to Leviathan (I, 201 ff.), and the fate of the small night-foundered skiff forecasts our own, and that of Adam and Eve. References to Pharaoh and to the Flood remind us that the biblical story extends beyond the Fall. All events are one in the eye of God, but the unity requires translation if it is to be apprehended by man. Hence the tradition of parallels between the Fall and the Passion:

> Man for man, tre for tre,
> Madyn for madyn; thus shal it be.
> . . . .
> Angell must to mary go,
> ffor the feynd was eue fo.
> ("The Annunciation," Towneley cycle)[7]

The tradition of reading in one event the prefiguration of another, of reading in the second a fulfillment of the first, is distinguished from other signifying systems (from allegory, from symbolism) by the nature of its existence in human time. The historicity of figural interpretation, one of Erich Auerbach's major points,[8] accords with the interpreter's temporal medium, but lodges necessity outside time, in the eternal. If, as in "The Annunciation," the relation between events seems causal, the cause is sheerly the will of God. The similes in *Paradise Lost* seldom invoke the Passion as a direct fulfillment of the Fall; they rather invoke the intervals between scenarios of completion: the time between the Fall and the Incarnation, the time between the comings of Christ, times when the Fall is enacted again and again.

The root of *interpret* corresponds to the Sanskrit *prath*—to spread abroad. Between what is spread abroad, the interpreter moves. The figure of speech, like the figurative event, stands for what elsewhere is unity. In *Ars amoris* (2,679), *figurae* are the positions of lovemaking.[9]

Discussions of "ornament" therefore mislead insofar as they conjure optional, detachable figures of speech.[10] There is no straighter rendering; we have only the translation into time. The text (in Bacon it is nature) has not the same form as the reader's mind.[11]

III. The poem is addressed to fallen man and points beyond the fallen state, both backward in time to the prelapsarian state and outside of time to divine omniscience. We seek, not more of the same, but what we know not by what we know: the perceptual task is demanding. The similes put us in training of a sort, give us sometimes a running start and sometimes the edge of the cliff:

> His Spear, to equal which the tallest Pine
> Hewn on Norwegian Hills, to be the Mast
> Of some great Ammiral, were but a wand.   (I, 292–94)

This is not altogether the radical undoing which Stanley Fish takes it to be. The pine, to be sure, is not commensurate in stature to the spear, but, as James Whaler has affirmed, a definite proportional relation is suggested: the spear is to the pine as the pine is to the wand.[12] Whaler's general point is well taken: there are coherent relations other than equivalence. His paraphrase also, I think, captures the sense we extract from the image, insofar as we continue to attend to size. The stricter grammatical cues, of course, tell us that the pine transformed to a mast is as a wand to the spear when an effort is made to equate the pine and the spear. This effort is hardly made by the tree; it no more seeks to be equal than it seeks to be a mast. Another perspective has entered and, I would argue, as far outweighs the question of size as the spear out-weighs the wand. The projections of human intentionality and imagina-tion have become the subject; man navigates on the ocean as he navigates in conceptual space. "Were but a wand" does not undo the project, but strips away its simplest guise to reveal its proper dimension. The dimen-sion at stake is not of a spear.

A wand, though small, is rich in connotation. It may be, for exam-ple, a walking stick or a magic rod. As the former, it modulates oddly back into the extrametaphorical territory. The pine, generated within the simile and transformed there to a mast, is compared to a wand, and, when we return to the tenor (spear), we find it being used as a walking stick (wand): "a wand / He walkt with to support uneasy steps" (I, 294–95). This is not, of course, its proper use. It is a measure of Satan's fall, in one respect, that he should use his weapon of war to support uneasy steps. It is not just the pine but the spear itself which is "but a wand." The spear, so far above our imaginative powers, falls below the image we have summoned to be its correlative, as far below it as a wand is to a pine.

As a magic rod, the wand has precedents. In the Towneley cycle, Moses perplexes Pharaoh with his "wand."[13] Milton himself used the word in Comus: "Nay Lady, sit; if I but wave this wand, / Your nerves are all chain'd up in Alabaster" (Comus, 659–60). The spear, less than fifty lines after it emerges from simile, is used to assemble the fallen an-gels as Moses' "potent rod" called up the locusts (I, 338 ff.). So a wand is more than a negligible item, even when compared to a pine tree or to

Satan's spear. The transformation of the middle term, the pine, to a mast that can move a ship, is awesome but not incomprehensible.[14] It bespeaks specifically human creativity and will. The nature of the spear is not so easily read. The magic stick used as a walking stick is, once more, a measure of diminishment, but we cannot assume that its powers are wholly gone.

In the fallen angels' new abode the powers of heaven undergo not mere erasure but a radical translation. "As one great Furnace flam'd, yet from those flames / No light, but rather darkness visible" (I, 62–63). Much of Hell is described in oxymoronic or paradoxical terms: "a fiery Deluge, fed / With ever-burning Sulphur unconsum'd" (I, 68–69). The normal exchange between earth and air (consummation) is abrogated, as is the normal antipathy between water and fire. The image makes no concessions to the familiar patterns of synthesis, but is not therefore a systematic disparagement of postlapsarian perceptual equipment. The mind does not stop before the paradox—that's the important thing. It rather gains new energy, as subatomic particles are accelerated in cyclotrons by being made to jump magnetic fields.

There are many ways of creating a verge to be jumped. There are only two requirements: that the elsewhere be neither assimilated nor so radically severed as to make what is here and now appear intact. Cut off from Eden, the realm of man is neither autonomous nor whole. The limbs of truth have been torn from her trunk and scattered (*Areopagitica*, pp. 741–42); this severance keeps the other in mind. The similes in *Paradise Lost* generate temporal and geographical maps in which the boundaries are both barriers and passageways. The fallen angels are

> A multitude, like which the populous North
> Pour'd never from her frozen loins, to pass
> Rhene or the Danaw, when her barbarous Sons
> Came like a Deluge on the South, and spread
> Beneath Gibraltar to the Lybian sands.   (I, 351–55)

The Rhene and Danaw give way before barbarian hordes as the Red Sea gave way before the Israelites. Fifty lines earlier, the fallen angels are as thick bestrown as the floating carcasses and broken chariot wheels of Pharaoh's men when the passageway becomes boundary again. North has flowed into south and the west for a time opened into the east. Norwegian pines make their entry amidst pictures of the Tuscan landscape. The four corners of the world are invoked in such a way as to assure us they are separate but not intact. "Pour'd never from her frozen loins": the event that did not take place is ambiguously insemination and birth; the Israelites, after wandering in the desert, beget a nation. As in "were but a wand," the logically extractable meaning is that the Vandal multitudes can no more be compared to fallen angels than a pine can be compared to Satan's spear. As in "were but a wand," the point is not mere size, but the quality of human imagination. We are certainly not encouraged to think we can embrace the numbers of the angels with our minds. "Comprehension" here is not containment, but an act which may be intuitively provoked. Comparison does not mean equation. We are taken to our conceptual limits as to the Red Sea, and told we must go beyond.

But "never" is a temporal modifier and is placed next to "pour'd." Unlike "were but a wand," the term of negation is placed, as it were, midstream. The Vandals never poured, but the subordinate passage extrapolates the deluge as though it had occurred, as indeed we know it did: "and spread / Beneath Gibraltar to the Lybian sands." The tension between "never" and "once" (in the mind, on the page) parallels the tension between north and south; they do not merge but interpenetrate. We have no more seen the Vandals pour than we have seen "Chineses drive / With Sails and Wind thir cany Waggons light" (III, 438–39). The process by which we know the events of human history and the reaches of human activity is not different in kind from the way in which we know the angels. We embody neither.

Barriers may be erected in the poem as in a landscape. When they are erected around similes, the figure will still inform the surrounding text:

> The Pilot of some small night-founder'd Skiff,
> Deeming some Island, oft, as Seamen tell,
> With fixed Anchor in his scaly rind
> Moors by his side under the Lee, while Night
> Invests the Sea, and wished Morn delays.   (I, 204–08)

The story is cut off before the morn, and menace looms all the larger. Lest chaos be come again, there is a movement to contain the threatening power within the "will / And high permission of all-ruling Heaven" (I, 211–12). The very suddenness of the closure underscores its inadequacy. Not that we doubt Providence, but that the level on which it is ordered is not the level on which we have anchorage. The rescue from night at sea has been rendered ominously ambiguous. Wished morn will presumably disclose to the pilot his doom.

IV. The similes focus attention upon the act of perception itself and make us aware that we are not looking alone. Whaler accounts for the introduction of "extraneous" human points of view by identifying this as a digressive device, a form of pleasant distraction.[15] Geoffrey Hartman talks of the observer "on the shore," who confirms by his presence the suspended quality internal to many of the similes, a quality that constitutes a "counterplot" about divine imperturbability.[16] It is not clear in the poem, however, that we have landed with perfect safety on the shore. The benignity Hartman points to exists in certain specific terms: the angels thick as autumnal leaves, the scattered sedge, the carcasses and chariot wheels so thick bestrown are alike in that they portray devastation as benevolent (I, 302ff.). But the shore from which the chosen people watch their enemies borders on the desert as well as on the Red Sea, the desert in which the Israelites will wander for forty years. No shore, till Christ come and come again, is the final refuge. We are offered the image of safety in order that we may not despair, may know that our state is different from that of Satan, who cannot repent. The images of danger remind us that we are not safe in an armchair as in a harbor when we read, but are active as on a ship.[17] We navigate by means of perceived alliances: with a pilot, a peasant, an astronomer. The patterns of alliance shift, because anchor is unsafe. The human figures planted within the poetic figures are part of a larger phenomenon of corroborative vision. We see through allusion and direct borrowings from previous traditions. Language itself is a medium of inherited, endowed imagination. What is logically condemned may be poetically affirmed. Those who look with us and what they see are no less present because the images that house them are condemned as "mere fabling." Hartman's point is that the "counterplot" of *Paradise Lost* is manifested by means other than overt theme, plot, and subplot. I would qualify his account of the subtext but see no reason to doubt the method by which it comes into being. The reading experience is not primarily governed by preexistent ordering structures, theological or otherwise. We are embroiled, for example, in simile. We form judgments by means of recognition.

    a. The observer *ab extra*.[18]

> As when the Sun new ris'n
> Looks through the Horizontal misty Air
> Shorn of his Beams, or from behind the Moon
> In dim Eclipse disastrous twilight sheds
> On half the Nations, and with fear of change
> Perplexes Monarchs. (I, 594–99)

The sun looks as we look upon it, but is not, as is usual, the light by which we see. This is Satan, shorn of half his brightness, that half of the sun (his beams) which normally lights our way. His fall has introduced disastrous division into the world. The sun from behind the moon sheds half light on half the nations. The monarchs, too, presumably look, and are perplexed. They read the event for implications, as does the peasant who sees, or dreams he sees, the revels of faery elves: "At once with joy and fear his heart rebounds" (I, 788). The moon above the peasant "sits Arbitress." The epithet is an odd one. Not simply the mistress of revels, the moon is arbitress, the one who goes between. The peasant sees by the moon and is judged by what he sees. Interpretation is difficult ("with joy and fear," "perplexes").

We look at and by the sun and the moon; the light is divided and reflected to boot. We look at and by the simile:

> his ponderous shield,
> Ethereal temper, massy, large and round,
> Behind him cast; the broad circumference
> Hung on his shoulders like the Moon, whose Orb
> Through Optic Glass the Tuscan Artist views
> At Ev'ning from the top of Fesole,
> Or in Valdarno, to descry new Lands,
> Rivers or Mountains in her spotty Globe.
> His Spear, to equal which the tallest Pine
> Hewn on Norwegian hills, to be the Mast
> Of some great Ammiral, were but a wand,
> He walkt with to support uneasy steps.   (I, 284–95)

The syntax is such that the shield and the spear attain a large degree of temporary independence from Satan. He throws the shield behind him; it changes from object to subject in the next clause, and its analogue, the moon, becomes the object of vision. The observer is observed by us: we locate the artist in Fesole *or* in Valdarno as he locates new lands, rivers *or* mountains in his glass. The spear generates an analogue that extends the purview to Norwegian hills and an Ammiral. The project, in several forms, is human navigation; it's the movement that maps a globe. And yet the structure is pendant to Satan's navigation in his fallen state; he is moving toward the shore. The globe is spotty, the monarchs perplexed with fear of change. The change that heralds others has already occurred.

    b. *Obiter dicta*.[19]

The simplest form is a phrase, "as Seamen tell" (I, 205), or a verb that makes us aware that others have looked or are looking as well: "So numberless were those bad Angels seen" (I, 344). More complex is to look by means of previous versions of experience:

he stood and call'd
His Legions, Angel Forms, who lay intrans't
Thick as Autumnal Leaves that strow the Brooks
In Vallombrosa, where th'Etrurian shades
High overarch't imbow'r; or scatter'd sedge
Afloat, when with fierce Winds Orion arm'd
Hath vext the Red-Sea Coast, whose waves o'erthrew
Busirus and his Memphian Chivalry,
While with perfidious hatred they pursu'd
The Sojourners of Goshen, who beheld
From the safe shore thir floating Carcasses
And broken Chariot Wheels; so thick bestrown
Abject and lost lay these, covering the Flood,
Under amazement of thir hideous change.   (I, 300–13)

The landscape immediately contrasts with that in which Satan is walking: his torrid clime is vaulted with fire, the Tuscan valley embowered with shade trees. Brooks and autumn are cool, as is evening, in which the Tuscan artist, fifteen lines ago, looked through his optic glass. But the contrast is not complete. The Etrurian shades may be spirits of the older (Etruscan) civilization, thus reinforcing what Merritt Hughes takes to be an allusion to Dante: spirits numberless as autumn leaves.[20] Orion armed has scattered the sedge as Orion, in Virgil, has risen with the winds that force the Trojans to land on Dido's Libyan shores. Virgil is to Dante as the Etruscans are to Tuscans. The landscape is old.

With the scattering of Pharaoh's men, we move from classical to Hebrew history, to greater violence and a more visible will in the simile. It is in relation to this will that we seek to orient ourselves. Men are wont to read their own mortality in the falling of leaves, but the cycle of seasons consoles us. The seas that shipwrecked Aeneas were raised by Juno's malevolent will, but the allusion is indirect and the will submerged. The exodus, on the other hand, is evoked directly: we know who made the Red Sea waters close. As Christians, we inherit the divine benevolence that overthrew the Memphian chivalry. As Britons (Trojans via Rome), we are part of a line that continued *despite* the raising of the wind. We seem to have arrived on the shores of simile as a chosen people, but back in the tenor the angels cover a flood. We are reminded of another flood, which was sent when men had wandered from God, as the Israelites are again about to do. When Satan's spear is raised to summon the angels, they swarm like the plague of locusts. The fallen angels will threaten men as the locusts threatened Egypt. A subsequent passage tells us how: the angels are named by the names they received from the sons of Eve, who fell into false belief. Our status as survivors, as the chosen, is complicated more than once.

   c. The instrument sees.

> As when by night the Glass
> Of Galileo, less assur'd, observes
> Imagin'd Lands.   (V, 261–63)

> But now my Oat proceeds,
> And listens to the Herald of the Sea.   (*Lycidas*, 88–89)

As with the sun, the thing we see by also sees. As with the poem, the thing we make is an instrument of perception. The eye dominates *Paradise Lost* as the ear dominates *Comus* and *Lycidas*. In the masque, characters are forewarned of one another by the sound of footsteps or songs. In the elegy, the birth of the final persona follows conception through the ear. Early attempts to enter are made and rejected: Phoebus "touch'd my trembling ears" (77); St. Peter comes as a "dread voice" (132). Lycidas' arrival in heaven is celebrated by an "unexpressive nuptial Song" (176), and the poet is finally freed for transformation by the song he sings himself.

    Ear becomes eye as speech moves to the page. *Comus* was of course written to be spoken aloud. The convention of the sung lyric still obtains in *Lycidas*, but is minimal in *Paradise Lost*. The word sees as the pipe once heard; this is the twofold nature of bearing witness. The witness perceives and testifies, is wholly implicated. Stanley Fish considers the act of composition primarily by implication, but his theory seems to me to maximize the difference between Milton's experience of the poem and that of the reader. Where the poet has received the understanding and control not granted to fallen man is never explained: presumably from his heavenly Muse. But dialogue with the Muse sounds strangely like a single voice; she answers quickly, for one thing: "Who first seduc'd them to that foul revolt? / Th'infernal Serpent; he it was" (I, 33–34). The Muse hasn't even a verse paragraph to herself. The voice is not distinct from numerous others that enter the poem; the inspiration is patently plural. I would posit the poet as a reader rather than a puppeteer, his poem a rendered reading of another text which he contemplates by our side. "And albeit whatever thing we hear or see, sitting, walking, travelling, or conversing, may be fitly called our book" (*Areopagitica*, p. 733). The inherited myths, the inherited structures of language are our book. The similes, highly allusive, heavily based upon classical and biblical texts, inhabited by suns and peasant and an artist who look, do much to foreground the act of reading. Milton's humanism seems to dominate his Puritanism on this point: we read in the company of those who have read before.

V. The navigation does not by itself get us to the other side; the landing on shore calls for grace. Milton's similes inculcate agility of mind: points diverse in human and divine history, in ordered philosophy, fable, nature observed, points which seem merely disparate to a man too comfortably lodged in his own space and time, are seen to have mutual relevance. There is an agility that is cultivated for purposes of evil (Satan's "ambivalent words"), and there is another that keeps us strong ("our faith and knowledge thrives by exercise, as well as our limbs and complexion," *Areopagitica*, p. 739). That which we cannot resolve but must continually posit is there for our good as well.

Galileo's astronomy is a going forth, an intellectual and creative project. The Copernican revolution was presumably long established but, in *Paradise Lost*, as elsewhere in Renaissance literature, the Copernican and Ptolemaic schemata are used alternately as sources for poetic image. Milton invokes the Prutenic tables in *Doctrine and Discipline of Divorce*,[21] though they had already been surpassed by Kepler's. Merritt Hughes (*Complete Poems*, p. 706n.) says that the perpetual revision of human understanding is precisely the point. However structured the wheel of day and night, it "needs not thy belief" (VIII, 136). The distances of celestial space are "inexpressible / By Numbers that have name" (VIII, 113–14). The unnamable has a singular potency. The power to name belongs in the created world to man alone, and is rightly the source of major confidence. When Adam named the animals, he knew at once their inmost natures. The significance of names extends beyond the human: the fallen angels have their names erased from the Book of Life, and we are to regard this as a dire consequence. We know them only by the names they have assumed as seducers of men. To be without name in the Book of Life is to have all opportunity for recovery of their heavenly state denied. The vessels that housed their former essences have been broken; they exist only as fallen. The creatures without name, like the spaces between the stars, their movements and patterns of subordination, so difficult to read, are not for naught. They exist "That Man may know he dwells not in his own" (VIII, 103).

As the space between celestial bodies instructs, so the space between vehicle and tenor instructs. There's slippage here, and space we cannot wholly resolve into either term. The poem resists complete synthesis in order that the reader may know there is more in the world than can be owned (made into himself) by man. Disjunctions are built into the figurative text to remind us of the space and our dependence. The starry lamps in Pandemonium yield light "as from a sky" (I, 730). The metaphor embodied in an adjective (starry) has encouraged this analogue, and the simile, paradoxically, calls attention to the falseness of the image. As from a sky: not only is there no sky in Pandemonium, there is no sky in Hell; there are only the vaults of fire. We think of any landscape as beneath a sky. The image betrays our assumptions, articulates as exceptional an analogue we tend to take for granted. Similarly, the angels spring up "as when men wont to watch / On duty, sleeping found by whom they dread, / Rouse and bestir themselves ere well awake" (I, 332–34). A homing instinct predisposes us to compare all things with ourselves. "As when men," oddly, warns us to respect the distance.

> and how he fell
> From Heav'n, they fabl'd, thrown by angry Jove
> Sheer o'er the Crystal Battlements: from Morn
> To Noon he fell, from Noon to dewy Eve,
> A Summer's day; and with the setting Sun
> Dropt from the Zenith like a falling Star,
> On Lemnos th'Aegean Isle: thus they relate,
> Erring.   (I, 740–47)

The error is identified as an error in dating: he fell much earlier than men relate. The laminations of time get complicated: Mulciber fell, not before Jove threw him, but before there were men to make up stories about the gods. One of the functions of this and similar anachronisms is to insist on the temporal precedence of the Christian God. Another is to cast doubt on the nature as well as the timing of myths. Achieved suspension is the quality that unites Pandemonium and the fall of its architect, as portrayed in classical myth. "From the arched roof / Pendant by subtle Magic many a row / Of Starry Lamps and blazing Cressets . . . yielded light" (I, 72–79); "From Morn / To Noon he fell, from Noon to dewy Eve, / A Summer's day," which is the longest day. We make a turning at the end of a line and encounter "Erring." The suddenness of the judgment is difficult to assimilate. Milton the poet has derived clear benefit from the classical image, has recreated it, and another to match, in distinctly attractive form. Time and space are extended as if to offer repose and consolation. "Nor aught avail'd him now / To have built in Heav'n high Tow'rs" (I, 748–49). The towers are built again in the poem, as the fall is built in fable and the capitol in Hell; their material is nostalgia, a longing backward to the forms of heaven. We are not to take up lodging in these structures, but to use them for moving on. "The light which we have gained, was given us, not to be ever staring on, but by it to discover onward things more remote from our knowledge" (*Areopagitica*, p. 742). We are warned, lest we be too much consoled.

The insubstantiality of Pandemonium is made even clearer by analogy to a straw-built citadel. The angels, even before their "actual" transformation in size, are like bees. But weakness and diminution are not the only points. A straw-built hive is built by the beekeeper, not by bees; their sweetness is all dependent. "When the sun in Taurus rides . . ." (I, 769): having dismissed the fable of the ancients, does Milton expect us to read Taurus as devoid of classical allusion? Or the earth's giant sons as less to be doubted than Mulciber's fall? Surely not.

> they but now who seem'd
> In bigness to surpass Earth's Giant Sons
> Now less than smallest Dwarfs, in narrow room
> Throng numberless, like the Pigmean Race
> Beyond the Indian Mount, or Faery Elves,
> Whose midnight Revels, by a Forest side
> Or Fountain some belated Peasant sees,
> Or dreams he sees.
> . . . .
> they on thir mirth and dance
> Intent, with jocund Music charm his ear.   (I, 777–87)

The "seem'd" casts doubt, not on the earth's giant sons, but on the relative size of the angels. The possible elves may be dreamt, but they take on enough reality to dance in the poem. If we, like the peasant, are belated because attached to the myths of earlier times, surely Milton is too. He employs the beauty and momentum of two constructs, and undoes them only to substitute others with similar materials. The warning may partly be, of course, that beauty formed without thought of God is no beauty to be trusted. Hartman affirms that we don't undo the work of the simile by being restored to "better judgment." The poem may caution us about the appetites to which similes appeal, the pleasures derived from stories, from the senses, but the figures are not therefore disposable. Milton builds with inherited stories and words. To read "dreams he sees" and "Erring" as signals of univocal control is like reading Othello's "It is not words that shakes me thus" as unparadoxical.

Raphael introduces the process of human understanding by means of a vegetative image:

> So from the root
> Springs lighter the green stalk, from thence the leaves
> More aery, last the bright consummate flow'r
> Spirits odorous breathes.   (V, 479–82)

If similes in *Paradise Lost* at times remind us of Eve's hair in wanton ringlets (IV, 306), they are trained to the elm of our greater inquiry.

We may look for unity too soon, or in the wrong place, miscalculating either our self-sufficiency or our helplessness, and thereby turn from God. Straight paths do exist. When Raphael stands at the opened gates of Heaven, he travels first with his eye: "From hence, no cloud, or, to obstruct his sight / Star interpos'd, however small he sees" (V, 257–58). Then, in borrowed shape he "Sails between worlds and worlds" (V, 268). Man's path, except to destruction, is "less assur'd." Satan, leading Eve to mischief swift, "made intricate seem straight" (IX, 632). The highway forged between Hell and Earth by Sin and Death is straight:

> a Bridge
> Of length prodigious joining to the Wall
> Immoveable of this now fenceless World
> Forfeit to Death; from hence a passage broad,
> Smooth, easy, inoffensive down to Hell.   (X, 301–05)

They have stopped all flux to pave their route:

> As when two Polar Winds blowing adverse
> Upon the Cronian Sea, together drive
> Mountains of Ice, that stop th'imagin'd way
> Beyond Petsora Eastward, to the rich
> Cathaian Coast.   (X, 289–93)

The way is not less crucial because it is imagined:

> As when by night the Glass
> Of Galileo, less assur'd, observes
> Imagin'd Lands and Regions in the Moon:
> Or Pilot from amidst the Cyclades
> Delos or Samos first appearing kens
> A cloudy spot.   (V, 261–66)

The imagination, though liable to fog or mirage, is our light. The truth, though single once and continuing so in the mind of God, is not so to her human friends. They must gather her scattered limbs as Isis gathered those of Osiris (*Areopagitica*, p. 742). We must not take the part for the whole; to do so is to despair of God and to ally with Belial, making hell more livable. We may not, on the other hand, treat as indifferent all earthly modes of understanding. The gathering is the way we wait for grace. Gatherers in a field do not walk in a single straight line, but their steps are not therefore unguided.

Stanford University

NOTES

1. Stanley Fish, *Surprised by Sin: The Reader in "Paradise Lost"* (New York, 1967), p. 311.
2. Page and line references to Miltonic texts are derived, unless otherwise noted, from *John Milton, Complete Poems and Major Prose*, ed. Merritt Y. Hughes (1957; rpt. Indianapolis, 1977).
3. The writer/persona of *Sonnet 19* hears in "stand and wait" his profoundest task in the service of God. But the mind and language are hardly at rest in the poem. Structures of stasis may encourage—indeed, require—movement within. The structure of the sonnet contributes to the accelerated momentum of enjambment. The consequent submergence of rhyme accentuates the starkness of the final demand, and withholds the comfort of re-sounding closure.
4. James Holly Hanford, "Milton's Style and Versification," in *A Milton Hand-book*, 4th ed. (New York, 1946), p. 319.
5. "Milton I," in *Selected Prose of T. S. Eliot*, ed. Frank Kermode (New York, 1975), p. 259, first published in *Essays and Studies of the English Association*, 1936.
6. James Whaler names this function in "The Miltonic Simile," *PMLA*, XLVI (1931), 1034, 1036, 1048-52, 1071.
7. *The Towneley Plays*, ed. George England and Alfred W. Pollard, *EETS*, ES LXXI (1897; rpt. London, 1966), Play X, lines 33-34, 61-62.
8. "Figura," trans. Ralph Manheim, in *Scenes from the Drama of European Literature* (Gloucester, Mass., 1973). The essay first appeared in *Neue Dantestudien* (Istanbul, 1944).
9. Ibid, p. 23.
10. To better illuminate the function and valence of ornament, Angus Fletcher revives the Greek term *kosmos* and reminds his readers of the etymological connection between such words as *cosmic* and *cosmetic*. See his discussion of the cosmic image in *Allegory: The Theory of a Symbolic Mode* (Ithaca, 1964), pp. 108-17.
11. See especially Aphorisms XXIII and XLV in Book I of *Novum Organum*, trans. James Spedding, in *The Works of Francis Bacon*, VIII, ed. James Spedding, Robert Ellis, and Douglas Heath (Boston, 1863).
12. P. 1064.
13. See "Pharaoh," in England and Pollard, *The Towneley Plays*, lines 160, 232, 247, 257, 388.
14. The periphrasis, moreover, has a history. The Roman poets commonly referred to the Argo as the "pine of Pelion." See Ernst Robert Curtius, "The Ship of the Argonauts," in *Essays on European Literature*, trans. Michael Kowal (Princeton, 1973), first published as *Kritische Essays zur europäischen Literatur*, 2nd ed. (Bern, 1954).

15. "The Miltonic Simile," p. 1057.

16. "Milton's Counterplot," *ELH*, XXV (1958), 8.

17. The comparison of poetic composition to a voyage by sea was a commonplace among the Roman authors and continues in such later poems as the *Paradiso* (II, 1–15) and *The Faerie Queene* (VI, xii, 1). In a short thesaurus of "nautical metaphors," E. R. Curtius surfaces only one direct reference, however, to the reader's part in the navigation (*European Literature and the Latin Middle Ages*, trans. Willard R. Trask, Bollingen Series XXXVI [New York, 1953], pp. 128–30; originally published as *Europäischen Literatur und lateinisches Mittelalter* [Bern, 1948]). In "The Ship of the Argonauts," Curtius traces a related theme from the Greeks to Goethe. Of special interest here is the emergence of an attendant figure: the observer on shore who finds the ship mysterious and attempts to "read" its nature and significance. Thus, though the Argo itself is not explicitly summoned as an image for the writing of the poem, it does figure as a stimulus to and representative of human inquiry.

18. The term is Hartman's, "Milton's Counterplot," p. 8.

19. The term is Whaler's, "The Miltonic Simile," p. 1060.

20. *Complete Poems*, p. 219n. The allusion to Virgil is documented here as well.

21. *The Doctrine and Discipline of Divorce*, in *Complete Prose Works of John Milton*, II, ed. Ernest Sirluck (New Haven, 1959), p. 243.

IRONIC AND AMBIGUOUS ALLUSION
IN *PARADISE LOST*

Douglas Bush, Harvard University

Criticism of *Samson Agonistes* has taken full account of the irony that invests the total structure, the outcome of the successive "acts," and the texture: ironic ambiguity begins with the title and the first line, "A little onward lend thy guiding hand." While Miltonic criticism has reached such bulk that one cannot readily take a precautionary review of it, ambiguity and irony in *Paradise Lost* seem to have been much less discussed, perhaps because these elements are less conspicuous in the more complex work or because they are accepted as obvious. Most of the examples I shall mention have been noted individually and incidentally but they have not, I think, been brought together. Those given here are only a sampling, especially on the biblical side, and they represent mainly one kind of ambiguity, that expressed through a particular but veiled allusion.

This technique seems to be regarded by some critics as the invention of Ezra Pound and T. S. Eliot, but it was used with subtle success by Spenser. The most exalted tribute Spenser paid to his bride is indirect:

> Open the temple gates unto my love,
> Open them wide that she may enter in.

The lines have their own emotional charge, but it is greatly heightened by our recollection of Psalm 24:7: "Lift up your heades ye gates, and be ye lift up ye everlasting dores, and the King of glorie shal come in." One example in *The Faerie Queene* (I, xii, 13, and 22–23) is the way in which the Red Cross Knight and Una merge with Christ and his "wife" through echoes of Christ's entry into Jerusalem and the marriage of the Lamb (Rev. 19:7–8).

The kind of allusion that we have in *Paradise Lost* had appeared in Milton as early as *In quintum Novembris* (1626). In the opening lines Satan, the roving exile from heavenly Olympus, counts over his faithful followers in crime, *sceleris socios*, a phrase Cicero used at least twice of Catiline's associates (*In Catilinam*, I, iv, 8, III, i, 4; cf. Lucretius, III, 61, *socios scelerum*). In line 11 these followers are described as *Participes regni post funera moesta futuros*, an ironical echo of Hebrews, 3:14, "For we are made partakers of Christ"; the echo is made still clearer by Tremellius' translation, *Participes enim facti sumus cum Christo* (cf. *De Doctrina Christiana, Works*, XVI, 4: *Christi participes facti sumus*).

There is a frequent difference between old and new methods, since in modern poets the whole significance may depend upon an allusion, sometimes a more or less esoteric allusion, which the reader may not catch and without which he is lost (until the critics have had time to hunt it down). In Spenser and Milton, however, the allusion is normally public, often biblical or classical, and supposedly within the ordinary reader's compass. Besides, even if it and its intensifying or complicating effect are missed, the loss, though real, is not fatal, since the main drift is clear without it.

Against this generality one partial exception might be lodged. Some lines in the epilogue to *Comus* are difficult in the modern way because—though the total context is a general guide—the meaning here is given through allusive symbols without anything in the way of "prose statement." The allusion to Venus and Adonis seems—as Professor Woodhouse showed in his well-known study (*University of Toronto Quarterly*, XI, 1941)—to be especially to Spenser's interpretation of the myth (*F.Q.*, III, vi, 46–49) in terms of the cycle of physical generation, the perpetual union of matter and form. Milton's allusion to Cupid and Psyche, which follows immediately (and is marked off by a distinct change of rhythm), is in a more fully orthodox tradition, since this late "myth" had long been understood as the marriage of Christ and the human soul, though it is uncertain here whether the poet is thinking of the life of grace on earth or of the full felicity of heaven.

While this short paper is concerned with particulars in *Paradise Lost*, we may remind ourselves of the larger ironies to which such details contribute. These larger and more familiar ironies are of the same dramatic kind that we have in *Samson:* that is, characters speak and act in ignorance of the outcome, which the reader already knows. But, because of the central theme of conflict in *Paradise Lost*, this dramatic irony has a further or clearer basis in the absolutes of Christian faith: Absolute Good, embodied in the Father and the Son, is completely and unshakably invincible, so that Satan—although he achieves a degree of success disastrous for man—can never be even imagined as winning. While in soliloquies he can recognize at least part of the truth, in his public harangues and actions he, like his followers, is in a state of spiritual blindness concerning the real issues. Thus all their futile activities are seen in an ironic light—"Hatching vain Empires," in Beelzebub's words.

This general conception, natural enough in a Christian writer, is carried out through a dramatic method, a character's self-revelation, which reminds us more of Shakespeare than of Sophocles. Like Shakespeare, Milton could rely on the moral and religious reactions of his audience, and he could also guide those reactions through his own comments. This sort of dramatic irony had been used in the speeches of Comus, as when he declares

> We that are of purer fire
> Imitate the Starry Quire . . . ;

and with him as with Satan we are not always certain of the line between unconscious and conscious self-deception. In *Paradise Lost* the first example of dramatic irony is Satan's first speech, delivered to Beelzebub—the place at which early romantic readers and their modern successors begin to show their inability to comprehend a Christian poem. Even if we had heard nothing of Satan's egocentric pride and hate, every phrase he utters reveals a completely perverted view of God and himself and the issues between them. In his second speech Satan is allowed to see the conflict between evil and good, even to state Milton's own conception of his epic theme (ll. 162–65; cf. 214–20), but only from the standpoint of Satan's own corruption. There is no need of remarking on the heterogeneous ironies and ambiguities that punctuate Satan's speeches, here and later, since we are, as I said, concerned with only one kind.

Paradise Lost has many certain and some uncertain examples of the veiled allusion. One of the most arresting is in the first two lines of Satan's first speech:

> If thou beest he; But O how fall'n! how chang'd
> From him, who in the happy Realms of Light . . . .

Milton's fusions of the Hebraic and the classical have usually a more than double potency, and here Isaiah's "How art thou fallen from heaven, O Lucifer, son of the morning" (14:12) is joined with Virgil's phrase about the bloodstained ghost of Hector, *quantum mutatus ab illo Hectore* who had been *lux Dardaniae* (*Aeneid*, II, 274, 281). Most of the general ironic ambiguities of Satan's speeches are quite clear, since they turn on two opposed sets of traditional values, religious and irreligious; but sometimes one is not sure how far the modern appetite for this sort of thing is entitled to go. One major premise at least is that Milton and his early readers knew the Bible and the common classics far better than we do and were far more likely to use and to catch overtones from both sources. For instance, when Satan grandly proclaims

> and thou profoundest Hell
> Receive thy new Possessor,

we know that he is really a prisoner, and in a mental as well as a local hell. We know that "Better to reign in Hell, then serve in Heav'n" embodies a false conception of power and freedom (and an echo in reverse of Achilles' shade in the *Odyssey*, XI, 489–91). But when in the same speech Satan refers to "this unhappy Mansion" (I, 268; cf. "this ill Mansion," II, 462), are we intended to remember "In my Father's house are many mansions" (John, 14:2)? (So too in *Samson*, where religious belief is kept within the Hebraic frame, are we to hear an ambiguous overtone in the grieving Manoa's "Home to his Fathers house"?) For another doubtful item, while the Red Sea's overwhelming of the Egyptians is the material of an elaborate simile (I, 304 ff.), we cannot be sure, a little earlier, if we are intended to see an ironic contrast with the Israelites' miraculous crossing when Satan

> rears from off the Pool
> His mighty Stature; on each hand the flames
> Drivn backward slope thir pointing spires, and rowld
> In billows, leave i' th' midst a horrid Vale.   (I, 221 ff.)

A longer passage (I, 549 ff.) prompts the question how far Milton, when utilizing a source not likely to come to everyone's mind, gives it an ironic effectiveness that is not dependent on recognition:

> Anon they move
> In perfect *Phalanx* to the *Dorian* mood
> Of Flutes and soft Recorders; such as rais'd
> To hight of noblest temper Hero's old
> Arming to Battel, and in stead of rage
> Deliberate valour breath'd, firm and unmov'd
> With dread of death to flight or foul retreat,
> Nor wanting power to mitigate and swage
> With solemn touches, troubl'd thoughts, and chase
> Anguish and doubt and fear and sorrow and pain
> From mortal or immortal minds. Thus they
> Breathing united force with fixed thought
> Mov'd on in silence to soft Pipes that charm'd
> Thir painful steps o're the burnt soyle; and now

Advanc't in view, they stand, a horrid Front
Of dreadful length and dazling Arms, in guise
Of Warriers old with order'd Spear and Shield,
Awaiting what command thir mighty Chief
Had to impose.

Commentators have noted that Milton is adapting a passage in Plutarch's *Lycurgus*, and North will serve our purpose (Temple Classics, I, 203–204):

So that it was a marvellous pleasure, and likewise a dreadful sight, to see the whole battell march together in order, at the sound of the pipes, and never to break their pace, nor confound their ranks, nor to be dismayed nor amazed themselves, but to go on quietly and joyfully at the sound of these pipes, to hazard themselves even to death. For it is likely, that such courages are not troubled with much fear, nor yet overcome with much fury: but rather they have an assured constancy and valiantness in good hope, as those which are backed with the assisting favour of the gods.[1]

Dr. Tillyard, writing without reference to Plutarch, said long ago (*Milton*, p. 269) what he probably would not say now, that "In this passage if anywhere Milton is on the Devils' side." The poet does certainly acknowledge, with a heightening of Plutarch, the order, courage, and dignity of the marching angels. At the same time he makes most of the borrowed matter into a simile and implies a contrast between the "Deliberate valour" of ancient heroes arming for battle in assurance of divine help and the "rage" that has inspired the defeated and evil host of hell; and after the simile the last lines (containing a bit of Plutarch) bring us back to these marchers and what and where they are. All this is made subtly clear even if we do not know of the "source."

A unique example of irony is the allegory of Sin and Death which Addison and Dr. Johnson disapproved of but which modern readers seem to find very powerful. Part of the effect, especially of the first episode, is the further and direct revelation of the true character and associations of the "heroic" Satan. But the chief effect, as modern critics have seen, comes from Milton's making Satan, Sin, and Death

[1] E. H. Gardner (*MLN*, LXII [1947], 360) pointed out that the parallel was perhaps first recognized by K. Chetwood in translating Plutarch (1683). It was noted by R. C. Trench, *Plutarch* (2nd ed. [London, 1874], pp. 75–76), and, more recently, by F. L. Jones, *MLN*, XLIX [1934], 44–45), G. Ethel (*MLQ*, XVIII [1957], 295–302), and P. Turner (*NQ*, IV [1957], 10–11. Turner spoke of the irony in Milton's use of a passage referring to courage and divine favor. Others have cited other and much less close parallels. Arnold Stein has an analysis of the whole passage, without reference to sources, in *ELH*, XVI (1949), 120–34.

a monstrous counterpart of the Trinity, and this is done through a few allusions—"thy only Son" (II, 728), "one for all / My self expose" (II, 827-28), and that climactic phrase which brings a special shock in the final inverted adjective,

> where I shall Reign
> At thy right hand voluptuous . . . .
> (II, 868–69; cf. III, 62–64)

In the continuation of the allegory in Book X, when Sin and Death set about building a bridge from hell to earth, they

> Flew divers, & with Power (thir Power was great)
> Hovering upon the Waters,

and the last phrase is again a grisly parody, of both Genesis and the exordium of the poem, where the creative spirit of God dove-like sat brooding on the vast abyss. In this whole passage, where Satan, returning to hell to report his triumph, congratulates Sin and Death on their bridge, the ironic parallel with the Trinity is carried on; the exchanges between Sin and Satan are like what might have been said by the Son and the Father after the Creation. The next incident (X, 504 ff.) involves no particular allusion but is a general reminder of Ovid, though the grotesque irony outdoes anything Ovidian—the wholesale metamorphosis of the triumphant Satan and his applauding followers.

Another and special Ovidian item may be added here, a mythological-topical allusion no less potent than obvious, and one which transcends irony. That is, in the invocation to Book VII, the appeal to Urania to

> drive farr off the barbarous dissonance
> Of *Bacchus* and his revellers . . . .

Part of the idea had just been presented in Milton's half-personal, half-impersonal way:

> On evil dayes though fall'n, and evil tongues;
> In darkness, and with dangers compast round,
> And solitude; yet not alone . . . .

At once, in terms that recall the passage on Orpheus in "Lycidas," he stridently depicts the savage murder of the ideal poet; but he asserts at the same time the protective guidance of his own Heavenly Muse. Through the mythological metaphor the blind John Milton in the London of Charles II is generalized into the inspired poet-priest in a world of corruption.

The irony that envelops Adam and Eve, like the irony that envelops Satan, arises from their ignorance of the future and of what is
at stake; partly also it goes along with the human weakness that
eventuates in sin like his. If Eden is a symbol of the poet's lifelong
vision of perfection, its perfection is brief. It is a master-stroke of
ironic presentation, as critics have amply recognized, that what
seems idyllic innocence and beatitude is from the start overshadowed
by Satan's presence. And if the finest of all Milton's similes, "Not
that faire field Of Enna," is a distillation of the beauty of Eden, it is
also a distillation of the pervasive irony, since, as every reader sees,
the reference to Proserpine and Dis is a clear though tacit anticipation of Satan's seduction of Eve. Although we think of Milton as an
exponent of moral choice, of conscious virtue, the impending ruin of
Adam and Eve evokes his nostalgic compassion for the simple innocence that is unaware of evil:

> Sleep on
> Blest pair; and O yet happiest if ye seek
> No happier state, and know to know no more. (IV, 773–75)

> thrice happie if they know
> Thir happiness, and persevere upright. (VII, 631–32)

In both utterances Milton is recalling Virgil's eulogy of the simple
Italian farmers who shun ambition and are content with their humble
life (*Georgics*, II, 458–60):

> O fortunatos nimium, sua si bona norint,
> agricolas! quibus ipsa, procul discordibus armis,
> fundit humo facilem victum iustissima tellus.

We know that Eve is to succumb to Satan's appeal to her ambition
and the reminder of Virgil's peasants adds a note of human actuality
to the pathos of idyllic innocence. Just before the first of these two
extracts (IV, 772–73) we have:

> And on thir naked limbs the flourie roof
> Showrd Roses, which the Morn repair'd.

The last phrase may echo *Georgics*, II, 201–202, where Virgil says
that what the herds crop in the long days the cool dew will restore in
one short night: "exigua tantum gelidus ros nocte reponet." In Virgil
the idea is merely nature's quiet, perpetual renewal; in Milton it becomes ironical because the morning's repairs will not go on much
longer. Apropos of this second *Georgic*, we may remember Milton's

echo, in the invocation to Light, of Virgil's lines 475 ff.; along with what Dr. Tillyard has finely said (*Poetry Direct and Oblique* [1934], pp. 189–90), we may note that Virgil's contrast between poetry of the cosmos and that of the countryside becomes in Milton a contrast between his beloved classics and the higher themes of Sion.

There has been in recent years a good deal of debate over the artistic problem of Milton's keeping Adam and Eve innocent while yet preparing the way for their fall; clearly the fall would be unreal and meaningless, a piece of melodrama, if it came as a sudden and complete surprise. The first hints of the possibility of weakness—they are no more than that—are given in a single speech of Eve's (IV, 460 ff.) and given through veiled allusions to two Ovidian myths. Though the first is made unmistakably clear—Eve's admiring her own face in a pool, like Narcissus—it achieves a quite subtle result, since the faint trace of latent vanity and self-centeredness is not incompatible with the naïve innocence of the newly created Eve. The second allusion is shorter and less obvious but would be immediately recognized by readers who knew their Ovid. Eve goes on to recall how, seeing Adam, she had turned away from a being less attractive than "that smooth watry image," whereupon he had followed, crying:

> Return faire *Eve*,
> Whom fli'st thou? whom thou fli'st, of him thou art,
> His flesh, his bone; to give thee being I lent
> Out of my side to thee, neerest my heart
> Substantial Life, to have thee by my side
> Henceforth an individual solace dear;
> Part of my Soul I seek thee, and thee claim
> My other half. . . .

These partly biblical words are an innocent declaration of pure love and devotion, yet they register Adam's potential weakness as Eve had registered hers, and chiefly because the first words recall those of Apollo as he pursues Daphne (*Metamorphoses*, I, 504 ff., 514 ff.):

> nympha, precor, Penei, mane! non insequor hostis . . .
> . . . nescis, temeraria, nescis,
> quem fugias, ideoque fugis. . . .

(The last phrase George Sandys rendered as "From whom thou fly'st, thou know'st not.") Milton's brief but clear echo of Ovid contributes to making his lines the germ, no more, of the extravagant avowal of idolatry in VIII, 521–59, where Adam is on the way toward letting Eve usurp his own proper place and come between him and God; later still, just before he surrenders to Eve's persuasions, he twice echoes the rest of the lines quoted above (IX, 911 ff., 952 ff.). In that dialogue in Book VIII, when Adam's excessive veneration for Eve has drawn a rebuke from Raphael, Adam, "half abash't," offers some defense, and in the course of it affirms (VIII, 610–11):

> yet still free
> Approve the best, and follow what I approve.

We do not share his confidence, partly because we know the story, but partly also because he is twisting the famous and more realistic saying of Ovid's Medea (*Metamorphoses*, VII, 20–21):

> video meliora proboque,
> deteriora sequor.

(Sandys' rendering is: "I see the better, I approve it too: / The worse I follow.")

A few examples may be taken from the drama of the fall. When Satan, working with specious logic upon Eve, argues from his own enlarged faculties to hers and Adam's, he says (IX, 713–14):

> So ye shall die perhaps, by putting off
> Human, to put on Gods. . . .

Whether or not Milton intended it, we think of the ironic difference between this argument and St. Paul's pleas for Christian rebirth, "put off . . . the old man" and "put on the new man" (Eph. 4:22–24; Col. 3:9–10). When Adam reaffirms his resolution to share Eve's fate, she exclaims "O glorious trial of exceeding Love" (IX, 961). If we met this phrase by itself, we would of course take it as an allusion to Christ's sacrifice for man;[2] here it is a large and ironic contrast to Eve's wholly selfish love. Fifty lines later, when Adam has eaten the fruit and Nature has given a second groan, the pair reach the height of their hubristic delusions (IX. 1008 ff.):

> As with new Wine intoxicated both
> They swim in mirth, and fansie that they feel
> Divinitie within them breeding wings
> Wherewith to scorne the Earth.

In *Comus*, lines 374 ff., Milton had used the image of wings in its Platonic sense, probably with direct reference to *Phaedrus*, 246 ff.:

> And Wisdoms self
> Oft seeks to sweet retired Solitude,
> Where with her best nurse Contemplation
> She plumes her feathers, and lets grow her wings. . . .

---

[2] Milton had so used "exceeding love" long before in "Upon the Circumcision," ll. 15–16 (E. S. LeComte, *Yet Once More*, p. 65).

And he may have blended the Platonic image with that of Pegasus when he wrote to Diodati on 23 September [November?] 1637: "Growing my wings and practising flight. But my Pegasus still raises himself on very tender wings" (*Complete Prose Works*, I [1953], 327). At any rate the lines in *Paradise Lost* recall, by ironic contrast, the Platonic ascent to the Good. The same ironic note attends the words of Sin to Death after the fall (X, 243–45):

> Methinks I feel new strength within me rise,
> Wings growing, and Dominion giv'n me large
> Beyond this Deep.

To come back to Adam and Eve, their sense of divinity sinks quickly into subhuman lust, and Adam indulges in a speech of repellent and sensual levity which ends thus (IX, 1029 ff.):

> For never did thy Beautie since the day
> I saw thee first and wedded thee, adorn'd
> With all perfections, so enflame my sense
> With ardor to enjoy thee, fairer now
> Then ever, bountie of this vertuous Tree.

The words, especially the aggressive crudity of "enjoy thee" from one who had been a reverent adorer, even idolater, are sufficient to show what Adam has become. Yet the effect is heightened for those who recognize a clear echo of the pagan sensuality of Paris addressing Helen, and Zeus addressing Hera (*Iliad*, III, 442 ff.; XIV, 313 ff.). The parallel with the second Homeric scene is carried further in lines 1039 ff.:

> He led her nothing loath; Flours were the Couch,
> Pansies, and Violets, and Asphodel,
> And Hyacinth, Earths freshest softest lap.

There is a double parallel here, with the hilltop bed of Zeus and Hera (*Iliad*, XIV, 346 ff.) and with the bower and nuptial bed of Adam and Eve in their first purity (*P.L.*, IV, 689–719); and Milton's picture, though largely Homeric, suggests the further contrast between innocent nature and corrupted man.

These scattered examples are enough to register what, as I said at the start, is often thought of as a very modern device. While *Paradise Lost* is not *The Waste Land* or *Finnegan's Wake*, such ironic allusions are one element in the poem's manifold richness of texture and reverberation.

114

MILTON'S ARMINIANISM
AND *PARADISE LOST*

Dennis Danielson

"**M**ILTON'S OBJECT," said Coleridge, "was to justify the ways of God to man! The controversial spirit observable in many parts of. . . . [*Paradise Lost*] is immediately attributable to the great controversy of that age, the origination of evil. The Arminians considered it a mere calamity. The Calvinists took away all human will."[1] Thus, in his laconic way, he pointed out the central connection between Milton's great interest in theodicy and the major rift in seventeenth-century Reformed theology. What I want to argue in this article is that understanding the issues involved in the controversy will contribute to an appreciation of *Paradise Lost*, particularly the end of Book X and the beginning of Book XI. Although it would not be right to claim that Milton was in any sense a "card-carrying" Arminian, there is no doubt that the term can be applied meaningfully, especially to his later writings. For it is true, as Samuel Johnson noted two centuries ago, that Milton's theological opinions can be said "to have been first Calvinistical, and afterwards, perhaps when he began to hate the Presbyterians, to have tended towards Arminianism."[2]

I hasten to add that—like "Calvinist"—"Arminian" is capable of various meanings. Strongest in England was the so-called Arminianism of the right, associated primarily with the ecclesiastical policies of Archbishop Laud, and unquestionably eschewed by Milton. This kind of Arminianism in fact made it difficult at first for Milton and his contemporaries to gain a clear understanding of Arminianism proper, of "Arminianism of the left."[3] In the earlier part of the seventeenth century, anything smacking of Arminianism of any sort was likely to be dismissed, by Puritans particularly, as Popish and Pelagian; and it would seem that Milton himself, as I shall show more fully later, initially accepted this caricature, implying in 1642 that Arminians "deny originall sinne."[4]

In the present discussion, however, I shall ignore those who might in fact have deserved the charge of Popery and Pelagianism, and take Arminianism to be the theology, especially as it concerns free will and grace, of Arminius and his followers condemned at the Synod of Dort, none of whom, so far as I can tell, denied "originall sinne." In doing so, I believe I follow most closely what Milton finally saw Arminianism as being. In 1673 he declared: "The *Arminian* . . . is condemn'd for setting up free will against free grace; but that Interpretation he disclaims in all his writings, and grounds himself largely upon Scripture only."[5] This, as I hope to show, is an accurate description of Arminius and his immediate followers. It also represents the nearest thing we have to an explicit declaration by Milton of his Arminian sympathies, since to say that a theologian "grounds himself largely upon Scripture only" was the highest compliment he could pay. Indeed, it was the claim he made for his own theology, the *Christian Doctrine:* "I devote my attention to the Holy Scriptures alone. I follow no other heresy or sect. I had not even studied any of the so-called heretical writers, when the blunders of those who are styled orthodox, and their unthinking distortions of the sense of scripture, first taught me to agree with their opponents whenever these agreed with the Bible."[6] It is the nature of Milton's agreement with some of these "so-called heretical writers" that I wish to explore.

The task is necessary because insufficient account has been taken of the evidence for Milton's Arminianism and its implications for *Paradise Lost.* Though few have gone as far as Joseph M. McDill, who claims "there can be no doubt that in *Paradise Lost* Milton teaches the five points of Calvinism,"[7] a major tendency among some Milton critics has been tacitly to presuppose that Milton's view of God and his ways agrees with that of orthodox Calvinist theology. William Empson, for example, in his discussion of the theory of the Fortunate Fall, assumes that Milton conceives of a God who "was working for the Fall all along"[8]—a conception that belongs to a good deal of Calvinist, but not to Arminian, teaching. Although Empson recognizes that Milton "came to give up" Calvinist predestination, he insists on referring to Milton's attempt "to make *his* God appear a bit less morally disgusting."[9] It is difficult to see what point there is in holding Milton responsible for a conception of God he had decided to reject.

A more specific difficulty is alleged by Thomas Greene's account of what he considers to be one of the seeds of destruction for the epic genre, namely "the questioning of the hero's independence":

Heroic independence in *Paradise Lost* is weakened by Milton's juggling with the theological categories of grace and merit. If we were to grant "the better fortitude of Patience and Heroic Martyrdom" as a proper notion of epic heroism, we should still want to feel that fortitude to be the painful achievement of the hero. But Milton in more than one passage suggests that this fortitude is the gift of God. It is a little anticlimactic for the reader, after following tremulously the fallen couple's gropings toward redemption in Book Ten, to hear from the Father's lips that he has decreed it—that all of this tenderly human scene, this triumph of conjugal affection and tentative moral searching, occurred only by divine fiat. One might have been tempted to alter his ideas of heroism to include Adam's contrition, did he not encounter God's own curt dismissal of it:[10]

> He sorrows now, repents, and prays contrite,
> My motions in him, longer than they move,
> His heart I know, how variable and vain
> Self-left. (XI, 90–93)[11]

Now if Greene were right—if Adam and Eve's repentance were the result merely of divine fiat—then we would indeed seem to be presented in *Paradise Lost* with a version of the theological determinism that accompanies Calvinist predestinarianism, as well as with the severe dramatic inconsistency or anticlimax Greene suggests. The same problem is alleged by C. A. Patrides, who, while denying that Milton presents the God of Calvinism, still feels that the passage referred to by Greene represents what he calls "the traditional 'inconsistency' of the Bible and St. Augustine": "upholding man's free will at one moment and denying it the next." The repentance we have witnessed, Patrides argues, accordingly seems "odd as well as unnatural," particularly "when we reach Milton's explanation of the episode":[12] "Prevenient Grace descending had removed / The stony from their hearts" (XI, 3–4). But I propose that, if we understand the Arminian character of the position Milton holds, the beginning of Book XI will be seen as neither theologically nor dramatically inconsistent with what precedes it.

John Peter has complained that a common fault "in Milton criticism is to wrench the characters and incidents of *Paradise Lost* from their artistic context, and then to consider them as if they were autonomous or as if they were simple copies of their doctrinal or traditional equivalents, disregarding the significance which has been conferred upon them by the poem."[13] Though this charge can, I believe, be laid against those who uncritically read Calvinism into *Paradise Lost*, their errors will not be remedied by

117

a similarly uncritical imposition upon the poem of Arminian doctrine. Therefore, I will try at the outset simply to show what Arminianism is and what motivated its development; then to indicate how the hypothesis of Milton's Arminianism can be supported by the artistic context in question. As we have seen, Patrides traces Milton's alleged brilliant "inconsistency" at least as far back in history as St. Augustine, and it is with him that we must begin.

Consider briefly Augustine's teaching on free will and grace. The former developed within the context of his doctrine of the Fall: he saw men as being created in a state of perfection, although "because they are not, like their Creator, supremely and unchangeably good, their good may be diminished and increased."[14] Such mutability exists in connection with man's free will, and Augustine accordingly sees sin—change for the worse—as consisting in a misuse of free will: "I inquired what iniquity was, and ascertained it . . . to be . . . a perversion of the will, bent aside from Thee, O God, the Supreme Substance, towards . . . lower things."[15] Furthermore, sin being thus seen in terms of man's agency, God is absolved of direct responsibility for the existence of evil. "Of course," says Augustine, "no one would dare to believe or declare that it was beyond God's power to prevent the fall. . . . But, in fact, God preferred not to use His own power, but to leave success or failure to the creature's choice. In this way, God could show both the immense evil that flows from the creature's pride and also the even greater good that comes from His grace."[16]

Now God's grace, in Augustine's thought, is that which enables any good to be accomplished. Even in Eden, Augustine believes, good acts were possible only through divine assistance, whereas to go wrong was completely within man's own power. Augustine points out an analogy to this in living:

The act of living in a body is a positive act which is not a matter of choice but is only possible by the help of nourishment; whereas the choice not to live in the body is a negative act which is in our human power, as we see in the case of suicide. Thus, to remain living as one ought to live was not a matter of choice . . . but depended on the help of God, whereas to live ill, as one ought not to live, was in man's power; therefore, man was justly responsible for the cutting short of his happiness and the incurring of the penalty that followed.[17]

On the surface, this position may appear to make a mockery of human freedom—as if the latter rendered man an agent culpable of all sin but capable of nothing but sin. Although man can clearly be an instrument of good, Augustine may seem to imply that if a man's actions are good, the agency is God's; if evil, the agency is his own. However, if we examine the matter more closely, we see that there is an interpretation of Augustine's words quite in keeping with the task of theodicy. It is not really relevant here that man is independently capable of sin, for in terms of Augustine's analogy a man's freedom either to carry on living or to commit suicide is not nullified by the fact that he could also involuntarily starve to death. Rather, the important question is this: Given the means of avoiding starvation, does one's continued existence really depend upon one's decision about whether or not to commit suicide? If it does, then one's free will is truly decisive with respect to one's living or dying; and, in the same way, Adam's free will would have operated as meaningfully in deciding not to eat of the forbidden fruit as it did in his act of disobedience, even though obedience presupposed divine assistance. What certainly would be inimical to theodicy is if God had withdrawn his grace and then accused Adam of willful disobedience—something that would amount to claiming that one who starved to death was a suicide. But, in the chapter of the *City of God* just quoted at least, Augustine does not go that far; and we ought to recognize in his analogy a coherent model of how man can be (on his own) incapable of good and yet responsible for evil.

The difficulty in evaluating Augustine's doctrine of grace is that elsewhere it does seem to imply a denial of the concept of free will upon which his theodicy depends. In arguing against the Pelagians, who "hasten to confide rather in it [free will] for doing righteousness than in God's aid, and to glory every one in himself, and not in the Lord,"[18] Augustine tended to depreciate free will to the point where it could no longer be seen as meaningfully decisive. In *On Grace and Free Will*, he says that "God works in the hearts of men to incline their wills whithersoever He wills, whether to good deeds according to His mercy, or to evil after their own deserts."[19] If this claim is correct, however, then a theodicy based on man's responsibility for sin is surely not possible; for, once man's will is seen as determined by the prior will of God, it can no longer be said in the case of any particular sin that the sinner could have chosen otherwise, and one is reduced to seeing all human actions, both good and evil, as the result of sheer divine will.[20] Thus it can appear, as N. P. Williams has put it, that Augustine tries "to run with the hare and hunt with the hounds. He wants to keep freedom in order to reserve man's responsibility for actual sin, and yet he wishes to throw it overboard in order to provide scope for irresistible grace."[21] The term *irresistible grace* anticipates the development of Augustine's thought by Reformers such as Luther and Calvin. Nevertheless, as suggested earlier, Augustine is not consistently predestinarian in the later Calvinist sense, and this discrepancy allowed his support to be enlisted on opposite sides of disputes .that were to arise in the future. As Williams says in a slightly different context, "the Reformation . . . was in great measure the posthumous rebellion of Augustine with Augustine."[22]

The classic instance of this conflict in the early Reformation is the debate on free will between Erasmus and Luther. Erasmus opposes Luther's determinism primarily in the interests of theodicy, saying that "care should be taken not to deny the freedom of the will, while praising faith. For if this happens, there is no telling how the problem of divine justice and mercy could be solved."[23] He agrees with Augustine insofar as "Augustine challenges the view that man, subject to sin, can better himself or act to save himself. Only undeserved divine grace can spur man supernaturally to wish that which will lead to eternal life. This is known to some as prevenient grace" (p. 28). Such teaching is, as I have argued, consonant with the purposes of theodicy as long as the gift of prevenient grace is in fact bestowed: one is culpable or not in respect to a given act only if one's own choice is meaningfully decisive in respect to that act, regardless of by whose power the decision is effected—just as the potential suicide will be responsible for his dying or not dying only if he has the means to avoid starving to death, regardless of the origin of those means. So, accordingly, Erasmus avoids rejecting the necessity of prevenient grace (thereby avoiding Pelagianism, with which Luther unjustly charges him) but, in order to safeguard theodicy, simply adds the assumption that "the goodness of God does not refuse to any mortals this . . . grace" (p. 29). Such a provision curbs the (determinist) predestinarian tendency of the doctrine of grace in Augustine (who "gained a more unfavorable view of the free will, because of his fight with Pelagius than he had held before" [p. 85]), and which tendency, as Erasmus recognized, led in some reformers to the opinion that he considered "worst of all": "that the free will is an empty name and . . . that rather God causes in us evil as well as good, and that everything happens of mere necessity" (p. 31).

In responding to Erasmus, Luther confirms and realizes the dangers that his opponent has pointed out, preferring to imperil the notion of divine justice rather than deny, as he thinks Erasmus' position does, divine prescience and omnipotence. Arguing that these two attributes of God entail our being under necessity (p. 132), Luther claims that God "foresees, purposes and does all things according to His immutable, eternal and infallible will. This thunderbolt throws free will flat and utterly dashes it to pieces" (p. 106). But Erasmus would maintain that such a position is inconsistent with any conception of either the goodness of God or the responsibility of man: "Everybody would judge . . . [a] lord cruel and unjust . . . were he to have his servant flogged for his stature, or protruding nose, or some lack of elegance. Would he not be justified in complaining against the lord who had him flogged: why should I suffer punishment for something that is not in my power to change?" (p. 83). Erasmus, recognizing the difficulty of reconciling foreknowledge with free will, suggests that possibly it is one of those things that "God wishes to remain totally unknown to us" (p. 9), although elsewhere he proposes that the matter has been explained sufficiently by Lorenzo Valla: "Foreknowledge does not cause what is to take place. Even we know many things which will be happening. They will not happen because we know them, but vice versa" (p. 49). However, this was not a position that had much influence on Luther.

The necessitarianism that Luther defended became fully worked into the system of Reformation theology, again with apparent disregard for the interests of theodicy, in Calvin's doctrine of double predestination. Predestination, says Calvin in his *Institutes of the Christian Religion*, is "the eternal decree of God," by which "some are preordained to eternal life, others to eternal damnation."[24] Calvin denies, moreover, that this decree is in any way contingent upon the foreseen free acts or choices of men, there being no such freedom as might be presupposed by those who would see predestination as a conditional decree. Rather, Calvin teaches, in giving an account of predestination "we must always return to the mere pleasure of the divine will, the cause of which is hidden in [God] himself" (III, xxiii. 4). "Nor ought it to seem absurd . . . [to say] that God not only foresaw the fall of the first man, and in him the ruin of his posterity; but also at his own pleasure arranged it" (III. xxiii. 7). And to Adam's posterity "there is a universal call, by which God . . . invites all men alike [to come to him], even those for whom he designs the call to be a savour of death, and the ground of a severer condemnation" (III. xiv. 8).

Thus, Calvin's doctrine of predestination can indeed appear to make God as cruel and unjust as the lord in Erasmus' little parable who had his servant flogged for something that he had no power to do anything about. It also thereby threatens to undermine the assumption (as Samuel Hoard put it in 1633) that "Justice, Mercy, Truth, and Holinesse in God are the same in nature with these virtues in men, though infinitely differing in degree"— an assumption without which "we may not safely imitate God, as we are commanded, Be ye perfect as your heavenly Father is perfect."[25] For the only way of preventing one's theology from throwing open the possibility of "devil-worship" is, as D. P. Walker has said, "to make the ideas of goodness, justice, etc., anterior to . . . God's decrees."[26]

Yet Calvin does face up to the charge that his position entails a denial of divine justice, though he rejects the charge on the basis of what he sees as the impossibility of man's in any way judging the will of God: for "truly does Augustine maintain that it is perverse to measure divine by the standard of human justice" (III. xxiv. 17); "the will of God is the supreme rule of righteousness, so that everything which he wills must be held to be righteous by the mere fact of his willing it" (III. xxiii. 2). In this connection, it is also important to note that Calvin would deny that he is a voluntarist. He does *not* say that something *is* righteous by the mere fact of God's willing it; nor will he be numbered among those who declare God to be "exlex."[27] However, when he says that men "are not to seek for any cause beyond [God's] will" (III. xxii. 11), one inevitably wonders whether this is not because the divine will is fundamentally arbitrary. With other "foolish men," one may indeed be inclined to "ask why God is offended with his creatures, who have not provoked him by any previous offence" or to suggest that "to devote to destruction whomsoever he pleases, more resembles the caprice of a tyrant than the legal sentence of a judge," as Calvin himself puts it (III. xxiii. 2). But as long as the divine will alone is considered the highest rule of justice, in practice it will follow that what God does is just, merely by definition, and the doubt concerning the meaningfulness of any assertion of God's goodness will thus be rendered insoluble. By placing the reason for God's will quite beyond human ken, Calvin ends up being a voluntarist in practice if not in theory, so that any argument he presents for the justice of God accordingly becomes circular and hence meaningless. And in this sense, I would suggest, Calvin begs the theodical question.

We can see, in any case, why Calvin's doctrine of predestination might have become the occasion for so much controversy. Though it was not in fact the main emphasis of his theology—he does not propound it until the third book of his *Institutes*—nevertheless, as that which was most strenuously attacked, it was also that which required to be most strenuously defended by orthodox Calvinists. In this way it became the most dominant feature of Calvinist theology in the seventeenth century and has remained such ever since.

Historically, the most significant expression of this doctrine of predestination, and also the main manifestation of its development as the Calvinists' shibboleth, is the so-called "five points" of Calvinism, which were set down in response to a major doctrinal rebellion within the Reformed confession: (1) unconditional election, (2) limited atonement, (3) the total depravity of man, (4) God's irresistible grace, and (5) the perseverance of the saints through God's preserving grace. In 1591, a Dutch Reformed pastor by the name of Jacobus Arminius was called upon to refute the errors of two Delft ministers, who had been assigned to argue against Coornhert, the humanist critic of Calvinism, but who in so doing had modified their own position to the extent that it, too, deviated from what was considered to be orthodox Calvinist teaching.[28] Arminius was a likely choice to represent Calvinism, as he had studied in Geneva with Theodore Beza, Calvin's successor. However, either the domino effect continued, with Arminius falling away from the position he was trying to justify, or else he secretly had disagreed with his former teacher for some time.[29] In any case, his refutation never appeared, and his deviation from the Calvinist norm became known. In 1603 he was installed as professor of divinity at the University of Leyden, where he began to come under fire for his views. The controversy grew, though Arminius himself died prematurely in 1609, and in 1610 his followers organized themselves under the leadership of a man named Uitenbogaert. These "Remonstrants" published in the same year "Five Arminian Articles," also known as the Remonstrance of 1610, to which the five points of Calvinism correspond.[30] The latter—the "Five Heads of Doctrine"—were formulated at the Synod of Dort of 1618–1619, which was convened expressly to deal with the views of Arminius and the Remon

strants. The upshot was a great ecclesiastical and political victory
for orthodox Calvinism, with the Remonstrants being forced into
one form of exile or another.

Arminius' ideas seem to have developed primarily out of an
attempt to bring Reformed theology into line with the requirements of theodicy. Like Erasmus before him, he placed emphasis
on human freedom, while at the same time insisting that "free will
is unable to begin or to perfect any true and spiritual good, without grace":

> That I may not be said, like Pelagius, to practice delusion with regard to
> the word "grace," I mean by it that which is the grace of Christ and which
> belongs to regeneration. I affirm, therefore, that this grace is simply and
> absolutely necessary for the illumination of the mind, the due ordering of
> the affections, and the inclination of the will to that which is good. It . . .
> infuses good thoughts into the mind, inspires good desires into the affec-
> tions, and bends the will to carry into execution good thoughts and good
> desires. This grace [praevenit] goes before, accompanies, and follows; it
> excites, assists, operates that we will, and co-operates lest we will in
> vain.[31]

However, Arminius avoids the problem that such a view of grace
seems to have in Augustine and almost certainly has in Calvin—
namely, that one's salvation depends on a sort of divine caprice in
respect to one's being granted grace or not. He avoids it in two
ways: First, like Erasmus, he believes that sufficient grace is
offered to all; "were the fact otherwise, the justice of God could
not be defended in his condemning those who do not believe" (II,
498). Second, in contrast to the orthodox Calvinists, he claims that
grace is resistible rather than irresistible, and again he clearly is
theodically motivated. In opposing those who represent grace "as
acting with such potency that it cannot be resisted by any free
creature," Arminius says, "it is not our wish to do the least injury
to Divine grace, by taking from it any thing that belongs to it. But
let my brethren take care, that they themselves neither inflict an
injury on Divine justice, by attributing that to it which it refuses;
nor on Divine grace, by transforming it into something else, which
cannot be called GRACE" (I, 366). Put in another way, if sufficient
grace were not offered to all, then those to whom it was not
offered would be incapable of willing good, and would thus in no
meaningful sense be free, so that God alone, in withholding grace,
would be responsible for those who perish without salvation. This
being clearly inconsistent with divine justice, a universal and suf-

ficient grace must be assumed. Furthermore, if grace were irresistible, then all those to whom it was offered would become regenerate. But not everyone becomes regenerate, so that either grace is resistible or else it is not universally offered. As shown in the preceding argument, we must assume sufficient grace to be offered to all, and must therefore conclude that grace is resistible.

Thus Arminius reasoned, opposing Calvinist predestinarianism and, within the context of Reformed theology, trying to work out the implications of the view that goodness and justice are anterior to God's decrees. Arminius' followers, as I have already said, published a list of these implications in 1610 in the form of five articles. The first, in accordance with the conviction that the human will plays a decisive role in accepting or rejecting salvation, declares that "God, by an eternal, unchangeable purpose in Jesus Christ his Son, before the foundation of the world, hath determined . . . to save . . . those who, through the grace of the Holy Ghost, shall believe on his Son Jesus, and shall persevere in this faith, through this grace."[32] This is conditional election, as opposed to the Calvinist assertion of unconditional election, by which God inexplicably decrees from eternity, without respect to any prior consideration of belief in men, that certain shall be saved, the rest damned. The second Arminian article, in accordance with the first, asserts that Christ "died for all men and for every man." For the Calvinist, on the other hand, since the decree of election to salvation preceded the decree of the means of salvation—namely, the sacrifice of Christ—the efficacy of that sacrifice was limited to the elect. Hence the doctrine of the "limited atonement," explicitly asserted at Dort.[33]

The third Arminian article is one that has occasionally been misunderstood. Seeing that the Calvinist tenet of the total depravity of man, as restated at Dort, was supposedly formulated in response to the third article, one might assume, as one modern writer has put it, that the latter expressed "man's partial depravity and the co-operative ability of his fallen will."[34] But in fact what the third article states is this: "That man has not saving grace of himself, nor of the energy of his free will, inasmuch as he, in the state of apostasy and sin, can of and by himself neither think, will, nor do any thing that is truly good; . . . but that it is needful that he be born again . . . and renewed in understanding, inclination, or will, and all his powers, in order that he may rightly understand, think, will, and effect what is truly good." Such teaching is clearly in the tradition of Reformed theology, which, as we have seen, has

its roots in Augustine's doctrine of grace. It resembles not at all
the Pelagianism of which the Remonstrants were accused. And, as
it stands, the Calvinist could scarcely find any objection to this
article short of misrepresenting it, although this is what the third
head of doctrine appears in fact to do. For the list of errors that the
Synod of Dort claims to reject includes the teaching that "a corrupt and naturall man can so rightly vse common grace (by which
they [the Remonstrants] meane the light of nature) or those gifts,
which are left in him after the fall, that, by the good vse thereof,
he may attaine to a greater, namely Euangelicall, or sauing grace,
and by degrees at length saluation it selfe."[35] This, however, is not
an opinion found in the statements of the Remonstrants, and appears rather to be a conveniently Pelagian-sounding version of the
Arminian insistence on the importance of free will—packaged, as
it were, for easy disposal.[36]

We must therefore take care not to join the detractors of Arminianism in misrepresenting it. Its teaching on divine grace, except for the insistence that grace is universally, sufficiently, but
not irresistibly bestowed, is scarcely to be distinguished from that
of Augustine or even of Calvin. The exceptions just mentioned
have far-reaching implications, certainly; but they do not alter the
view of the essential necessity of divine grace. The fourth Arminian article, for example—the one famous for its rejection of irresistible grace—is devoted primarily to reiterating the weakness of
man and accordingly his need for the power of grace: "this grace
of God is the beginning, continuance, and accomplishment of all
good, even to this extent, that the regenerate man himself, without
prevenient or assisting, awakening, following and co-operative
grace, can neither think, will, nor do good, nor withstand any
temptations to evil; so that all good deeds or movements, that can
be conceived, must be ascribed to the grace of God in Christ." It
is vital that we recognize this emphasis, for otherwise we shall be
liable either to accept a caricature of Arminianism as Pelagian, or
else to see as Calvinistic a teaching that is in fact not necessarily
allied with Calvinist predestinarianism.

The fifth Arminian article is connected with the fourth: if
grace is resistible, then the Christian may be free to reject his
salvation even after it has first been accepted. However, the article avoids dogmatism and expresses only an uncertainty about
whether those who have once received God's offered grace "are
capable . . . of forsaking again the first beginnings of their life in
Christ, . . . of becoming devoid of grace."[37] The Remonstrants de-

clared that this is something that "must be more particularly determined out of the Holy Scripture, before we ourselves can teach it with full persuasion of our minds." But a doubt is all that was needed to mitigate the sense of security that often accompanied Calvinist predestinarian teaching and had in certain cases encouraged antinomianism such as that of the Ranters in England. In this sense, the fifth article (though the least theoretically developed of the five) may be seen as the one of greatest practical importance, since it took away the overconfidence that could lead to moral laxity and irresponsibility. I mention this aspect of Arminianism, not because the fifth article is very important for our present discussion of *Paradise Lost*, but because it completes the picture we have of the moral motives that informed Arminian teaching: Arminianism was concerned to produce good and righteous people, as well as to make theology conform to the view that there is a good and righteous God.

Now Milton rejected the same aspects of Calvinism as did Arminius and the Remonstrants; and he did so, it seems, out of a similar concern for righteousness, particularly divine righteousness. The main expression of this rejection on Milton's part is found in his *Christian Doctrine*, where, in the interests of theodicy, free will is asserted in opposition to the doctrine of absolute predestination. "We must conclude," declares Milton, "that God made no absolute decrees about anything which he left in the power of men, for men have freedom of action. The whole course of scripture shows this":[38]

As a vindication of God's justice, especially when he calls man, it is obviously fitting that some measure of free will should be allowed to man . . . and that this will should operate in good works or at least good attempts. . . . For if God . . . turns man's will to moral good or evil just as he likes, and then rewards the good and punishes the wicked, it will cause an outcry against divine justice from all sides. (p. 397)

As we have seen in the case of the Remonstrants, such a position entails a rejection of the doctrine of "limited atonement," and Milton accordingly affirms that God "has omitted nothing which might provide salvation for everyone" (p. 175; cf. pp. 447, 455). This general conviction leads in turn to the doctrine, already discussed in connection with Erasmus and Arminius, that each individual is granted sufficient grace. God "considers all worthy of sufficient grace, and the cause is his justice" (p. 193; cf. p. 446). The doctrine is important for our discussion because, like his Arminian predecessors, Milton held that God's grace is necessary in every stage of salvation and sanctification, even in the act of will by which one accepts God's gift in the first place, so that for all men to be free to accept or reject God's salvation presupposes that enabling grace be withheld from no one. At the same time, an insistence that the power to will comes from God prevents any sort of Pelagian self-reliance. Milton's doctrine is thus "absolutely in keeping with justice and does not detract at all from the importance of divine grace. For the power to will and believe is either the gift of God or, insofar as it is inherent in man at all, has no relation to good work or merit" (p. 189).

Thus, in his major theological treatise, Milton consistently restates the basic Arminian position. It is important not only to recognize this fact, but also to see what a divergence it represents from the opinions Milton held in his earlier prose works, and from the opinions of many of his contemporaries. Calvinist teaching was a powerful force in English politics and religion of the seventeenth century, and even James I had sent a delegation to the Synod of Dort, where they added their votes in denunciation of the Remonstrant articles. Perhaps typical of the anti-Arminian attacks that abounded from that time through the mid-seventeenth century is the work written by William Prynne, Milton's fellow Puritan and one of the great polemicists of the age, entitled *The Church of Englands Old Antithesis To New Arminianisme. Where in 7 . . . Arminian (once Popish and Pelagian) Errors are manifestly disproved.* In it he encourages Parliament "to further . . . the discouery and suppression of those Hereticall and Grace-destroying Arminian nouelties, which haue of late inuaded, affronted, and almost shouldered out of doores, the ancient, established, and resolved Doctrines of our Church."[39] Moreover, Milton's own works of the early 1640s reveal that he considered himself part of the Calvinist, anti-Arminian mainstream of Puritan thought. As we have already noted, in his *Apology Against a Pamphlet* (1642), Milton implies that Arminians "deny originall sinne." Furthermore, in the *Doctrine and Discipline of Divorce* (1643), he mentions that "the Jesuits, and that sect among us which is nam'd of *Arminius*, are wont to charge us of making God the author of sinne."[40] Then in 1644, in *Areopagitica*, he refers to the circumstances of Arminius' coming to doubt certain points of Calvinism, as mentioned earlier: "the acute and distinct *Arminius* was perverted meerly by the perusing of a namelesse discours writt'n at *Delf*, which at first he took in hand to confute."[41] While there is indicated here almost an admiration for the man, Milton clearly assumes Arminius' teaching to be a perversion of the truth—the truth of orthodox Calvinist theology.

Yet, only a decade and a half later, Milton was himself arguing an Arminian position against what he had previously accepted as the truth. This truth had been set down in 1647 in the Westminster Confession, which taught, in opposition to the Arminian position (as had the Canons of Dort), that grace is bestowed not universally but only upon "those that are ordained unto life." It followed that, since "God did, from all eternity, decree to justify all the elect," the atonement was limited, and "Christ did, in the fullness of time, die for their sins, and rise again for their justification."[42] But, as I have already mentioned, the *Christian Doctrine* argues from an assumption of divine justice to the conclusion that "no one should lack sufficient grace for salvation. Otherwise it is not clear how [God] can demonstrate his truthfulness to mankind" (p. 193). Milton also contradicts Westminister by denying absolute predestination and asserting free will, lest "we should make [God] responsible for all the sins ever committed, and should make demons and wicked men blameless" (pp. 164–65). Of course, this teaching is extremely important with respect to the Fall of Man, for on it hinges the question of God's responsibility for Adam's lapse, or even of his complicity in it. Calvinist theologians taught both absolute predestination and human culpability, although it may be hard for us, as it was for Milton, to see this as anything but a bald assertion of contraries. The position that in some sense God, as Empson puts it, "was working for the Fall all along," though opposed by Milton, is clearly set forth in the Westminster Confession: "the almighty power, unsearchable wisdom, and infinite goodness of God so far manifest themselves in his providence that it extendeth itself even to the first fall, and all other sins, . . . and that not by a bare permission, but such as hath joined with it a most wise and powerful bounding; . . . yet so as the sinfulness thereof proceedeth only from the creature, and not from God."[43] In dealing with the same issue in his *Christian Doctrine*, Milton says: "Everyone agrees that man could have avoided falling. But if, because of God's decree, man could not help but fall (and the two contradictory opinions are sometimes voiced by the same people), then God's restoration of fallen man was a matter of justice not grace" (p. 174).

How can we account for such a reversal in Milton's theological position in scarcely fifteen years? Only the merest hypothesis can be suggested here, but I think the key to understanding Milton's rejection of the "contradictory opinions" held by those among whom he would once have numbered himself is to recognize his constant efforts to show that his God, above all, is good and just. In his great personal misfortunes of the 1650s and in the decline of the revolutionary cause, ending finally in the Restoration, Milton's relationship to his nation and to God must have had to undergo a painful reorientation. As Arthur Sewell puts it:

England had forsaken God, and Milton's belief in God had to find ground more assured than the high mission and triumph of his native country. More, he himself must have felt alone and chastened; his own mission was called in question. Is it not probable that now he was left with a conception of God which suddenly appeared as a."bundle of impossibles and inconceivables"; with the Calvinist conception of God without that high social optimism which made such a conception tolerable and reasonable?[44]

As long as one was of the elect and history was the working-out of God's good purposes for the elect, it could not have been too hard to believe that something was right and good merely because God willed it. But when the course of history, which God presumably had been directing, turned against the chosen people themselves, the apparent arbitrariness of the divine will must have presented itself as a great difficulty, and the possibility of "devil-worship" lurking in Calvinist predestinarianism may have started to look like an actuality. As Christopher Hill suggests, "Milton was not of the devil's party without knowing it: part of him knew," and he had somehow to eliminate this element from his theology. "If Milton had allowed himself consciously to accept the view of Winstanley, Erbery and some Ranters, that the God whom most Christians worshipped was a wicked God, his life would have lost its structure, would have fallen in ruins about his head like the temple of the Philistines. He had to justify the ways of God to man in order to justify his own life."[45] As Milton himself says of those who see God's decree or foreknowledge as shackling supposedly "free causes" with necessity, "to refute them . . . would be like inventing a long argument to prove that God is not the Devil" (p. 166).

Now it seems to me that if we keep in mind the foregoing broad hypothesis of Milton's adoption of an Arminian solution to some of the problems concerning divine justice, then we shall find a great deal less problematical the utterances of God in *Paradise Lost* in particular, and the theme of regeneration in Milton's later poetry generally. We shall also avoid treating too casually the dogma we find Milton's God expressing. For example, although

John Steadman has called a "theological commonplace" God's assertion "that neither 'impulse or shadow of Fate' nor 'absolute Decree Or high foreknowledge' has caused Adam to sin,"[46] having considered the Westminster Confession and the arguments in Milton's *Christian Doctrine,* we should see in it greater significance than the word "commonplace" suggests. Such an assertion represents an important divergence from Westminster's, and—it would seem—the younger Milton's, Calvinist position. Of course I am not suggesting that the Arminian theology of Milton's prose should be imposed uncritically on his poetry, but it is surely fair to assume that, where a Calvinist and non-Calvinist reading of a given passage are possible, the greater burden of proof will rest upon those who would argue the former.

The *Christian Doctrine* provides grounds at least for the hypothesis that the theology of *Paradise Lost* is also Arminian, especially since both works plainly reveal a strong theodical motivation. Maurice Kelley has pointed out parallels in the two works to suggest, for example, that God's promise in Book III of *Paradise Lost,* that "Man shall not quite be lost, but saved who will, / Yet not of will in him but grace in me / Freely vouchsafed" (173–75), expresses both the decisive character of the will and the instrumentality of grace[47]—central points, as we have seen, of Arminian teaching. Moreover, in the *Christian Doctrine,* Milton says that the elect are simply those who freely accept God's gift and that predestination is accordingly a contingent decree; Christ's atonement is not "limited" to a predetermined few. "God, out of his supreme mercy and grace in Christ, has predestined to salvation all who shall believe" (p. 183). Therefore, as Kelley concludes, the lines "Some I have chosen of peculiar grace / Elect above the rest," although capable of a Calvinist interpretation, "considered in their context and in relation to the *De doctrina* . . . express an Arminian view."[48]

The scene in heaven in Book III repeats other themes we have seen in our consideration of Arminianism, and as usual it is primarily a concern for theodicy that informs their expression. Many readers have found the God of Book III an unappealing figure. For example, as Peter has pointed out, "in representing God anthropomorphically and then obliging him to speak his own defences at some length, Milton has conveyed a most unfortunate impression of uneasiness."[49] Yet, despite their arguably unhappy dramatic context, God's words deal frankly and effectively with the issue of divine justice as it concerns the Fall of Man and his need for salvation. God declares he made man free, since other-

wise man "had served necessity, / Not me" (110–11), and thereby
dissociates himself from the theology of the Westminster Confession, which conceives of God's predeterminings as including
"even . . . the first fall, and all other sins." And, whereas for the
orthodox Calvinist "the will of God is the highest rule of justice,"
in Book III of *Paradise Lost* the Son himself suggests that some
more-than-self-referential justification of his Father's will is in
order. His question is as blunt a challenge to divine benevolence
and omnipotence as any posed by Empson, although the Son's use
of the subjunctive shows that he has not closed his mind to the
possibility of receiving an answer:

> should man finally be lost, should man
> Thy creature late so loved, thy youngest son
> Fall circumvented thus by fraud, though joined
> With his own folly? That be from thee far,
> That far be from thee, Father, who art judge
> Of all things made, and judgest only right.
> Or shall the adversary thus obtain
> His end, and frustrate thine, shall he fulfil
> His malice, and thy goodness bring to nought,
> Or proud return though to his heavier doom,
> Yet with revenge accomplished and to hell
> Draw after him the whole race of mankind,
> By his corrupted? Or wilt thou thy self
> Abolish thy creation, and unmake,
> For him, what for thy glory thou hast made?
> So should thy goodness and thy greatness both
> Be questioned and blasphemed without defence.   (150–66)

What follows is essentially the Arminian teaching of sufficient and
universal grace. Even the nonelect—meaning, as suggested earlier, those who freely refuse salvation—shall be offered grace. God
will, he promises,

> clear their senses dark,
> What may suffice, and soften stony hearts
> To pray, repent, and bring obedience due.
> To prayer, repentance, and obedience due,
> Though but endeavoured with sincere intent,
> Mine ear shall not be slow, mine eye not shut.   (188–93)

And the grace of God manifest in the atonement of Christ is not
limited but universal, sufficient to save "the whole race lost"
(280). Provided one accepts and values man's freedom of choice,
one must admit that the Son's request for theodicy has been met.

Those who freely "neglect and scorn" God's grace will indeed be lost, but "none but such from mercy" he excludes (202).

Now it is important for us to understand the relationship between man's freedom and the grace that is offered him, for when later in *Paradise Lost* they are shown operating, their relationship to each other is not spelled out so explicitly; and, if we fail to understand or remember what we have been told in Book III, we may be liable to misread what happens. As we have seen, the Synod of Dort asserted the depravity of man in response to what they believed was the Remonstrants' teaching on man's only partial depravity and the cooperative ability of his fallen will, although in fact the Arminian articles taught that "man has not saving grace of himself, nor of the energy of his free will, inasmuch as he, in a state of apostasy and sin, can of and by himself neither think, will, nor do anything that is truly good," and that accordingly there is a need for prevenient grace. It is precisely this doctrine, I would suggest, that the Son is expressing when he refers to grace as something that is sent to all God's creatures, "and to all / Comes unprevented, unimplored, unsought." And it is "happy for man" that it comes in this manner, since "he her aid / Can never seek, once dead in sins and lost" (III, 230–33). This prevenient grace, moreover, is granted universally and sufficiently, so that one's salvation depends on what one does with it once it has been granted. Grace is not, as it is in orthodox Calvinist theology, irresistible; rather, its efficacy depends, strictly speaking, on one's freely deciding not to resist it. As we recall from Augustine's analogy of suicide, human choice can in fact be decisive without being sufficient by itself to produce any positive result, just as "the act of living in a body is a positive act which is not a matter of choice but is only possible by the help of nourishment; whereas the choice not to live . . . is a negative act which is in our human power." The distinction is subtle, but it provides an instructive parallel to the one God makes when he promises that "Man shall not quite be lost, but saved who will, / Yet not of will in him, but grace in me" (III, 173–74): will is decisive but not efficacious; grace is efficacious but does not overrule the human will. For the orthodox Calvinist, the divine will alone is decisive; for the Pelagian, the unaided human will can be efficacious.

By adopting the Arminian position with respect to predestination, grace, and free will, therefore, Milton is able to avoid both Pelagianism on the one hand and the theodically dissonant aspects of Calvinism on the other. As Arminianism teaches, suffi-

cient grace is offered to all human beings, so that their wills are
truly decisive, despite the fact that they would be incapable of
desiring or producing good without that grace. But at the same
time, men are also meaningfully free with respect to evil, and so
God is not made the author of sin. Such, it would seem, is the
view presented in *Paradise Lost,* where it thus consistently fur-
thers Milton's justification of the ways of God.

From this view, moreover, there emerges a peculiar though
meaningful conception of the nature of human virtue. Put briefly,
divine agency accounts for good; human agency accounts for the
evil of sin. But, given God's offer of divine grace, man is free
either to reject it and use his own power to sin, or else to accept it
and use the power received from God to refrain from sinning. The
peculiarity of the view is that, strictly speaking, as far as man is
concerned, sin is by commission and moral virtue by omission,
just as in Eden virtue was to be achieved through abstaining from
eating the forbidden fruit, whereas sin consisted in the commissive act of disobedience.[50] As Milton says in commenting on Romans ix, 16 ("it does not depend on him that wills or on him that
runs but on God who is merciful"), "I am not talking about anyone
willing or running, but about someone being less unwilling, less
backward, less opposed" to divine grace (p. 187).

Now supposing that such a view of virtue were to be presented in a piece of literature, the difficulty might be that, failing
to understand the respective functions of grace and free will, the
reader would suspect some essential inconsistency between being
led to believe that certain actions are humanly virtuous and praiseworthy, and being told that in fact they result from divine agency.
Of course this is just what occurs at the end of Book X and in the
earlier part of Book XI of *Paradise Lost,* although any suspicion of
inconsistency, I would argue, is unwarranted. Bewailing the results of fallenness and the evil prospects before her and her husband, Eve proposes suicide as a way of escape (X, 1001). But
Adam responds with counsels of hope, and he and Eve, acting
upon them, penitent and remorseful,

> forthwith to the place
> Repairing where [God] judged them prostrate fell
> Before him reverent, and both confessed
> Humbly their faults, and pardon begged, with tears
> Watering the ground, and with their sighs the air
> Frequenting, sent from hearts contrite, in sign
> Of sorrow unfeigned, and humiliation meek.   (1098–1104)

Thus ends Book X, and Book XI begins with what might look like a reductive explanation of the human drama we have just witnessed:

> Thus they in lowliest plight repentant stood
> Praying, for from the mercy-seat above
> Prevenient grace descending had removed
> The stony from their hearts, and made new flesh
> Regenerate grow instead, that sighs now breathed
> Unutterable.   (XI, 1–6)

Then the Son, already fulfilling his role as mediator, presents to the Father Adam and Eve's humble request for pardon:

> See Father, what first fruits on earth are sprung
> From thy implanted grace in man, these sighs
> And prayers, which in this golden censer, mixed
> With incense, I thy priest before thee bring,
> Fruits of more pleasing savour from thy seed
> Sown with contrition in his heart, than those
> Which his own hand manuring all the trees
> Of Paradise could have produced ere fallen
> From innocence.[51]

If our minds are uncluttered with theological preconceptions, how we understand these lines—which on their own admit of various interpretations—will depend on the context provided by the poem as a whole. And, as we have seen, the grace mentioned here in Book XI was in Book III promised by God himself, even to those who, unlike Adam and Eve, would "neglect and scorn" his "long sufferance" and his "day of grace" (198–99): "I will clear their senses dark, / What may suffice, and soften stony hearts / To pray, repent, and bring obedience due" (188–90). It makes no sense to see this grace as the sole explanation for Adam and Eve's sighs and prayers when it clearly does not produce any such "fruits" in those who reject God's offer. The efficacy of God's grace explains how man's repentance *can* come about, once he is "dead in sins and lost" (III, 233), but does not finally account for the fact that it *does*. Grace is not irresistible, and we must recognize that the human will (although not efficacious) is decisive, since it is free not to resist, as well as to resist, God's will—something well understood by Adam when he counsels against suicide on the grounds that it "cuts us off from hope, and savours only / Rancour and pride, impatience and despite, / Reluctance against God and his just yoke" (X, 1043–45; cf. *Christian Doc-*

trine, p. 295). There is no reason for thinking Adam mistaken in assuming this possibility of "reluctance against God" to be real, even though we are subsequently told that the decision not to be reluctant was effected through God's grace. For here Augustine's analogy is virtually the fact; *mutatis mutandis,* his words accurately describe the situation in which Adam and Eve find themselves: "to live was not a matter of choice . . . but depended on the help of God, whereas to live ill . . . [here, to cease living altogether] was in man's power."

The opening of Book XI, therefore, does not deny the validity of the reader's feeling that what he has just seen is the virtuous behavior of freely acting human beings; what it does is to place within the context of divine grace the limited but real freedom we have seen operating.[52] What Adam and Eve have done is genuinely righteous, and there is no need to doubt that their contrition is truly their own; as Michael implies when he tells Adam he must leave Paradise, what God has provided is "grace wherein thou mayst repent."[53] Although human freedom must be recognized as meaningful and important, it is even more important that one recognize God as the ultimate source of that power whereby righteous deeds are possible. If we keep in mind the context provided by the rest of *Paradise Lost*, the passage in question can be seen thus to complement rather than contradict what has immediately preceded it. We may conclude that there is no justification for the charge that Milton "juggles" with grace and merit, or that he upholds man's free will at one moment and denies it the next. Certainly Patrides is right to point out that "grace is no philosophical tenet to be dissected but an experience to be lived";[54] I am not suggesting that it can be reduced to a simple formula. How God removes "the stony" from hearts and makes "new flesh / Regenerate grow instead" must remain a great mystery, and how the operation of such grace is experienced may be ineffable, even at times paradoxical. But human experiences have philosophical implications, and what an understanding of Milton's Arminian view of grace reveals is that the experience of grace he presents in *Paradise Lost* implies no contradiction.[55]

Further, the foregoing analysis suggests that *Paradise Lost* does indeed present a meaningful version of that notion which Greene would seem to accept as fulfilling the minimum requirements of epic heroism, namely something like "the better fortitude / Of patience and heroic martyrdom" (IX, 31–32). Milton's position does seem to be, as suggested earlier, that virtue, strictly speaking, is more importantly an omission to do what is evil than a commission of good. To this extent, to serve God is but to stand and wait, and to refrain from sin oneself while observing God's providence, which alone actually has the power to overcome evil with good.[56] And yet a central tenet of such a view is that the human will is able to resist the grace God offers; so that, although the human will is in itself powerless to effect good, it is still meaningfully decisive with respect to the good that can be accomplished through divine assistance. Thus, Adam and Eve's decision to repent is unambiguously as we have perceived it: a heroically significant "painful achievement," and not the result merely of divine fiat.

Finally, the view of grace and freedom that we encounter in *Paradise Lost* accords with a predominant motive of Milton's later theology, as well as of Arminianism generally: to show how God is good and just, as well as omnipotent. The reason for God's actions is ultimately to be found, not in his will alone, but in the justice and goodness that are part of his nature. Just as God's bestowing prevenient grace on Adam and Eve fulfills an earlier promise, so, in the fallen couple's anticipation of God's response to their repentance, we are reminded of the promise in Book III that the divine policy will be "mercy first and last" (134). In *Christian Doctrine*, Milton defines saving faith as divinely implanted persuasion, "by virtue of which we believe, on the authority of God's promise, that all those things which God has promised us in Christ are ours"; and in *Paradise Lost* it is precisely such a recognition of God's gracious purpose that informs Adam's speech opposing suicide: "Remember," he urges Eve, "with what mild / And gracious temper he both heard and judged / Without wrath or reviling" (X, 1046–48). If they do repent of their sin, God undoubtedly

> will relent and turn
> From his displeasure; in whose look serene,
> When angry most he seemed and most severe,
> What else but favour, grace, and mercy shone? (X, 1093–96)

"Thus the excellence of faith appears," as Milton says in *Christian Doctrine*, "which is that it attributes the supreme glory of veracity and justice to God" (p. 473). In Adam and Eve's regeneration in *Paradise Lost*, Milton demonstrates the same divine qualities. In his presentation of the manner of God's gracious cultivation of the fruits of repentance, he affirms both God's sovereign purpose and man's genuine creaturely freedom. And in so doing he achieves a

70   MILTON STUDIES

theologically consistent artistic fusion of both aspects of his poem's "great argument": to "assert eternal providence, / And justify the ways of God to men."[57]

St. John's College, Oxford

NOTES

1. Lecture X, "Milton," February 27, 1818, in *The Complete Works*, ed. W. G. T. Shedd (New York, 1853–), IV, 303.

2. *Lives of the English Poets*, ed. George B. Hill (Oxford, 1905), I, 154. Milton's Arminianism has also been acknowledged by James Holly Hanford in his *Milton Handbook*, 3d ed. (New York, 1939), pp. 228–31, and by Maurice Kelley in *This Great Argument* (Princeton, 1941), pp. 14–20, as in note 47 below. Kelley's introduction to the *Christian Doctrine*, trans. John Carey, in *Complete Prose Works of John Milton*, ed. Don M. Wolfe et al. (New Haven, 1953–), VI, 74–86 (hereafter cited as YP), contains probably the best account of Milton's Arminianism yet available. Also valuable in this connection are William B. Hunter's articles "The Theological Context of Milton's *Christian Doctrine*," in *Achievements of the Left Hand: Essays on the Prose of John Milton*, ed. Michael Lieb and John T. Shawcross (Amherst, 1974), pp. 269–87; and "John Milton: Autobiographer," *Milton Quarterly*, VIII, no. 4 (December 1974), 100–04.

3. The two branches of Arminianism were described in the following way by the Presbyterian Robert Baillie, in his *Antidote Against Arminianisme* (London, 1641), pp. 18–20: "The Arminian spirit in *Holland* leads men to hell another way then here in Britaine; . . . a *Netherlandish Arminian* will scorn the superstitions, the Idolatries, the Tyrannies of the *Romish* Church, but is much inclined after *Vorstius* and *Socinus* . . . : On the contrary, a *British Arminian* . . . will abhor the Extravagancies of *Vorstius* and *Socinus*, yet their heart is hot and inflamed after the abominations of *Rome*."

4. *An Apology against a Pamphlet*, in *The Works of John Milton*, ed. Frank Allen Patterson et al. (New York, 1931–38), III, 330 (hereafter cited as CM).

5. *Of True Religion*, CM, VI, 169.

6. YP, VI, 123–24, cited hereafter by page number in the text.

7. "Milton and the Pattern of Calvinism" (Ph.D. dissertation, Vanderbilt, 1938), p. 368.

8. *Milton's God* (London, 1961), p. 190. The genealogy of this view is traced by J. Martin Evans in *Paradise Lost and the Genesis Tradition* (Oxford, 1968), pp. 187–90.

9. *Milton's God*, pp. 202, 200, italics added.

10. *The Descent from Heaven: A Study in Epic Continuity* (New Haven, 1963), p. 407.

11. Quotations of *Paradise Lost* are from *The Poems of John Milton*, ed. John Carey and Alastair Fowler (London, 1968).

12. *Milton and the Christian Tradition* (Oxford, 1966), pp. 194–95, 201–02, 211.

13. A *Critique of Paradise Lost* (London, 1960), pp. 126–27.

14. *Enchiridion*, chap. 12, in *The Nicene and Post-Nicene Fathers*, ed. Philip Schaff (Buffalo and New York, 1866–), vol. III.

15. *Confessions*, VII, xvi, 22, in *Nicene Fathers*, vol. I.

16. *City of God*, trans. G. Walsh et al., in *Fathers of the Church*, ed. R. J. Deferrari et al. (Washington, D.C., 1950–54), XIV, 27.

17. Ibid.

18. A *Treatise Against Two Letters of the Pelagians*, I, 5 (II), in *Nicene Fathers*, vol. V.

19. Chap. 43 (XXI), in *Nicene Fathers*, vol. V.

20. For modern discussions of "compatibilism," as this position is often called, and its implications for theodicy and the "Free Will Defence," see Alvin Plantinga, *God, Freedom, and Evil* (London, 1975), pp. 31–32; and Antony Flew, "The Free Will Defence," in *The Presumption of Atheism* (London, 1976), pp. 81–99.

21. *The Ideas of the Fall and of Original Sin* (London, 1927), pp. 369–70.

22. Ibid., p. 321.

23. *Erasmus-Luther: Discourse on Free Will*, trans. Ernst F. Winter (New York, 1961), p. 84; cited hereafter by page number in the text.

24. Trans. Henry Beveridge (Grand Rapids, 1975), III, xvi. 5; cited hereafter by book, chapter, and section in the text.

25. I quote from the 1656 edition of *Gods Love to Man-Kinde, Manifested, By Dis-proving that Doctrine which telleth us of an Absolute Decree for their Damnation* (London), p. 49.

26. *The Decline of Hell* (London, 1964), p. 55.

27. See *Institutes*, III, xxiii. 2; and *Concerning the Eternal Predestination of God*, trans. J. K. S. Reid (London, 1961), p. 179: "I detest the doctrine of the Sorbonne . . . that invents for God an absolute power. For it is easier to dissever the light of the sun from its heat . . . than to separate God's power from His righteousness. . . . The faithful . . . understand His power . . . to be tempered with righteousness and equity." Contrast with this the much more extreme, voluntarist position of William Twisse, prolocutor of the Westminster Assembly, who declares "the Will of God" to be "the very Essence of God" (*The Riches of Gods Love . . . consistent with His Absolute . . . Reprobation* [Oxford, 1653], p. 6).

28. I follow the account of Carl Bangs, *Arminius: A Study in the Dutch Reformation* (New York, 1971), pp. 138 ff. and passim. See also *The Writings of James Arminius*, trans. James Nichols and W. R. Bagnall (Grand Rapids, 1956), I, 9–15.

29. The latter conclusion is favored by Bangs, *Arminius*, p. 141.

30. See Louis Praamsma, "The Background of the Arminian Controversy (1586–1618)," in *Crisis in the Reformed Churches*, ed. Peter Y. De Jong (Grand Rapids, 1968), pp. 22–38.

31. *The Writings of James Arminius*, II, 472. Cited hereafter by page number in the text.

32. All five articles are in *The Creeds of Christendom*, ed. P. Schaff (New York, 1877), III, 545–49.

33. For the suggestion that it was Beza and Calvin's *soi-disant* followers rather than Calvin himself who were responsible for this doctrine, see Brian G. Armstrong, *Calvinism and the Amyraut Heresy* (London, 1969), pp. 38–42.

34. Fred H. Klooster, "The Doctrinal Deliverances of Dort," in De Jong, *Crisis*, pp. 52–53.

35. *The Ivdgement of the Synode Holden at Dort, Concerning the fiue Articles*

(London, 1619), p. 37. Again, on this point Calvin himself would seem to be less extreme than his followers. His teaching on total depravity was clearly motivated by a desire to show that not only some but "all the parts of the soul" (including intellect and will) were affected by the Fall. Accordingly, man's depravity is total in the sense of being comprehensive, though not necessarily in the sense of being utter. See the *Institutes*, II. ii. 8–10.

36. For the Remonstrants' (I think convincing) defense of themselves against the charge of Pelagianism, see "Articulus Tertius et Quartus de Gratia Dei in Conversione Hominis," in *Acta et Scripta Synodalia Dordracena Ministrorum Remonstrantium in Foederato Belgio* (Herder-wiici, 1620), pp. 22–24.

37. As Kelley points out, in discussing the perseverance of the saints and its related issues, Milton explicitly cites the Remonstrants: *Christian Doctrine*, YP, VI, p. 512.

38. Ibid., p. 155.

39. (London, 1629 and 1630), the first page of "The Epistle Dedicatorie." See also Prynne, *God, No Imposter Nor Deluder: Or, An Answer To A Popish Arminian Cauill, in the defence of Free-Will, and universal Grace* (London, 1629 and 1630); as well as William Pemble, *Vindiciae Gratiae. A Plea for Grace . . . Wherein . . . the maine sinewes of Arminius doctrine are cut asunder* (Oxford, 1627, 1629, 1635, and 1659); William Twisse, *Vindiciae Gratiae, Potestatis, ac Providentiae Dei. Hoc est, Ad Examen Libelli Perkinsiani de Praedestinationis modo et ordine, institutum a Iacobo Arminio* (London, 1632); Baillie, *Antidote Against Arminianisme* (1641 and 1652); John Owen, *A Display of Arminianism* (London, 1643); John Ball, *A Treatise of the Covenant of Grace: Wherein . . . divers errours of Arminians and others are confuted* (London, 1645); Samuel Lane, *A Vindication of Free-Grace: In Opposition to this Arminian Position* [of John Goodwin] (London, 1645); Anthony Burgess, *Vindiciae Legis: Or, A Vindication of the Morall Law and the Covenants, From the Errours of the Papists, Arminians, Socinians, etc.* (London, 1646 and 1647); Richard Allen, *An Antidote Against Heresy: or A Preservative for Protestants against the poyson of Papists, Anabaptists, Arrians, Arminians, &c.* (London, 1648); Samuel Rutherford, *Disputatio Scholastica De Divina Providentia . . . adversus Jesuitas, Arminianos, Socinianos, etc.* (Edinburgh, 1650); Thomas Whitfield, *The Doctrines of the Arminians & Pelagians Truly Stated and clearly Answered* (London, 1652); and so on.

40. YP, II, 293.

41. Ibid., pp. 519–20.

42. VII, iv; XI, iv; in Schaff, *Creeds of Christendom*, vol. III.

43. Ibid., V, iv. Cf. Calvin: "Man therefore falls, divine providence so ordering, but he falls by his own fault" (III. xxiii. 8).

44. *A Study in Milton's Christian Doctrine* (London, 1967), p. 62.

45. *The World Turned Upside Down* (London, 1972), pp. 326, 325.

46. "Man's First Disobedience: The Causal Structure of the Fall," *JHI*, XXI (1960), 194.

47. "The Theological Dogma of *Paradise Lost*, III, 173–202," *PMLA*, LII (1937), 75–79.

48. Ibid., p. 78.

49. *Critique*, p. 11.

50. Of course, as Evans rightly points out, prelapsarian virtue does, in the cultural area, have its commissive aspect, in that Adam and Eve must "dress the

garden and . . . keep it." See his discussion in *Paradise Lost and the Genesis Tradition*, pp. 246 ff.

51. X, 22–30; cf. Calvin's indirect reference (based on Matthew xv, 13) to the elect as those whom God has "been pleased to plant as sacred trees in his garden," *Institutes*, III. xxiii. 1.

52. For a different, though not necessarily incompatible, reading of XI, 3 and 91, see Stanley Fish, *Surprised by Sin* (London and Berkeley, 1971), pp. 19–20.

53. XI, 255; italics added.

54. *Milton and the Christian Tradition*, p. 204.

55. A view very similar to the one I am suggesting Milton presents, including reference to prevenient grace and use of the seed metaphor (*PL* XI, 3, 26 ff.), was expressed by Milton's (Arminian) contemporary Henry Hammond: Obedience to the call of grace "may reasonably be imputed to the humble, malleable, melting temper . . . owing to the preventing Graces of God, and not to the naturall probity, or free will of man. . . . [This opinion] attributes nothing to free will, considered by it self, but the power of resisting . . . , yielding the glory of all the work of conversion . . . to his sole Grace, by which the will is first set free, then fitted and cultivated, and then the seed of eternal life successfully sowed in it" (*A Pacifick Discourse of Gods Grace and Decrees* [London, 1660], pp. 58–59).

56. See *PL* XII, 561 ff.

57. *PL* I, 25–26. My sincere thanks to John Carey, Martin Evans, Patrick Grant, and Philip Sampson for the extremely helpful—and friendly—criticism each of them has offered on earlier drafts of this essay.

CHAPTER 4

Milton's Arianism: why it matters

John P. Rumrich

In a preliminary report by the committee studying the provenance of *de doctrina Christiana*, Gordon Campbell stated that arguments based on the treatise's coherence with the accepted canon of Milton's works remind him of Fluellen's case for the resemblance between Henry V and Alexander the Great: "There is a river in Macedon, and there is also more-over a river at Monmouth ... and there is salmons in both."[1] Though Campbell assumed authorial responsibility, C. A. Patrides was the original wag. He quoted Fluellen a generation ago to deride Maurice Kelley's use of *de doctrina* as a theological guide to *Paradise Lost*.[2] Ironically, Patrides authored *Milton and the Christian Tradition*, a work that to characterize Milton's epic theology casts its nets into the boundless deep of more than fifteen centuries of Christian religious writing.[3] Kelley at least was fishing for trout in a peculiar river – one that he had, moreover, definitively charted.

Campbell's unacknowledged revival of Patrides's resile mockery indi-cates that the controversy over Milton's authorship of *de doctrina* springs in part from obscure sources. More than half a century ago, Kelley first argued systematically that the coherence of *Paradise Lost* and *de doctrina Christiana* is far-reaching, detailed, and, in their shared deviations from Christian orthodoxy, distinctive.[4] Perhaps Kelley's original description of the theology as a gloss on the poetry slights the integrity of distinct modes of discourse. But he did not overstate the broad intellectual coherence and large consistency of the poet-theologian who produced both. Others – Barbara Lewalski, William Kerrigan, and Stephen Fallon notable among them – have fortified Kelley's general claim through credible interpreta-tion of Milton's poetry that rests substantially on reference to *de doctrina*. Such amplification by pertinent contextualization and discriminating comparison lies at the heart of philology and literary studies, including the assessment of provenance. Yet the committee's final report retains Campbell's skepticism "about argument arising from congruence or contradictions with works indisputably written by Milton" (section 10).

William Hunter, on the other hand, has repeatedly affirmed the vital part that "congruence or contradictions" plays in determining authorship: "The points of greatest interest . . . are the heresies that *Paradise Lost* supposedly shares with the *Christian Doctrine*, a major part of both of Kelley's comparative studies of the two works."[5] Hunter candidly admits his stake in divorcing Milton from the treatise – so that we might see the poet as "closer to the great tradition of Christianity, no longer associated with a merely eccentric fringe."[6] His case against Milton's authorship rests largely on the claim that *Paradise Lost*, taken alone, seems orthodox, while *de doctrina* fairly bursts with heresies: "such heresies are not evident to the objective reader who limits himself to the poem and ignores the interpretations of it derived from ideas in the treatise."[7]

In support of this claim, Hunter repeats the familiar allegation, also more than half a century old, that prior to the discovery of *de doctrina* in 1825, readers found *Paradise Lost* "exemplary of Protestant dogma."[8] He acknowledges only two exceptions: Daniel Defoe's insistence that the epic offers an Arian representation of the Son and "another minor upheaval" caused by John Dennis's similar complaint in the early eighteenth century.[9] Michael Bauman has shown, however, that many more than two early readers thought the poem heretical, as John Toland indirectly testified in 1698: "As to the choice of his subject, or the particulars of his story, I shall say nothing in defence of them against those people who brand 'em with heresy and impiety." Similarly, in 1734, Jonathan Richardson, though defending the orthodoxy of Milton's epic, acknowledges "another Conjecture which some have made; I mean that Milton was an Arian." Antitrinitarianism seems indeed to have been early readers' common complaint. Charles Leslie in 1698 condemned Milton for making "the Angels ignorant of the blessed Trinity." The aforementioned John Dennis, commenting in 1704 on Book 3.383–95, claimed that "Milton was a little tainted with Socinianism, for by the first verse 'tis evident that he looked upon the Son of God as a created Being." When Bishop Charles Sumner published his translation of the treatise, he listed Newton, Trapp, Todd, Symmons, Warton, and Calton as previous readers who, without ever having seen *de doctrina*, regarded Milton's poetry as heretically Arian. Finally, Thomas Macaulay, commenting on Milton's Arianism just after the treatise was published, asserts that "we can scarcely conceive that any person could have read *Paradise Lost* without suspecting him of [it]."[10]

Far from supposing Milton's epic orthodox, early readers persistently suspected it of heresy, most often the "archetypal heresy" – Arianism –

which denies orthodox formulations of the trinity and in the late seventeenth century represented "the prime exemplar of heresy in general."[11]
The focal power and overdetermined significance of this heresy, originally
defined at the Council of Nicaea in 325, endures in Milton criticism of the
present day. Not only in the essays questioning the provenance of *de doctrina*, but also in many earlier works over four decades, Hunter has
doggedly contended that unlike the treatise, *Paradise Lost* presents an
orthodox if subordinationist vision of the Son of God. Similarly, the committee's final report on the authorship controversy – despite its skepticism
over "congruence or contradictions" – identifies a passage concerning the
status of the Son of God as one of "a hard core of four points, all of them
local, in which treatise and *Paradise Lost* are curiously and gratuitously at
odds" (section 10). The local point it cites regarding the Son has also been
raised previously in discussions of Milton's alleged Arianism – first by
Patrides (1971) and then by committee member Campbell (1980). Michael
Bauman answered their arguments (1987).[12] Yet the committee's report
ignores previous controversy over this "local point."

In short, the evidence suggests that an unacknowledged critical history
has predisposed current arguments, especially when the theological issue
at stake is Milton's view of the Son of God. Hunter is moreover certainly
correct to suggest that the reception history of *Paradise Lost* fairly cries out
for explanation, though we must reverse his formulation: namely, how is it
that so many early readers identified the epic as Arian, when most twentieth-
century readers, despite the added evidence of *de doctrina*, have accepted
the claim that *Paradise Lost* conforms to orthodoxy? The answer to this
question is multiple and, as it concerns twentieth-century reception history, complicated by the quirky and competing agendas of Milton scholarship. The theological sensitivities of earlier readers, however, seem at this
historical distance straightforward and relatively easy to explain.

Once a settlement of the ecclesiological battles of mid-century had been
imposed, christology occupied the center stage of seventeenth-century
English theological disputes. "Between 1687 and approximately 1700,"
notes John Marshall, "there was a major debate over the trinity in England
which became known as the 'Unitarian Controversy.' "[13] The resurgence
of antitrinitarianism featured an emphasis on the disciplined application
of reason – purged of metaphysical complication – and preference for
scriptural evidence over human authority. Milton's characterization of
Arian and Socinian beliefs in *Of True Religion* (1673) is illustrative:

The Arian and Socinian are charg'd to dispute against the Trinity: They affirm to believe the Father, Son, and Holy Ghost, according to Scripture, and the Apostolic Creed; as for terms of Trinity, Triunity, Coessentiality, Tripersonality, and the like, they reject them as Scholastic Notions, not to be found in Scripture, which by a general Protestant Maxim is plain and perspicuous abundantly to explain its own meaning in the properest words, belonging to so high a Matter and so necessary to be known; a mystery indeed in their sophistic Subtilties, but in Scripture a plain Doctrin. (*CP* VIII: 424–25)

Milton here plainly states that Arians and Socinians reject orthodox trinitarian formulations as scholastic obscurities lacking scriptural warrant. The author of *de doctrina* rejects trinitarian orthodoxy on the same basis: "I shall state quite openly what seems to me much more clearly deducible from the text of scripture than the currently accepted doctrine" (*CP* VI: 201). The appeal for toleration of opinions based on scripture and the disciplined application of reason is a common theme in the mature Milton's writings.

Hunter also quotes the passage above, but contends that it endorses "the perspective of the Church of England," which in the late seventeenth century explicitly condemned antitrinitarian beliefs. To make the identification of Milton with this perspective seem plausible, Hunter recommends that we replace the final semi-colon with a period and indicate with a bracketed insertion – "[response]" – that the subsequent clause is Milton's judgment of the Arians and Socinians, rather than a description of the scholastic notions they forsook.[14] Extensive refutation of this modest editorial proposal is unnecessary, since the obvious contextual referent for "their sophistic Subtilties" is "Scholastic Notions." "Sophistic Subtilties" is, furthermore, diction that Milton typically reserves for criticism of scholasticism. Consider, for example, his condemnation of the "scholastick Sophistry" of "Canon iniquity" in *The Doctrine and Discipline of Divorce* – canon iniquity embraced by the Church of England, much to Milton's dismay (*CP* II: 351).

As with other antitrinitarians of the late seventeenth century, Milton's trust in human reason is deeply qualified in matters of religious knowledge; he, like Locke, insisted "on the impossibility of making significant deductions that take us beyond the expressions given in scriptural revelation."[15] Both of them firmly and consistently rejected what they regarded as excessive, speculative reasoning embodied in customary church doctrines like "the bizarre *troika* of Athanasius," as Hugh Trevor-Roper phrases it.[16] This methodological conviction confirmed for both Milton and Locke "long-standing anticlerical suspicions of clerical orthodoxy and . . . support for toleration."[17] It has yet to be recognized how extensively Locke and other prominent late-century intellectuals recapitulate Milton's progression from anticlericalism and an Arminian tolerationist stance to serious consideration, if not endorsement, of antitrinitarian tenets. As the introduction to this volume suggests, Milton's paradigmatic religious development may be taken as a rough guide to the history of seventeenth-century theological controversy.

By the early eighteenth century so many had followed Milton's path that antitrinitarian deviations from orthodoxy "found widespread support in Britain."[18] Consciousness of antitrinitarian tendencies was unusually well developed, therefore, and the recorded responses of a reader with theological training – like Defoe, for example – ought to guide us as to what would register as unorthodox with a religiously informed reader of his time. As for later, relatively desensitized readers, it should not startle us that the Arianism of the epic has escaped notice. Though neither a whimsy put aside nor inept doctrine forsaken, the Arianism of the epic, as Balachandara Rajan has observed, is mixed in with the narrative fiction tactfully enough to avoid offending the orthodox, or, perhaps more to the point, to evade their ire.[19] The notorious Restoration Milton first published *Paradise Lost* in 1667, when the growing tendency toward toleration had suffered a shocking setback. Even when the tide of enforced conformity receded with the Toleration Act of 1689, antitrinitarians alone of Protestant sectaries suffered exclusion with the papists. At Glasgow in 1697 they hanged Thomas Aikenhead, aged eighteen, for denying the trinity.[20]

I use "Arian" rather than "antitrinitarian" to indicate Milton's beliefs concerning the Son of God. Part of England's theological vocabulary at least since the sixteenth century, "Arian" is the term Milton himself uses, almost exclusively, to describe antitrinitarian heresy (*CP* I: 533, 555, 557; VIII: 424). Though the term is vexed and has been polemically compromised for most of two millennia, "Arianism," as Maurice Wiles maintains, "has certainly existed as a powerful concept throughout Christian history."[21] As opposed to its cloudy origins in fourth-century church politics, the theological definition of Arianism is straightforward enough for summary in a few sentences. The foundation of the Arian position is the insistence that the essence of true Godhood is unique and unbegotten (*agenetos*). This unbegotten essence belongs only to the paternal God, not to the Son or to the Holy Spirit. As *de doctrina* insists, "really a God cannot be begotten at all," a blanket statment that covers figurative and literal meanings of begotten (*CP* VI: 211). From this perspective, even the standard Nicene formulation "begotten not made" registers the Son's real inferiority to the

Father. Arians deny the Son the essential divine attribute of unbegotten-
ness – or eternal existence – and also deny him related attributes such as
omnipotence, omniscience, and ubiquity. Inferior to the Father, the Son is
not "very" or "true" God, but instead, per the formulation in *de doctrina*, "a
God who is not self-existent, who did not beget but was begotten, is not
a first cause but an effect, and is therefore not a supreme God" (*CP* VI:
263–64).[22]

Long before launching the controversy over the treatise's provenance,
Professor Hunter argued that, unlike *de doctrina*, *Paradise Lost* offers an
orthodox, trinitarian depiction of God. In his view, the epic indicates that
Milton was not an Arian but instead a "subordinationist": "The poem
indeed has, as C. A. Patrides, J. H. Adamson, and I have shown, a subordi-
nationist underpinning: the Son is divine but subordinate to the Father as
Eve is human but subordinate to Adam."[23] Many have since followed
Hunter, Adamson, and Patrides in applying the term *subordinationist* to
Milton's epic presentation of the Son. The relevant entries from *A Milton
Encyclopedia* are revealing as to why:

> On the basis of . . . highly competent theological analyses, what had earlier been
> regarded by some as the Arian heresy is now generally recognized as a seven-
> teenth-century expression of the "subordinationism" of early Fathers of the
> Church up to the Council of Nicaea, a position that was held by many orthodox
> writers.

> Milton's view . . . has by some been identified with the Arian heresy, but this con-
> tention has been successfully questioned and corrected by meticulous and com-
> petent historical analysis.[24]

Part of the point seems to be that these theological affairs are complicated
enough to require extraordinary expertise and analytical powers, that
ordinary readers should submit to the authoritative judgment of the com-
petent few. This attitude resembles that prevalent among civil and religious authorities concerned with heresy in the seventeenth century. It
also implies that readers like Defoe, Macaulay, David Masson, Rajan, and
Kelley, all of whom identified Milton as consistently Arian, are relatively
incompetent.

The excerpts quoted above do not exaggerate the general acceptance of
the term "subordinationism" among Milton scholars. Almost everyone
who has had occasion to discuss the Son's status uses it, though (or perhaps
because) no one seems to know what it signifies concerning Milton's relation to orthodoxy. Dennis Danielson, for example, warns that we should
not let Milton's subordinationism mislead us into underestimating "the

extent to which Milton is scriptural and orthodox in his presentation of the relationship between Father and Son."[25] Though the term was introduced in the defense of Milton's orthodoxy, Danielson clearly wishes to guard against the possibility that it implies unorthodoxy. The inclusiveness of "subordinationism" thus allows a convenient critical doublethink: (1) by using it, scholars acknowledge that Milton's representation of the Son differs significantly from customary representations of the Son; (2) by using it, scholars agree that Milton's version of the Son is nonetheless orthodox. For Milton scholarship "subordinationism" has in effect come to mean unorthodox orthodoxy.

If "subordinationism" already refers to orthodox doctrine, why should an exact scholar like Danielson need to qualify it as he does? I believe that its chief value to Milton criticism lies in its vagueness. Unlike the term "antitrinitarianism," which Kelley preferred, "subordinationism" does not explicitly deny the trinity. Instead, suggesting a grammatical model, it lumps together various ways in which the Son has been considered dependent on the main clause of paternal deity. Aside from the grammatological analogy it offers those disposed to parse the Godhead, "subordinationism" holds little descriptive value, bears no historical relevance to Milton's century (the *OED* records no usage of "subordinationism" before 1843), and indeed, outside of Milton studies is so obscure a piece of jargon that general encyclopedias (e.g., *Britannica, Americana*) ignore it, as do various specialized sources (e.g., *The Encyclopedia of Religion* edited by Mircea Eliade). *The New Catholic Encyclopedia* does include a short entry, but contrary to the definition of the term provided by Milton studies' theological experts, it begins, "the *heresy* . . . that admitted only the Father as truly God and taught the inferiority . . . of the Son" (italics mine). It never existed for condemnation as the name of a heresy until the nineteenth century, and even then only taxonomically, as a forbidden category. To say that something called subordinationism was "upheld by the early Christian writers to the Council of Nicaea," as Patrides would have it, is to perpetuate a grotesque anachronism.[26]

As Michael Bauman has argued, the depiction of the Son in *Paradise Lost* agrees with the doctrine presented in chapter 5 of *de doctrina*, which characterizes the Son as a limited, localized, mutable being, not eternal but derived in time from an eternal, substantially omnipresent Father.[27] During the course of the epic action, the Son increases in stature, authority, and power, all at the Father's pleasure – an augmentation of being that would not be possible or needed if he were unlimited, infinite, immutable, and eternal. The undeniable differences between the exposition of doctrine and epic narration need not signal a difference in theology. The Arianism of the epic is clear enough. As William Empson observed, "the poem makes the Son and the Father about as unidentical as a terrier and a camel." Empson even suggests that Milton discovered his Arianism as a consequence of his epic composition, deciding "that what his imagination had produced amounted to being an Arian."[28] Bauman presents the case in compelling detail, addressing each relevant passage in the epic and convincingly explicating its consistency with Arian belief. I do not have the scope here to reiterate his arguments, but because they have been ignored by Hunter and by most other Milton scholars, a sample seems warranted.

In a section entitled "Milton's Arian Angels," Bauman cites the following hymn of praise:

> Thee next they sang of all creation first,
> Begotten Son, divine similitude,
> In whose conspicuous countenance, without cloud
> Made visible, the almighty Father shines.[29]

Bauman observes that the angels here, as always, address the Son after praising the Father, "the only one who, in Milton's theology, is 'omnipotent, / Immutable, immortal, infinite' and 'eternal' " (3.372–4). The Son is never addressed as possessing such traits, though on occasion he is afforded access to them according to his Father's will.

In line 383, the phrase "of all creation first" alludes to Colossians 1:15; Bauman cites the explication of this passage in *de doctrina*:

The first born of all created things . . . Here both the Greek accent and the verbal passive *protótomos* show that the Son of God was *the first born of all created things* in the same sense as the Son of man was the *protótomos* or *first born* of Mary, Matt. i. 25 . . . That can only mean that he was the first of the things which God created. How, then, can he be God himself? (*CP* VI: 302–03)

Bauman considers other Arian passages in the epic without adducing such substantiating evidence from the treatise. This example is useful, however, because it indicates how closely the poetry and theology correspond to each other.

To describe Milton as an "orthodox subordinationist" is hardly more precise than simply to describe him as orthodox. Orthodox believers are all subordinationist in that they posit an inequality of function, office, or subsistence among the persons of the trinity. In the Nicene creed, the Father begets the Son; the Son does not beget the Father. The Son sits at the right hand of the Father, not the other way round, and so on. The theological basis for Hunter's claim that Milton was an orthodox subordinationist is that for Milton the Son derives from God's own substance ("one substance [*homoousia*] with the father," according to one translation of Nicene ortho-doxy). For the monist materialist Milton, however, *all* creatures derive from God's own substance. By this criterion, to borrow the words of John Fry, an Arian supporter of Parliament present for Charles's trial, "I might be said to be God too, as well as Jesus Christ, and the like might be affirmed of all other creatures whatsoever."[30] Milton's cosmos begins with "one first matter all" and ends when "God shall be All in All" (*Paradise Lost* 5.472; 3.341). The Son's material being may originally be more refined and exalted than that of other creatures, but eventually parakeets and pachy-derms would also qualify as participants in the Godhead.[31]

The import of Milton's monistic ontology should figure into any com-parison with the strongly dualistic subordinationism of the Gnostics, who are cited by Hunter as historical precedent. Divinity of constituent sub-stance is for Milton a universal condition of being, not a privilege in itself sufficient to warrant divine status. Another famous seventeenth-century Arian, Isaac Newton, criticized those Gnostics who thought it proper to worship Christ simply because he emanated from the substance of "the supreme God": "he that is of this opinion may believe Christ to be of one substance with the father without making him more then a meer man. Tis not cosubstantiality but power and dominion which gives a right to be worshipped."[32] The author of *de doctrina Christiana* is, like Newton, unmis-takably explicit on the subject: "[God is] in a real sense Father of the Son, whom he made of his own substance. It does not follow, however, that the Son is of the same essence as the Father" (*CP* VI: 209). The treatise repeat-edly insists that "the attributes of divinity belong to the Father alone," par-ticularly the attribute of "supreme domination both in heaven and earth: the highest authority and highest power of making decisions according to his own absolutely free will" (*CP* VI: 227). God's eternal essence and thus his absolute causal priority qualify him alone as truly, unconditionally, divine.

When Hunter still acknowledged Milton's authorship of *de doctrina*, he elaborated his claim for Milton's orthodoxy by arguing that in the poet-theologian's opinion the Son is really eternal and absolute because, as the *Logos*, he has always existed in the mind of God. Hunter called this the "two-stage logos theory" and traced it, too, to Neoplatonic and Gnostic speculation within the early church.[33] Newton's meticulous knowledge of early church theological controversy is generally acknowledged to meet the highest standard of competence so that we can feel confident in turning to his writings for historical background: "The Gnosticks after the manner of

the Platonists and Cabbalists considered the thoughts or Ideas or intellectual objects seated in Gods mind as real Beings or substances." Newton
disparages this notion as crude and heathen, and as G. L. Prestige – an
authority often cited by Hunter – asserts, Christians "early opposed and
soon repudiated" the two-stage logos theory.[34] Ignoring Prestige on this
point, Hunter insists that the two-stage logos theory "entirely escaped condemnation by the early church."[35] True, as a theory it was too insignificant
to be condemned specifically at Nicaea. Yet it certainly falls under the
Nicene anathemas. For one thing, the transition between two states of
being entailed by the theory violates the Nicene insistence on the
immutability of the Son.

   As Bauman observes, not only is the two-stage logos theory not orthodox; Milton never endorsed it.[36] Milton has no more patience than
Newton with the ontological premises of such a theory, insisting in the *Art
of Logic* that a thing that exists only in the mind of a subject does not in reality exist at all (*CP* VIII: 236). If, on the contrary, Milton had agreed that
divine consciousness of a phenomenon constitutes its existence, what
would become of the distinction he so carefully draws between foreknowledge and free will? Furthermore, supposing that Hunter were correct in
ascribing such arcane Gnostic notions to Milton, the idea of all creation –
indeed, of all possible creations – would also have eternally existed in the
mind of an omniscient God. Again the Son would enjoy no special ontological distinction from the rest of creation.

   I have been appealing to the work of Isaac Newton because it contains
such detailed knowledge of the early church and because his arguments
are close to those presented in *de doctrina*. He is also, like Locke, a prime
example of the wave of antitrinitarian heresy that swept over late-seven-
teenth and early eighteenth-century England. For Newton as for the
author of *de doctrina*, trinitarianism confused causes and as a species of
polytheism, was an instance of the gravest sin, idolatry.[37] Both insisted on
the Arian position primarily because each viewed God as indivisibly one.
As the author of *de doctrina* wryly observes, "it would have been a waste of
time for God to thunder forth so repeatedly that first commandment
which said that he was the one and only God, if it could nevertheless be
maintained that another God existed as well" (*CP* VI: 212). (Carey's translation is fairly exact here, and the diction – e.g., *intonoare*, thunder forth –
strikes my ear as authentically Miltonic.) The Son, on the other hand,
according to Newton's theology, "had assumed and would assume many
shapes and forms . . . a messenger, an agent, a vice-ruler under God, a
judge," and as "the one Mediator between God and Man."[38] Similarly,

de doctrina suggests that scripture calls the Son *only begotten* chiefly because he is the only mediator between God and man (*CP* VI: 210–11): "However the Son was begotten, it did not arise from natural necessity, as is usually maintained, but was just as much a result of the Father's decree and will as the Son's priesthood, kingship, and resurrection from the dead (*CP* VI: 208). It so happens that, as Milton, Newton, and most of their contemporary Arians agree, the Father chooses to do everything in creation through the Son.

Hence, in *Paradise Lost*, once the Father has determined to show humanity mercy, the Son volunteers to act as redeemer and rescue humankind from death and the Father enables him to do so: "all Power / I give thee" (3.317–18; see also 203–302). Similarly, the Father assigns him the task and provides the means of defeating the rebel angels: "Two days are therefore past, the third is thine; / For thee I have ordain'd it ... / ... Into thee such Virtue and Grace / Immense I have transfus'd" (6.699–704). Creation, too, occurs at the Father's pleasure, through the Son: "thou my Word, begotten Son, by thee / This I perform" (7.163–64). The angels sum up the unequal, complementary relationship between Father and Son quite explicitly:

> Hee Heav'n of Heavens and all the Powers therein
> By thee created, and by thee threw down
> Th' aspiring Dominations: thou that day
> Thy Father's dreadful Thunder didst not spare,
>
> . . .
>
> Son of thy Father's might,
> To execute fierce vengeance on his foes:
> Not so on Man; him though their malice fall'n,
> Father of Mercy and Grace, thou didst not doom
> So strictly, but much more to pity inclin'd,
> No sooner did thy dear and only Son
> Perceive thee purpos'd not to doom frail Man
> So strictly, but much more to pity inclin'd
> Hee to appease thy wrath . . .
>
> . . .
>
> offer'd himself to die
> For man's offense.   (3.390–410)

Such power, knowledge, and position as the Son enjoys derive from the Father and are contingent on the Son's voluntary and therefore meritorious obedience. The Son's designation as judge of fallen humanity follows the same pattern: "Vicegerent Son, to thee I have transferr'd / All Judgment"; to which the Son replies, "Father Eternal, thine is to decree, /

Mine both in Heav'n and Earth to do thy will" (10.56–57, 68–69). Finally, when the Son acts as priest and intercessor on humanity's behalf, the Father observes that even here his own will preceded the Son's apparent agency: "all thy request was my Decree" (11.47).

In every guise, the contingent Son as represented in *Paradise Lost* acts to fulfill the will of the one absolute being. This exemplary obedience entitles him to divine honors and worship, but not to the status of true divinity. The demotion of the Son to finite if still divine status reflects again the insistently theodical point of Milton's theology. In *Paradise Lost*, the Son's freely made decisions to obey the Father's will function as a striking counter-example to the decisions of Satan and Adam, his angelic adversary and human predecessor, respectively. Through *voluntary* obedience both God's ways and the human race are justified.

Some might object that, regardless of Milton's own usage, the label "Arian," deriving from a fourth-century controversy, is as inappropriate to the seventeenth century as the nineteenth-century label "subordination-ist." In the late seventeenth century, Arianism undoubtedly reflects a historically specific inclination on the part of individual believers to apply their own reason and logic to religious doctrine, and an associated tendency to scrutinize rigorously doctrinal and scriptural history. It also manifests the growing conviction among secular, educated men that the individual conscience alone must dictate in matters of faith. This distinctly early modern profile, retrospective though it may be, certainly fits figures like Newton, Locke, and the surprisingly large number of their intellectually eminent circle who held Arian opinions. Arguably, it is a profile that fits Milton as well. It does not of course fit fourth-century Arians, and in that respect the label "Arian" seems misleading.

Yet we should also consider another side to the intellectual–historical picture. Although for many scholars, seventeenth-century debates over the unity of God seem like irrelevant distractions from more pressing sociopolitical questions, such debates were not without much broader cultural ramifications. Nor was the theological position signified then and now by the term Arianism treated as a curious relic of fourth-century Christianity. Many different opinions of what was essential in Christian belief existed during Milton's time, but most included the trinity. Those in power in church and state, whether in London, Rome, or Geneva, were even in an intolerant age remarkably unyielding on the subject. In England, at least eight antitrinitarian heretics were burned at the stake from 1548 to 1612. One of the last was Bartholomew Legate. In a characteristic moment of personal involvement, the scholarly King James tried himself to convince the heretic of his error, but after listening to Legate, broke into "choler, spurn[ing] at him with his foot" and commanding him out of his presence.[39] That Legate was one of the last Arians burnt to death in England does not seem to have owed to a softening of official attitudes. As Thomas Fuller remarks, after Legate went up in flames, the King "politicly preferred that Heretics hereafter ... should silently and privately waste themselves away in Prison rather than to grace them and amuze others with the solemnity of a public Execution."[40] Perhaps the impulse toward demystification expressed in Arianism was dimly perceived as a threat to the ideological basis of monarchical power. If awe for the mystery of Christ's essential but unapparent divinity was lacking, what would become of the awe for kings as Christ's representatives, or indeed of any of the similarly unapparent ontological distinctions supposed to separate noble from common in a hierarchical society? Whatever it was that drove an outraged James to kick at Legate, the profession of Arian opinions provoked authorities across seventeenth-century Europe as no other heresy could.

Agents of the Enlightenment like Newton formed their consciously Arian opinions deliberately and knowledgeably in the vocabulary of fourth-century church history, a century for various reasons considered highly relevant by many educated and forward-looking men in seventeenth-century England, early and late. Newton corresponded with Locke about the trinity and at Locke's behest nearly allowed his arguments concerning the lack of scriptural evidence for the trinity to be published. Richard Westfall observes that a fairly wide circle of Arians was "connected with Newton"; Frank Manuel lists Edmund Halley, David Gregory, Fatio de Duillier, Hopton Haynes, and Samuel Clarke.[41] Newton's successor at Cambridge, William Whiston, was ejected from his chair when his Arian opinions became known.[42] Professional ruin is a far cry from incineration, yet there seems to have been sufficient reason even in the eighteenth century for an Arian to suppress his heretical belief. Though an Arian of deepest conviction, Newton, like Milton, "received a Church of England burial," which in Milton's case Hunter takes to mean, "that he had not voiced to anyone ... [his] heretical ideas."[43] Such public silence does not indicate that Milton was orthodox on the trinity, however, any more than Newton's public silence signals his orthodoxy. Unless he were seeking imprisonment or a martyr's death, certainly Milton, like Newton after him, would have kept his Arianism hidden from the authorities.

The nature of Newton's heretical beliefs was suppressed after his death, and his voluminous, unpublished, religious writings were, as Manuel again puts it, "bowdlerized, neglected, or sequestered."[44] It is a history that should not seem altogether strange to Milton scholars. By the early 1670s, Newton's massive and what would be sustained efforts in biblical and historical analysis centered on early church history, and especially on the trinitarian controversies of the fourth century. He repeatedly and variously builds the case for Arius while construing Athanasius as a vile politician symbolic of humanity's evil inclination to substitute man-made intricacy and superstition for the unity and singularity of divine truth. Newton convinced himself that "a universal corruption of Christianity had followed the central corruption of doctrine," according to Westfall, a corruption especially evident in church government, where the former polity was replaced by "concentration of ecclesiastical power in the hands of the hierarchy."[45] Like Milton, Newton refused to take orders in such a church – "accept ordination he could not" – though he became a fellow, ironically, of Trinity College.

For the author of *de doctrina*, too, Christianity had been "defiled with impurities for more than thirteen hundred years" – that is, since the time of Constantine and the institutionalization of Christianity as the state religion (*CP* VI: 117). Milton and Newton's opinions reflect the profound influence of the revisionist millenarian calculations of Joseph Mead, a tutor at Christ's College during Milton's time there. Presbyterians and Independents agreed that some apocalyptic history had passed, though more was to come. But while Presbyterians typically sought to institute an order defined by historical and legal precedent, Independents tended to see the imminent future as precipitating an ideal order, one that would transcend previous laws and institutions. Representative of Presbyterian belief on the subject, Richard Baxter supposed that the paradigm for the millennium had already occurred, under Constantine, and that Christians should work toward a return to the ideal represented by the Holy Roman Empire. Hence, amidst the many vacillations in Baxter's writings, one consistent theme, as William Lamont has shown, is his yearning for the reign of a godly prince, one who would use civil authority to promote the interests and discipline of true religion – under the guidance of divines like Baxter.[46] This ideal, and an associated adherence to preexisting forms of scriptural and national law, was the basis for Presbyterian allegiance to the monarchy and outrage at the regicide. Preferring Mead's interpretation of apocalyptic scripture, Independents like Milton looked back not to the first thousand years of the Holy Roman Empire, but forward to an unprecedented millennium when the true King, Christ, would return and rule.[47] The expectation of a new and just order – Augustine's invisible city of God made visible on Earth in real time – had the effect of rendering the institution of monarchy, as well as ecclesiastical policies and even civil law, less sacred and more open to question.

For Milton as for Newton, in line with Mead's chronology, the papal Antichrist originated in the fourth century, not the fourteenth, and was a product of the union of civil and ecclesiastical powers. Hence, as Newton would, Milton disapproved of the institution of Christianity as a state church and of the hierarchical exaltation of its clergy. Milton berated Constantine for promoting prelates to luxurious lives and giving them authority over matters better left to individual believers.[48] This early malediction of Constantine (1641) indicates that Milton's skeptical attitude toward supposedly sacred rulers and clerical authority preceded and perhaps prepared the way for his Arian convictions (*CP* I: 554–59; see also I: 420). The definition of Arianism at the Council of Nicaea indeed represented a crucial, politically charged moment in the establishment of a set doctrine for a unified state church.[49] Milton's aversion to such an alliance of civil authority and religious concerns, furthermore, is of a piece not only with his Arianism but also with the millenarian, tolerationist, historical perspective evinced by the opening argument of *Areopagitica*. For it was under the "Roman *Antichrist . . .* bred up by *Constantine*" that religious persecution, and with it pre-publication censorship, waxed strongest (*CP* I: 559).

Early readers recognized Arianism in *Paradise Lost* and, once *de doctrina Christiana* was discovered and published, various Milton scholars, Maurice Kelley most notably, recognized the consistency of its heretical theology with Milton's poetic fiction. Arianism is implicit, not effaced, in Milton's epic and consistent with his political ideology and view of apocalyptic history. An exemplary heresy in the seventeenth century, its adherents manifest an intellectual posture adopted by some of the best minds of the time, one for which they contended, sincerely if discreetly, in terms of fourth-century church history. The Arianism of *de doctrina Christiana* presents no obstacle to the assignment of the treatise to its author, John Milton. Is Milton scholarship so committed to the orthodoxy of *Paradise Lost* that it will continue in its refusal to acknowledge Milton's Arianism, even if it means denying the evident provenance of his theology?

NOTES

1. William Shakespeare, *King Henry V*, ed. Andrew Gurr (Cambridge, 1992), 4.7.20–25. The occasion for the report was the 1995 International Milton Symposium in Bangor, Wales.

90 JOHN P. RUMRICH

2. C. A. Patrides, "Milton and the Arian Controversy," *Proceedings of the American Philosophical Society* 120 (1976), 245–52.
3. For more extensive criticism of Patrides's argument and method, see my *Milton Unbound: Controversy and Reinterpretation* (Cambridge, 1996), pp. 29–34.
4. Maurice Kelley, *This Great Argument* (Princeton, 1941).
5. William B. Hunter, "The Provenance of the *Christian Doctrine,*" *SEL* 32 (1992), 132.
6. Hunter, "Forum: Milton's *Christian Doctrine,*" *SEL* 32 (1992), 166.
7. Hunter, "Provenance," 132.
8. *Ibid.* C. S. Lewis was the first to insist that Milton's epic "was accepted as orthodox by many generations of acute readers well grounded in theology." See *A Preface to Paradise Lost* (Oxford, 1942), p. 82.
9. Hunter, "Provenance," 132.
10. I list evidence drawn from Michael E. Bauman, "Heresy in Paradise and the Ghost of Readers Past," *College Language Association Journal* 30 (1986), 59–68. He relies primarily on John T. Shawcross, ed., *Milton: The Critical Heritage* (New York, 1970), and records only those instances that "may easily be discovered by any interested student of Milton" (p. 66). For a fuller discussion of early readers' reactions to the heretical potential of Milton's epic, see Joseph Wittreich's essay, chapter 12 of this volume.
11. Maurice Wiles, *Archetypal Heresy* (Oxford, 1996), p. 63.
12. William B. Hunter, C. A. Patrides, J. H. Adamson, *Bright Essence* (Salt Lake City, 1971), p. 10; Gordon Campbell, "The Son of God in *de doctrina Christiana* and *Paradise Lost,*" *Modern Language Review* 75 (1980), 507–14; Michael E. Bauman, *Milton's Arianism* (Frankfurt, 1987), pp. 238–42.
13. John Marshall, *John Locke: Resistance, Religion, and Responsibility* (Cambridge, 1994), p. 389.
14. William B. Hunter, "The Provenance of the *Christian Doctrine*: Addenda from the Bishop of Salisbury," *SEL* 33 (1993), 195.
15. Wiles, *Archetypal Heresy*, p. 70.
16. Hugh Trevor-Roper, "Toleration and Religion after 1688," in Ole Peter Grell, Jonathan I. Israel, and Nicholas Tyacke, eds., *From Persecution to Toleration* (Oxford, 1991), p. 402.
17. Marshall, *Locke*, p. 329.
18. Wiles, *Archetypal Heresy*, p. 4.
19. Balachandara Rajan, *Milton and the Seventeenth Century Reader* (1947, 1962; rpt. London, 1966), pp. 23–31. It was C. S. Lewis, *A Preface to Paradise Lost*, p. 91, who described Milton's theology as whimsical, and Patrides, n. 3 above, who thought it inept.
20. Jonathan I. Israel, "William III and Toleration," *From Persecution to Toleration*, p. 153. See also Trevor-Roper, "Toleration and Religion," pp. 391, 400–2.
21. Wiles, *Archetypal Heresy*, p. 4.
22. My analysis follows Bauman, *Milton's Arianism*. See also Wiles, *Archetypal Heresy*, pp. 5–17.
23. Hunter, "Provenance," 132–33. This chapter's discussion of subordinationism repeats arguments from *Milton Unbound*, pp. 41–47.

24. *A Milton Encyclopedia*, ed. William B. Hunter, et al., 9 vols. (Lewisburg, PA, 1978–83), vol. VIII, pp. 14, 90.
25. Dennis Danielson, *Milton's Good God* (Cambridge, 1982), p. 54.
26. C. A. Patrides, *Milton and the Christian Tradition* (Oxford, 1966), p. 16.
27. Bauman, *Milton's Arianism*, pp. 203–318.
28. William Empson, *Milton's God*, rev. edn. (London, 1965), p. 278. My thanks to Stephen Dobranski, who brought this reference to my attention.
29. *Paradise Lost* 3.383–86. All citations of Milton's poetry are taken from *The Poetical Works of John Milton*, ed. Helen Darbishire, 2 vols. (Oxford, 1952).
30. John Fry is quoted by H. J. McLachlan, *Socinianism in Seventeenth-Century England* (Oxford, 1951), p. 241.
31. Against Hunter, Barbara K. Lewalski observes that though for Milton the Son shares in divine substance, this does not fundamentally distinguish him from the rest of creation. See *Milton's Brief Epic* (London, 1966), pp. 138–46.
32. Frank E. Manuel, *The Religion of Isaac Newton* (Oxford, 1974), p. 60, cites this passage from the *Yahuda Manuscript*, 15.5, fol. 98ᵛ.
33. See Hunter's "Milton's Arianism Reconsidered," in *Bright Essence*, pp. 38–41. Hunter's claims are critiqued by Bauman, *Milton's Arianism*, pp. 126–32.
34. Newton, *Yahuda Manuscript*, 15.7, fol. 108ᵛ; cited by Manuel, *Religion of Isaac Newton*, p. 69. G. L. Prestige, *God in Patristic Thought* (London, 1952), p. 128.
35. Hunter, "Milton's Arianism Reconsidered," p. 43.
36. Bauman, *Milton's Arianism*, p. 133.
37. Manuel, *Religion of Isaac Newton*, pp. 42–43.
38. *Ibid.*, p. 60.
39. Thomas Fuller, *The Church History of Britain*, vol. X, section iv, as cited by McLachlan, *Socinianism*, p. 33.
40. *Ibid.* See also McLachlan, *The Religious Opinions of Milton, Locke and Newton* (Manchester, 1941), pp. 103–04.
41. Richard S. Westfall, *Never at Rest* (Cambridge, 1980), p. 650; Manuel, *Religion of Isaac Newton*, p. 7.
42. Westfall, *Never at Rest*, p. 332.
43. Hunter, "Provenance," 132.
44. Manuel, *Religion of Isaac Newton*, p. 10.
45. Westfall, *Never at Rest*, p. 315.
46. William Lamont, *Richard Baxter and the Millennium* (London, 1979), p. 13, observes that Baxter's position hearkens back to that of John Foxe, *Acts and Monuments*, 8 vols. (rpt., New York, 1965), who portrayed Elizabeth as following Constantine's example (vol. I, pp. xvi–xxiv, 4–5, 248–50, 285).
47. Robert Baillie, in *A Dissuasive from the Errors of the Time* (London, 1645), expressed the common Presbyterian opinion that the notion of a literal reign of Christ was a heretical misreading of mystical and allegorical apocalyptic scriptures (pp. 80–85, 224–27). For the opposed, Independent position, see, for example, the sermon *A Glimpse of Sion's Glory* (published in London, 1641) usually attributed to Thomas Goodwin, in *The Works of Thomas Goodwin*, ed. Thomas Smith, 12 vols. (Edinburgh, 1861–66), vol. XII, p. 66. Hugh Peters preached on the same,

implicitly anti-monarchical theme before Parliament in April of 1645, *Gods Doings and Mans Duty* (London, 1646), pp. 9–25. John Cooke, Charles's prosecutor in 1649, wrote to similar effect and explicitly counter to the Presbyterian position in *Reintegration Amoris* (London, 1647), pp. 80–84. Or refer to various works of John Goodwin, including *Theomachia* (London, 1644), p. 48, *Innocency and Truth* (London, 1646), p. 10, and, with particular relevance to the Independents' disagreement with the Presbyterians, *The Obstructours of Justice* (London, 1649), p. 85.

48. Ironically, in the same passage, Milton, who in 1641 was certainly an orthodox trinitarian, also berates Constantine for Arian inclinations.

49. Wiles, *Archetypal Heresy*, pp. 1–6.

The Mortalist Heresy in 'Paradise Lost'

Gordon Campbell

In Book III of *Paradise Lost* Christ accepts his mission to redeem mankind with the words

> Though now to Death I yield, and am his due
> All that of me can die, yet that debt paid,
> Thou wilt not leave me in the loathsom grave
> His prey, nor suffer my unspotted Soule
> For ever with corruption there to dwell.[1]
>
> (III. 245-249)

And in Book X, Adam speculates on the nature of his impending death:

> it was but breath
> Of Life that sinn'd; what dies but what had life
> And sin? the Bodie properly hath neither.
> All of me then shall die: let this appease
> The doubt, since humane reach no further knows.
>
> (X. 789-792)

I should like to explore the relationship between Christ's "All that of me can die" and Adam's "All of me then shall die" with a view to showing that these statements are deliberately similar in diction because the truth of Christ's statement is meant to point to the faultiness of Adam's. Both statements have understandably been compared to the mortalism which Milton espoused in his *De Doctrina Christiana;*[2] accordingly, we shall begin with a brief examination of the views expounded in Milton's theological treatise.

In his discussion "Of the Death which is Called the Death of the Body" in *De Doctrina Christiana,* Milton acknowledges that man has traditionally been viewed as a trichotomous being composed of body, soul, and spirit.[3] Although Milton was not wholly convinced that these elements were distinguishable,[4] he accepted the distinction as the basis of his argument

for the total death of man. Milton initially tries to prove that the whole man dies,[5] and then argues that each separate part—body,[6] spirit,[7] and soul[8]—experiences death. That the body dies, no one doubts. And if we accept Milton's idea "that the spirit is not divine but merely human,"[9] there is little room for disagreement about the death of the spirit. But Milton's contention that the soul dies is a conscious departure from orthodoxy, and he therefore devotes the greatest part of his argument to the death of the soul, or as he says more precisely in another chapter, the sleep of the soul.[10]

As one of the passages in *Paradise Lost* with which we are concerned deals with the death of Christ, we should take note of Milton's observations on that subject in *De Doctrina.* Like man, Christ is said to have a soul, a spirit, and a body,[11] and Milton argues that "even Christ's soul succumbed to death for a short time when he died for our sins."[12] The soul of Christ to which Milton refers is part of Christ's human nature[13] (even though it was generated supernaturally[14]), and should not be confused with His divine nature.[15] Milton considers the question of whether or not Christ died in His divine nature, arguing that

> the fact that Christ became a sacrifice both in his divine and in his human nature, is questioned by no one. It is moreover, necessary for the whole of a sacrifice to be killed. So it follows that Christ, the sacrificial lamb, was totally killed.[16]

In *De Doctrina,* then, Milton argues that the death of man is total, involving body, soul, and spirit. He also argues that the death of Christ was total, involving both His human nature—body, soul, and spirit—and

His divine nature. In *Paradise Lost* Milton's characters discuss the death of man and the death of Christ, and in both cases they contradict the opinions forwarded in *De Doctrina Christiana*.

When Adam says "All of me then shall die," he seems to be upholding the mortalism of the theological treatise. An exact parallel also seems apparent in Adam's idea that the body can have neither life nor sin, for Milton had noted in *De Doctrina* that the body "is in itself lifeless"[17] and "had no actual part in the sin."[18] In Adam's ascription of sin to the "breath / Of life," however, there is a hint that Milton has changed his mind about the validity of the mortalist position. In *De Doctrina* Milton had insisted that "all sin proceeds in the first instance from the soul,"[19] and that the soul was "the part which sinned most."[20] Adam's assertion is therefore at variance with Milton's, for Milton had argued that "the breath of life mentioned in Genesis was not . . . the soul, but a kind of air or breath of divine virtue, fit for the maintenance of life and reason and infused into the organic body."[21] Milton does not identify the "breath of life" with the soul, but with the spirit,[22] and in the poem Adam is seen to hold the same opinion when he refers to "that pure breath of Life, the Spirit of Man / Which God inspir'd" (X. 784-785). Adam maintains that the spirit sinned, and Milton, in the theological treatise, that the soul sinned. Adam's justification for advocating the mortalist heresy was not quite the same as Milton's.

Nor were Milton and Adam prompted by the same considerations. Milton argued that the question of the mortality of the soul could "be debated without detriment to faith or devotion, whichever side we may be on," and therefore "put forward quite unreservedly the doctrine which seems . . . to be instilled by . . . scripture."[23] Adam did not share Milton's dispassionate scholarly approach. For Adam, the sole function of the mortalist heresy was to "appease / The doubt" (X. 792-793), the doubt in question being the possibility of "a living Death" (X. 788), which followed on the fear "least all I cannot die" (X. 783). Adam's affirmation of total mortality is nothing more than an attempt to deny the consequences of his fall, to "appease" the possibility of a living death. The final proof that Adam's speech is not a vehicle for Milton's mortalist sympathies is that Adam goes on to entertain an alternative hypothesis: "But say / That Death be not one stroak, as I suppos'd" (X. 808-809). The affirmation has become a supposition, which when repudiated, brings Adam's fear of a living death "thundring back" (X. 814). It is this fear that brings about the first stage of Adam's repentance,

his conviction of sin (X. 831). Adam's defence of mortalism was therefore nothing more than an attempt to deny the consequences of his fall, to appease the fear of living death. Only when he denies mortalism and faces the truth of death does he begin to repent. This denial of mortalism conflicts with Milton's defence of that doctrine in *De Doctrina Christiana*.[24]

Adam's temporary advocacy of mortalism is shown to be erroneous not only because of its psychological context and its immediate repudiation, but also because of the contrast between Adam's "All of me then shall die" and Christ's "All that of me can die." The Son's phrase clearly introduces a qualification to the effect that He is not capable of total death.[25] The Son does not explain in detail which parts of Him will be subject to death, but clearly His body will die, and His "unspotted Soule" will go to the grave.[26] According to *De Doctrina*, the Son also has a human spirit and divine nature,[27] and Milton argues that the Son's human nature—body, soul, and spirit—and divine nature both experienced death.[28] In the poem, the Son is saying that either His spirit or His divine nature (or both) cannot die. Milton is firm in *De Doctrina* that the soul and body of Christ died,[29] but is less confident about His divine nature and spirit. Although his conclusion is that these elements must have participated in Christ's total death,[30] Milton admits that "as for his divine nature, it is more questionable whether that also succumbed to death;"[31] and on the problem of the death of Christ's spirit, Milton argues that if the spirit was brought to life it must have first been dead, unless by "spirit" we mean "the cause of life," in the which case "this must be understood to mean the spirit of God the Father,"[32] which Milton presumably thought incapable of death.

In the theological treatise Milton is dogmatic about the total death of man—body, soul, and spirit; on the death of Christ, he is insistent that the Son's body and soul died, but not absolutely certain about the death of the Son's spirit and divine nature. In the poem the dogmatism about the total death of man is placed in a context where it will be shown to be false, and the uncertainty about the totality of Christ's death is resolved into a definite qualification about the totality of His death. This qualification is expressed in a way that is at once succinct and prudently unspecific in the phrase "All that of me can die." And when seven books later Adam says "All of me then shall die," we recognize that the echo of the Son's phrase is meant to warn us that Adam is being incautiously dogmatic. This realization is confirmed a few lines later when Adam, approaching repentance, casts off the mortalism which had given false security against living death.

University of Liverpool

NOTES

[1]Quotations from Milton's poetry, and the Latin text of *De Doctrina Christiana* (hereafter abbreviated as *DDC*) are taken from *The Works of John Milton*, gen. ed. F. A. Patterson (18 vols, New York, 1931-1940). This edition will be cited as *CE* (Columbia edition). The English translation of *DDC* cited in the text is by John Carey, in Volume Six of *Complete Prose Works of John Milton*, gen. ed. D. M. Wolfe (6 vols to date, New Haven, 1953 ff). This edition will hereafter be cited as *Yale*.

[2]The discussion may be traced through the following publications: Denis Saurat, *Milton: Man and Thinker* (New York, 1925), pp. 310-322; Arthur Sewell, "Milton's *De Doctrina Christiana,*" *E&S*, 19 (1934), 49-50; G. Williamson, "Milton and the Mortalist Heresy," *SP*, 32 (1935), 553-579; Denis Saurat, "Two Notes on Milton," *RES*, 12 (1936), 323-324; W. A. Sewell and Denis Saurat, "Two Notes on Milton," *RES*, 15 (1939), 73-75, 78-80; Maurice Kelley, *This Great Argument: A Study of Milton's "De Doctrina Christiana" as a Gloss upon "Paradise Lost"* (Gloucester, Mass., 1941), pp. 31-32, 67, n. 230, and 153-155; G. N. Conklin, *Biblical Criticism and Heresy in Milton* (New York, 1949), pp. 75-85; N. H. Henry, "Milton and Hobbes: Mortalism and the Intermediate State," *SP*, 48 (1951), 234-249; C. A. Patrides, "*Paradise Lost* and the Mortalist Heresy," *N&Q*, 202 (1957), 250-251; idem, "Psychopannychism in Renaissance Europe," *SP*, 60 (1963), 227-229; idem, *Milton and the Christian Tradition* (Oxford, 1966), pp. 264-266; Virginia Mollenkott, "Milton's Mortalism: Treatise vs. Poetry," *Seventeenth-Century News*, 26 (1968), 51-52; Maurice Kelley, "Thnetopsychism," in *Yale*, VI, 91-95; see also Kelley's notes in *Yale*, VI, 405, n. 15 and 408, n. 20. For an admirable general study of English mortalism see N. T. Burns, *Christian Mortalism from Tyndale to Milton* (Cambridge, Mass., 1972).

[3]*DDC* I.13; *Yale*, VI, 400; *CE*. XV, 218.

[4]For details of the distinctions and Milton's reservations about them see *DDC* I.7; *Yale*, VI, 318-319; *CE*, XV, 40-42. The disparagement of the writings of the heathen authors on the soul is echoed by Milton's Christ in *Paradise Regain'd*. IV. 313.

[5]*DDC* I.13; *Yale*, VI, 401-403; *CE*. XV, 218-226.

[6]*DDC* I.13; *Yale*, VI, 339-400, 403; *CE*, XV, 214-218, 226.

[7]*DDC* I.13; *Yale*, VI, 403-404; *CE*, XV, 226-228.

[8]*DDC* I.13; *Yale*, VI, 404-414; *CE*, XV, 228-250.

[9]*DDC* I.13; *Yale*, VI, 404; *CE*, XV, 226, Milton's argument is set out in detail in *DDC* I.7; *Yale*, VI, 318-319; *CE*, XV, 40-42.

[10]*DDC* I.16; *Yale*, VI, 452; *CE*, XV, 340. Although Milton is referring back to his earlier discussion in *DDC* I.13, in that chapter he talks about the death of the soul rather than the sleep of the soul, despite the fact that he quotes Scriptures in which the key word is "sleep" and suggests that Lazarus was "asleep" in death *(DDC* I.13; *Yale*, VI, 405-406; *CE*, XV, 232-234).

[11]*DDC* I.13; *Yale*, VI, 413; *CE*, XV, 246. More fully, *DDC* I.14; *Yale*, VI, 426; *CE*, XV, 276.

[12]*DDC* I.13; *Yale*, VI, 405; *CE*, XV, 230.

[13]*DDC* I.14; *Yale*, VI, 426; *CE*, XV, 276, and *DDC* I.16; *Yale*, VI, 439; *CE*. XV, 306.

[14]*DDC* I.7; *Yale*, VI, 324; *CE*, XV, 52. The human soul, on the other hand, "is generated by the parents in the course of nature" *(DDC* I.7; *Yale*, VI, 319; *CE*, XV, 42).

[15]On Christ's divine nature see *DDC* I.5; *Yale*, VI, 203-280; *CE*, XIV, 176-356. On man not having a divine nature see *DDC* I.7; *Yale*, VI, 317; *CE*, XV, 38.

[16]*DDC* I.16; *Yale*, VI, 440; *CE*, XV, 308.

[17]*DDC* I.13; *Yale*, VI, 408; *CE*, XV, 238.

[18]*DDC* I.13; *Yale*, VI, 401; *CE*, XV, 218.

[19]*DDC* I.7; *Yale*, VI, 321; *CE*, XV, 46.

[20]*DDC* I.13; *Yale*, VI, 401; *CE*, XV, 218.

[21]*DDC* I.7; *Yale*, VI, 318; *CE*, XV, 40.

[22]*DDC* I.7; *Yale*, VI, 317; *CE*, XV, 38. The distinction is a fine one, for Milton later notes that the soul was "breathed from the mouth of God" *(DDC* I.7; *Yale*, VI, 323; *CE*, XV, 48).

[23]*DDC* I.13; *Yale*, VI, 400; *CE*, XV, 218.

[24]Henry, Patrides (1957 and 1966), and Mollenkott support the idea that the treatise and the poem conflict on this point, while Kelley *(Yale*, VI, 408, n. 20) dissents from the view of these critics.

[25]Kelley (1941), p. 32, disagrees, arguing that "the passage says merely this: though now I yield to death and am his due, all of me that can die (that is, body, soul, and spirit), yet when I have paid . . .," and that Milton's mortalism is "tersely presented" in these lines. In Alastair Fowler's edition of *Milton: Paradise*

Lost (London, 1971), Fowler acknowledges Kelley's interpretation, but argues that "the doctrine could only be extracted from the present passage by force" (pp. 156-157, in the note on Book III lines 245-249).

[26]Kelley (*Yale*, VI, 408, n. 20) suggests that Christ's soul being consigned to the grave refutes the idea that Adam's speech does not reflect Milton's mortalism.

[27]See the passages documented by notes 11, 13, and 15 above.

[28]See the passages documented by n. 16 above.

[29]See *DDC* I.16; *Yale*, VI, 493; *CE*, XV, 306, and the passage documented by n. 12 above.

[30]*DDC* I.16; *Yale*, VI, 440; *CE*, XV, 308.

[31]*DDC* I.16; *Yale*, VI, 439; *CE*, XV, 306.

[32]*DDC* I.16; *Yale*, VI, 440; *CE*, XV, 308.

THE FALLACY OF THE FALL IN *PARADISE LOST*

By Millicent Bell

THE OLD QUESTION: Why did Milton's Adam and Eve disobey the Divine Commandment? continues to provoke conflicting answers and consequently diverse accounts of the meaning of *Paradise Lost*. That Milton's epic is, like *King Lear*, or *Faust*, or *Moby Dick*, a work able to sustain many seemingly-contrary interpretations—that in fact it contains them all to some degree—is clear to anyone who will reread the poem at intervals, following the lead first of one and then another critical guide. But this richness of implication has obscured the real logical handicap assumed by anyone who attempts to find the ultimate origins of the narrative action in what is familiar to us as occasion or motivation—in a word, in *cause*.

Inherent in Milton's ancient material is the paradox of the essential *causelessness* of the Fall. The many-times-retold story presents us with: *one*—the myth of unfallen perfection, and *two*—a set of standard observations concerning the human nature visible in Adam and Eve after their sin. The transition between Man and Woman uncorrupt and mankind corrupted is simply to be accepted as having happened. Yet the mind cannot accept the fact that perfection was capable of corruption without denying the absoluteness of perfection. In terms of the story, we cannot imagine any reason why Adam and Eve should, in the face of repeated warning, have violated God's injunction, not, that is, if we conceive the father and mother of the race to have been unfallen before the Fall. For all possible temptations—those traditionally offered and any we might add—appeal to impulses characteristic of *fallen* mankind. Between perfection and imperfection, the unimaginable and the familiar, the fable constructs a bridge. This bridge is the temptation, an event which could not understandably occur before the Fall, an event which must actually be explained by motivations characteristic of men as we find them now—ambition, curiosity, vanity, gluttony, or lust. It is a bridge built of the material of fallen human nature, that is, from the substance of only one bank of the chasm, the one nearer us. From the farther bank, the anterior condition of unfallen perfection, the bridge takes nothing at all. For there is nothing in the Paradisal state that can furnish cause for Man's lapse from perfection. What is commonly identified as cause is actually result.

This fundamental difficulty in the story "of man's first disobedience" was not troubling to Milton as it may be to us, for Milton took the account in Genesis as received truth. In the unquestionable record of the Holy Spirit we are told that the first of humankind were tempted. The

Fall is "given." Consequently to Milton it was obvious that tempted they were; moreover, one had only to look upon the world about one to observe the effects of their surrender. I do not think that Milton seriously tried to find an exact name for the initiating defection other than "disobedience." This word is the oftenest repeated of all characterizations of the Fall in *Paradise Lost*, but its sense, as we shall later see, is equivalent to "disorder"; it stands for all those unbalances in the universe and the soul which the Fall itself created. "Disobedience" is merely a description of what has happened, for after all it is no explanation that our Grandparents disobeyed because they were disobedient. Unavoidably, Milton's picture of the original sin which he calls "disobedience" is a complex of its results made to appear as causes, since if Adam and Eve were to be thought of as motivated in the way we are familiar with motivation, the causes of their Fall would have to be sought among the familiar frailties of their descendants. Milton was not concerned—as modern critics have obsessively been—to identify a *prime* cause. The causes of the Fall were, for him, a backward reflection of the complex results, as if to say—out of undisciplined curiosity, or overreaching aspiration, or intemperate will, or inordinate appetite Man fell to a condition in which those propensities were natural to him.

A paradox? A confusion of cause with result. But Milton would not have concerned himself about scientific dissection of our most reliable knowledge about the beginning of things. What he did do is the consummate triumph of an art just in that degree unconscious of itself, founded on the absolute conviction that what we are told is true, that perfection is susceptible of imperfection. The logical flaw in the fable—as it appears to a different order of mind—never presented itself to him. But as an artist he must have felt two things. First, that it would be impossible to present the Fall as beginning only at that awful moment when Eve did eat and Nature groaned. In one way or another it was necessary to create an Eve liable to temptation, and so to remove the threshold of her transition to sin to some indefinite moment in the past. It was necessary to infect prelapsarian Eden with the symptoms of fallen Nature. Secondly he must have conceived that the effects of the Act of Disobedience were so closely consequent upon the deed itself as to be indistinguishable from it; the disorders that immediately manifested themselves in the erring pair could only be seen as an exaggeration of susceptibilities by which they were tempted. And so he constructed an account of the Fall which subtly obscured any sharp division in the drama, any "before" and "after."

Instead of asking what caused the Fall, Milton was preoccupied, I think, in employing the somewhat intractable legend to characterize the state of fallen Man—Man as he knew him. Paul Elmer More has suggested that the theme of Milton's poem is the lost Paradise,[1] but it may be objected that Milton's cast of mind was the reverse of nostalgic; his interests would be directed, not towards an irrecoverable past, but towards the present condition of humankind. Now Biblical scholars recognize that the Genesis story itself is not an attempt to arrive at a "first cause" for sin, but an attempt to explain the conjunction of facts in the human situation. We are presented in experience with Man, knowing beyond the rest of Creation, yet bound to toil, and to anguish in child-bearing, cruel to his own kind like no other species, wasteful of his energies, and ashamed of his nakedness. For the first item, in which Man was more fortunate than any other creature, he would appear to have paid well; the price of the knowledge which lifts him above the other animals is the surrender of the freedom and innocence of some imagined past in which he was at one with the rest of Nature. I am not suggesting that Milton approached the myth in just these terms. But in expanding the terse account in Genesis to epic proportions he was bound to come across the difficulty inherent in the story which is, as I have said, that it does not deal with causes at all. What it does do is contemplate the compound nature of experience, and imply that somehow good had been paid for by bad, knowledge by the loss of Eden's enormous bliss. And we shall discover that this primitive idea is not unlike the sophisticated philosophic monism which governs *Paradise Lost*. We see this not merely in the *felix culpa* itself, which balances the Redemption against the Fall, but in every turn of the action in Heaven, Earth, and Hell, in which good is converted out of evil.

That Man had once been without sin, then, Milton of course believed, but he did not attempt to explain the endorsed account of the Biblical narrative—in this sense his interpretation is as limited as that of the first seven sentences of the Third Chapter of Genesis in which the fable is told entire. What he did was to analyze, out of an impulse not dissimilar to that which stirred the first teller of the story, perhaps, the human condition as found. He studied the operation of the manifest disorders which he saw in men and nations in the seventeenth century, determined to prove, despite all the confusion life presents, that the universe is a seamless unity.

If we reconcile ourselves to the fact that from the very start Milton is presenting us with the effects of temptation rather than with causes we are better prepared, I feel, to profit by the full richness·of his analysis. What he wanted to understand—what it was a bitter personal necessity

---

[1] "The Theme of Paradise Lost," *Shelburne Essays*, 4th Ser. (New York, 1906).

for him to understand—was the fallen state itself. It was his state, and it is our own.

The question of the cause of Man's Fall did not seriously trouble Milton's commentators until they began to take the Bible account less literally than he. To Addison the matter was self-evident: "The great moral which reigns in Milton," he said, "is the most universal and most useful than can be imagined, that obedience to the will of God makes men happy and that disobedience makes them miserable" (*Spectator*, No. 369). Among contemporary critics, on the other hand, only C. S. Lewis is enough of a Biblical literalist to find disobedience a sufficiently satisfactory definition of what takes place in Milton's Eden. Other commentators have chased what seems to me to be, actually, a sort of marsh-fire—identifying the cause of the Fall with the triumph of unreason over temperance (Greenlaw), of sensuality over asceticism (Hanford), of the sense of "injured merit" over self-abnegation (Williams), or of mental levity over self-knowledge (Tillyard),[2] to name four modern writers whose contributions to Milton criticism have been notable. As I have been suggesting, Milton's method does not permit us to isolate a single cause, for all these "causes" are really consequences of the fallen character.

Of late there has been some tendency to admit that the Fall, as Milton really depicts it, is a complex affair not to be compassed by any one-factor explanation. Of the critics named above, Tillyard has recently confessed (*Studies in Milton*, London, 1951) that in his earlier work he may have overstressed a single motive, and that Milton made use as well of some of the traditional explanations of the primal sin, Eve's desire to get ahead and her defective understanding, and Adam's uxoriousness, for example. Tillyard has seen the necessity for a closer scrutiny of *all* stages of the narrative for the multiple temptations to which Adam and Eve are subjected. In the close reading which underlies his present account, he has, of course, been preceded by a number of American scholars, notably Bush and Diekhoff.[3] These writers would probably agree with his observation that the "crisis" of the poem is not, after all, confined to those culminating lines in the Ninth Book which Raleigh singled out as the "main event" (*Milton*, London, 1900, p. 77), when Eve's "rash hand

---

[2] C. S. Lewis, *A Preface to Paradise Lost* (London, 1942); Edwin Greenlaw, "A Better Teacher than Aquinas," *SP*, xiv (1917), 196–217; James Holly Hanford, "The Temptation Motive in Milton," *SP*, xv (1918), 176–194; Charles Williams, introd. *The English Poems of Milton* (London, 1940); E. M. W. Tillyard, *Milton* (London, 1930).

[3] Douglas Bush, *Paradise Lost in Our Time* (New York, 1945); John S. Diekhoff, *Milton's Paradise Lost* (New York, 1946).

in evil hour / Forth reaching to the Fruit, she pluck't, she eat" (IX.780–784).[4] In the original story the Fall does not begin until this moment, and it comes to a stop when Adam, undeterred by fuller knowledge of what he is about to do, also bites into the forbidden apple. But in the poem, the transition from innocence to sin can be felt very early in the narrative—most strikingly in Book IV, where the rehearsal of the temptation presented in Eve's dream already moves her across the border this side of innocence, and in Book VIII, where Adam in conversation with Raphael reveals that thus early Eve's influence over his judgment is no longer compatible with a state of innocence. "The' Fall, then," Tillyard concludes, "must be extended back in time; it has no plain and sensational beginning; and the actual eating of the apple becomes no more than an emphatic stage in the process already begun, the stage when the darker and stormier passions make their entry into the human heart" (*Studies in Milton*, p. 13). The crisis of the Fall must be extended forward also, for the progress in sin of Eve and Adam is intensified and continued after they eat of the tree, and disaster and disorder widen out of the bounds of Paradise to include, in Book X, the entire created universe. Only with the penitence and reconciliation of Adam and Eve does the process stop, and, says Tillyard, the poem comes to its true climax.

Carried to its logical conclusions such a rereading accomplishes far more than anyone has claimed for it. As I shall show, the indications of Adam and Eve's common humanity are distributed pervasively throughout the entire narrative; we can find evidence of their susceptibility to corruption almost from our earliest encounter with them. There is, in effect, no longer a Fall as the Bible plot presents it—there is, possibly, no longer a Fall at all. And as a consequence, there is no possibility of discerning cause—from the very first we are after the Fall; we are dealing with results and not preliminaries. Of these diverse effects no one is necessarily earlier than the rest.

One does less than justice to Milton's plan if one considers the early evidences of Adam's and of Eve's frailty to be merely artistic foreshadowing. Tillyard comments that Milton "resorts to some faking; perfectly legitimate in a poem, but faking nevertheless; he anticipates the Fall by attributing to Eve and Adam feelings which though nominally felt in the state of innocence are not compatible with it" (*Studies in Milton*, pp. 10–11). But the result of these effects is more serious than this, I propose. By blurring the transition from innocence to experience as he does, Milton changes the significance of his plot entirely. What is called "faking" is really the very essence of the poem's structure, for it establishes a

---

[4] All quotations from *P.L.* follow the text of the poem edited by Merritt Y. Hughes (New York, 1935).

continually active tension between the fable, with its donnée of Man's inconceivable perfection, and Milton's personal knowledge of the human quality which is in essence imperfection. The real turn of the inner plot of *Paradise Lost* does come upon the occasion Tillyard discerns. It is, unlike the Fall, an occasion perfectly understandable to us, and hence motivated, dramatic. It is a change from worse to better, the prosperous outcome which Dryden missed,[5] the birth of the redemptive impulse in man as we know him. Up to this point the graph of the story is a long descent, an aftermath to a change—if there was one—inscrutably in the past.

Since 1941, when Maurice Kelley established the dating of the *De Doctrina Christiana*, we have been able to assume that the dogmas set forth in the treatise are substantially those Milton held when writing *Paradise Lost*. And in the *De Doctrina* we find confirmation of our belief that Milton saw in the Fall no single temptation, but the loosening of Man's nature to include all varieties of corruption:

If the circumstances of this crime are duly considered, it will be acknowledged to have been a most heinous offence, and a transgression of the whole law. For what sin can be named, which was not included in this one act? It comprehended at once distrust in the divine veracity, and a proportionate credulity in the assurances of Satan; unbelief; ingratitude; disobedience; gluttony; in the man excessive uxoriousness, in the woman a want of proper regard for her husband, in both an insensibility to the welfare of their offspring, and that offspring the whole human race; parricide, theft, invasion of the rights of others, sacrilege, deceit, presumption in aspiring to divine attributes, fraud in the means employed to attain the object, pride and arrogance.[6]

For each entry in the terrifying catalogue given in the treatise, the poem, as Kelley points out,[7] furnishes illustration. No simple formula defines Milton's view of the Fall, but the poet deliberately complicates the evidence of his narrative to indicate the manifold nature of Eve's and Adam's errors. Satan's speech of seduction in Book IX with its talk of the alluring odor and taste of the fruit, the smell of the fruit itself, Eve's eager appetite, and the very fact that the conversation takes place at lunch-time, all suggest that her temptation is one of "gluttony." Then the Serpent's assertion of his own growth of intellectual power, his assurance that for Eve, too, the taste of the apple will bring enlightenment

---

[5] "As for Mr. Milton, whom we all admire with so much justice, his subject is not that of an heroic poem, properly so called. His design is the losing of our happiness; his event is not prosperous, like that of all other epic works" (*Essay on Satire*, 1693).

[6] *De Doctrina Christiana* I, x, Columbia Univ. Press edition of Milton's works (New York, 1931-38), xv, 113.

[7] *This Great Argument* (Princeton, 1941), pp. 143–150.

and even divinity rather than the penalty of death—these are induce-
ments to "distrust in the divine veracity" and "presumption in aspiring
to divine attributes." Milton's description of Eve as "unwarie" and
"credulous," and her ready acceptance of the Serpent's account are illustrations of "credulity in the assurances of Satan." When Adam resolves
to share her fate he falls, of course, into the sin of "excessive uxoriousness,"
but in rationalizing his decision before he takes action he compounds
Eve's "presumption in aspiring to divine attributes," "unbelief," "arrogance," and "credulity in the assurances of Satan." It will be noticed
that even at the critical moment of actual capitulation to the Tempter,
Milton has studiously multiplied the appeals drawing Adam and Eve
to their destruction. We are dealing, it is obvious, with individuals capable not only of one kind of surrender to vice, but indeed, like the rest
of us, of surrender to many kinds.

We then are prompted to go back from this, the brink itself of their
collapse, to some point earlier in the narrative where the temptation
may better be said to begin. The debate of Adam and Eve and her departure to her gardening tasks alone (IX.205–385) is a significant preparation for the technical Fall. Eve's insistent urging of her whim is
patently Milton's "in the woman a want of proper regard for her husband." And Adam's uxoriousness was never more obvious than at this
critical point, as Eve herself afterwards reproaches him:

> why didst not thou the Head
> Command me absolutely not to go,
> Going into such danger as thou said'st?
> Too facile then thou didst not much gainsay,
> Nay didst permit, approve, and fair dismiss.
> Hadst thou been firm and fixt in thy dissent,
> Neither had I transgress'd, nor thou with mee. (IX.1155–61)

His laborious and mild dissuasion (IX.226–269) is a dull recital of principles she is as familiar with as he is. Provoked by the barbs beneath her
"sweet austere composure" and "accent sweet," he finally does go more
penetratingly into the dangers against which they must guard themselves (343–369), but it is really too late—Eve has managed to arouse
in herself a small head of willful steam. And Adam, at the very climax of
his most forceful argument, suddenly collapses—perhaps, though Milton doesn't tell us so, it is the look on her face which is responsible. Weakness rather than chivalry seems to produce his sudden yielding (370–
375).

Already, as their dispute illustrates, Eve and Adam are changed from
ideal prototypes. Eve's argument especially anticipates much of the
Serpent's most telling urgings, for like him she proposes that experience is

a necessary ingredient of virtue. "If what is evil / be real, why not known, since easier shunn'd?" the Serpent will say (IX.698-699), giving a sophistic twist to *Areopagitica*. But Eve has very nearly been there before him with "and what is Faith, Love, Virtue unassay'd / Alone, without exterior help sustained" (IX.335-336)? We cannot help feeling that, considering the hazards, Eve is already displaying a rather decadent appetite for trouble; Adam himself observes: "Seek not temptation then, which to avoid / Were better, and most likely if from mee / Thou sever not: Trial will come unsought" (IX.364-366).

So here too we must confess that we have arrived too late. The onset of temptation is past. And one must add that it is difficult to explain altogether Eve's sudden, unprecedented inclination for working away from her husband's side. Well may Adam later wonder at "that strange / Desire of wand'ring this unhappy Morn, / I know not whence possess'd thee" (IX.1135-37). Tradition did not dictate this episode to Milton; it was only necessary that he contrive that Eve meet the Serpent alone, and this might have happened quite innocently and accidentally. But as we read Milton's version it seems almost as though she *expected* to meet someone rather interesting in the shade of the fruit trees. Her use of the arts of persuasion seems quite accomplished for one so uncorrupt, almost a slighter instance of the Serpent's own superb proficiency in argument which overwhelms her in its turn. So she charges Adam with distrusting her, with the not altogether reliable indignation of a woman bent on getting her own way:

> His violence thou fear'st not being such,
> As wee, not capable of death or pain
> Can either not receive, or can repel.
> His fraud is then thy fear, which plain infers
> Thy equal fear that my firm Faith and Love
> Can by his fraud be shaken or seduc't;
> Thoughts, which how found they harbour in thy breast,
> Adam, misthought of her to thee so dear? (IX.282-289)

She has all the careful guile and gentle persistence of a woman planning to deceive her husband!

So our search for the borderline between innocence and corruption takes us still further back. In the case of Eve we go straight to the experience the Freudians would have directed us to all along, that curious anticipatory dream which she relates to her spouse in Book V. Now this preliminary temptation, which we observed being manipulated by Satan crouching at the ear of the sleeping Eve in Book IV, occurs nowhere in the traditional and literary versions of the story. Grant McColley explains that Milton may have wanted to make use of two accounts of the temptation—one saying that Adam fell on the day of his creation, the other putting his fall a week later.[8] But the deliberate artistry of Milton's design can hardly be the result of mere husbandry of materials.

In Book IV we are told just how Satan produced this dream in Eve, Zephon and Gabriel catching the Devil at his work and booting him spiritedly from the lady's bower. In Book V, however, we relive with Eve the amazing night in which a gentle male voice ("I thought it thine," she says to Adam) calls her into the moonlit woods and leads her to the "Tree of interdicted Knowledge." The handsome Angel (for so he seems) serenades first the Tree and then Eve herself. He endeavors to persuade her to taste the fruit of the Tree, urging the virtues of the knowledge it might impart to the eater and even suggesting boldly that she may henceforth become "among the Gods / Thyself a Goddess" (77–78).

In the seventeenth century such an episode would be taken as just what it is presented to be, the intrusion into the sleeping mind of an evil spirit, and we must restrain our modern proneness to suspect the sleeper of wish- or anxiety-phantasies, or the like. But even a contemporary reader would have felt the ominousness of the incident. Eve sleeps "with Tresses discompos'd, and glowing Cheek," and wakes in a state of intense excitement. Adam tells her soothingly that "evil into the mind of God or Man / May come and go, so unapprov'd and leave / No spot of blame behind" (v.117–119). But we cannot believe it, knowing already the outcome of the story. His speculations on the wandering action of the Fancy during the hours when sleep overcomes the Reason are wide of this particular mark. And he is not convincing when he says "Yet evil whence? In thee can harbour none, / Created pure" (99–100).

Was this the portal of temptation? There could hardly be any previous occasion, for Eve may at this point be only a few hours old. Yet already we suspect her receptive to the Tempter's choice flattery and to his adroit fanning of an ego that might respond to the impulse for self-advancement. And so we will take one look at the earliest Eve. Newborn she awakes by the side of a clear lake and looking down at its reflecting surface is pleased by her own delightful form. A voice leads her to Adam "fair indeed and tall, / Under a Platan, yet methought less fair, / Less winning soft, less amiably mild, / Than that smooth wat'ry image" (IV.478–480). Though she soon admits that "beauty is excell'd by manly grace / And wisdom, alone is truly fair," we have glimpsed a dainty vanity in "our general Mother" which the Serpent will put to use.

---

[8] *Paradise Lost* (Chicago, 1940), pp. 158 ff.

Adam's earlier history is still more significant than Eve's, however. Our first indication of danger comes in Book VIII when Raphael is forced to admonish his pupil against too intemperate a zest for useless knowledge. Adam has requested that Raphael help him to decide between the Copernican and the Ptolemaic versions of celestial motion, and brought upon his head an impatient reproof (VIII.167–176). Raphael's meaning is perfectly clear. He does not condemn knowledge, but he condemns a delusive craving of knowledge for its own sake (this thought is expressed even more strongly by Adam's other angelic instructor, Michael, in XII.575–587). He says that the end of knowledge is Man's happiness in what has been assigned him. And Adam seems to be "cleared of doubt," promptly repeating the lesson, like a good schoolboy (VIII.182–195). Yet part of Adam's speech at this point is curiously significant, for it expresses an instinct of waywardness which he finds implanted in his own nature:

> But apt the Mind or Fancy is to rove
> Uncheckt, and of her roving is no end;
> Till warn'd, or by experience taught, she learn
> That not to know at large of things remote
> From use, obscure and subtle, but to know
> That which before us lies in daily life
> Is the prime Wisdom; what is more is fume,
> Or emptiness, or fond impertinence   (VIII.187–195)

Fine words. But the lesson does not really take, as the outcome of the tale will show, the desire for knowledge of hidden matters being not the least notorious of the appetites flaring into expression at the Fall. And since the Fancy will not be disciplined by warning, it is only "by experience taught" that Adam is to apprehend "the prime Wisdom." His title to perfection, meanwhile, is none too clear.

Adam, tactfully changing the subject after this rough passage, proceeds to relate his own brief remembrances of his creation, his first conversations with his Creator, and the interesting instructions received concerning a particular tree in his Paradisal home. He describes the creation of Eve and his delight in her. And then he begins to talk in a vein that causes the angel to pull him up still more sharply than before. Adam speaks of a "commotion strange" awakened by the beauty of Eve, a disturbance different from that caused by the taste, smell, or sight of herbs and flowers which "works in the mind no change / Nor vehement desire." He wonders if this again does not indicate some weakness in him, whether Nature failed in him, leaving him unable to stand "against the charm of Beauty's powerful glance," or whether Eve has been endowed with too much of outward and too little of inward quality (VIII. 533–539). For he confesses

All higher Wisdom in her presence falls
Degraded, Wisdom in discourse with her
Loses discount'nanct and like folly shows;
Authority and Reason on her wait,
As one intended first, not after made
Occasionally. (VIII.551–556)

Quickly and sternly, "with contracted brow," Raphael answers in an elaborate speech which reviews prophetically the complex hazard which Adam will encounter and succumb to (VIII.561–594). A. J. A. Waldock has protested that Raphael is here being "unpleasant" and "untruthful," for Adam in his reply (VIII.596 ff.) seems to indicate that he knows wherein true love consists.[9] But Adam *has* given occasion for Raphael's reproaches; the poetry of Adam's defense cannot vitiate the angel's judgment. Milton has pitched against one another the strong virtue of human love and the greater virtue of *l'amor che move il sole e l'altre stelle.* But in the scale of Raphael's vision, which represents Milton's own deepest convictions concerning the ultimate proportions of things, Adam's love is sinful. It causes him to lose the sense of what is preeminent in importance ("attributing overmuch to things / Less excellent"); it makes him admire surface rather than essence ("what transports thee so, / An outside?"); it leads him to subject himself to the woman when he should rule her; it leagues him with the beasts in sensuality and causes him to subordinate reason to passion; in sum, it makes of love, which might be a ladder by which Man can ascend the scale of perfection, a pitfall through which he may fall to sin. Looking back at the speech which aroused Raphael's condemnation we see its perversity: it represents the mind of fallen Man. Adam's worship of Eve would have seemed idolatrous to Augustine, as it does to Milton.

In the Argument to Book v, Milton tells us that Raphael has been sent to visit Adam and "admonish him of his obedience, of his free estate, of his enemy near at hand" in order "to render Man inexcusable." It might seem that the lectures with which Book VIII ends are simply designed as warnings. But it cannot be overlooked that the angelic instructor is *provoked* to them, contracting his brow at words that, read carefully, are plain evidences of Adam's perilous state of mind. Even more than in the case of Eve are we compelled to suppose that unfallen Man was congenitally Man as we know him, subject to temptations and excesses, for there has been no Satan at Adam's ear to instill poisonous thoughts. And already human nature is shown in its full complexity of motivation—the lust of forbidden knowledge, uxoriousness, the subordination of Reason to passion, and so forth, are ready for their operation at the Fall.

[9] *Paradise Lost and Its Critics* (Cambridge, 1947), p. 43.

As Williams and Hughes have illustrated,[10] the description of the pristine perfection of Adam and Eve was a favorite exercise of the Renaissance commentators on Genesis. Hexameral tradition declared that Adam was created possessed of all knowledge, or at least of all needful knowledge. Joseph Glanvill portrayed the soul of "this medall of God," as "not clogged by the inactivity of its masse, as ours; nor hindered in its actings, by the distemperature of indisposed organs. Passions kept their place, as servants of the higher powers, and durst not arrogate the Throne, as now: no countermands came hence, to repeal the decretals of the Regal faculties; that *Batrachomyomachia* of one passion against another, and both against reason, was yet unborn" (Hughes, *P.L.*, p. xxxiv). Though Milton would have agreed that Adam's power and knowledge were almost divine,[11] he nevertheless exhibits to us an Adam who in contrast with Glanvill's is, as Hughes says, "a very human sort of person" (p. xxxv). And in this he was supported by another strain in the traditional thinking of his time which justified God in laying Man open to the temptation because it was a demonstration to Man of his own weakness and dependence upon divine grace. Even the unfallen soul was not, to such thinkers, the self-regulating mechanism Glanvill described; hence the need of the trial. "God is said to try man," wrote the seventeenth-century theologian David Pareus, "not that he may discover what he does not know (he knows even our inmost thoughts), but that we may discover our weakness, which we do not know" (*The Common Expositor*, p. 113).

Is it correct then to say, as does Dickhoff, that this Adam and this Eve "needed no purification?"[12] As the distinction between them and ourselves dissolves in Milton's narrative, it becomes possible to see that their situation is like our situation. As it is true that "we bring not innocence into the world, we bring impurity much rather: that which purifies is triall, and triall is by what is contrary" (*Areopagitica*, IV, 311), Adam also had the obligation to learn self-discipline, if not by accepting instruction, then by painful experience. That human nature is subject to temptation of all kinds does not lessen our responsibility to strive for virtue, and the vulnerability of Adam and Eve likewise did not diminish their duty or their Free Will. Adam's plea that he is unable to withstand Eve's charm cannot be accepted, as Milton has Raphael indignantly indicate. Peter Martyr, whose commentary on Genesis was published in 1579, had declared that a nature incapable of sin would have been unsuit-

---

[10] Arnold Williams, *The Common Expositor* (Chapel Hill, 1948), pp. 80–82; Merritt Y. Hughes, ed. *Paradise Lost*, Introd. pp. xxxiv–xxxv.

[11] Cf. *De Doctrina Christiana* I, vii (*Works*, XV).

[12] *Milton's Paradise Lost*, p. 46.

able to a rational creature. The essence of being a creature is weakness. The essence of being rational is free choice. Hence Man must be able to fall. He can be confirmed in grace only after the opportunity to sin has been met (*The Common Expositor*, p. 113). Given judgment as well as passion, Free Will as well as openness to temptation, Man must do more than passively accept God's gifts. He must complete himself by action, by choice. The opening of Raphael's final speech of advice in Book VIII is significantly worded: "Accuse not Nature, she hath done her part; / Do thou but thine."

It is such an Adam and it is such an Eve who come to their fatal moment of trial beneath the forbidden Tree of the knowledge of Good and Evil. There, it is not the onset of sin we witness, so much as it is the be-ginning of self-discovery by creatures essentially human, which is to say, imperfect in a hundred ways, moved by the complex springs of impulse listed in the *De Doctrina Christiana*. And it seems to be Milton's thought that only by becoming conscious of these qualities does Man have hope of attaining that inner harmony and the unity with the cosmic purpose which is his true Paradise.

And so what of the apple? The old story implied that it was a magical fruit which brought the eater new sorts of knowledge, but in Milton's poem this is only Satan's declaration—and not even his opinion. We recall that the hymn to the Tree which he inserts into Eve's dream (v. 58–73) speaks of the power of the fruit to "make Gods of Men," and asks in humanist indignation "O fair Plant . . . Deigns none to ease thy load and taste thy sweet, / Nor god, nor Man; is Knowledge so de-spis'd?" Upon this theme Satan expands more fully in the actual tempta-tion, saluting the Tree: "O Sacred, Wise, and Wisdom-giving Plant, / Mother of Science" (IX.679–680). To Eve he says:

> Why then was this forbid? Why but to awe,
> Why but to keep ye low and ignorant,
> His worshippers; he knows that in the day
> Ye eat thereof, your Eyes that seem so clear,
> Yet are but dim, shall perfetly be then
> Op'n'd and clear'd, and ye shall be as Gods,
> Knowing both Good and Evil as they know. (IX.703–709)

But obviously, if the tree could really make Gods of the violators, Satan, their enemy, would not be so ready to act the part of Prometheus. His grudge is based on the fact that the newly-created pair have already been exalted to favored status with the promise of further advancement, and he rightly suspects that he can accomplish their ruin by exploiting' the ambiguity in the Tree's title. It will be cause for a Satanic cackle that Man "by fraud I have seduc'd / From his Creator, and the more to increase / Your wonder, with an Apple" (x.485–487).

The interpretation of the apple which Satan offers Eve has misled many readers of *Paradise Lost*, even Walter Raleigh.[13] But Satan's hypocrisy had already taken in Uriel. Significantly, it is as the idealist searching for the truth, a youthful angelic seeker after knowledge, that Satan poses in order to outwit the sharpest-sighted of the angels (iii.662 ff.). Satan's actual attitude seems, on the other hand, to have been shared by Voltaire who remarked in the *Essai sur la poésie épique* that the French are inclined to laugh when told that England has an epic in which Satan struggles against God, and a serpent persuades a woman to eat an apple (*Œuvres*, Paris, 1757, i, 372).

Neither Satan's pretended nor his sincere interpretation of the apple is Milton's. The apple did not instruct Adam and Eve in astronomy, but on the other hand it is not a Divine hoax either. Adam and Eve had nothing new to learn from the mysterious fruit except the nature of their own hearts. And this they learned from *themselves*, from the act of fulfilling their own desires to the final degree. As I have tried to show, they come to the occasion mature in the possession of every passion, yet ignorant of their own natures. In developing self-consciousness they do become as one of the Gods, but, as their ironic Creator observes, only because they have experienced "Good lost and Evil got" (xi.87). It is for this reason that their first impulse upon realizing what has happened to them is to be ashamed, to cover their nakedness. Their self-consciousness has been purchased by the fulfillment in action of what has hitherto lain hidden in the mind.

This is illustrated by the course of their sensations during and immediately after they eat the fruit. Eve, "jocund and boon," gluttonously stuffs herself with the delicious apple at the same time that her thoughts insatiately race towards the idea of Godhead (ix.785–793). She then falls to the sin of idolatry, worshipping the tree (795–809). Fatuously she imagines that she may even be unobserved by Omniscience (811–816). Her credulity is followed by the consequences of "a want of proper regard for her husband," for she considers exploiting her discovery to become Adam's equal, even his superior (817–825), and finally, having remembered the penalty of death which may still ensue, and the even more wrenching possibility that Adam may live to enjoy another Eve, she resolves that he must share her fate, whether "bliss or woe" (826–831). This last decision, as Lewis rightly observes, is properly titled—Murder (*Preface to Paradise Lost*, p. 121).

---

[13] "Satan unavoidably reminds us of Prometheus, and although there are essential differences, we are not made to feel them essential" (*Milton*, p. 134).

Making a "low reverence" to her new idol, she leaves the Tree. Her first words to Adam are hypocritical. She declares that she has missed him, though it is obvious that she has been having the time of her young life. Then she tells him what she has done at the Serpent's prompting— gained hold of Godhead "which for thee / Chiefly I sought, without thee can despise"—a conscious deceit, as we know from the preceding passage.

Adam's resolution to follow her into Sin is taken in a moment. Through human love, not lust, he falls into all the dangers of which Raphael warned him.

> O fairest of Creation, last and best
> Of all God's Works, Creature in whom excell'd
> Whatever can to sight or thought be form'd,
> Holy, divine, good, amiable, or sweet! (IX.896–899)

he begins. We cannot help but find his words affecting, for we recognize in them the magic of the entire Western tradition of mundane love with its persistent identification of the Woman and the Goddess. But to the Puritan Milton nothing could be more obvious than the impiety implied by Adam's epithets. And by his worship Adam subjects himself to the creature he should rule, for he, not she, is "the fairest of Creation." His poignant and unforgettable declaration (908–916) that he will share her fate is posed in awful tension against the judgment Milton has prepared us to make. Certainly there is conflict in our reaction. But this is the conflict which Milton has been making poetic use of throughout the work —the conflict between our fallen human values—the only ones we can prove upon our pulses—and an ultimate measure of perfection represented by the myth of Paradise.

Immediately Adam proceeds to demonstrate that as he is a man, nothing human is alien to him. Despite the fact that it is "against his better knowledge, not deceiv'd / But fondly overcome with Female charm" (998–999) that he joins Eve in sin, he sets about infecting himself with credulity in the assurances of Satan and distrust in the Divine veracity. Perhaps the Serpent actually told the truth about the marvellous efficacy of the fruit (928–937); perhaps, in any case, God may not keep His word concerning the penalty (938–951). Then he eats, and drunken with the taste of the fruit itself he descends to wisecracks: "If such pleasure be / In things to us forbidden, it might be wish'd, / For this one Tree had been forbidden ten" (1024–26). And love becomes lust.

Upon the soiling the sexual act follows depression, shame, and inward turmoil. "For Understanding rul'd not, and the Will / Heard not her lore, both in subjection now / To sensual Appetite, who from beneath / Usurping over sovran Reason claim's Superior sway" (1127–30). With the sound of their pitiable and unmistakably human quarreling, the Ninth book finally closes.

We may now consider whether this Fall has been a loss, or whether it has indeed been fortunate, the result of a *felix culpa*. The bare story makes no mystery of it. It was infinite disaster. But if, as I have been contending all along, the Fall is only the climax of self-realization reached by human-kind already fallen, then it was not only inevitable, but necessary. Once the sinfulness of Adam and Eve is established, it is only along this road followed to its bitter terminus that they may pass to redemption. And this redemption is not merely release from sin, but the acquired moral ability which enables Man to vanquish Evil.

Adam and Eve's deficiency had been that they were insufficiently aware of their own qualities, repeat though they might the academic lessons concerning the relation of the Will, and Reason, and Passion. What they lacked was the inner regulator of conscience, that agency of Right Reason which instructs the soul concerning the majestic scheme of order ruling Man and Nature. Their redemption involves the awareness that for them virtue can never be instinctive. Like the bearing of children or the tilling of the ground, virtue must henceforth be the fruit of pain and vigil.

Milton makes mention of another possibility. God may once have planned that Man might ascend to a higher level of consciousness not through a Fall and a redemption but by a ripening of unfallen powers. In his little after-dinner chat with Adam, Raphael explains that even angels eat, for all of nature is linked by a Divine chain to its source in infinite perfection, and the lower sustains the higher (v.469 ff.). He hopefully remarks that the time may come when men will eat the more ethereal diet of angels and their bodies become entirely spiritual so that they will be able to fly up to Heaven, "If ye be found obedient" (v.493–503). Later we learn from Raphael that God had declared his intention of creating Man with this plan in mind, in order that the new race will come in time to take the place vacated in Heaven by Satan's followers,

> till by degrees of merit rais'd
> They open to themselves at length the way
> Up hither, under long obedience tri'd,
> One Kingdom, Joy and Union without end.   (vi.157–161)

This, the original plan, suggests that even "unfallen" Man was not really perfect. A process of progressive improvement would have been necessary for him if he had escaped the particular experience which caused his expulsion from Eden. But it is obvious that Milton could not imagine Man achieving such improvement without the harsh education of error and suffering. He must be worse ere he can be better.

It is plain that Adam and Eve misunderstand the plan completely. It will be recalled that Raphael told Adam that true love is the "scale by which to heav'nly Love thou may'st ascend" (VIII.591–592), but in Adam's heart is no such ladder. He simply does not understand the principle involved in this proposal for his gradual promotion. And it is this misunderstanding that assists the Serpent so effectively. Adam notes that the Serpent gained

> Higher degree of Life, inducement strong
> To us, as likely tasting to attaine
> Proportional ascent which cannot be
> But to be God, or Angels Demi-Gods. (IX.934–937)

And Eve is ready to accept the suggestion of the Serpent that a few rungs may easily be skipped by a bold climber:

> And what are Gods that Man may not become
> As they, participating God-like food?
> The Gods are first, and that advantage use
> On our belief, that all from them proceeds;
> I question it, for this fair Earth I see,
> Warmed by the Sun, producing every kind,
> Them nothing: (IX.716–722)

Adam and Eve do not sin simply because they aspire above their limitations—Milton could not imagine a God who would curse the yearning for greater wisdom and goodness. But they had to learn how to make this upward progress. They did not know the terrible irony of that boast by the Serpent who is Satan in disguise that he "'life more perfet [had] attained than Fate / Meant mee, by vent'ring higher than my Lot" (IX.689–690).

In their aspiring they show that they do not know themselves, for they cannot establish the checks and balances of order in their souls which God has established in the universe. The principle involved in that order is represented, of course, by the word "obedience," which is the announced theme of the poem. Just as Man was to be elevated *up* the scale of being by means of obedience, the fallen angels had suffered degradation *down* the scale, as Mammon observes in Book II (275 ff.). By failing to obey, Adam and Eve themselves pass downward in the scale of faculties, lowering Reason beneath Will and Passion, transmuting love to the lower form of lust.

Raleigh called Milton's God a "whimsical tyrant" for demanding assent to an incomprehensible interdict, the taboo of the apple. The command was provoking, tempting violation rather than inducing compliance because it was laid upon Man with no reasons given. But as Adam states,

> of this Tree we may not taste nor touch;
> God so commanded, and left that command
> Sole Daughter of his voice; the rest, we live
> Law to ourselves, our Reason is our Law.   (ix.651–654)

As a Puritan Milton believed that it was necessary finally to reach God by an accession of confidence which Reason knoweth not. The prohibition, to be a test of faith, *had* to be incomprehensible, for it represented all those aspects of life which demand our trust in God, whatever human logic declares. In refusing this assent, Adam and Eve displayed unreadiness to accept God's ordered scheme as the ultimate support of their behavior. Setting aside that "easy, sole command" (vii.46), "this one, this easy charge" (iv.421), "the sole command, / Sole pledge of his obedience" (iii.93), Man violates the whole structure of the created order: "Man disobeying, disloyal breaks his fealty and sins / Against the high supremacy of Heav'n" (iii.203).

Obedience is freedom, Milton says repeatedly in *Paradise Lost.* This is because it depends upon one's consciousness of one's place in the scheme of things. Unconsciousness is bondage, and unconsciousness is the condition of Adam and Eve until instructed by their own experience of disaster. It is not surprising that when Adam and Eve sin the universal order groans (ix.782–784, 1000–03) and even Satan's rebellion is represented as having brought pain and disorder into Nature (vi.267–278). Ignorant of order in the human microcosm—of the correct status of the faculties in their fealty to Right Reason—Adam and Eve defy the entire ordained order of things. Naturally Adam forgets that he is the "Head" and Deity asks him afterward, "Was shee thy God . . . " (x.145)? Naturally Eve cherishes her little rebellious plot against both husband and Deity.

So God employed an alternate plan for Man's elevation. There has been much discussion of those lines in the Twelfth Book in which Michael suggests to Adam the possibility that the Second Coming shall make of Earth a happier Paradise than Eden ever was—to some this has seemed a paradox, for has not the purpose of all the preceding thousands of lines been to demonstrate the terrible consequences of the lapse from primal perfection? Adam himself stands amazedly in doubt when he wonders "whether I should repent me now of sin / By me done or occasioned, or rejoice / Much more that much more good thereof shall spring" (xii.474–476). But if it be granted that the Fall never takes place before us at all, but that what Milton has shown us throughout the action is *fallen* Man, then Adam's case has never been other than our case, and the Redemption is his only real hope, as it is ours, of Paradise. So the upward motion that begins in Book Ten with the repentance of Adam and Eve is the first real change in direction taken by the plot, and these final words far from being paradoxical are the triumphant victory which is the only possible "prosperous outcome."

A. O. Lovejoy, who brilliantly displayed the traditional roots of the idea of the *felix culpa* some years ago, felt nevertheless that this culminating passage placed the theme of the poem in an ambiguous light, and suggested that Milton solved the problem of a contradiction in his structure by keeping the two ideas of misfortune and fortune entirely separated in the narrative: "In the part of the narrative dealing primarily with the Fall, the thought that it was after all a *felix culpa* must not be permitted explicitly to intrude; that was to be reserved for the conclusion, where it could heighten the final consummation by making the earlier and unhappy episodes in the story appear as instrumental to that consummation, and, indeed, as its necessary conditions."[14] I find, on the contrary, that the idea of a *felix culpa* has been present throughout the poem, for Milton has conceived all along of a fallen world in need of what St. Francis de Sales called God's "gentle and loving antiperistasis."

Like the Cambridge Platonists Milton seems to have rejected Cartesian dualism, veering towards a monism which made God alone accountable for all that is. That Milton's God has no rivals in responsibility may help to account for his well-known anti-Trinitarianism[15] and for his use of the unorthodox *omnia ex Deo* to explain the origin of the world.[16] Even chaos is of God, and that primal chaos from which God "retires" yet which is a part of Him from which He withdraws His majestic discipline (*P.L.* vii.170–172) seems revealed again in Milton's description of the state of human and cosmic Nature after the Fall. Evil is self-generated in Satan, sprung from the Devil's brow; Adam was free to sin or to abstain and so responsible for the evil set loose by him. Yet Milton seems to hold that all is contained within God's inscrutable managing. In *Paradise Lost* God is pictured as continually engaged in converting apparently evil phenomena into an ultimate sum of Good. The *felix culpa* would be only an instance of the unsleeping process by which the moral unity of the cosmos is maintained and Evil "cancelled out" by the Divine use to which it is ultimately put.

[14] "Milton and the Paradox of the Fortunate Fall," *ELH*, iv (1937), 179, 177.

[15] Explicit in *De Doctrina Christiana*, i, v (*Works*, xiv), but also implicit in *Paradise Lost* though this has been energetically debated. The evidence for the Arianism in the poem has been comprehensively gathered together by Kelley, *This Great Argument*, passim.

[16] *De Doctrina Christiana* v, vii (*Works*, xv); *Paradise Lost*, v.469 ff.

As Man must be a creature capable of temptation, so the universe at large requires the existence of evil, or at least of potential evil. Such was the view of Peter Martyr, Pererius, Marsenne, and other Renaissance theologians (cf. *The Common Expositor*, pp. 113–114). God permits sin because it calls forth his goodness and makes the victory of virtue still more glorious than it would otherwise be, just as the penitence and redemption of fallen Man and Woman opens the way to their more resplendent future. And this is what seems continually to be in Milton's mind in *Paradise Lost*.

God's maintenance of the Divine unity is a process the reverse of that attempted by Satan who cries "Evil be thou my Good" or "all good to me becomes bane" (IX.122). Satan is determined to thwart God's intention "out of our evil to bring forth good," and resolves "out of good still to find a means of evil" (I.162–168). And Heaven permits him to pursue his dark designs in order to make still more clear "how all his malice serv'd but to bring forth / Infinite goodness, grace and mercy shown on Man" (I.210–220). The theory of the fortunate Fall has been applied to Satan's fall; the creation of Man is the countermove of Goodness, which makes of every triumph of Evil a still greater triumph for Virtue. Evil's next attack upon the balance is, of course, the Fall of Man, for which God has prepared the overwhelming compensation of the Redemption.

The process is noted by Milton at every point of the narrative. During the infernal councils in Hell, when the fallen spirits plot "Earth with Hell / to mingle and involve, done all to spite / The great Creator," Milton comments: "But their spite still serves His glory to augment" (II.383–386). And as God witnesses the battle in Heaven, it is remarked that he "permitted all, advis'd / That his great purpose he might so fulfil" (VI.674). Man is himself the result of God's care "Good out of Evil to create, instead / Of Spirits malign a better Race to bring / Into their vacant room, and thence diffuse / His good to Worlds, and Ages infinite" (VII.188–191). Thus sings the Heavenly choir:

> Who seeks to lessen thee, against his purpose serves
> To manifest the more thy might: his evil
> Thou usest, and from thence creat'st more good,
> Witness this new made World . . . .   (VII.613–617)

In turn this "new made World" becomes the seat of the new evil, the Fall, which by the same system of cosmic balances will necessarily be fortunate, for it results in the coming of the Messiah. Just as God permits the battle to rage in Heaven in order to honor the Son who has occasion to show himself "worthiest to be Heir / Of all things" (VI.707-

708), so the Fall of Man is occasion for a still grander victory. As Death and Sin build their causeway between Hell and the home of Man, the jest is God's:

> I called and drew them thither
> My Hell-hounds, to lick up the draff and filth
> Which man's polluting Sin with taint hath shed
> On what was pure, till cramm'd and gorg'd, nigh burst
> With suckt and glutted offal, at one sling
> Of thy victorious Arm, well-pleasing Son,
> Both *Sin*, and *Death*, and yawning *Grave* at last
> Through Chaos hurl'd, obstruct the mouth of Hell
> For ever, and seal up his ravenous Jaws.   (x.629–637)

Death itself, the ordained penalty of eating the fruit of the Tree of Good and Evil knowledge, becomes Man's final remedy.

> and after Life
> Tri'd in sharp tribulation, and refin'd
> By faith and faithful works, to second Life
> Wak't in the renovation of the just
> Resigns him up with Heav'n and Earth renew'd.   (xi.62–66)

The spectacle laid before us in *Paradise Lost* is of a universe in which Evil is an active, ever-present element, constantly transmuted by God's design into a part of the total Good. The soul of Man is such a place too. Though Man be ready to debase his higher qualities and give the throne to his lower ones, God will make it possible for him to order them aright. I think that this viewpoint is all-present in *Paradise Lost* and that it helps to account for the fact that Milton's Adam and Eve, like the universe at large, are never purely Good, but fallen and capable of redemption from the start.

BROWN UNIVERSITY
Providence 12, R. I.

Milton's Rejection of the Fortunate Fall

Virginia R. Mollenkott

Like many before him, John R. Mulder has recently assumed that in *Paradise Lost* Milton accepts the paradox of the Fortunate Fall. Writes Mulder, "As a type, paradise is inferior to its antitype: If Christ is the greater Man, the original Garden is the habitat of a smaller Man, a place of external amenities, which become superfluous in Christ's 'blissful seat.' . . . Once Adam understands God's redemptive history and adds 'Deeds to thy knowledge answerable,' the loss of his local Eden no longer matters, because he will 'possess/A Paradise within thee, happier farr' (XII. 586-589)."[1] Happier far than what? Mulder apparently believes that Michael's words are meant to compare the results of redeemed, holy living with the unfallen life Adam would have continued to live had he never sinned; the meaning then would be "Happier far than remaining in Eden in an unfallen state." To this Arthur O. Lovejoy would have agreed: "No devout believer could hold that it would have been better if the moving drama of man's salvation had never taken place . . . . Moreover, the final state of the redeemed . . . would far surpass in felicity and moral excellence the pristine happiness and innocence of the first pair in Eden—the state in which, but for the Fall, man would presumably have remained."[2] Frank L. Huntley concurs: "In the first stage of the plot of *Paradise Lost*, the union with God is good and stable because it is beneficent and easy and natural for Adam and Eve constantly to affirm it. But for them to remain in that stage would rob them of a more difficult perfection."[3]

In the face of these remarks, it should be emphasized that Milton takes great pains to suggest what would have happened had man never fallen; and the prospect as he viewed it was neither static nor inferior to the "moving drama of man's salvation." It involved meaningful struggle to be perfectly obedient to the will of God, and it progressed toward a magnificent goal, as Raphael explained to Adam:

O *Adam*, one Almighty is, from whom
All things proceed, and up to him return,
If not depraved from good, created all
Such to perfection, one first matter all,
Indu'd with various forms, various degrees
Of substance, and in things that live, of life;
But more refin'd, more spirituous, and pure,
As nearer to him plac't or nearer tending
Each in thir several active Spheres assign'd,
Till body up to spirit work, in bounds
Proportion'd to each kind . . . .
. . . time may come when men
With angels may participate, and . . .
Your bodies may at last turn all to spirit,
Improv'd by tract of time, and wing'd ascend
Ethereal, as wee, or may at choice
Here or in Heav'nly Paradises dwell;
If ye be found obedient, and retain
Unalterably firm his love entire
Whose progeny you are. (*PL* V. 469-503).[4]

And Adam got the point, for he praised Raphael's description of how "In contemplation of created things/By steps we may ascend to God" (511-512). Like John Hales and others, Milton believed that God had ordained a law for Adam "by observation of which, as the Angels by *Jacobs* ladder, he should ascend up to supernatural and heavenly bliss."[5] And Irene Samuel reminds us that in the process, Adam and Eve are not forbidden "to think, to raise questions, to have impulses and notions, to correct false impressions, to deal with the world out of their own developing natures and knowledge." In fact, far from being static, Eden can include everything—everything, that is, except its own cancellation.[6]

Because the matter was not revealed in Scripture, Milton could do no more than speculate about what would have occurred had man not fallen; hence he makes Raphael speak diffidently. But since Raphael's comments all tend in the same direction, clearly the result of Milton's speculation was that unfallen man could indeed have worked his way up to supernatural and heavenly bliss.[7] And he could thus have engaged in a noble struggle for higher and higher good without the constant alloy of evil, without that inevitable result of eating of the Tree of the Knowledge of Good and Evil, "Knowledge of good bought dear by knowing ill" (*PL* IV. 222). It is only *in a fallen world* that Milton cannot praise a fugitive and cloistered virtue which fails to run a race entailing dust and heat. For *unfallen* man there would have been another sort of race, free of dust and heat but full of glory, "shining more and more until the perfect day" (Prov. 4:18). It would be strange indeed if, after establishing this magnificent possibility, Milton should identify the future of fallen-but-redeemed man as happier far than never having fallen at all!

As a matter of fact, Milton touches only lightly upon the paradox of the Fortunate Fall, putting the concept into the mouth of an Adam who is full of doubt about its validity:

O goodness infinite, goodness immense!
That all this good of evil shall produce,
And evil turn to good; more wonderful
Than that which by creation first brought forth
Light out of darkness! full of doubt I stand,
Whether I should repent me now of sin
By mee done and occasion'd, or rejoice
Much more, that much more good thereof shall spring,
To God more glory, more good will to Men
From God, and over wrath grace shall abound.
(XII.469-478).

Of course, Adam does not doubt that God's goodness is infinite and immense; he wonders only whether he should repent or rejoice about his own sin, about his fall which has supplied the opportunity for that goodness to make itself manifest. Had he decided to rejoice, he would have decided in favor of the Fortunate Fall. But he does not make up his mind either way, turning instead to further questions concerning the fate of Christ's followers.

Milton has, however, subtly tipped the scales against the concept of the fall as fortunate by putting into Adam's mouth an allusion to Romans 5:20 and 6:1-2: "But where sin abounded, grace did much more abound . . . . What shall we say then? Shall we continue in sin, that grace may abound? God forbid." In this passage, St. Paul has recognized the libertine implications of the doctrine of the Fortunate Fall: if sin gives opportunity to the grace of God, then let us sin repeatedly, rejoicing rather than repenting. And Paul has immediately repudiated that implication: "God forbid." The *grace* is fortunate; the sin is not, and it would be extremely ungrateful to abuse God's graciousness with deliberate and repeated falling.

C. A. Patrides thought Milton put the concept of the Fortunate Fall into the mouth of a doubtful Adam in order to escape "the theological traps inherent in the paradox" (p. 143); but while this may be part of the reason, the major one is Milton's faithfulness to his vision of unfallen man's glorious future and his insistence on the enormity of the loss of that future. A. O. Lovejoy recognized the difficulty by asserting that Milton simply had to keep the two themes separate: "In the part of the narrative dealing primarily with the Fall, the thought that it was after all a *felix culpa* must not be permitted explicitly to intrude; that was to be reserved for the conclusion when it would heighten the happy final consummation by making the earlier and unhappy episodes in the story appear as instrumental to that consummation, and indeed as necessary conditions."[8] But there is no such fragmentation in Milton's handling of the Fall, and the "final consummation" of *Paradise Lost* is not "happy." That was the emphasis of Richard Bentley's famous "restoration" of the final lines: "They hand in hand with social steps their way/Through Eden took with Heavenly Comfort cheered." But the fact is that Adam and Eve were crying, and wandering, and solitary because they were missing the overt presence of the God who had walked with them in the Garden. They had Providence as their guide and the promise of a Redeemer to keep them from despair; but they had suffered a great loss, and they knew it. Michael had achieved his mission, for he sent them forth "though sorrowing, yet in peace" (XI. 117). It is Milton's genius that the conclusion neither denies the loss with Bentley's cheerfulness nor sinks beneath it into total depression. Instead of either half-truth, there is a wonderful mingling of hope and resignation, tragedy and comedy, which is characteristic of Milton's complex vision.

What then did Milton mean by having Michael assure Adam that he could possess "A paradise within . . . . happier far?" Mary Ann Radzinowicz' suggestion, "the paradise of the quiet conscience is better than an unquiet and desolate expulsion,"[9] has the disadvantage of a ridiculous comparison: since there was nothing happy about a desolate expulsion in the first place, why should Michael use the comparative degree in speaking of the happiness of the paradise within? John S. Diekhoff's opinion is more plausible: "The paradise within . . . that Adam is to achieve even in this life is . . . happier far than the merely physical paradise that he is loath to leave" (p. 131). For it must be conceded that the *immediate* context does indeed suggest that the inner paradise will be better than the local Paradise of Eden. There is, however, a *larger* context; and the larger context indicates that this comparison has a special meaning which by no means offers support to the doctrine of the Fortunate Fall.

Michael tells Adam that if he will live up to his newly expressed insight that "to obey is best," he and Eve will be no longer "loath/To leave this Paradise, but shalt possess/A Paradise within thee, happier far." When had Adam and Eve expressed their loathing to leave the local Paradise? Not in the immediate context, but before Michael gave Adam his course in the History of Civilization, back in Book XI.263-333. Eve had lamented that she was used to her home and could not leave it, and had been reminded that Adam's presence was her home. Adam had lamented the loss of the "Presence Divine," but had been assured that God is everywhere. Immediately thereafter, Michael had launched into the history of mankind, precisely to preserve Adam and Eve from despairing over their lot; but the heart of their desire was revealed in Eve's lament:

How shall I part, and whither wander down
Into a lower World, to this obscure
And wild, how shall we breathe in other Air
Less pure, accustom'd to immortal Fruits?
(XI.282-285).

In other words, both Adam and Eve wanted to go on living in Eden, breathing the pure air, eating their customary immortal fruits, walking with God, and pretending that nothing had ever happened: "Here let us live, though in fall'n state, content" (XI.180). It was therefore necessary for the Angel to make clear to them that honest acceptance of reality is a much better way; one cannot go on eating immortal fruits after one has suffered the sentence of death and thus become painfully mortal. Michael is performing the task assigned to him by God the Father: he must bring Adam to understand that

longer in that Paradise to dwell
The law I gave to Nature him forbids;
Those pure immortal elements that know
No gross, no unharmonious mixture foul,
Eject him tainted now, and purge him off
As a distemper, gross to air as gross,
And mortal food . . . (XI.48-54).

Michael's summary of human history is intended to help Adam face this painful reality and accept with equanimity what must now happen to him; hence, when he sees that to obey is best, Michael reverts to the earlier discussion and assures Adam that obedient confrontation with his fate in the "subjected Plain" will provide an inner paradise that will be happier far than staying on in an external paradise where he no longer belongs, pretending that the Fall has never taken place and thus living a lie.[10]

Immediately after his promise that for a fallen man, obedient godliness outside of Eden will be happier far than disobedient pseudo-godliness within Eden, Michael says, "Let us descend therefore from this top/Of Speculation; for the hour precise/Exacts our parting thence." Supported by his new-found knowledge, Adam is able to make the descent.

Contrary to widespread opinion since Lovejoy, Milton does not espouse the doctrine of the Fortunate Fall; nor does he remain doubtful about it, as Diekhoff concludes. While he clearly demonstrates that a gracious God brings good out of evil by providing redemption, Milton suggests through Raphael that the alternative might have been even *more* glorious. (If God can do so much in the presence of human disobedience, what might He have done had man been "found obedient"!) Milton does not, as Lovejoy claims, show that human sinfulness is the condition of "a greater manifestation of the glory of God and of immeasurably greater benefits for man than could conceivably have been otherwise obtained."[11] Neither does he picture redemption as the "ultimate result" of the Fall.[12] Redemption is the result of God's concern for fallen man; apart from the loving nature of God, there is no necessary connection between the Fall and the Atonement. Redemption is therefore the remedy, not the result, of the Fall. As Irene Samuel comments in this connection, "cancer is not a great good because it enables surgeons to show their skill."[13]

In other words, Milton demonstrates that once sin is a *fait accompli*, God manages to do something wonderful about it. There can be no doubt that to Milton the goodness of God surpasses the evil of Satan; but that is not the same thing as claiming that God's goodness to fallen man surpasses what God's goodness would have provided if man had never fallen. Such a claim runs counter to common sense: in the daily routine of life, which of us would lavish more love and rewards on our children when they are disobedient than we are willing to provide when they are living in obedient harmony with us? Although we may kill the fatted calf to celebrate a prodigal's return, yet "all that we have" belongs to the child who lives in cooperation with us (Luke 15:31).

Milton gives the concept of the Fortunate Fall short shrift in Adam's tentative speculations; he does not imply it in the statement concerning inner paradise; and above all, he flatly disavows it in *PL* XI.84-89, the words of the Almighty Father to His assembled Angels (italics mine):

O Sons, like one of us Man is become
To know both Good and Evil, since his taste

3

Of that defended Fruit; but let him boast
His knowledge of Good lost, and Evil got,
*Happier, had it suffic'd him to have known
Good by itself, and Evil not at all.*

— William Paterson College of New Jersey

FOOTNOTES

[1]John R. Mulder, *The Temple of the Mind: Education and Literary Taste in Seventeenth-Century England* (New York, 1969), p. 143. Arthur O. Lovejoy's article on "Milton and the Paradox of the Fortunate Fall" first appeared in *ELH*, IV (Sept., 1937), 169-179. That it is still exerting a strong influence is evident from several reprintings: in A. O. Lovejoy, *Essays in the History of Ideas* (New York, 1948), pp. 277-295; in *Milton's Epic Poetry*, ed. C. A. Patrides (Baltimore, 1967), pp. 55-73; and in *Critical Essays on Milton from ELH* (Baltimore, 1969), pp. 163-181. Lovejoy asserts that "an intelligent reader could hardly have failed to conclude that his [Adam's] doubt [concerning whether to repent or rejoice about the Fall] was to be resolved in favor of the second alternative [i.e., in favor of the Fortunate Fall]" (*Essays*, p. 282).

[2]Lovejoy, *Essays*, p. 278.

[3]Frank L. Huntley, "Some Miltonic Patterns of Systasis," *Approaches to Paradise Lost*, ed. C. A. Patrides (Toronto, 1968), p. 7.

[4]Merritt Y. Hughes, ed. *John Milton Complete Poems and Major Prose* (New York, 1957), pp. 313-314. It should be noted that in *Milton's Paradise Lost: A Commentary on the Argument* (New York, 1958), John S. Diekhoff quotes this very passage in refutation of Lovejoy (pp. 129-130); but rather than recognizing that Milton repudiated the doctrine of the Fortunate Fall, Diekhoff concludes that Milton "was unwilling to choose between the horns of the dilemma. With Adam he might say 'full of doubt I stand' upon this point, and like Adam come to no conclusion. Apparently he had not made up his mind . . ." (p. 131).

[5]John Hales, as quoted by C. A. Patrides, *Milton and the Christian Tradition* (Oxford, 1966), p. 108. For Milton's explicit use of Jacob's ladder as symbolizing open access to Heaven before the Fall, and the possibility of gradual spiritualization, see *PL* III.510-530. Milton's concept of a ladder of spiritualization, obviously Platonic, accords with Calvin's interpretation of Plato: "Now, if the end for which all men are born and live, be to know God, . . . it is evident, that all who direct not every thought and action of life to this end, are degenerated from the law of their creation. Of this the heathen philosophers themselves were not ignorant. This was Plato's meaning when he taught that the chief good of the soul consists in similitude to God, when the soul, having a clear knowledge of him, is wholly transformed into his likeness" (*Institutes of the Christian Religion*, ed. John Allen [Phila., 1932], I, 53). In *Comus* Milton also uses Platonic imagery concerning fallen but redeemed man; the ladder of physical transformation to the spiritual which was open to unfallen man is thus re-opened on an internalized basis through Christ's act of redemption. But it is a mistake to apply Milton's imagery of gradual spiritualization to fallen and *unredeemed* humanity.

[6]Irene Samuel, "*Paradise Lost* as Mimesis," *Approaches to Paradise Lost*, ed. C. A. Patrides (Toronto, 1968), pp. 22-23.

[7]It is amusing that although C. A. Patrides recognizes Milton's belief in the gradual spiritualization of unfallen man, he worries that "The obvious problem of how our physical frame could have withstood the effect of centuries does not seem to have troubled commentators" (*Milton and the Christian Tradition*, p. 108). Perhaps it has not troubled commentators for the reason that if man's body were gradually taking on the characteristics of pure spirit, it would no longer be subject to the ravages of time. The speech of God the Father in III.98-111 indicates that Milton did not think of the unfallen state as passive and static. In the case of all created beings, unfallen obedience required the vigilant use of free will and reason.

[8]Lovejoy, *Essays*, p. 295.

[9]Mary Ann Radzinowicz, "Man as a Probationer of Immortality," *Approaches to Paradise Lost*, ed. C. A. Patrides (Toronto, 1968), p. 36.

[10]Cf. H. V. S Ogden's discussion, utilizing different evidence but arriving at similar conclusions: "The Crisis of Paradise Lost Reconsidered," *Milton: Modern Essays in Criticism*, ed. A. E. Barker (1965), pp. 324-326.
In *De Doctrina Christiana*, where there is no speculation concerning what would have happened had man never fallen, Milton says that through redemption, man is "raised to a far more excellent state of grace and glory than that from which he had fallen" (I. 14). This divergence from *Paradise Lost* parallels other divergences on topics like mortalism and subordinationism.

[11]Lovejoy, *Essays*, pp. 278-279. Another possible support for the Fortunate Fall, the promise that "A fairer Paradise is founded now/For *Adam* and his chosen Sons" (*PR* IV.613-614) collapses when it is remembered that had they not fallen, Adam and Eve would not have been confined to the earthly Paradise, but would also have had the option of living in Heaven if and when they so desired: see *PL* V.499-500.

4

[12]Huntley, p. 6. In the same symposium, Mary Ann Radzinowicz claims that the institution of Christian liberty is the "completest expression" of the paradox of the Fortunate Fall (pp. 47-48). But Christian liberty is neither a result nor an expression of the Fall, but of the Atonement, which in turn stemmed not from the Fall but from God's loving nature. Earlier, Miss Radzinowicz rightly recognizes that nowhere does Milton suggest that Adam and Eve will "receive a better reward for the struggle to repair what they needlessly defaced" (p. 36).

[13]Samuel, p. 29.

PARADISE LOST AND THE COLONIAL IMPERATIVE

Paul Stevens

And God blessed them, and God said unto them, Be fruitful, and multiply, and replenish the earth, and subdue it: and have dominion over the fish of the sea, and over the fowl of the air, and over every living thing that moveth upon the earth.

Genesis i, 28

Colonies . . . have their warrant from God's direction and command; who as soone as men were, set them to their taske, to replenish the earth and subdue it.

The Planter's Plea, 1630[1]

WHILE THERE HAS been a great deal of interest over the last several years in the relationship between Renaissance literature and the rhetoric of colonialism, and while at the same time there has been a dramatic renewal of interest in Milton's politics, surprisingly little has been written on Milton and colonialism. The most important exception is David Quint's recent book, *Epic and Empire* (1993). Quint, who approaches the issue through a somewhat ambivalently postmodern analysis of the political implications of genre, comes to the conclusion that the Milton of *Paradise Lost* is a poet against empire. In this essay I wish to challenge Quint's reading in order to suggest how exactly and to what extent *Paradise Lost* authorizes colonial activity even while it satirizes the abuses of early modern colonialism.[2]

I

Until fairly recently, "cultural" in the context of literary studies was understood as something which was by definition apolitical. It was, as Terry Eagleton in an uncharacteristically nostalgic mood has suggested, "the 'other' of political society—the realm of being as opposed to doing, the kingdom of ends rather than of means, the home of transcendental spirit rather than the dreary prose of everyday life."[3] For many scholars the exhilaration of professing literature lay precisely in the discipline's promise to transcend the quotidian. All that has clearly changed. After two or three decades of "theory," for most active critics, the distinction between culture and politics has largely disappeared, and the net result for Renaissance studies as for most other areas of literary study is political criticism.

While the long-term consequences of this change may be significant, its immediate manifestations are rarely as radical or disturbing as the newspapers still like to claim.[4] What political criticism tends to mean—to use Thomas Kuhn's well-worn but still useful vocabulary—is that political readings of literary texts and the culture in which they were produced have become "normal science," that is, an institutionally sanctioned, normative practice.[5] While it is certainly true that many critics are well informed and passionate in their political commitment, at least as many simply acquiesce in the prevailing discourse and often allow the rhetoric of their critical practice to make them sound far more radical than they actually are. Political criticism in Renaissance studies seems to take two predominant forms. On the one hand, it seems to mean integrating literary texts into exciting new homologies of contemporary political issues, thus satisfying the critic's need not only to analyze but to act or effect an "intervention." On the other hand, it seems to mean simply figuring out the immediate political context of a literary work for no other purpose than a positivist determination to get at the "facts." In the first form, agency is much more likely to be granted to ideology or discourse; in the second, to local contingencies or the will of the individual. Even in the first.form, however, ideology often figures, though certainly not always, as an increasingly limited or mannerist category. In this context, David Quint is especially interesting because, while routinely invoking ideology in *Epic and Empire,* he appears to be in transit from the first form of critical practice to the second, and in so moving helps to illustrate my point about the domestication of political criticism.

In *Epic and Empire,* Quint appears as a traditionally trained literary historian, simultaneously eschewing the "bad history" of new historicism's political homologies (pp. 14, 370) while busily adapting the well-tried methods of genre analysis to meet the discipline's apparently insatiable demand for political readings. Quint's first move in this process is to credit familiar literary genres with specific political or ideological implications. Literary history as the history of genres is thus represented as possessing a political life of its own. The two genres he is most interested in are epic and romance. Epic after Virgil, he feels, is the peculiar property of empire, and by *empire* he means the centralized, expansionist Western state, the Roman Empire and its various early modern heirs. Seen from the perspective of Virgilian epic, romance is the aimless, meaningless fate of the enemies of empire. "To the victors," so the *Aeneid* implies, "belongs epic, with its linear teleology;

to the losers belongs romance, with its random and circular wandering. Put another way, the victors experience history as a coherent, end-directed story told by their own power; the losers experience a contingency that they are powerless to shape to their own ends" (p. 9). But the power of romance is not mocked, and the contingency it articulates, so Quint argues, eventually comes to be seen by the defeated as a means of escaping, contesting, or subverting the power of the victors. To be specific, the contingency of romance enables the defeated to see all kinds of liberating possibilities beyond the totalizing and totalitarian closure of epic narrative.

Thus, in the same way that Patricia Parker in the 1970s—in the heyday of Yale deconstruction—made romance thematize Derridean *différance*, the distancing, difference, and deferral "intrinsic to language," so now Quint politicizes it.[6] Just as in Parker's account, to which Quint is immediately indebted, romance is understood as anticipating Derrida's critique of "Presence"—that is, "the metaphysical assumption of an ultimate Origin, Center, or End, and the various social and intellectual hierarchies it authorises" (p. 220)—so in Quint's account romance stands in opposition to what not surprisingly turns out to be a familiarly Foucauldian version of the imperial state's power. To the degree that Milton's great epic, for instance, turns to romance, so it may be construed, like its sequel *Paradise Regained*, as "a defense of the individual against the state, against its instruments of surveillance and control" (p. 324). It is difficult at this point not to feel that in Milton Quint is allegorizing his own commonsense belief in individual agency and his desire to distance himself from the Foucauldian moment of early new historicism. In a footnote he refers us to David Bromwich, who valorizes common sense and excoriates theory and "the erosion of [the] secular individualism" it signifies as "perhaps the worst intellectual disaster of the 1970s and 1980s."[7]

The place of *Paradise Lost* in Quint's story of politics and generic form is central. The logic of his literary history would seem to demand that Milton's great poem be consigned to the ash heap of beautiful but obsolete imperial epics. The poem is, however, saved by the "turn to romance" which Quint claims is the distinguishing feature of what he calls "the losers' epic" (p. 9), a subgenre inaugurated by Lucan's *Pharsalia*. In *Paradise Lost*, the triumphalist epic plot first given a specific ideological direction in Virgil's *Aeneid* and reproduced in Renaissance poems like Tasso's *Gerusalemme Liberata* and Camoëns's *Lusiads* is satirized by Milton in the way Satan's would-be colonial epic collapses into a "bad romance" (p. 248) and transumed in the way Adam and Eve's tragic story turns into a good romance. "Reserving the imperial typology of the Virgilian epic for its God alone,"

Quint concludes, "*Paradise Lost* effectively moves away from epic altogether" (p. 248). Like a more quietist version of the Romantic Milton of
Wordsworth's sonnet or Masson's biography, Quint's Milton gradually
emerges as a poet against empire, and his poem comes to be seen as "an
indictment of European expansion and colonialism that includes his own
countrymen and contemporaries" (p. 265). Most important, Milton emerges
as an individual who seems so able to manipulate generic form that ideology
seems to have little constraining force for him.

Despite Quint's impressive erudition and many brilliant local insights,
this reading of *Paradise Lost* may be questioned on a number of grounds,
all of them requiring the reader to step outside the narrow bounds of Quint's
politically inflected literary history. Two points, both suggestive of Milton's
lack of freedom from ideological constraint, immediately come to mind.
First, that Satan's journey to the new world is not so much a satire on colonialism as on the abuses of colonialism. There is, for instance, no evidence
to suggest that Milton ever felt the Protestant colonization of New England,
Virginia, or Ulster, in principle at least, anything but admirable. Nor does
reserving the imperial typology of Virgilian epic to God alone constitute a
rejection so much as a displacement of an extraordinarily deep-rooted and
tenacious will-to-order which is often hard to distinguish from a will-to-
power. *Second,* that the representation of Adam and Eve in Paradise, especially in the way that representation both amplifies and idealizes the colonial
imperative embedded in Scripture, confounds the postmodern distinction
Quint wishes to make between the political implications of epic and romance. For the new world that Adam and Eve are commanded to replenish
and subdue in Genesis—the world Milton calls their "neather Empire" (IV,
145)—is precisely the end that so many early modern colonialists desire and
feel themselves duty-bound to seek.[8] In other words, the image at the heart
of the poem of a paradise that is lost, the romance vision of a garden that is
to be regained when "the Earth / Shall all be Paradise" (XII, 463–64), is
central to the *mentalité* responsible for the building of European colonial
empires. In drawing attention to the imperative of Genesis i, 28, Milton's
contemporary, John White, for instance, offers a glimpse of the biblical origin of empire. If we allow, says White in *The Planter's Plea,* God's command
to replenish and subdue the earth "to bind *Adam,* [then] it must binde his
posterity, and consequently our selves in this age, and our issue after us, as
long as the earth yields empty places to be replenished" (p. 2). As long as
the earth yields empty places to be replenished. With the last clause, it
suddenly becomes apparent that the endless deferral of fulfillment in romance is not the antithesis of empire but in the case of Western colonialism
its scriptural genesis.

II

In order to develop these points let me begin with Satan's journey to the New World. As Martin Evans demonstrated in a brilliantly succinct analysis over twenty years ago, there is abundant evidence to suggest that the journey parodies a colonial venture.[9] The project that governs the poem's satanic plot is the discovery and colonization of a new land. It is true that in one version of this plan colonization is understood simply as a means of precipitating the land's destruction, but much more insistently it is imagined as a permanent settlement. Beelzebub talks of possessing "All as our own," of driving out "as we were driven, / The punie habitants" (II, 366–67). Satan imagines dwelling secure "in some milde Zone" where "the soft delicious Air" shall breathe her balm and heal his scars (II, 397–402). This satanic colonizing project is mediated through multiple frames of reference: classical, biblical, and of course, not least, contemporary. The journey to the New World is, for instance, repeatedly described in terms of recent overseas "adventures" for trade or settlement. As Satan approaches the gates of hell he is seen as a fleet of merchant ships returning from the East Indies, Bengal, or the Spice Islands (II, 636–42); as he approaches Paradise he is imagined on board ship, sailing from the Cape of Good Hope and cheered by the spicy odors of Arabia (IV, 159–65); and, most important, when he finally encounters the naked inhabitants of the New World, he speaks the words any patriotic Englishman in the late 1650s would expect a rapacious adventurer or conquistador to let slip:

> And should I at your harmless innocence
> Melt, as I doe, yet public reason just,
> Honour and Empire with revenge enlarg'd,
> By conquering this new World, compels me now
> To do what else though damnd I should abhorre.   (IV, 388–92)

In the event, in what seems like a ringing indictment of colonialist ambition, honor and empire are shown to mean fraud and dispossession; the poor natives are cheated of their birthright and fall prey to the ghastly hellhounds of Sin and Death.

At this point, it is important to emphasize that, despite Quint's assertion to the contrary, the early modern discourse of English colonialism was consistent in its efforts to distinguish legitimate from illegitimate activity.[10] Though much of this moralizing was of course disingenuous, much of it was agonizingly sincere, and in *The Reason of Church-government* (1642) Milton himself contributes to the debate when he deploys a colonial metaphor to distinguish himself from the Bishops. When it comes to bearing God's truth, the difference between the Bishops and himself is the difference between two kinds of colonial entrepreneur: on the one hand there are those false merchants who "abuse the people, like poor Indians with beads and glasses," while on the other there are those resolute adventurers who bear themselves honestly at the trading post, "uprightly in this their spiritual factory," offering stones of "orient lustre" at bargain prices, "at any cheap rate, yea for nothing to them that will" (CM III, pp. 229–30). Thus, at the same time that he is justifying himself for speaking out against the Bishops, he is also justifying colonial trade by distinguishing the true from the false. In effect, he is offering his own merchant class an idealized view of itself, tacitly accepting the legitimacy of establishing factories or trading colonies like those set up at Jamestown in Virginia (1607) or Surat in India (1612).[11]

The metaphor of treasure, the stones of "orient lustre," the pearl of great price (Matt. xiii, 45–46), is especially relevant because the image is a staple of those tracts and pamphlets whose main purpose is to demonstrate the lawfulness of colonization. As Milton gives this image of "heavenly traffic" a colonial setting to dramatize his religious vocation, so propagandists deploy it to lend the religious aspirations of their readers a colonial outlet. We offer native peoples "the incomparable treasure of the trueth of Christianity and of the Gospell," says Richard Hakluyt, "while we use and exercise common trade with their merchants." We "doe buy of them the pearles of the earth," says the Virginia Company's *True Declaration,* "and sell to them the pearls of heaven."[12] In practice, of course, the pearls of heaven often got lost in the rush for the pearls of the earth. In 1622, for instance, an English fleet from the East India Company's factory at Surat joined forces with a Moslem army from Persia to bloodily relieve the Christian Portuguese of that pearl of the orient, Ormus, the center of the Persian Gulf pearl trade.[13] For Milton such excess is to be censured, and it is precisely for reasons of excess that "the wealth of Ormus and of Ind" is associated with Satan (II, 1–5). Milton's pride in English colonial adventure and his disapproval of mercantile excess are simultaneously made explicit in his *Brief History of Muscovia* (1682): "The discovery of *Russia* by the northern Ocean, made first, of any Nation that we know, by *English* men, might have seem'd an enterprise almost heroick; if any higher end than the excessive love of Gain and Traffick, had animated the design" (YP VIII, p. 524).

The class into which Milton was born, it needs to be remembered, was mercantile. The parish of All Hallows, Bread Street, London, the first social group of which the poet became conscious, was largely composed of successful merchants, more than half of them dealers in cloth, and many, including Milton's maternal grandfather, members of the Merchant Taylors' Company.[14] His next-door neighbor, Ralph Hamor, was a merchant-tailor but also a member of the Virginia Company and his son, also called Ralph, wrote one of the best known defenses of the colony, *A True Discourse of the Present Estate of Virginia* (1615). The rector of the parish in 1626 was Samuel Purchas, whose great collection of colonizing voyages, *Purchas His Pilgrimes*, Milton combed through for his history of Russia and is said to have planned to abridge.[15] For people like this, whether domestic merchants or members of overseas companies, the commonplace shorthand or metonym for colonial excess was Spanish imperialism.

From the first English translation of Bartolomé de Las Casas's *Brevisima Relación de la Destrucción de las Indias* in 1583,[16] English colonialism had defined itself in opposition to Spain's excessive love of gain and traffic—a lust for land and treasure which, according to Las Casas, had led to a series of genocidal atrocities. Las Casas's detailed account of these cruelties enabled the English to represent themselves as a kinder, gentler type of colonialist, indeed as protectors of the Indians.[17] Throughout his 1596 tract, *The Discovery of Guiana*, for instance, Sir Walter Ralegh presents himself to his readers as a knight from Spenserian romance come to do Gloriana's bidding by protecting the Indians from the depredations of the Spanish:

I made them understand that I was a servant of a Queene, who was the great *Casique* of the north, and a virgin, and had more *Casiqui* under her then there were trees in their Iland: that she was an enemy to the *Castellani* in respect of their tyrannie and oppression, and that she . . . had sent me to free them. . . . I shewed them her maiesties picture which they so admired and honored, as it had beene easie to have brought [thought] them Idolatrous thereof.[18]

This self-representation is part of a continuous tradition of national propaganda from the 1580s to the late 1650s, and it impinges directly on Milton's career. Between 1655 and 1658, while Milton was still employed on government business, and at about the same time, according to his nephew Edward Phillips, that he was beginning work on *Paradise Lost*, the rhetoric of Spanish colonial abuse was redeployed in a concerted effort to justify Cromwell's Western Design—that is, his plan to carve out a colonial empire in the Caribbean.[19] In Sir William Davenant's 1658 masque, *The Cruelty of the Spaniards in Peru*, for instance, the New Model Army, complete with red coats, arrives to rescue the racked and tortured Incas in a vision of things to come. In *The Tears of the Indians*, the 1656 translation of Las Casas's pamphlet made by Milton's other nephew, John Phillips, Cromwell appears making ready to avenge the Indians—for they had been devoured by the Spanish, "not as if they had been their Fellow-Mortals, but like Death it self."[20] And in the official 1655 *Declaration Against Spain*, which may or may not have been written by Milton, the self-imposed English obligation to avenge the blood of so many slaughtered Indians becomes a warrant by which the English can legitimately inherit Indian land.[21]

Given the immediacy and intensity of this tradition, given Milton's social background and his participation in articulating government policy (including his work on an abortive colonial treaty with the Spanish), it seems unlikely that his critique of colonial abuses in *Paradise Lost* would be uninfluenced by what the Spanish in self-defense called the Black Legend. And indeed if it is uninfluenced by it, then the significance of Milton's explicit characterization of the Spanish as "*Geryons* Sons" (XI, 410) at the only moment in the poem when the politics of contemporary colonialism is directly referred to remains unclear. For there on the mountaintop of Speculation, as Adam is shown the future empires of the world, Milton rehearses the argument of Ralegh's *Discoverie of Guiana:* the riches of Mexico and Peru are juxtaposed with the "yet unspoil'd" riches of Guiana, "whose great Citie *Geryons* Sons / Call *El Dorado*" (XI, 409–11). In Spenser, Geryon's son is the monstrous progeny of Spanish imperialism devouring the children of the Netherlands; in Milton, "*Geryons* Sons" is an allusion to a specific historical example of the way contemporary colonialism may reenact the entry of Death itself into the world.[22]

John Phillips's description of Spanish excess as "Death it self," of the Spanish murdering Indians "to satisfie the contemptible hunger of their Hounds" (sig. A8ʳ), suggests the degree to which the representation of Sin and Death in *Paradise Lost* continues the colonial critique. One of the distinguishing features of Las Casas's text is the recurrent reference to the Spanish use of war dogs, "which they teach and instruct to fall upon the Indians and devour them" (p. 130). In *Paradise Lost*, the denouement of Satan's conquest of the New World is the arrival of Sin and Death as hellhounds specifically charged by "the folly of Man" (X, 619) to devour the inhabitants: "See with what heat these Dogs of Hell advance / To waste and havoc yonder World," cries God the Father (X, 616–17). What is most important here is that Death and the havoc he causes are not the necessary outcomes of colonialism but of the perversion of colonialism, of excess, fraud, and dispossession, that is, of Sin. The extent to which the colonial triumph of Sin and Death is a counterfeit imitation of the good is suggested in the way their satanic charter is made to parody the colonial ideal of Genesis i, 28:

> right down to Paradise descend;
> There dwell and Reign in bliss, thence on the Earth
> Dominion exercise and in the Aire,
> Chiefly on Man, sole Lord of all declar'd,
> Him first make sure your thrall, and lastly kill.   (X, 398–402)

III

The strongest argument for doubting Milton's conversion to any kind of blanket anticolonial stand is not, as I have just tried to suggest, that his satire on colonialism can so easily be construed as a satire on its abuses, but that his depiction of Adam and Eve in Paradise turns out to be such a powerful representation of its ideal. And because that ideal has the quality of a romance, it undermines the explanatory force of Quint's binary opposition between the political implications of epic and romance.

The most obvious difference between Satan's colonial project and that of Adam and Eve is explained by Sir Francis Bacon: "I like a *Plantation* in a Pure Soile; that is, where people are not *Displanted*, to the end, to *Plant* in Others. For else it is rather an Extirpation, then a *Plantation*."²³ Satan does not have a pure soil; Adam and Eve do. Satan and his fellow adventurers are forced to rehearse various self-serving arguments to extirpate the territorial rights of the natives: they are "punie," *puis né*, born later, says Beelzebub (II, 367); "Into our room . . . advanc't," says Satan (IV, 359). Their very chthonic origins are turned against them: they are denigrated as people of clay, children of despite, as though they were tainted by the ground out of which they had come (IX, 176). Adam and Eve, however, have no need for such arguments. Not only do they have a pure soil, but the world they enter conforms in almost every way with the ideal of English colonial discourse. If the New World of that discourse is frequently recreated in the image of a biblical paradise, so Milton's biblical Paradise is indebted to his familiarity with colonial accounts of the New World.²⁴ The land Adam and Eve enter is gendered female, virginal, and stands ready to be husbanded. It is a place like Robert Johnson's Virginia, where "valleys and plaines . . . [stream] with sweete Springs, like veynes in a naturall bodie," where the soil is so strong and lusty that it "sendeth out naturally fruitfull vines running upon trees, and shrubbes." It is place like Samuel Purchas's Virginia of such "luxuriant wantonesse" that it is well "worth the wooing and loves of the best Husband."²⁵ Adam and Eve are imagined like the settlers of Virginia, not only as husbandmen, but paradoxically as the plants to be husbanded: they are rooted in the soil, "earth-born" (IV, 360), like the vine and the elm, indigenous, almost autochthonous. But most important, like Purchas's settlers, they have the charter of Genesis i, 28, "a Commission from . . . [God] to plant" (XIX, pp. 218–19). "Not only these fair bounds," says Milton's God to Adam, amplifying the biblical text,

> but all the Earth
> To thee and to thy Race I give; as Lords
> Possess it, and all things that therein live,

Or live in Sea, or Aire, Beast, Fish, and Fowle.
In signe whereof each Bird and Beast behold
After thir kindes; I bring them to receave
From thee thir Names, and pay thee fealtie
With low subjection.   (VIII, 338–45)

What is most seductive about this fantasy of world dominion is that it articulates both the complete possession of power and its deferral. For in Milton's fiction not only Adam and Eve's nether empire but the Garden itself has to be replenished and subdued, that is, cultivated. Adam and Eve are confronted with "a Wilderness of sweets" where nature "Wantond as in her prime, and plaid at will / Her Virgin Fancies" (V, 294–96): as Eve explains,

what we by day
Lop overgrown, or prune, or prop, or bind,
One night or two with wanton growth derides
Tending to wilde.   (IX, 209–12)

Their struggle to cultivate the wilderness is, as in any other early modern colonial romance, a metonym for the struggle toward civility. Implicit in Adam's response to Eve's plan to divide their labors is the suggestion that she has overemphasized the vehicle at the expense of the tenor, the gardening at the expense of the civility it is meant to convey: "Yet not so strictly hath our Lord impos'd / Labour" (IX, 235–36) so as to debar them from the daily delights of civil intercourse—"whether food, or talk between, / Food of the mind, or this sweet intercourse / Of looks and smiles, for smiles from Reason flow" (IX, 237–39). As their ensuing quarrel indicates, with its carefully plotted account of the disintegration of the language of politeness, civility is understood not simply as refreshment or relief from work but as a different kind of work—a community-defining social practice that takes skill and energy, an art that needs to be joined to nature. Because this task is at the heart of their quest, the failure of Adam and Eve is causally linked to their subsequent moral and epistemological failures, that is, the collapse of civility is not accidental but central to Milton's representation of the Fall.

My point here is twofold: first, that what is frustrated or deferred in Milton's story of Adam and Eve is the desire for a culturally specific form of civility and the membership of the ideal, imagined community it signifies; and second, that this desire is the lack that most powerfully animates early modern colonial settlement at its most idealistic: "if bare nature be so amiable in its naked kind," wonders Robert Johnson of his brave new world, "what may we hope, when Arte and Nature both shall joyne, and strive together."[26] It is a solipsistic desire because it is a longing for the ideal form of a civility that already identifies colonists as English, Christian, European. It is a desire that renders the literary historian's distinction between epic's imagined completion of history and romance's imagined wandering toward that completion relatively insignificant. It is not clear, for instance, that Ralegh's digressive and ultimately fruitless Spenserian quest in *The Discoverie of Guiana*—as much a courtly demonstration of temperance as a search for El Dorado[27]—is any less a manifestation of Western imperialism's will-to-power than the *Aeneid* or the *Lusiads*. Both epic and romance are perfectly capable of articulating an imperial ideology.[28]

If one of the ways in which ideology may be understood is as "identity-thinking," that is, as the network of "discursive formations" that give a particular culture or community its coherence or integrity, then ideology in *Paradise Lost* may be most usefully approached through the discourse of civility.[29] The civility that constitutes the daily practice of Adam and Eve is, however, more than just a discourse in the sense of one particular tradition; it is more like a master code that generates and demands adherence to a series of moral and epistemological rules so deeply ingrained as to be hardly open to question—rules such as the need to restrain the luxuriant growth of wanton fancy, to subdue sensual appetite, and to maintain the sovereignty of reason (IX, 1127–31).[30] These imperatives are aestheticized in art's power "to allay the perturbations of the mind, and set the affections in right tune" (*The Reason of Church-government*, CM III, p. 238). As Ferdinand in *The Tempest*, in what many claim to be Shakespeare's colonial romance, unwittingly bears witness, such civility so aesthetically conceived is precisely the end of Prospero's art: the magician's strange and rare music crept by him on the waters, he says, "Allaying both their fury and my passion / With its sweet air" (I, ii, 392–94).[31] For both Milton and Shakespeare, civility so understood is not relative, particular, or contingent, but absolute and universal, in Milton's case especially empyreal and imperial.

What needs to be emphasized at this point is the degree to which the early modern discourse of civility *is* contingent, from our perspective both culturally specific and solipsistic. In colonial narratives this may be seen most tellingly in those moments of wonder when what is discovered is not the disconcerting strangeness of the other so much as an idealized form of the familiar in the midst of the other. Contrary to Stephen Greenblatt's argument, in epiphanies of wonder ideology is just as likely to be reasserted as resisted.[32] What most moves Ralegh, for instance, is not the incomprehensibility or alterity of Guiana, but marvellous moments of recognition like this:

On both sides of the river, we passed the most beautiful countrie that ever mine eies beheld: and whereas all that we had seen before was nothing but woods, prickles, bushes, and thornes, heere we beheld plaines of twenty miles in length, the grasse short and greene, and in divers parts groves of trees by themselves, as if they had been by all the art and labour in the world so made of purpose and stil as we rowed, the Deere came downe feeding by the waters side, as if they had been used to a keepers call. (p. 48)

The same discovery of a civility so wonderful because of its unexpected familiarity is recounted by George Percy as he and his companions negotiate the labyrinthine woods of Nevis in the West Indies:

We past into the thickest of the Woods where we had almost lost our selves, we had not gone above half a mile amongst the thicke, but we came into a most pleasant Garden, being a hundred square paces on every side . . . we saw the goodliest tall trees growing about the Garden, as though they had beene set by Art, which made us marvel very much to see it.[33]

In *Paradise Lost*, Milton's immersion in colonial discovery narratives is evident in the way he reproduces the same wonderful moment of recognition. What we discover in his Paradise, so remote in time and exotic in location, is not so much a transcendent ideal as an idealized English quotidian. Following Satan, traveling east of Eden, beyond the undergrowth "so thick entwin'd" of "shrubs and tangling bushes," the "new wonder" that greets us is "A happy rural seat of various view" (IV, 174–76, 205, 247)— "almost laughably," says John Broadbent, registering his own moment of recognition, "the England of Penshurst, Cooper's Hill, and Appleton House."[34] The civility Adam and Eve seek and lose is precisely what Milton himself cannot give up. It is a discourse so pervasive and constitutive of other discourses—moral, epistemological, aesthetic—that it functions as his *habitus;* that is, in Pierre Bourdieu's explanation of ideology, the complex of "principles which generate and organize practices and representations that can be objectively adapted to their outcomes without presupposing a conscious aiming at ends"—in Eagleton's words, "the relay or transmission mechanism by which mental and social structures become incarnate in daily social activity."[35]

If the implication of Adam and Eve in a colonial romance is as deep rooted as I am suggesting, then one might expect their failure to be represented in terms of the ultimate colonial failure of civility, that is, of "going native." The fear that animates English colonial texts as diverse as Spenser's *View of the Present State of Ireland,* or John Rolfe's letter explaining his marriage to Pocahontas, is the fear of degeneration, of becoming savage, of being excluded from the civil community.[36] And that is, of course, exactly the fate that overtakes Adam and Eve. In their fall, the first settlers are metamorphosed into Indians. The difference between guilt and shame i. the difference between moral failure on the one hand and social transgression and exclusion on the other.[37] At their most intense moment of shame, Adam and Eve are excluded from the community into which they were born: "How shall I behold the face / Henceforth of God or Angel," cries Adam, "O might I here / In solitude live savage" (IX, 1080–81, 1084–85). In attempting to cover their "uncleanness" with fig leaves, they only confirm their excluded, degenerate status: "O how unlike / To that first naked Glorie," comments the poet. Now in their shame they look like the American Indians "*Columbus* found . . . so girt / With featherd Cincture, naked else and wilde / Among the Trees on Iles and woodie shores" (IX, 1114–18). For Milton, guilt and shame seem inseparable. That the Fall, the original moral failure of all humankind, is imagined in terms of what for many of us now is largely a matter of the cultural difference of a specific part of humankind suggests the degree to which moral failure in Milton cannot be imagined in terms other than those of the failure of civility or community transgression. Adam and Eve have not only broken God's commandment, but they have become the defining other of English or European culture. Covered with fig leaves, they imagine themselves back within the community—"Thus fenc't, and as they thought, thir shame in part / Coverd" (IX, 1119–20)—when in fact they are still outside the fence, beyond the pale: "distemperd," "estrang'd," "tost and turbulent" (IX, 1131, 1132, 1126).

To the extent that Adam and Eve are capable of regeneration, however, so the colonial quest can continue, and, as the evidence of American colonial writers like Cotton Mather suggests, the image of these first settlers will inspire generations of English colonists on their errand into the wilderness. In his *Magnalia Christi Americana* (1702), for instance, Mather imagines the garden as New England overgrown and threatened by Satan and his followers in the form of the Indians:

About this time *New-England* was miserably *Briar'd* in the Perplexities of an *Indian War;* and the Salvages, in the *East* part of the Country, issuing out from their inaccessible *Swamps,* had for many Months made their Cruel Depredations upon the poor *English* Planters, and surprized many of the Plantations on the Frontiers, into Ruin. . . . They [the English] found, that they were like to make no weapons reach their Enswamped Adversaries, except Mr. *Milton* could have shown them how

> To have pluckt up the Hills with all their Load,
> Rocks, Waters, woods, and by their shaggy tops,
> Up-lifting, borne them in their Hands, therewith
> The Rebel Host to've over-whelm'd.[38]

IV

Milton as a poet against empire is too easy. In his "Digression on the Long Parliament," which he sought to publish with his *History of Britain* long after the Restoration in 1670, Milton urges his readers to learn the lessons of political failure.[39] Unless the conduct of affairs is given to "men more then vulgar," he says, men "bred up . . . in the knowledge of Antient and illustrious deeds, invincible against money, and vaine titles," men whose minds are "well implanted with solid & elaborate breeding," then "wee shall else miscarry still and com short in the attempt of any great enterprise" (YP V, p. 451). Though this was written in 1649, the fact that Milton wanted it published in 1670 does not suggest that he was someone who had given up on England's need to cultivate its nether empire. This is even more apparent in his last polemical pamphlet, *Of True Religion* (1673), in which he proudly recalls England's defining act of independence in throwing off the "*Babylonish* Yoke" of the pope's authority and happily joins in the common work of the nation in hindering "the growth of this Romish Weed": "I thought it no less then a common duty to lend my hand, how unable soever, to so good a Purpose" (YP VIII, pp. 430, 417–18).

The *locus classicus* for the quietist Milton's rejection of empire is Jesus' excoriation of the Roman Empire's corruption in *Paradise Regained* (1671). But Jesus' rejection of Rome turns out to be highly ambiguous. First, the rejection comprises a traditional, humanist civility argument. Jesus makes it clear that though Rome has become degenerate, it had actually started out well: the Romans "who once just, / Frugal, and mild, and temperate, [had] *conquer'd well*" (IV, 133–34; my emphasis). Thus, presumably, for a state or people bound by the civil imperatives of justice, frugality, mildness, and temperance, it was still possible to conquer well. Second, the affective attraction of power is evident in Jesus' intensely threatening millenarian prophecy:

> Know therefore when my season comes to sit
> On *David's* Throne, it shall be like a tree
> Spreading and over-shadowing all the Earth,
> Or as a stone that shall to pieces dash
> All Monarchies besides throughout the world
> And of my kingdom there shall be no end.   (IV, 146–51)[40]

The anger of the dispossessed in this apocalyptic passage makes it difficult not to recall D. H. Lawrence's comments on the Book of Revelation: "For Revelation, be it said once and for all, is the revelation of the undying will-to-power in man, and its sanctification, its final triumph." And as Laura Knoppers has recently shown, the allusions to the Book of Daniel in this

prophecy had immediate, aggressively political, "Fifth Monarchy" ramifications for Restoration England.[41]

The strongest evidence in *Paradise Lost* (1674) for Milton's rejection of
empire is Michael's quietist admonitions, but the poem's closing books are
an act of public humiliation and it is in this context that the archangel's
admonitions are best understood. Even then they are every bit as ambiguous as Jesus' rejection of Rome. It is true that Michael encourages Adam to
focus on obedience rather than what he once possessed in Paradise, "all the
rule, one Empire" (XII, 581), but at the same time Adam makes it clear that
the imperial imperative of Genesis i, 28, has not lapsed: "that right we hold /
By his donation" (XII, 68–69). It is true, we are somewhat belatedly told,
that the imperative was never meant to legitimize "Dominion absolute" of
"Man over men" (XII, 68–70), but in Michael's nostalgic glance back at
what might have been, Adam's empire is imagined as a patriarchal dominion
in which the garden might have been

> Perhaps thy Capital Seate, from whence had spred
> All generations, and hither come
> From all the ends of th'Earth, to celebrate
> And reverence thee thir great Progenitor.   (XI, 343–46)

And outside the poem, it is clear that Milton does not stop believing in the
necessity for a civil community in which some people will be subject to
others: the vulgar will still have to be led, the corrupt punished, the Romish
weeded out, the savage civilized, and so on. There is, for instance, no evidence to suggest that Milton ever felt the need to revise his view that the
Irish were degenerate and had merely proved their obdurate willfulness by
refusing to take advantage of England's "civilizing Conquest" to "improve
and waxe more civill" (*Observations upon the Articles of Peace*, YP III, p.
304). Finally, it is true that Michael urges Adam to concentrate on the "paradise within thee, happier farr" (XII, 587), but, if my argument is true, then
that admonition to turn inward and forget the expansiveness of the Genesis
imperative will be undermined by the logic of daily practice—the quotidian
demands of early modern civility. Not least, it will be undermined by the
extraordinary, affective power of those demands' ideal representation in
Milton's version of Paradise, and the consequent longing or lack that that
aesthetic achievement creates in the readers of Milton's great poem.

As all his writings testify, Milton was an intensely idealistic and moral
man, and what is most challenging about him, like Las Casas and other
putative early modern anticolonialists, is that it is his very virtue, his desire
for civility and his refusal of any thoroughgoing relativism, that makes it so
difficult for him to stand outside the discourse of colonialism. To argue oth-

erwise is to underestimate the power of ideology and to continue the work of diluting the truly important insights of the political criticism that we associate with cultural materialism and the now much-denigrated new historicism.

Queen's University, Canada

NOTES

1. John White, *The Planter's Plea* (London, 1630; rpt. New York, 1968), p. 1.

2. David Quint, *Epic and Empire: Politics and Generic Form from Virgil to Milton* (Princeton, 1993). Other works on Milton and early modern colonialism include Robert Ralston Cawley, *Milton and the Literature of Travel* (Princeton, 1951); James H. Sims, "Camoëns' 'Lusiads' and Milton's 'Paradise Lost': Satan's Voyage to Eden," in *Papers on Milton*, ed. Philip Mahone Griffith and Lester F. Zimmerman (Tulsa, 1969); *John Milton: Paradise Lost: Books IX–X*, ed. J. Martin Evans (Cambridge, 1973), esp. pp. 46–47; I. S. MacLaren, "Arctic Exploration and Milton's 'Frozen Continent,'" *N&Q*, new ser. XXXI, no. 3 (1984), 325–26; Gordon Campbell, "The Wealth of Ormus and of Ind,"*MQ* XXI, no. 1 (1987), 22–23; V. J. Kiernan, "Milton in Heaven," in *Reviving the English Revolution*, ed. Geoff Eley and William Hunt (London, 1988), pp. 161–80; Thomas N. Corns, "Milton's *Observations upon the Articles of Peace*: Ireland Under English Eyes," in *Politics, Poetics, and Hermeneutics in Milton's Prose*, ed. David Loewenstein and James Grantham Turner (Cambridge, 1990), pp. 123–34; Andrew Barnaby, " 'Another Rome in the West?': Milton and the Imperial Republic, 1654–70," *Milton Studies* XXX, ed. Albert C. Labriola (Pittsburgh, 1993), pp. 67–84; Paul Stevens, " 'Leviticus Thinking' and the Rhetoric of Early Modern Colonialism," *Criticism* XXXV, no. 3 (1993), 441–61; "Spenser and Milton on Ireland: Civility, Exclusion, and the Politics of Wisdom," *ARIEL* XXVI, no. 4 (1995), 151–67; and David Armitage, "John Milton: Poet Against Empire," in *Milton and Republicanism*, ed. David Armitage et al. (Cambridge, 1995). I should also mention three unpublished papers: Paul Brophy, " 'So Many Signs of Power and Rule': Colonial Discourse, Pastoralism, and the Representation of Autochthony in *Paradise Lost*," 1990; Balachandra Rajan, "Banyan Trees and Fig Leaves: Some Thoughts on Milton's India," 1991; and Bruce McLeod, "The 'Lordly Eye': Milton's Imperial Imagination," 1995.

3. Terry Eagleton, "Discourse and Discos," *Times Literary Supplement*, 15 July 1994, p. 3.

4. See Peter Brooks, "Frighted with False Fire," *Times Literary Supplement*, 26 May 1995, pp. 10–11.

5. Thomas S. Kuhn, *The Structure of Scientific Revolutions*, 2nd ed. (Chicago, 1970), esp. pp. 10–34.

6. Patricia A. Parker, *Inescapable Romance: Studies in the Poetics of a Mode* (Princeton, 1979), p. 220.

7. David Bromwich, *A Choice of Inheritance: Self and Community from Edmund Burke to Robert Frost* (Cambridge, Mass., 1989), p. 279. For Quint's praise of Bromwich's "searching" critique, see *Epic and Empire*, p. 370.

8. Milton's poetry is quoted from *The Works of John Milton*, ed. Frank Allen Patterson et al., 18 vols. (New York, 1931–38), and his prose, unless otherwise indicated, from *Complete*

Prose Works of John Milton, ed. Don M. Wolfe et al., 8 vols. (New Haven, 1953–82). Here .⁶ cited as CM and YP, respectively.

9. Evans, *Paradise Lost: Books IX–X*, pp. 46–47.

10. See Quint, *Epic and Empire*, p. 169: "Unlike the other European nations engaged in imperial and colonial expansion in the New World, the Spaniards seriously worried about the legality and morality of their project."

11. Much more pointedly, he may also be offering his readers an idealized view of those smaller, domestic merchants who were excluded from overseas commerce by the increasingly Royalist "great Marchants" of the chartered companies. For the rivalry between the two groups, see Robert Brenner, *Merchants and Revolution: Commercial Change, Political Conflict, and London's Overseas Traders, 1550–1653* (Princeton, 1993), esp. pp. 83–89.

12. Richard Hakluyt the younger, Epistle Dedicatory, *The Principal Navigations of the English Nation*, Vol. II of *The Original Writings & Correspondence of the Two Richard Hakluyts*, ed. E.G.R. Taylor, 2 vols. (1589; rpt. Nendeln, Liechtenstein, 1967), p. 400; *A True Declaration of the State of Virginia*, vol. V of *New American World: A Documentary History of North America to 1612*, ed. D. B. Quinn, 5 vols. (New York, 1979), p. 250.

13. "And so the Inhabiters of Hormuz doe say, that all the world is a ring, and Hormuz is the stone of it." "Relations of Ormuz," in vol. X of Samuel Purchas, *Hakluytus Posthumus, or Purchas His Pilgrimes* (1625), 20 vols. (1905–07; rpt. New York, 1965), p. 324. See also Campbell, "The Wealth of Ormus," pp. 22–23, Cawley, *Milton and the Literature of Travel*, pp. 78–79, and Sir William Foster, *England's Quest of Eastern Trade* (London, 1937), pp. 295–313.

14. See William Riley Parker, *Milton: A Biography*, 2 vols. (Oxford, 1968), vol. I, pp. 6–8; vol. II, pp. 698–701.

15. See YP VIII, p. 459.

16. M.M.S., *The Spanish Colonie* (London, 1583); rpt. in Purchas, *Hakluytus Posthumus*, vol. XVIII, pp. 83–180.

17. Richard Hakluyt the younger sets the tone in his *Discourse of Western Planting* (London, 1584); rpt. in *Original Writings*, ed. Taylor, vol. II, pp. 211–326, esp. pp. 257–65. See also Richard Helgerson, *Forms of Nationhood: The Elizabethan Writing of England* (Chicago, 1992), pp. 151–91, esp. p. 185.

18. Sir Walter Ralegh, *The Discoverie of the Large, Rich, and Bewtiful Empyre of Guiana* (1596; rpt. New York, 1968), p. 7. On Ralegh's Spenserian self-representation, see Louis Montrose, "The Work of Gender in the Discourse of Discovery," *Representations* XXXIII (1991): 177–217, esp. 187. See also Mary C. Fuller, "Ralegh's Fugitive Gold: Reference and Deferral in *The Discoverie of Guiana*," *Representations* XXXIII (1991), 42–64.

19. On the propaganda for the Western Design, see Karen Ordahl Kupperman, "Errand to the Indies: Puritan Colonization from Providence Island through the Western Design," *William and Mary Quarterly*, 3rd ser., XLV, no. 1 (1988): 70–99, and Janet Clare, "The Production and Reception of Davenant's *Cruelty of the Spaniards in Peru*," MLR XXXIX, no. 4 (1994): 832–41.

20. Sir William Davenant, *The Cruelty of the Spaniards in Peru*, in *The Works of Sir William Davenant*, 2 vols. (1673; rpt. New York, 1968), vol. II, pp. 103–14, esp. pp. 111–14. John Phillips, *The Tears of the Indians* (1656; rpt. Stanford, n.d.), sig. A8ˇ.

21. CM XIII, pp. 509–63, esp. pp. 517, 555. Since J. Max Patrick's rejection in YP V, pp. 711–12, the tide of critical opinion has turned against Milton's authorship of the *Declaration*. While Kiernan, "Milton in Heaven," p. 175, and Clare, "Production and Reception," p. 835, seem unaware that there is an issue, Kupperman, "Errand to the Indies," p. 94, concludes that the manifesto "was written by a committee headed by Nathaniel Fiennes." Robert T. Fallon, *Milton in Government* (University Park, Pa., 1993), pp. 99–100, follows Patrick, and

Dustin Griffin, *Regaining Paradise: Milton in the Eighteenth Century* (Cambridge, 1986), p. 279, persuasively argues that Thomas Birch's attribution of the Manifesto to Milton in 1738 was conditioned by impending hostilities with Spain and the parliamentary opposition's desire to enlist the prestige of Milton's name in its attacks on Walpole's reluctance to go to war.

22. See Fallon, *Milton in Government*, pp. 88–100, 229–46; *The Faerie Queene* V, x, 8ff.

23. Sir Francis Bacon, "Of Plantations," in *The Essayes or Counsels, Civill and Morall*, ed. Michael Kiernan (1625; rpt. Oxford, 1985), p. 106. The same point, but with the added authority of Genesis i, 28, is made in the *Declaration Against Spain*: "The best Title, that any can have to what they possess in those parts of America, is Plantation and Possession, where there were no Inhabitants, or where there were any, by their consent, or at least in such waste and desolate parts of their Countries, as they are not able in any measure to plant, and possesse; (God having made the world for the use of men, and ordained them to replenish the same.)" (CM XIII, p. 555).

24. Compare Cawley, *Milton and the Literature of Travel*, and Joseph E. Duncan, *Milton's Earthly Paradise: A Historical Study of Eden* (Minneapolis, 1972), esp. pp. 188–233, 234–42.

25. Robert Johnson, *Nova Britannia* (London, 1609), in Quinn, *New American World*, vol. V, p. 239. Compare Annette Kolodny, *The Lay of the Land: Metaphor as Experience and History in American Life and Letters* (Chapel Hill, 1975), esp. pp. 10–25. "Virginias Verger," in Purchas, *Hakluytus Posthumus*, vol. XIX, pp. 243, 242.

26. Quinn, *New American World*, vol. 5, p. 238. On the centrality of civility, see, for instance, Nicholas Canny's seminal article, "The Ideology of English Colonization: From Ireland to America," *William and Mary Quarterly*, 3rd ser. XXX (1973): 575–98.

27. Compare Montrose, "The Work of Gender," 186–88.

28. For a different way of interpreting the colonial uses of romance, see Stephen Greenblatt, *Marvelous Possessions: The Wonder of the New World* (Chicago, 1991), esp. pp. 132–33.

29. Especially suggestive is Terry Eagleton's critique of Adorno in *Ideology: An Introduction* (London, 1991), esp. pp. 126–27, 221–24, and Fredric Jameson, *The Political Unconscious: Narrative as a Socially Symbolic Act* (Ithaca, N.Y., 1981), pp. 103–50.

30. Compare Paul Stevens, *Imagination and the Presence of Shakespeare in "Paradise Lost"* (Madison, 1985), pp. 11–45, esp. pp. 21–22.

31. Quoted from *The Tempest*, ed. Stephen Orgel (Oxford, 1987). For *The Tempest* as a colonial romance, see especially Paul Brown, " 'This Thing of Darkness I Acknowledge Mine': *The Tempest* and the Discourse of Colonialism," in *Political Shakespeare: New Essays in Cultural Materialism*, ed. Jonathan Dollimore and Alan Sinfield (Manchester, 1985), pp. 48–71.

32. Greenblatt, *Marvelous Possessions*, pp. 17–19: "The experience of wonder seems to resist recuperation, containment, ideological incorporation."

33. George Percy, "A Discourse of the Plantation of the Southern Colonie in Virginia" (1606–07), in Quinn, *New American World*, vol. V, p. 268.

34. John B. Broadbent, *Some Graver Subject: An Essay on "Paradise Lost"* (1960; rpt. London, 1967), p. 184.

35. Pierre Bourdieu, *The Logic of Practice*, trans. Richard Nice (Stanford, Calif., 1990), p. 53; Eagleton, *Ideology*, p. 156.

36. Compare Edmund Spenser, *A View of the Present State of Ireland*, ed. W. L. Renwick (Oxford, 1970), esp. pp. 63–69, and John Rolfe, "Letter to Sir Thomas Dale," in Ralph Hamor, *A True Discourse of the Present Estate of Virginia* (1615; rpt. New York, 1971), pp. 61–68.

37. On the difference between moral rules and pollution rules, see Mary Douglas, *Purity and Danger: An Analysis of Concepts of Pollution and Taboo* (London, 1966), esp. pp. 129–39.

38. Compare *Paradise Lost* VI, 644–47. Cotton Mather, *Magnalia Christi* \ ⋅ ⋅⋅⋅⋅, Books I and II, ed. Kenneth B. Murdock (Cambridge, Mass.. 19⁷⁻ˀ, ⵏ ⵣⵊ ﹚. George F. Sensabaugh, *Milton in Early America* (Princeton, 1964) is the strongest advocate for the shaping influence of Milton in colonial America. Sensabaugh's views are contested by Keith W. F. Stavely, especially in "The World All Before Them: Milton and the Rising Glory of America," *Studies in Eighteenth-Century Culture* XX (1990): 147–64. However, in his effort to distance the poet, whom he considers increasingly antimillenarian and antinationalist, from the imperialism of American revolutionary rhetoric, Stavely inadvertently reveals just how imperial a poem many colonial Americans took *Paradise Lost* to be. Their "misreading," if it is one, constitutes eloquent testimony to the poem's ideological force.

39. The "Digression" was written in 1649 and, according to Edward Phillips, could not pass the licensor in 1670. For the complex but fascinating political and textual history of the "Digression," see Nicholas von Maltzahn, *Milton's "History of Britain": Republican Historiography in the English Revolution* (Oxford, 1991), pp. 1–21, 22–48, esp. pp. 45–46.

40. Compare Barnaby, "Milton and the Imperial Republic," pp. 78–81.

41. Lawrence, *Apocalypse* (1931; rpt. London, 1972), p. 13; Knoppers, *Historicizing Milton: Spectacle, Power, and Poetry in Restoration England* (Athens, Ga., 1994), pp. 123–41, esp. pp. 137–41.

PARADISE LOST AND MILTON'S POLITICS

Barbara Kiefer Lewalski

INTO *PARADISE LOST* Milton poured all that he had learned, experienced, desired, and imagined about life, love, artistic creativity, theology,
work, history—and politics. He had been thinking about writing some kind of
epic for decades, on the model of Homer and Virgil and Tasso, and with a
great national hero like King Arthur. When he came to doubt Arthur's historicity he considered King Alfred. We cannot be sure just when Milton decided
that the great epic subject for his own times had to be the Fall and its
consequences: not the founding of a great empire or nation, but the loss of an
earthly paradise and with it any possibility of founding an enduring version of
the City of God on earth.[1] He probably settled on this subject for epic
sometime in the 1650s—"long choosing, and beginning late," as he put it in
the proem to Book Nine.[2] He may have begun writing around 1658 and
completed some part of the poem before the Restoration of 1660 brought
Charles II back to the throne. John Aubrey reports, citing Edward Phillips as
source, that Milton began the poem "about 2 yeares before the K. came-in,
and finished about 3 yeares after the K's Restauracion," working on it only
during the winter months and spending about four or five years on it (*EL*,
13).[3] The proem to Book Seven, with its dark references to the bard fallen on
"evil dayes" and encompassed round with dangers, suggests that much of the
final six books postdate the Restoration. He evidently had a complete draft in
hand by August, 1665, when his Quaker friend Thomas Ellwood reported
seeing it.[4] Most likely he continued working on it at Chalfont and in London,
during the eighteen months before its publication in 1667.

But those dangers and disappointments did not lead Milton, as some
critics believe, to write an epic that abandons politics and honors a quietistic
retreat to the spiritual realm, the "paradise within."[5] Several recent studies—
by, among others, Joan Bennett, Laura Lunger Knoppers, Sharon Achinstein, and most recently David Norbrook[6]—have challenged that view, underscoring some political issues the poem engages. I mean to argue here that
Milton's poem is a more daring political gesture than we often realize, even as
it is also a poem for the ages by a prophet poet who placed himself with (or
above) Homer, Virgil, Ariosto, Tasso, and the rest. It undertakes a strenuous
project of educating readers in the virtues, values, and attitudes that make a

people worthy of liberty, and we need to recognize just how emphatic its political lessons were and are. In the moral realm the Miltonic bard exercises his readers in discernment, rigorous judgment, imaginative apprehension, and choice by setting his poem in relation to other great epics and works in other genres, thereby prompting a critique of the values associated with those other heroes and genres.[7] In the political realm, he involves them in thinking through the ideological and polemic controversies of the recent war, engaging them to think again, and think rightly, about monarchy, tyranny, rebellion, liberty, hierarchy, and republicanism. The long reception history of *Paradise Lost* demonstrates that it was quite possible to ignore, or to misread, the poem's politics. But that is not, I think, because Milton has obscured these issues out of confusion or misjudgment, or sought to give himself cover from the censors,[8] or multiplied difficulties in the reading process as a deliberate educational strategy. These considerations cannot be discounted, especially Sharon Achinstein's view that Milton's readers are made to struggle for right understanding as a means to form them as revolutionary readers. But it seems to me that Milton intends to make his political meanings clear, though of course when he challenges stereotypes he runs the inevitable risk of activating them. His fit readers may be few, but he wanted his poem to produce as many more of them as possible.

Throughout the revolutionary period, as Milton engaged his pen to the cause of reform, regicide, and a more nearly ideal church, state, and society, he continually sought to prod, goad, and educate his countrymen to understand the evils of monarchical government, the virtue of a republic, and above all the need to secure religious toleration for all Protestants and to separate church and state. Like others in the tradition of Plato, Aristotle, and Machiavelli, he believed that kinds of government—monarchy, aristocracy, democracy—must conform to the nature of the people, and that people get the government they deserve and are fit for. Monarchy is justified only when the king is vastly superior to the rest, but that condition seldom obtains, and when it does it should not: monarchy, and especially absolute monarchy, Milton came increasingly to believe, is a debased form of government only suited to a servile, debased people. Properly, government should be shared among the large body of worthy citizens who are virtuous and love liberty: as he put it in the *First Defense*, "It is neither fitting nor proper for a man to be king unless he be far superior to all the rest; where there are many equals, and in most states there are very many, I hold they should rule alike and in turn."[9] But the continuing disaffection of the majority of the English people after the regicide forced restrictive governments: first, by the unrepresentative Rump, and then by a Protectorate veering ever closer to monarchy. In supporting those governments, Milton recognized that England was not becoming the nation of prophets he had so hopefully envisioned in *Areopagitica*, nor yet the republic of worthy, virtuous, liberty-loving citizens he had projected in the *Tenure of Kings and Magistrates*.

Yet early to late he continued his efforts to educate his countrymen to the moral and political virtues he thought necessary to sustain a republican commonwealth. In *Of Education* (1645) he laid out a curriculum intended to fit students to be citizens, "to perform justly, skillfully and magnanimously all the offices both private and publike of peace and war" (YP 2:378–79). In his *History of Britain* (c. 1648–49) he sought to help Englishmen recognize and counter what he saw as a worrisome characteristic, displayed over and over again in their history: though valorous in war, they sadly lacked the civic virtues needed to sustain free governments and their own liberties, and should supply that lack by gaining "ripe understanding and many civil vertues . . . from forren writings & examples of best ages" (YP 5:451). In his *First Defense* he laments the disaffection of "a great part of the people [who] . . . longed for peace and slavery" [i.e., a restoration of the monarchy] but he hopes that a republican ethos will teach them better values:

I can still say that their sins were taught them under the monarchy, like the Israelites in Egypt, and have not been immediately unlearned in the desert, even under the guidance of God. But there is much hope for most of them, not to enter on the praises of our good and reverent men who follow earnestly after truth.   (YP 4:386–87)

In that tract and yet more earnestly in the *Second Defense* (1654), even as he justifies Cromwell's Protectorate on the ground that he alone has proved superlatively worthy to lead, he pleads passionately with his countrymen to display the political virtue that will fit them to participate in government:

By the customary judgment and, so to speak, just retaliation of God, it happens that a nation which cannot rule and govern itself, but has delivered itself into slavery to its own lusts, is enslaved also to other masters whom it does not choose. . . . Learn to obey right reason, to master yourselves. Lastly, refrain from factions, hatreds, superstitions injustices, lusts and rapine against one another. Unless you do this with all your strength you cannot seem either to God or to men, or even to your recent liberators, fit to be entrusted with the liberty and guidance of the state.   (YP 4:684)

In the *Readie and Easie Way to Establish a Free Commonwealth* (1660), published on the eve of the Restoration, he again proposes schools in each locale to train up children in "all liberal arts and exercises," as a means of spreading "knowledge and civilitie, yea religion through all parts of the land," and to make the people "flourishing, vertuous, noble and high spirited" (YP 7:460). And though he recognized that it was then all but hopeless to try to prevent the king's return, he still dared to hope his argument might have some effect: "I trust I shall have spoken perswasion to abundance of sensible and ingenuous men, to som perhaps whom God may raise of these stones to become children of reviving libertie" (YP 7:463).

After Charles II and the Anglican Church were restored in all courtly magnificence, Milton saw several of his regicide friends executed and Puritan dissenters harshly repressed. He himself was for some months in danger of execution for treason and spent some weeks in prison; in the proem to Book Seven of *Paradise Lost* he laments that he has fallen "On evil dayes . . . / In darkness, and with dangers compast round" (PL 7.26–27). He had reason to fear that his epic and any high poetry might be drowned out by the "barbarous dissonance" of the Restoration court's Bacchic revelers, and that he might meet the fate of the archetypal bard, Orpheus, who was killed and dismembered by other followers of Bacchus:

> But drive farr off the barbarous dissonance
> Of *Bacchus* and his revellers, the Race
> Of that wild Rout that tore the *Thracian* Bard
> In *Rhodope*, where Woods and Rocks had Eares
> To rapture, till the savage clamor dround
> Both Harp and Voice; nor could the Muse defend
> Her Son. So fail not thou, who thee implores:
> For thou art Heav'nlie, shee an empty dreame.   (7.32–39)

But he does not despair, because he can rely on the protective powers of his muse Urania, who is in part a figure for heavenly aid and inspiration. Nor does he hide or change his politics.

The poem's form makes its first overt political statement. For the first edition in 1667 Milton set aside Virgil's and Tasso's twelve-book epic format and chose instead the ten-book model of the Roman republican poet Lucan. That choice distances Milton's epic from Virgil's celebration of the glorious empire of Augustus predestined by the Gods, and from Tasso's celebration, through the story of the first crusade, of Counter-Reformation hegemony restored over all varieties of rebellion and dissent.[10] It also signals that *Paradise Lost* is not an epic of conquest and empire, though Satan conceives of his adventure in such terms. But another reason for Milton to gesture toward Lucan was surely that royalists had appropriated the Virgilian heroic mode both before and after the Restoration. John Denham's translation in heroic couplets of Book Two of the *Aeneid* under the title, *The Destruction of Troy* (1656), makes Aeneas' narrative of and lament for the death of King Priam and the destruction of Troy resonate with the regicide and the royalist defeat. Denham's poem ends well before Virgil's Book Two does, with a scene of Priam's beheading that evokes the beheading of Charles: "On the cold earth lies th'unregarded King, / A headless Carkass, and a nameless Thing."[11] After the Restoration, in what Laura Knoppers terms the "politics of joy," poets hailed the new era in Virgilian terms as a golden age restored, celebrating Charles II as a new Augustus; his coronation procession was designed as a magnificent Roman Triumph through elaborate Roman arches mythologizing him as Augustus, Aeneas, and Neptune.[12] Dryden's *Astraea Redux* (1660) rings changes on those motifs: "Oh Happy Age! Oh times like those alone / By Fate reserv'd for Great *Augustus* Throne."[13]

Also, Milton probably obtained and had someone read to him Dryden's *Annus Mirabilis,* which appeared in January, 1667.[14] Treating the naval losses and the great fire of 1666, that poem was carefully designed to recoup the king's reputation in the face of intense criticism. Patriarchal imagery covers over his barrenness and profligacy, representing him as a pious and tender father of his people: rebuilding the destroyed navy, directing rescue efforts in the fire, and giving shape to the vision of a reborn and far grander "Augustan" city.[15] With his own epic at some prepublication stage, Milton would have been especially interested in Dryden's essay defending this new model of a heroic poem based on contemporary events and serving royalist interests. Terming his poem "Historical, not Epick," Dryden nonetheless claims that kind as a branch of epic, insisting that his poem's "Actions and Actors are as much Heroick, as any Poem can contain." He also lays claim to the Virgilian legacy: his master, he proclaims, is Virgil and he has "followed him every where."[16] This new claimant to the modern heroic poem would surely goad Milton to offer the fit reader, promptly, his better version of epic. If Milton had not yet given his poem its Lucanian ten-book structure, Dryden's new royalist poem so explicitly claiming Virgil's mantle could have prompted republican Milton to find a formal means of withholding his poem from such Virgilian appropriations, even as he emphasizes in the opening lines of his epic that the true restoration will not be effected by an English Augustus, but must await a divine hero: "Till one greater Man / Restore us, and regain the blissful Seat."

Lucan's unfinished epic, *Pharsalia,* or *The Civil War,* was the font of a counter tradition. It celebrates the resistance of the Roman republic and its heroes, Pompey and Cato, who were finally defeated by the victorious tyrant Caesar in a bloody civil war. But, by ascribing that event to contingency and chance, not the Gods, and by having the spirit of the butchered Pompey enter into the future tyrannicide, Brutus (9.1–17), Lucan suggests an ongoing struggle against Caesarism.[17] Lucan's own career was readily assimilated to his story, since he was forced to commit suicide at age twenty-six for involvement in a botched conspiracy against Caesar's infamous successor, Nero. As David Norbrook has demonstrated, by Milton's time Lucan's epic was firmly associated with antimonarchical and republican politics through several editions and translations, especially the English version by the Long Parliament's historian-to-be, Thomas May (1627).[18]

Milton did organize his poem in twelve books for the second edition, 1674, by the simple expedient of splitting two books and adding a few lines. He did not intend to blunt the political import, but rather, I would suggest, to reclaim the central epic tradition for his better subject and nobler heroism, at a time when royalist Virgilianism was no longer such an issue. While Milton's poem includes the full range of topics and conventions common to the Homeric and Virgilian epic tradition,[19] it explicitly rejects the traditional epic subject (wars and empire) and the traditional representation of the epic hero as the epitome of courage and battle prowess. *Paradise Lost* celebrates, not an emperor or a debauched Charles II, but the only true king and kingdom in heaven; not the heroism of war but the "better fortitude / Of Patience and Heroic Martyrdom"; not a Virgilian earthly empire and new golden age but an earthly paradise now tragically lost. His protagonists are a domestic pair, Adam and Eve; the scene of their action is a pastoral garden, not a battlefield;[20] and their primary challenge is, "under long obedience tri'd" (7.159), to make themselves, their marital relationship, and their garden (as the nucleus of the human world) ever more perfect. The combats they fight and lose—but will ultimately win in conjunction with the "greater man" Christ— are moral and spiritual. Milton's epic in twelve books formally enlists that noblest genre in the service of his dearest values.

Another formal element of Milton's poem, blank verse, also carried political resonance, since rhyme, and especially the heroic couplet, had become the norm for heroic poetry and drama in the Restoration court. In *Annus Mirabilis* Dryden claimed that, while classical unrhymed verse gave poets more freedom, his four-line stanzas in alternating rhyme are "more noble, and of greater dignity, both for the sound and number, then any other verse in use amongst us."[21] Also, by coincidence Dryden's essay *Of Dramatick Poesie* was registered with the Stationers the same month as Milton's epic, August 1667, and it probably greeted the reading public at about the same time.[22] At the end of the essay Neander, Dryden's persona, makes a case for rhyme as the distinguishing excellence of modern poets and the best verse form for tragedy and heroic drama.[23] He affirms, categorically, that "Blank Verse is acknowledg'd to be too low for a Poem, nay more, for a paper of verses; but if too low for an ordinary Sonnet, how much more for Tragedy"— or for epic, he implies, since he considers drama and epic to be of the same genus.[24] Moreover, in the preface to the work Dryden notes that rhyme enjoys the favor of the court, "the last and surest judge of writing."[25] If

Milton's printer Samuel Simmons recognized that in this cultural milieu readers expected rhyme and needed an explanation for its absence, Milton was no doubt happy to take up the gauntlet thrown down by his erstwhile colleague in Cromwell's Secretariat, now the rising star on the poetic and critical horizon. He did so for the 1668 printing, challenging not only the new poetic norms but also the debased court culture and royalist politics that nurture them:

The measure is *English* Heroic Verse without Rime, as that of *Homer* in *Greek*, and of *Virgil* in *Latin*; Rime being no necessary Adjunct or true Ornament of Poem or good Verse, in longer Works especially, but the Invention of a barbarous Age, to set off wretched matter and lame Meeter; grac't indeed since by the use of some famous modern Poets, carried away by Custom, but much to thir own vexation, hindrance, and constraint to express many things otherwise, and for the most part worse then else they would have exprest them. Not without cause therefore some both *Italian* and *Spanish* Poets of prime note have rejected Rime both in longer and shorter Works, as have also long since our best *English* Tragedies, as a thing of it self, to all judicious ears, trivial and of no true musical delight. . . . This neglect then of Rime so little is to be taken for a defect, though it may seem so perhaps to vulgar Readers, that it rather is to be esteem'd an example set, the first in *English*, of ancient liberty restored to Heroic Poem from the troublesome and modern bondage of Riming. (sigs. a 3v–a 4)

This language elevates Milton's blank verse above the practices of the barbarous gothic age and the vulgar taste of the present, and associates it not only with ancient poetic liberty but also, as Steven Zwicker notes, with the restoration of English liberty from the modern bondage of Stuart tyranny.[26] Milton makes his choice of blank verse the aesthetic complement to republican politics and culture.

Early responses to the poem indicate that it aroused political suspicion. As required by the Press Act of 1662 that revived the system of censorship for all books and periodicals, Milton submitted the *Paradise Lost* manuscript to the censors before its initial publication, and the censor, Thomas Tomkyns, who was a royalist, a high churchman, and domestic chaplain to the Archbishop of Canterbury, Gilbert Sheldon, reportedly denied it a license at first.[27] That censor would surely check carefully for subversion a poem by the notorious Milton, whose regicide and divorce treatises were still being cited and vigorously denounced in the press in the mid-1660s.[28] John Toland reports that Tomkyns objected especially to a passage in Book One:

I must not forget that we had like to be eternally depriv'd of this Treasure by the Ignorance or Malice of the Licenser; who, among other frivolous Exceptions, would needs suppress the whole Poem for imaginary Treason in the following lines.

----------As when the Sun new risen
Looks thro the Horizontal misty Air
Shorn of his Beams, or from behind the Moon
In dim Eclipse disastrous Twilight sheds
On half the Nations, and with fear of change
Perplexes Monarchs.   (*EL*, 180; *PL* 1.594–99)

At first blush it seems odd that Tomkyns singled out these lines rather than, say, the overt republicanism of the Nimrod passage in Michael's prophecy (12.24–71). But the recent series of English calamities—the Great Plague of 1665, the Great Fire of 1666, and losses in the Dutch Wars—were being read as God's punishment for the nation's sins and linked with dire predictions attaching to comets and a recent solar eclipse (June 22, 1666), which church and government were eager to suppress. As one tract put it, eclipses are always attended by astounding effects such as "the death of Kings and Great persons, alterations of Governments, change of Laws."[29] However, Tomkyns probably thought that this complex poem posed little danger to the masses by comparison with the more overt subversion from dissenters' sermons and treatises, and so was prevailed upon to give it his (undated) imprimatur in late 1666 or early 1667.[30] The poem may have escaped harsher scrutiny because it was submitted, perhaps by Milton's design, at a time of weakened government and relaxed severities against nonconformists in the wake of the plague, the fire, and the fall of Charles's chief minister, Clarendon.[31] The first documented response to the poem, in letters from the royalist John Beale to John Evelyn, points to the Nimrod passage as evidence that "Milton holds to his old Principle"; he also found the "blasphemies" of the devils deeply disturbing.[32]

The early publication history of the poem also testifies to uneasiness about it and its author. *Paradise lost, a Poem in Tenne Bookes* was registered with the Stationers by Samuel Simmons on August 20, 1667; Milton is identified only by his initials, J. M.[33] The text of the first edition, a quarto, was well printed, in an attractive format and on good paper—gilt edged in some copies. But readers may well have been surprised at the stark presentation of the poem in the first three issues: it had no dedicatory or commendatory verses, no epistle from author or bookseller, no prefatory matter at all to engage the reader's interest or sympathy—not even the bookseller's name. That Milton's poem was sent forth into the world bare and unaccommodated suggests that the likely presenters and commenders had qualms about associating themselves with the rebel Milton's return to print. Yet Milton may have been willing enough to see his poem presented without the usual apparatus, wishing to separate himself decisively from the system of patronage and to present himself, as he had in his prose tracts, as a new kind of author in the market-oriented system aptly termed by Peter Lindenbaum a "Republican Mode of Literary Production."[34] Over the next three years the first edition was issued with six different title pages and distributed by six different booksellers—a strategy for making it more widely available, spreading the risk, and promoting sales.[35] The changing title pages with changing styles indicate continued anxiety on Simmons's part that a poem by the notorious Commonwealth polemicist might be shunned by prospective readers as treasonous or heretical. The title pages of the first three issues include, in large type, a message intended to reassure them: "Licenced, and Entred according to order." Two title pages dated 1667 bear Milton's name, but the second reduces that name to very small type, as if to avoid calling attention to it; a third (1668) identifies the author only as J. M.[36] With the fourth title page (1668) Simmons had gained confidence: Milton's name appears in full as does, for the first time, Simmons's name as printer, and the "Licenced, and Entred" line is omitted.

Milton's Arminianism, so vigorously defended in *De Doctrina Christiana*,[37] lies at the heart of the poem's politics, even as it also grounds the theodicy which is the stated intent of *Paradise Lost:* To "justifie the wayes of God to men." As a poet Milton works out that theodicy, not primarily by theological argument, but by the imaginative vision the entire poem presents of human life and the human condition as good, despite the tragedy of the Fall and "all our woe." That seems a quixotic, though also rather wonderful, affirmation from a poet who endured the agony of total blindness throughout his most creative years and experienced the utter defeat of the political cause to which he gave over twenty years of his life. But that continued belief in the goodness of the human condition is inextricably linked with the ideas of human freedom, moral responsibility, and especially the capacity for growth and change that make education, and politics, still possible for Milton.

Milton's politics are embedded in his representations of hell, heaven, and Eden, all of which challenge readers' stereotypes, then and now. All reflect aspects of human society and all are in process: their respective physical conditions are fitted to the beings that inhabit them, but the inhabitants then interact with and shape their environments, creating societies in their own images. By representing both Satan and God as monarchs and portraying Satan as a self-styled grand rebel against what he calls the "tyranny of heaven,"[38] Milton directly confronts the familiar royalist analogies—God and the king, Satan and the Puritan revolutionaries—and teaches his readers to find those analogies entirely false. The royalist analogy was spelled out very clearly in James I's celebrated speech to Parliament in 1609:

Kings are justly called Gods, for that they exercise in a manner or resemblance of Divine power upon earth. . . . They make and unmake their subjects: they have power

of raising, and casting downe: of life, and of death: Judges over all their subjects, and
in all causes, and yet accomptable to none but God onely. . . . Kings are not onely God's
Lieutenants upon earth, and sit upon God's throne, but even by God himself they are
called Gods.[39]

Continuing the analogy, James declared that as it would be blasphemy to
"dispute what God may doe" so "is it sedition in Subjects, to dispute what a
King may do in the height of his power." Milton's polemic antagonist Salmasius applied that analogy to Charles I: "If we lift up our eyes to the sovereign
patron of all things, we will find that this fashion of commanding [absolute
monarchy] is copied from that of God, who is the sole Sovereign of the world
as he is therein the sole maker of it."[40] A few weeks before the Restoration,
Matthew Griffith preached on Proverb 24:1: "My Son, feare God, and the
King, and medle not with them that be seditious," deriving the familiar
royalist analogy from its terms: "God is an heavenly King, and eternal . . . but
the King is an earthly, and dying God . . . And yet in a qualified sence, they
are both *Gods*, and both *Kings*."[41] Royalists commonly described the king
as God's anointed and his vicegerent on earth, thereby making revolution
against the king rebellion against God. As Sharon Achinstein illustrates, after
the regicide and in the months just before and after the Restoration several
royalist treatises described "parliament in hell" scenes in which famous revolutionaries—Bradshaw, Vane, Cromwell, Nedham, and sometimes Milton—
join forces with Satan to carry out the English revolution.[42]

Milton's treatises not only deny the analogy between the Heavenly King
and earthly kings but also charge earthly monarchs with inspiring idolatry
precisely because they seek to imitate God's rule. He also insists that God's
preferred government for humans is a republic. A few examples must suffice.
Answering Salmasius' claim that monarchy was patterned on the example of
one God, Milton asks rhetorically in his *Defense:* "who, in fact, is worthy of
holding on earth power like that of God but some person who far surpasses all
others and even resembles God himself in goodness and wisdom? The only
such person, as I believe, is the Son of God whose coming we look for" (YP
4:427–28). Milton's *Eikonoklastes* is a book-long critique of what he calls the
peoples' "civil kinde of Idolatry in idolizing thir Kings," ascribing it to the
"servility" taught them by prelates and Presbyterian ministers, and to King
Charles's complicity in making himself an idol in *Eikon Basilike*.[43] In the
Ready and Easy Way (1660) Milton finds evidence of God's disapproval of
monarchy in the much-debated text in 1 Samuel 8, in which the Israelites ask
God for a king and God chastises them for wanting to replace his kingship
over them with that of gentilish kings who will be tyrants; he also finds that

Christ's reproof to the sons of Zebedee (Matthew 20:25–27) shows his strong preference for republics:

> A free Commonwealth [is] not only held by wisest men in all ages the noblest, the manliest, the equalest, the justest government . . . most cherishing to vertue and true religion, but also (I may say it with greatest probabilitie) planely commended, or rather enjoind by our Saviour himself, to all Christians, not without remarkable disallowance and the brand of *gentilism* upon kingship. God in much displeasure gave a king to the *Israelites*, and imputed it a sin to them that they sought one: but *Christ* apparently forbids his disciples to admitt of any such heathenish government: *the kings of the gentiles, saith he, exercise lordship over them; . . . but ye shall not be so; but he that is greatest among you, let him be as the younger; and he that is chief, as he that serveth.* . . That he speaks of civil government, is manifest. (7:424)

Earthly kingship is idolatry in that the king usurps a role belonging only to God and his Son, and it is tyranny because the king exercises wrongful dominion over those who are "for the most part every way equal or superior to himself" (YP 7:429). Magistrates in a Commonwealth, Milton declares, "walk the streets as other men, may be spoken to freely, familiarly, friendly, without adoration. Wheras a king must be ador'd like a Demigod, with a dissolute and haughtie court about him" (YP 7:425). Kingship rightly belongs only to Christ, "our true and rightfull and only to be expected King, only worthie as he is our only Saviour, the Messiah, the Christ, the only heir of his eternal father, the only by him anointed and ordaind since the work of our redemption finishd, Universal Lord of all mankinde" (YP 7:445). On this understanding, kings themselves are the greatest rebels against God, and rebelling against kings may be piety to God.

This is the perception Milton asks the readers of *Paradise Lost* to adopt as, in Books One and Two, he portrays hell as a monarchy in the making, with royalist politics, perverted language, perverse rhetoric, political manipulation, and demagoguery. He presents hell first in traditional terms, with Satan and his crew chained on a lake of fire. But they soon rise up and begin to found a society: they mine gold and gems, build a government center (Pandemonium), hold a parliament, dispatch Satan on a mission of exploration and conquest, explore their spacious and varied though sterile landscape, engage in martial games and parades, perform music, compose epic poems, and argue hard philosophical questions. Hell's monarch, Satan, is not God's vicegerent but his presumptuous imitator: "To reign is worth ambition though in Hell: / Better to reign in Hell, then serve in Heav'n" (1.262–63). Satan has some claim to kingship according to the theory by which Milton and others justified rule by one who is out of all measure superior to the rest: he is "By

merit rais'd / To that bad eminence" (2.5–6); and he readily assumes "as great
a share / Of hazard as of honour" when (in parody of the Son's offer to die for
fallen humankind) he offers to go as hell's emissary to subvert Adam and Eve.
But his superiority is only relative: it bears no comparison to that of God over
his creatures, or that of the Son of God who sacrifices himself for them.
Satan's ambition has led him, the narrator reports, to "set himself in Glory
above his Peers." To reinforce the evil of kingship, Milton's hell abounds in
kings. Death, Satan's son by incestuous intercourse with his daughter Sin,
wears "the likeness of a Kingly Crown" (2.673) and claims hell as his realm:
"Where I reign King, and to enrage thee more, / Thy King and Lord" (2.678–
79). Moloch, introduced first as the idol he will become in human history, is
termed a "horrid king besmear'd with blood" (1.392). And Belial is introduced in terms of his continuing reign on earth in kingly courts:

> In Courts and Palaces he also Reigns
> And in luxurious Cities, where the noyse
> Of riot ascends above their loftiest Towrs,
> And injury and outrage.   (1.497–500)

During his long reign, the sons of Belial, "flown with insolence and wine"
(1.502), riot not only in Sodom but also in Restoration England.

Pandemonium is "the high Capital / Of Satan and his Peers" (1.755–56);
within it the "great Seraphic Lords and Cherubim" sit in conclave while the
common angels, reduced to pygmy size, swarm without (1.777–97). The
parliament in hell evokes, not a republican House of Commons, but a House
of Lords controlled by a monarch.[44] Satan always addresses these superior
angels as "Peers" and by their noble titles: "Powers and Dominions, Deities
of Heav'n" (2.11); "Thrones, Dominations, Princedomes, Virtues, Powers"
(5.772). He opens his council in hell in the style of an oriental sultan, a figure
for the most extreme absolutism, luxury, and tyranny: "High on a Throne of
Royal State, which far / Outshon the wealth of *Ormus* and of *Ind*, / Or where
the gorgeous East with richest hand / Showrs on her Kings *Barbaric* Pearl
and Gold / Satan exalted sat" (2.1–8). In the uneasy position of defeated
military leader and de facto ruler, he begins by summarizing the grounds—all
of them true enough—upon which his leadership of the angels was founded:
first, "just right, and the fixt Laws of Heav'n" (legitimacy); next, their own
"free choice" to follow him; and finally, his proven merit in counsel and in
battle (2.18–20). In Book One he is addressed or referred to in terms relating
to that leadership role, as "Chief of many Throned Powers" (128), "Leader of
those Armies bright" (272), "their General" (337), "Their great Commander"
(358), "Their dread commander" (589). But then, by a piece of rhetorical
legerdemain, he simply assumes that these bases for *leadership* justify his

assumption of *kingship*, and he proceeds to claim a "safe unenvied Throne / Yielded with full consent" (2.23–24). However, he cannot appeal to Heaven's laws to legitimate such a power grab, and he does not risk another free vote. Rather, he relies on the Hobbesian principle that a society's passive acceptance of a sovereign's power and protection establishes a binding social contract. Like a Machiavellian prince, he seeks to secure a new throne by manipulating his followers, and works to advance his goal—continued war against God—by Machiavellian force and fraud, "open Warr or covert guile" (2.41). He constructs his parliament as Charles I constructed his, as a consultative body only, not an independent legislature: "who can advise, may speak" (2.42). When the powerful peers venture to debate their own agendas, Satan sways the council to his will through the agency of his chief minister and spokesman, Beelzebub (Milton's readers might think of Strafford or Laud or Clarendon). The scene closes with Satan accorded divine honors: "Towards him they bend / With awful reverence prone; and as a God / Extoll him equal to the highest in Heav'n" (2.477–79). This is an exaggerated version of the idolatry Milton regularly associated with the Stuart ideology of divine kingship. As monarch of hell Satan alludes to Charles I but also to other Stuart Kings and to monarchs generally—including, perhaps, Cromwell, insofar as he was assuming quasi-monarchical powers and trappings in 1657, under the new constitution, *The Humble Petition and Advice;* he was also offered and was thought to be considering a crown.[45]

Some evidence that Milton's careful readers recognized his radical rewriting of the royalist "parliament of hell" trope is afforded by John Dryden's *State of Innocence.* Sometime in the 1670s Dryden sought and won Milton's permission to turn his epic into a drama in rhymed couplets—"Tagg'd his Lines" as Milton put it with wry humor (*EL,* 296). If Milton encountered the result he would not have been pleased. Not only were his soaring lines tamed and bounded by rhyme; Dryden also took care to restore the parliament in hell trope to the royalist meaning it conventionally carried, and to reinstate the royalist analogy between divine and human kingship. He does this by dividing Satan's speeches among several fallen angels (including new characters not in Milton's poem) so that the entire community, which he terms a "senate" or "States-General of Hell," plots the continuing rebellion against heaven and the seduction of Adam and Eve. In Milton's poem, rebellion is the act of a would-be usurping monarch against the only rightful kings, God and his vicegerent Son; for royalist Dryden it is the act of a parliament rising against a divine king, in analogy to the English revolution against a king claiming office by Divine Right.

In the temptation scene in heaven, when Satan tempts his followers to revolt after the Son is proclaimed king, Milton gives to Satan the rhetoric of republican virtue and the rights of a free citizenry that he himself used in the *Tenure of Kings and Magistrates*. In that work, Milton's argument for popular sovereignty and government based on contract begins with the declaration, "No man who knows ought, can be so stupid to deny that all men naturally were borne free, being the image and resemblance of God himself, and were by privilege above all the creatures, born to command and not to obey, and that they liv'd so" until the Fall (YP 3:198–99). It concludes with a declaration that kings and magistrates hold authority from the people, who retain sovereign power fundamentally in themselves, and so have always the right "as oft as they shall judge it for the best, [to] either choose him or reject him, retain him or depose him though no Tyrant, meerly by the liberty and right of free born Men to be govern'd as seems to them best" (YP 3:206). Satan offers a parallel argument:

> Will ye submit your necks, and choose to bend
> The supple knee? ye will not, if I trust
> To know ye right, or if ye know your selves
> Natives and Sons of Heav'n
> . . . .
> Who can in reason then or right assume
> Monarchie over such as live by right
> His equals, if in power and splendor less,
> In freedome equal? or can introduce
> Law and Edict on us, who without law
> Erre not, much less for this to be our Lord,
> And look for adoration to th'abuse
> Of those Imperial Titles which assert
> Our being ordain'd to govern, not to serve?   (5.787–802)[46]

This surprising republican rhetoric has led some readers to assume that Milton had a measure of sympathy with Satan the revolutionary, or that he had come to repudiate as Satanic the rebellion he had before promoted, or that he here convicts Cromwell of having used republican language to cover personal ambition, or that he intentionally or unintentionally sends a mixed message, confusing the reader.

But as the scene plays out, it demonstrates yet more decisively the fallacy of the royalist claim that rebellion against kings is rebellion against God, by showing that kings and aspirants to kingship are the true rebels. They usurp a role that belongs to God and take his place as false idols: "Affecting all equality with God," Satan addresses the angels from a splendid "Royal seat" high on a mount, like the one from which Messiah was pronounced king (5.756–66). Directly challenging Satan's republican argument, Abdiel underscores the absurdity of the royalist analogy between God and any other monarch: God is absolute monarch of heaven because he created all other beings, and the Son enjoys regal status by God's "just Decree" and as God's agent in Creation. Abdiel makes the crucial distinction that while Satan's republican argument against monarchy on grounds of equality is generally true, it is beside the point here because there can be no equality between Creator and creature:

> But to grant it thee unjust,
> That equal over equals Monarch Reigne:
> Thy self though great and glorious dost thou count,
> Or all Angelic Nature joind in one,
> Equal to him begotten Son, by whom
> As by his Word the mighty Father made
> All things, ev'n thee, and all the Spirits of Heav'n
> By him created in thir bright degrees.   (5.831–36)

Abdiel and Satan continue this political debate on the battlefield as Satan derides the loyal angels "traind up in Feast and Song" for having a servile and slothful spirit such as Milton often ascribed to royal courts and courtiers. The loyal angels will come off badly, Satan scoffs, when they match their "Servilitie" with the rebels' "freedom" (6.164–69). Abdiel counters with the natural law argument Milton spelled out in the *Second Defense* to support Cromwell's Protectorate: monarchy is justified "When he who rules is worthiest, and excells / Them whom he governs"—patently true of God if almost never of other rulers. Abdiel also makes the familiar Miltonic and Platonic distinction that relates liberty and tyranny in the first instance to states of soul, which are then replicated in the state:

> This is servitude,
> To serve th'unwise, or him who hath rebelld
> Against his worthier, as thine now serve thee,
> Thy self not free, but to thy self enthrall'd.   (6.177–81)

It is the followers of aspiring kings, not God's servants, who are servile since they mostly serve rulers enslaved to their own ambitions and passions.

Milton's presentation of the ensuing battle in heaven further identifies earthly kings as rebels against God. Observing that battle from his "gorgeous Throne," Satan is "exalted as a God / . . . Idol of Majesty Divine" (6.99–103). The rebel angels are referred to, significantly, as "Rebel Thrones" (6.199), and Moloch as a "furious King" (6.357). Finally, in sending the Son forth to end the battle, God proclaims that the title of divinely anointed king belongs to him alone: he only is "worthiest to be Heir / Of all things, to be Heir and to be King / By Sacred Unction, thy deserved right" (6.707–9). The reader also

knows that the Son will display his superlative merit by his offer to die for
fallen man: in Book Three God refers to that offer as proof that he indeed
deserves his kingly office, "Found worthiest to be so by being Good, / Farr
more then Great or High" (311–12).

Milton affirms republican principles quite explicitly in Book Twelve, as
they pertain to the future history of the postlapsarian world. In the exchange
between Michael and Adam about Nimrod, monarchy is equated with tyranny because it involves a man usurping over his equals the dominion that
belongs only to God. Reporting that Nimrod subjected men to his empire by
force, Michael explains the epithet ascribed to him, "mightie Hunter," in
terms that associate him with Charles I's claims of Divine Right kingship and
castigation of his opponents as "rebels": Nimrod, Michael states, claimed
"from Heav'n . . . second Sovrantie; / And from Rebellion shall derive his
name, / Though of Rebellion others he accuse" (12.33–37). Adam's immediate and fierce denunciation of Nimrod shows him to be, in Norbrook's terms,
"instinctually republican."[47] He understands and appropriately applies the
republican theory of Milton's *Tenure:*

> O execrable Son so to aspire
> Above his Brethren, to himself assuming
> Authoritie usurpt, from God not giv'n:
> He gave us onely over Beast, Fish, Fowl
> Dominion absolute; that right we hold
> By his donation; but Man over men
> He made not Lord; such title to himself
> Reserving, human left from human free.   (12.64–71)

Michael commends Adam for "justly" abhorring this descendant but reminds
him—in terms reminiscent of many Milton tracts—that political liberty depends on inner liberty, which is the product of reason and virtue, and that the
Fall allows "upstart Passions" to "catch the Government / From Reason, and
to servitude reduce / Man till then free" (12.83–90). That analysis accounts
for the Stuart Restoration and for absolute monarchy wherever it exists: inner
servility leads to deprivation of outward freedom either as a natural consequence or as a punishment from God—but that does not justify tyranny or
imply that it should not be resisted. Milton's poem means to help create a
virtuous and liberty-loving people who might deserve, and so take steps to
gain, a free commonwealth.

Heaven, of course, is not a republic but an absolute monarchy: it has no
parliament, only assemblies in which the angels hear divine pronouncements
or a dialogue between God and the Son. The imagery Milton uses to portray
God, and the attributes Milton assigns him, often invite association with

earthly monarchs, an association that many readers find disconcerting. That the Bible uses such imagery to portray God is a partial but not a sufficient explanation. A better one is that by this association Milton definitively removes absolute monarchy from earth to heaven, as the only place it rightly belongs.

Milton's heaven combines courtly magnificence and pastoral nature. Though hierarchical, it is designed to promote happiness, growth in virtue, and responsible citizenship in all its inhabitants. In this complex social order, God, though an absolute monarch, delegates power (presumably for merit) to many "Scepter'd Angels," described as "Princes, whom the supreme King / Exalted to such power, and gave to rule, / Each in his Hierarchie, the Orders bright" (1.734–37). Heaven's citizens of all ranks engage in a wide range of activities: elegant hymns suited to various occasions, martial parades, warfare, pageantry, masque dancing, feasting, lovemaking, political debate, the education of Adam and Eve, the protection of Eden. Their diverse pleasures and responsibilities give the lie to Satan's disparagement of their life as courtly servility. As messengers, Raphael and Michael have large liberty to decide how to carry out their educative and admonitory missions to Adam and Eve. Angels guard the Garden of Eden and its inhabitants against violent attack, though they cannot secure Adam and Eve against temptation. At God's command they fight heroically against the rebels threatening their society, though they cannot extirpate this evil by their own military might. That fact, along with the grotesque cannon-barrages and hill-hurlings, the near-destruction of Heaven's lovely landscape, and Michael's later denunciation (12.688–99) of the giants who sought glory in battle and conquest, suggests to some that Milton has become a pacifist, or that he means to repudiate the recent armed rebellion in England.[48] But these scenes rather invite a sober estimation of the costs and limitations of warfare, while allowing its necessity as a response to blatant evil. They undermine the epic ideal of *aristeia,* battle glory, by demonstrating that war is always, in its essence and its effects, tragic, not glorious. They also demonstrate war's limitations: however good the cause, however heroic the warriors, however divinely authorized and necessary—as the war in heaven clearly was, and as Milton always thought the English war had been—war cannot by itself eradicate evil.

The angels' mix of heroic, georgic, and pastoral activities and modes offers an ideal of wholeness, but an ideal involving process, not stasis, complexity not simplicity, and the continuous and active choice of good rather than the absence of evil. Most exegetes held that the loyal angels always were unable to swerve from grace, or that they at least became so after withstanding Satan's temptation. But Milton's angels, as Raphael explains to Adam, are exactly like prelapsarian humans in that they must continually and freely choose to act from obedience and love:

My self and all th'Angelic Host, that stand
In sight of God enthron'd, our happie state
Hold, as you yours, while our obedience holds;
On other surety none; freely we serve,
Because wee freely love, as in our will
To love or not; in this we stand or fall.   (5.535–40)

Also, though Milton's God does not hold parliaments, his decrees invite free
and thoughtful, not blind, obedience. At times he stages scenes that require
active participation by his creatures, to determine just what the decree means
for them, as is the case with the Dialogue in Heaven between God and the
Son, who in Milton's antitrinitarian theology is not omniscient or coequal to
God (3.80–343).[49] God first explains and defends his "high Decree" that
mandates contingency and freedom from all eternity and thereby secures to
both angels and humans a genuine freedom of choice, whose results he
foresees but does not determine. Responding to the dilemma God sets when
he foresees the Fall—the apparent conflict between Justice and Mercy that
seems to require damnation of Adam and Eve—"Dye hee or Justice Must"—
the Son works out for himself how Justice and Mercy might be reconciled
through his own sacrificial act and freely makes the appropriate offer. In
much the same way God stages a scene in which Adam must defend his
desire for and need of a mate in the face of God's apparent dismissal of his
request (8.354–451).

Another issue probed in Milton's epic is the politics of empire and
colonization. Language relating to those enterprises came readily to him,
given its contemporary currency.[50] Eden is described in terms often used of
the new world: lush, beautiful, prodigeously prolific, requiring to be cultivated and tamed. And both God and Satan seek to hold it as a satellite
colony.[51] However, God's relation to Eden is in virtually all respects the
obverse of Satan's. God created the lush garden and its inhabitants, he does
not discover it and conquer them. The epithet "sovran Planter" (5.641),
might seem to associate him with the plantation of settlements, but in context
it defines him as the gardener who produced the delights of Adam and Eve's
garden. The purpose of the angelic military guard in Eden is not to control
the inhabitants but to ward off external force. God forbids Adam and Eve one
tree but allows them free use of all else. He does not need or want any of
Eden's products but leaves them wholly to the inhabitants, whose labor he
requires, not for himself but because they themselves need to control the
garden's prolific growth and take responsibility for their environment. God
does not intend to settle any of the heavenly host on earth but wants the
inhabitants to increase, multiply, and spread through all the earth, cultivating

it for their own uses. At length he intends to bring Adam and Eve and their descendants to a still better place, heaven.

By contrast, Satan is represented as an explorer bent on conquest and colonization. He sets out courageously, like the sailors in Camoëns' *Lusiads*, to sail through an uncharted sea (Chaos), enduring as-yet-unknown dangers and difficulties. The fallen angels in Hell think of him as "their great adventurer" gone to seek "Forrein Worlds" (10.440–41). He discovers the Paradise of Fools and prepares for a future colony there. He discovers the paradise of Eden and intends, after conquering Adam and Eve, to settle the fallen angels in it. He practices fraud on Eve and causes her to lose her rightful domain. Upon first seeing Adam and Eve, he makes clear in soliloquy that he means to use Eden and its inhabitants for his own purposes, that his excursion aims at empire-building and the takeover of this idyllic place:

> League with you I seek,
> And mutual amitie so streight, so close,
> That I with you must dwell, or you with me
> Henceforth. (4.375–79)

He justifies his enterprise by "public reason just, / Honour and Empire with revenge enlarg'd"—characterized by the narrator as "necessitie, / The Tyrants plea" (4.389–94).

This does not mean that Milton thought all exploration and colonization in the Americas necessarily Satanic, though, as with Satan's degradation of various versions of heroism, his language indicates how susceptible such enterprises are to evil purposes. Milton does formally link Satan's depredations with those of Spain: Michael's prophecy refers to "as yet unspoil'd / *Guiana*, whose great Citie *Geryons* Sons / Call *El Dorado*" (11.409–11), an allusion to Spanish conquests and exploitations of new world lands and peoples in their search for gold.[52] As for the English conquest and colonization of Ireland, nothing in *Paradise Lost* suggests that Milton has changed his mind about his earlier vigorous defense of that enterprise on the score of Irish barbarism and savagery in his *Observations upon the Articles of Peace, Made and Concluded with the Irish Rebels* (1649). Still, the imaginative force of Milton's representations may reach beyond his conscious intention. As the Genesis text prescribes, Milton's God gave Adam and Eve absolute dominion over the earth— a gift often cited in contemporary tracts to justify exploitation and subjugation of other races. But Milton does not allow such a gloss, for Michael's denunciation of Nimrod explicitly forbids such dominion to humans.

What then of the politics of Eden?[53] At the center of his epic, Milton set a richly imagined representation of prelapsarian love, marriage, and domestic society. It is a brilliant though sometimes conflicted representation, in which Milton's ideal of companionate marriage, contemporary views of gender hierarchy, his own life experiences, and his deeply felt psychic needs strain against each other. Some authoritative statements in the poem affirm gender hierarchy. Adam, after admitting to Raphael his unsettling passion for Eve, states that he knows she is inferior to himself in qualities both of mind and body; Raphael confirms Adam's judgment; and the Son, judging Adam after the Fall, reiterates that Adam's proper role is to act as Eve's head and governor:

> Was shee thy God, that her thou didst obey
> Before his voice, or was shee made thy guide,
> Superior, or but equal, that to her
> Thou did'st resigne thy Manhood, and the Place
> Wherein God set thee above her made of thee,
> And for thee, whose perfection far excell'd
> Hers in all real dignitie: Adornd
> She was indeed, and lovely to attract
> Thy Love, not thy Subjection, and her Gifts
> Were such as under Government well seem'd,
> Unseemly to beare rule, which was thy part
> And person, had'st thou known thy self aright.   (10.145–56)

Yet this conventional view of gender hierarchy is destabilized by elements of Milton's imaginative vision that invite a more egalitarian conception: if Milton could not fully work through these conflicts, he did provide liberalizing perspectives upon which later feminists could and often did build.[54] One such is the poem's unusually fluid concept of hierarchy, the concomitant of its monism: if, as Raphael explains to Adam and Eve, humans and angels differ only in degree, and humans can expect the gradual refinement of their natures to angelic status, the distance between male and female on the hierarchical scale must be minimal. Moreover, the fact that creatures hold their place on that scale "As neerer to him [God] plac't or neerer tending" (5.476) allows that their final places will depend on how they develop, whither they "tend." In Milton's unique representation of the state of innocence, Adam and Eve are both expected to grow, change, and develop in virtue by properly pruning and directing their own erroneous apprehensions and sometimes unruly impulses as well as their burgeoning garden.

Another complicating element is Milton's advanced notion of companionate marriage, argued in the divorce tracts and dramatized in more gracious terms in the poem. Adam asks God for an equal life partner: "Among unequals what societie / Can sort, what harmonie or true delight? / . . . Of fellowship I speak / Such as I seek, fit to participate / All rational delight" (8.383–91). In answer God states that he always intended exactly such a mate for Adam, "Thy likeness, thy fit help, thy other self, / Thy wish exactly to thy hearts desire" (8.450–51). Consonant with this vision of marriage, Adam and Eve's roles and talents are not sharply segregated by gender, as convention would dictate. Eve performs certain domestic tasks, ornamenting the couple's bedroom bower and preparing and serving the noonday meal when Raphael visits. Otherwise she shares with Adam in all the physical and intellectual activities of Edenic life and she enjoys certain areas of autonomy and initiative. The couple take equal responsibility for their world, laboring together to maintain its ecosystem and keep the garden from returning to wild. Unique to Milton is the role he assigns to Eve in naming the plants of Eden, and in thereby sharing in the authority over nature, the intuitive knowledge, and the power of symbolization that Adam's naming of the animals signifies, albeit in lesser degree. She also receives the same education as Adam, though not in the same manner. As decorum dictated, Adam asked Raphael questions (often framing them faultily) while Eve listened in silence, sitting at a distance but within earshot: for both, therefore, the Edenic curriculum included ontology, metaphysics, moral philosophy, history, epic poetry, and divine revelation.⁵⁵ Eve missed the astronomy lesson when she left to tend her flowers, but the Miltonic bard insists that she both delighted in and was fully capable of that knowledge and would obtain it later in discussion (mixed with kisses) with Adam—thereby gaining the educational benefit of dialogic interaction that Adam enjoyed with Raphael (8.48–50). She is portrayed as an accomplished reasoner and debater in the marital dispute in Book Nine, she often proposes issues for discussion and initiates action, and she constructs the first autobiographical narrative as she recounts her earliest recollections—with the implications autobiography carries of coming to self-awareness, probing one's own subjectivity, interpreting one's own experience, and so becoming an author (4.449–91). Also, she is as much a lyric poet as Adam—perhaps more so—with her elegant love lyric to Adam that begins "Sweet is the breath of morn" (4.641–56) and her lament-plea to Adam that opens the way to repentance, forgiveness, and reconciliation.

Milton further destabilizes the ideology of gender hierarchy by his treatment of Adam and Eve's different experiences and psychology. As a striking example, they offer very different accounts of their creation, first meeting, and marriage, producing versions of self that evidently reflect Milton's reading of female and male psychology. Eve tells of constructing herself first through pleasurable self-contemplation mistaken as response to another shape in the water, and then, after brief continued attraction to that "wat'ry image," freely accepting a marriage relationship urged by two who claim paternity over her, God and Adam. But she evidences no felt sense of need or lack, as Adam does, and her narrative resists interpretation of her story as a simple submission to patriarchy.[56] As she recounts the words spoken to her by God, they almost suggest that Adam was made for her, not vice versa, and they almost seem to institute matriarchy, not patriarchy:

> hee
> Whose image thou art, him thou shalt enjoy
> Inseparablie thine, to him shalt beare
> Multitudes like thy self [not, like himself], and thence be call'd
> Mother of human Race.   (4.471–76)

By contrast, Adam's narrative (8.355–99) testifies to a psychological and emotional neediness that in some ways undercuts gender hierarchy and recalls Milton's similar testimony in the divorce tracts.[57] Recounting his eloquent pleas with God for a mate, Adam emphasizes his keenly felt sense of incompleteness and loneliness; and he explains Eve's hesitation not as she herself did but by projecting onto her a serene consciousness of self-worth "That would be woo'd, and not unsought be won" and a demeanor of "obsequious Majestie" in accepting his suit (8.500–10). He also expresses a tension between what he "knows" of Eve's inferiority to him and what he experiences when he is with her:

> when I approach
> Her loveliness, so absolute she seems
> And in herself compleat, so well to know
> Her own, that what she wills to do or say,
> Seems wisest, vertuousest, discreetest, best;
>
> .   .   .   .
>
> Authority and Reason on her waite,
> As one intended first, not after made
> Occasionally; and to consummate all,
> Greatness of mind and nobleness thir seat
> Build in her loveliest, and create an awe
> About her, as a guard Angelic plac't.   (8.546–59)

After Eve's fall, Adam's instant decision to fall with her arises from his desperate fear of a return to his lonely life before she came to him:

> How can I live without thee, how forgoe
> Thy sweet Converse and Love so dearly joyn'd,
> To live again in these wilde Woods forlorn?
> Should God create another *Eve*, and I
> Another Rib afford, yet loss of thee
> Would never from my heart.   (9.908–13)

If the politics of Milton's Eden remain uneasily hierarchical and patriarchal, he does dare to bring that ideology up against the testimony of experience and allow the conflicts to stand. He also explores through Adam and Eve the fundamental challenge of any love relationship: the uneasy, inevitable, and ultimately creative tension between autonomy and interdependence.

Milton designed the last segment of his poem, Michael's prophecy of the future history of humankind, around the issue of postlapsarian education for Adam, Eve, and the reader. Adam and Eve have to learn how to interpret the messianic promise of redemption signified by the metaphorical curse on the serpent: that the seed of the woman will bruise his head. But Milton also incorporates into Michael's prophecy the political issue closest to his heart: the misuse of civil power to force consciences. In a long passage that begins with popes and Roman emperors in the early Christian ages and then surveys subsequent history, Michael restates principles Milton urged in *Areopagitica, Of Civil Power, The Likeliest Means, De Doctrina Christiana*, and elsewhere: Christian liberty, the separation of spiritual and civil powers, the inviolability of conscience and individual faith, and the gift of the Spirit to all believers. That long passage also invites application to the harsh repression of Puritan dissent after the Restoration by prelates and magistrates who appropriate to themselves the "Spirit of God, promisd alike and giv'n / To all Beleevers," and who seek to force "Spiritual Lawes by carnal power / On every conscience" (12.519–22). Milton's voice echoes behind Michael's stern judgments:

> What will they then
> But force the Spirit of Grace it self, and binde
> His consort Libertie; what, but unbuild
> His living Temples, built by Faith to stand,
> Thir own Faith not anothers: for on Earth
> Who against Faith and Conscience can be heard
> Infallible? yet many will presume:
> Whence heavie persecution shall arise
> On all who in the worship persevere
> Of Spirit and Truth; the rest, farr greater part,
> Will deem in outward Rites and specious formes
> Religion satisfi'd; Truth shall retire
> Bestruck with slandrous darts, and works of Faith
> Rarely be found. (12.524–35)

Adam and the reader are also to learn how to respond to the tragic course of history. They are shown, over and over again, one or a few righteous humans standing against the many wicked but at length overwhelmed. Michael sums up that pattern as he comments on the way of the world after Christ's ascension: "so shall the World goe on, / To good malignant, to bad men benigne, / Under her own weight groaning" until Christ's second coming (12.537–51). That tragic vision of an external paradise irretrevably lost, along with the promise of "A paradise within thee, happier farr" might indeed seem a recipe for quietism and retreat from the political arena, but it is not. The thrust of Michael's prophecy is against any kind of passivity, spiritual, moral, or political. He shows instead that in every age the few just have the responsibility to oppose, as God calls them to do so, the Nimrods, or the Pharaohs, or the royalist persecutors of the Church, even though (like the loyal angels in the battle in heaven) they can win no wholly decisive victories and can found no permanent City of God on earth until the Son appears. Michael's history-as-prophecy offers Adam and his progeny examples of two kinds of heroism: heroic martyrdom and heroic action. And Adam learns the lesson. He has come to understand that "suffering for Truths sake / Is fortitude to highest victorie," but also that God often accomplishes great things by unlikely means, "by things deemd weak / Subverting worldly strong" (12.565–70).

Harvard University

NOTES

1. Milton's nephew Edward Phillips saw the lines that now form the opening of Satan's address to the Sun (*PL* 4.32–41) some years before the poem was begun; the speech was then designed for the beginning of a tragedy on the subject of the Fall. See *The Early Lives of Milton*, ed. Helen Darbishire (London, 1932), 72–73 (hereafter, *EL*). John Aubrey had information from Phillips that he had seen the lines intended for a tragedy "about 15 or 16 yeares before ever his Poem was thought of" (*EL*, 13).

2. *PL* 9.26. Here and hereafter I cite book and line number of *Paradise Lost* (1674) from *John Milton's Complete Poetical Works, reproduced in Photographic Facsimile*, ed. Harris Francis Fletcher, 4 vols. (Urbana, 1943–48), vol 3.

3. Phillips's own account is less specific as to the years involved but suggests a somewhat longer period of composition and revision.

4. Thomas Ellwood, *The History of the Life of Thomas Ellwood*, ed. J[oseph] W[yeth] (London, 1714), 233.

5. Blair Worden offers a recent restatement of this common view in "Milton's Republicanism and the Tyranny of Heaven," *Machiavelli and Republicanism*, eds. Gisela Bock, Quentin Skinner, and Maurizio Viroli, (Cambridge, 1990), 244.

6. Joan Bennett, *Reviving Liberty: Radical Christian Humanism in Milton's Great Poems* (Cambridge, Mass., 1989); Laura Lunger Knoppers, *Historicizing Milton Spectacle, Power, and Poetry in Restoration England* (Athens, Ga., 1994); Sharon Achinstein, *Milton and the Revolutionary Reader* (Princeton, 1994); David Norbrook, *Writing the English Revolution: Poetry, Rhetoric, and Politics, 1627–1660* (Cambridge, 1999).

7. See Barbara K. Lewalski, *Paradise Lost and the Rhetoric of Literary Forms* (Princeton, 1993).

8. Recently argued by Achsah Guibbory in *Ceremony and Community from Herbert to Milton: Literature, Religion, and Cultural Conflict in Seventeenth-Century England* (Cambridge, 1998).

9. *Complete Prose Works of John Milton*, ed. Donald M. Wolfe et al., 8 vols. (New Haven, Conn., 1953–1982), 4:366–67. Subsequent references to Milton's prose are from this edition, hereafter cited parenthetically in the text as YP, followed by volume and page number).

10. See David Quint, *Epic and Empire: Politics and Generic Form From Virgil to Milton* (Princeton, 1992), 21–31, 50–96, 213–47.

11. John Denham, *The Destruction of Troy* (London, 1656). Denham claims to have written it around 1636, but if so, he surely revised it after the regicide. He sets forth as his theory of translation a wish to make Virgil speak "not only as a man of this Nation, but as a man of this age."

12. Knoppers, *Historicizing Milton*, 67–122.

13. John Dryden, *Astraea Redux* (London, 1660), lines 320–21. The epigraph is from Virgil's fourth Eclogue, line 6: "Iam redit et Virgo, redeunt Saturnia regna" (Now the Virgin [Astraea] returns, and the reign of Saturn [the golden age] begins)."

14. Dryden, *Annus Mirabilis: The Year of Wonders* (London, 1667). It was dated in Dryden's prefatory letter to Sir Robert Howard, November 10, 1666.

15. For the skillful rhetoric of that attempt, see Steven N. Zwicker, *Lines of Authority: Politics and English Literary Culture 1649–1689* (Ithaca, N.Y., 1993), 90–107.

16. "An account of the ensuing Poem, in a Letter to the Honorable, Sir Robert Howard," *Annus Mirabilis: The Year of Wonders* (London, 1667), sig. A 5v.

17. See Quint, *Epic and Empire*, 131–57.

18. See Norbrook, *Writing the English Republic*, 23–62. Norbrook traces the association of Lucan with anticourt critique and an aristocratic republicanism in translations of the *Pharsalia* by Arthur Gorges (1614), Hugo Grotius (1614) and Thomas Farnaby (1619), as well as May.

19. Among many studies of such debts, see C. M. Bowra, *From Virgil to Milton* (London, 1944); Francis Blessington, *Paradise Lost and the Classical Epic* (Boston, 1979); and Lewalski, *Paradise Lost and the Rhetoric of Literary Forms*.

20. See Harold Toliver, "Milton's Household Epic," in *Milton Studies* 9, ed. James D. Simmonds (Pittsburgh, 1976), 105–20; and T. J. B. Spencer, "*Paradise Lost:* The Anti-Epic," in *Approaches to Paradise Lost: The York Tercentenary Essays*, ed. C. A. Patrides (Toronto, 1968).

21. Letter to Sir Robert Howard, *Annus Mirabilis*, sigs. A5v–A6v.

22. John Dryden, *Of Dramatick Poesie, An Essay* (London, 1668). The bookseller Herringman registered the work in the *Stationers' Register* on August 7, 1667. The title page bears the date 1668, as was usual with late year publications.

23. He is answering the case against rhyme urged by Crites, the dramatist Sir Robert Howard, who was described by John Toland as a "particular Acquaintance" and "a great admirer of *Milton* to his dying day," as well as "a hearty Friend to the Liberty of his Country" and a vigorous critic of the "Heathen and Popish" Anglican clergy (*EL*, 185–86). Howard's strictures against rhyme in drama first appeared in the preface to his *Four New Plays* (London, 1665), sigs a 4v–b 1r, which includes *The Indian Queen* written with Dryden. It sets the topics for Dryden's defence of rhyme in his *Essay*. Howard excuses his own use of rhyme against his principles, "since it was the fashion," and he thought best "as in all indifferent things, not to appear singular."

24. Dryden, *Dramatick Poesie*, 66–67.

25. Ibid., sig. A 3.

26. See Steven N. Zwicker, "Lines of Authority: Politics and Literary Culture in the Restoration," in *Politics of Discourse: The Literature and History of Seventeenth-Century England*, eds. Kevin Sharpe and Steven N. Zwicker (Berkeley, 1987), 249.

27. Shortly after he dealt with Milton's poem Tomkyns published a tractate urging enforced uniformity in religion and strict control of dissenters, to obviate the dangers toleration would pose to political stability. [Thomas Tomkyns], *The Inconveniences of Toleration, or, An Answer to*

a Late Book, Intituled, A Proposition Made to the King and Parliament, for the Safety and Happiness of the King and Kingdom (London, 1667). See also [Thomas Tomkyns], *The Rebel's Plea Examined: or Mr. Baxter's Judgment concerning the late War* (London, 1660).

28. *Eikonoklastes* is cited as a "Villanous Book" in Thomas Sprat's *Observations on Monsieur de Sorbier's Voyage into England* (London, 1665), 58–59; [Pierre Nichole], *The Pernicious Consequence of the New Heresie of the Jesuits against the King and the State* (London, 1666), sig. A 4v, links Milton and the late republicans with the Jesuits as advocates of regicide. David Lloyd attacked *Eikonoklastes* in *Memoires of the Lives, Actions, Sufferings, and Deaths of those Noble, Reverend, and Excellent Personages that Suffered . . . in our Late Intestine Wars* (London, 1668), 221. Also, for seven consecutive years beginning in 1664 "Blind Milton" was mentioned as an object of ridicule in *Poor Robin*, a satiric almanac.

29. John Gadbury, *Vox Solis: or, an Astrological Discourse of the Great Eclipse of the Sun* (London, 1667), 2. See Nicholas von Maltzahn, "The First Reception of *Paradise Lost* (1667)," *RES* 47 (1996): 481–87.

30. "IMPRIMATUR: Tho. Tomkyns, RRmo. in Christo Patri ac Domino, Dno. Gilberto, Divina Providentia Archiepiscopo Cantuariensi, a sacris domesticis. Richard Royaston. Intr. per Geo: Tokefeilde Ck:" [Let it be Printed: Thomas Tomkyns, one of the religious servants of the most reverend father and lord in Christ, Lord Gilbert, by divine providence Archbishop of Canterbury. Entered by George Tokefield, clerk]," in *The Life Records of John Milton*, ed. J. Milton French, 5 vols. (New York, 1966), vol. 4, 433–34. The entry is now barely legible in the manuscript. The contract Milton signed with the printer Samuel Simmons on April 27, 1667 describes the poem as "lately licensed to be printed."

31. Maltzahn, "First Reception," 488–89.

32. Also, Beale cannot forget Milton's polemics: "he writes so good verse, that tis pitty he ever wrote in prose." And he mistakenly supposes that the elaborate demonology of the poem shows Milton's harsh Calvinism (British Library MSS, Evelyn Papers, 1EA 12, fal. 71). See Nicholas Von Maltzahn, "Laureate, Republican, Calvinist: An Early Response to Milton and *Paradise Lost* (1667)," in *Milton Studies* 29, ed. Albert C. Labriola (Pittsburgh, 1992), 187–94.

33. The entry reads: "Master Sam. Symons. Entred for his copie under the hands of Master Thomas Tomkyns and Master Warden Royston, a booke or copie intituled *Paradise lost A Poem in Tenne bookes* by J. M." *Stationers' Registers*, vol. 2, 381.

34. The legal contract Milton signed with Samuel Simmons was for sums that seem roughly consistent with contemporary levels of payment to writers, Lindenbaum, "John Milton and the Republican Mode of Literary Production," in *The Yearbook of Literary Studies* 21, ed. Andrew Gurr (London, 1991), 121–36. Also see Lindenbaum, "The Poet in the Marketplace: Milton and Samuel Simmons," in Paul G. Stanwood, ed., *Of Poetry and Politics: New Essays on Milton and His World* (Binghamton, N.Y., 1995), 258. The contract shows Milton exercising an author's right to his intellectual property at a time when copyright was granted only to stationers through entry in the Stationers' Register.

35. The first title page reads: "*Paradise lost. A Poem. Written in Ten Books By John Milton.* London: Printed, and are to be sold by Peter Parker under Creed Church near Aldgate; And by Robert Boulter at the Turks Head in Bishopsgate-street; And Matthias Walker, under St. Dunstons Church in Fleet-street, 1667." The first three issues list these three booksellers.

36. Von Maltzahn speculates that the poem may have been first presented for sale with the 1668 title page bearing just the initials, since that formula corresponds most closely to entry in the Stationers' Register, and that the 1667 title pages, though printed earlier, were used later. "First Reception," 488.

37. YP 6:151–202 . Also see Lewalski, "Milton and *De Doctrina Christiana*," in *Milton Studies* 36, ed. Albert C. Labriola (Pittsburgh, 1998), 203–28.

38. For some cogent analyses of God and Satan as monarchs, see Mary Ann Radzinowicz, "The Politics of *Paradise Lost,*" in *Politics of Discourse,* ed. Sharpe and Zwicker, 204–29; Michael Wilding, *Dragons Teeth: Literature in the English Revolution* (Oxford, 1987), 204–58; Stevie Davies, *Images of Kingship in Paradise Lost: Milton's Politics and Christian Liberty* (Columbia, Mo., 1983); and Joan S. Bennett, *Reviving Liberty,* 33–58.

39. James I, *The Political Works of James I,* ed. C. H. McIlwain (Cambridge, Mass., 1918), 307–8.

40. Claude Saumaise [Salmasius], *Defensio Regia, Pro Carolo II . . .* ([The Hague]: Elzevir, 1649), 136 (my translation).

41. Matthew Griffith, *The Fear of God and the King.* London, 1660 (March 25), 53. Milton answered Griffith in *Brief Notes upon a Late Sermon* (London, 1660).

42. See Achinstein, *Milton and the Revolutionary Reader,* 187–99.

43. For historical perspective on this gesture, see Richard F. Hardin, *Civil Idolatry: Desacralization and Monarchy in Spenser, Shakespeare, and Milton* (Newark, 1992).

44. See Wilding, *Dragons Teeth,* 205–31.

45. See Bennett, *Reviving Liberty,* 33–58; and Blair Worden, "Milton's Republicanism and the Tyranny of Heaven," in *Machiavelli and Republicanism,* 242–44.

46. Satan's misapplication of this rhetoric is contextualized by Cataline's exhortation to his greedy and dissolute soldiers, as reported by Sallust: "Awake, then! Lo, here, here before your eyes is the freedom for which you have yearned, and with it riches, honor, and glory . . . unless haply I delude myself and you are content to be slaves rather than to rule" (Sallust, *The War with Cataline,* 20.1–17, trans. J. C. Rolfe [Loeb, Cambridge, Mass., 1965], 35–39).

47. Norbrook, *Writing the English Revolution,* 463.

48. For a critique of this position from another standpoint, see Robert T. Fallon, *Captain or Colonel: The Soldier in Milton's Life and Art* (Columbia, Mo., 1984), 202–34.

49. See *De Doctrina Christiana,* YP 6:203–80; also see Lewalski, "Milton and *De Doctrina Christiana,*" in *Milton Studies* 36, ed. Albert C. Labriola (Pittsburgh, 1998), 203–28.

50. For such echoes see especially Quint, *Epic and Empire,* 253–67. J. Martin Evans, in *Milton's Imperial Epic: Paradise Lost and the Discourse of Colonialism* (Ithaca, 1996), argues that the pervasive influence of the conflicted discourses of exploration, Spanish, Portugese, and English produced a conflicted representation of that enterprise in Milton's poem.

51. Evans, *Milton's Imperial Epic,* 77–103, unwarrantably in my view, assimilates Adam and Eve to the condition of indentured servants working for God, or to new world Indians needing to be evangelized and controlled.

52. Spenser had presented Geryon as a type of political tyranny in *The Fairie Queen* 5.10.8–9, associating him specifically with Spain. Montezuma's empire had been spoiled by Cortez and Peru by Pizarro, but the fabulous El Dorado was not yet plundered by the Spanish explorers.

53. For a range of views on this point, see Diane K. McColley, *Milton's Eve* (Urbana, 1983; Christina Froula, "When Eve Reads Milton: Undoing the Canonical Economy," *Critical Inquiry* 10 (1983): 321–47; and Julia Walker, *Milton and the Idea of Woman* (Urbana, 1988).

54. For evidence of such liberalizing uses, see Joseph A. Wittreich, *Feminist Milton* (Ithaca, 1987).

55. See Barbara K. Lewalski, "Innocence and Experience in Milton's Eden," in *New Essays on Paradise Lost,* ed. Thomas Kranidas (Berkeley, 1969), 86–117.

56. For different readings of this episode, see Mary Nyquist, "The Genesis of Gendered Subjectivity," in *Re-membering Milton,* eds. Mary Nyquist and Margaret Ferguson (New York, 1987), 99–127, and Janet Halley, "Female Autonomy in Milton's Sexual Politics," in Walker, ed., *Milton and the Idea of Woman,* 230–53.

57. The leitmotif of man's loneliness without a wife fit for intelligent conversation echoes

through both versions of *The Doctrine and Discipline of Divorce,* even to the point of identifying the "burning" in the Pauline text (1 Cor. 7:9) as loneliness rather than lust: "What is it [that burning] then but that desire which God put into *Adam* in Paradise before he knew the sin of incontinence; that desire which God saw it was not good that man should be left alone to burn in; that desire and longing to put off an unkindly solitarines by uniting another body, but not without a fit soule to his in the cheerfull society of wedlock" (YP 2:251).

When Eve Reads Milton: Undoing the Canonical Economy

Christine Froula

Let a woman learn in silence with all submissiveness. I permit no woman to teach or to have authority over men; she is to keep silent.
—1 Tim. 2:11–12

In *Jacob's Room*, with her nose pressed against a Cambridge window, Virginia Woolf's narrator describes the don within holding forth in speech that is at once coin and communion wafer to an audience of admiring undergraduates:

> Sopwith went on talking . . . The soul itself slipped through the lips in thin silver disks which dissolve in young men's minds like silver . . . manliness. He loved it. Indeed to Sopwith a man could say anything, until perhaps he'd grown old, or gone under, gone deep, when the silver disks would tinkle hollow, and the inscription read a little too simple, and the old stamp look too pure. and the impress always the same—a Greek boy's head. But he would respect still. A woman, divining the priest, would, involuntarily, despise.[1]

In the sixty years since Woolf wrote this passage, women in significant numbers have broken the barriers which excluded Woolf herself from "Oxbridge," and now inhabit some of the rooms formerly occupied by Jacob and his dons. I begin with it, however, not to measure women's

I am indebted to Adrienne Munich, Paul Wallich, Maureen Quilligan, and Robert von Hallberg for provocative dialogue on the issues of this paper and helpful criticism of the manuscript.

Critical Inquiry 10 (December 1983)

progress from cultural exclusion but because in contrasting the places and stances of "man" and "woman" in the cultural economy, Woolf opens a more complicated question concerning the effects of women's inclusion: How are the dynamics of canonists selecting, readers interpreting, teachers teaching, and students learning affected by what is beginning to be a critical mass of women in the academy? Woolf's image is useful to a feminist critique of the literary canon because, rather than focusing on a canonical work, it abstracts what we might call the canonical mode of authority embodied in the don's speech and presents different responses of "man" and "woman" to this authority. The don, as "priest," mediates between his sacred books and his flock. A man, partaking of the "silver disks," respects; a woman, for whom the male-impressed currency is both inaccessible and foreign, involuntarily despises priestly authority. That woman can "divine" for herself challenges such authority, implying independence of the don's exclusive mediation. Further, even if we suppose her to have acceded to the don's role as cultural mediator, both her historical exclusion and her independent view suggest that she must play that part in a different way, reforming the traditional model of cultural authority in fidelity to her own experience.

But how might Woolf's "woman" transform the priestly model that has been instrumental in her own cultural oppression? To ask this question is to conceive cultural authority not merely as a commodity which women seek to possess equally with men but as power which has a political dimension realized in particular stances toward literary texts and literary history, toward language and stories, students and curricula. As the traditional literary canon exists in problematic relation to women, so do the modes of literary authority enshrined in those texts, upon which the social authority that institutes the canon and draws our models of literary history patterns itself. Sixty years after Woolf wrote, it is not only—nor even all—women who are alienated from the modes of authority invoked by cultural canons and priests; for present purposes, therefore, I will borrow Woolf's representation of "man" as one who "respect[s] still" the don's mystified cultural authority and "woman" as one who, "divining the priest," raises questions about the sources, motives, and interests of this authority. This definition identifies "woman" not by sex but by a complex relation to the cultural authority which has traditionally silenced and excluded her. She resists the attitude of blind submission which that authority threatens to imprint upon her; further, her resistance takes form not as envy of the "priest" and desire to possess his authority herself

Christine Froula, associate professor of English at Yale University, is the author of *A Guide to Ezra Pound's "Selected Poems"* and of the forthcoming *"To Write Paradise": Style and Error in Pound's Cantos*. She is currently working on a book about literary authority in James Joyce and Virginia Woolf.

but as a debunking of the "priestly" deployment of cultural authority and a refusal to adopt that stance herself. Women, under this local rule, can be "men," as men can be "women."[2]

Following the ground-breaking studies of Simone de Beauvoir, Mary Ellmann, and Kate Millett, many feminists have explored the politics of reading the patriarchal canon, which, as Elaine Showalter points out, holds up to the female no less than to the male reader the ideal of thinking "like a man."[3] Judith Fetterley, for example, has shown how the study of the traditional American literary canon presses the female reader to identify with the male point of view—the position of power—against herself.[4] In the last fifteen years, women professors of literature have begun to redress the male bias, both by including women authors in the curriculum—in established courses which their very presence exposes as having been previously, and invisibly, preoccupied with "men's studies," as well as in courses focused on women writers—and by employing the critical and pedagogical strategies of the "resisting reader" exemplified by de Beauvoir, Millett, Fetterley, and many others.

The effect of this work has been not simply to balance male bias with female (or marginal) bias—the "opening" of the canon—but to disrupt the canonical economy as such, the dynamics of cultural authority.[5] Feminists have moved from advocating representation of voices formerly silenced or "marginalized" by the established curriculum to recognizing that such representation implies and effects a profound transformation of the very terms *authority* and *value*—cultural and aesthetic or literary—that underwrite the traditional idea of the canon.[6] As Fetterley puts it: "To expose and question that complex of ideas and mythologies about women and men which exist in our society and are confirmed in our literature is to make the system of power embodied in the literature open not only to discussion but . . . to change."[7] Since the opening of the literary canon has been in some degree accomplished, we can now begin to analyze the impact of formerly silenced voices on the political economy of the literary canon, on the "system of power" that controls which texts are taught and how they are taught. How are "women" writers and teachers, formerly excluded from positions of cultural authority, affecting the economy of literature? I will take up two aspects of this large question: first, the radical challenge that feminist perspectives pose to the concept of a canon as such—not merely to the history and politics of canon-formation but to the *idea* (and ideal) of "the canon"—and, second, the critique of traditional modes of literary authority that emerges from reading "canonical" and "marginal" texts side by side.

1. The Politics of Orthodoxy: Canonists vs. Gnostics

I begin by extrapolating from Elaine Pagels' book, *The Gnostic Gospels*, to the power dynamics of literary authority, first, as claimed by texts and, second, as "respected" or "despised" by readers, teachers, and students. Pagels' study of the second-century gnostic writings discovered at Nag Hammadi in 1945 illuminates the politics implied in the canonist's stance by showing how the rediscovery of the gnostic texts—successfully suppressed by the church fathers in the struggle to establish a unified Church—dispels the widespread myth that all Christians shared the same doctrine in the apostles' time. She shows that early Christianity appears to have been "far more diverse than nearly anyone expected before the Nag Hammadi discoveries" and that the establishment of the "one, holy, catholic, and apostolic Church" required the suppression not merely of dissenting voices but of an antithetical conception of spiritual authority embodied in certain gnostic writings.[8]

There are, of course, many important differences between the deployment of cultural authority in the social context of second-century Christianity and that of twentieth-century academia. The editors of the *Norton Anthology*, for example, do not actively seek to suppress those voices which they exclude, nor are their principles for inclusion so narrowly defined as were the church fathers'. But the literary academy and its institutions developed from those of the Church and continue to wield a derivative, secular version of its social and cultural authority. Since Matthew Arnold, the institution of literature has been described in terms which liken its authority to that of religion, not only by outsiders—Woolf's woman "divining the priest"—but by insiders who continue to employ the stances and language of religious authority; see, for instance, J. Hillis Miller's credo in a recent issue of the *ADE Bulletin:* "I believe in the established canon of English and American literature and in the validity of the concept of privileged texts. I think it is more important to read Spenser, Shakespeare, or Milton than to read Borges in translation, or even, to say the truth, to read Virginia Woolf."[9] Such rhetoric suggests that the religious resonances in literary texts are not entirely figurative, a point brought out strikingly by revisionary religious figures in feminist texts. In her recent essay " 'The Blank Page' and the Issues of Female Creativity," Susan Gubar cites as some of the "many parables in an ongoing revisionary female theology" Florence Nightingale's tentative prophecy that "the next Christ will perhaps be a female Christ," H. D.'s blessed Lady carrying a "Bible of blank pages," and Gertrude Stein's celebration of *The Mother of Us All.*[10] The *revisionary* female theology promoted in *literary* writing by women implicitly counters the patriarchal theology which is *already* inscribed in literature. The prophesied female Christ, blank Bible, and female Creator revise images familiar in the literary tradition, and, in contrast to earlier appropriations of religious imagery by Metaphysical, Pre-Raphaelite, and other poets, make visible the patriarchal preoccupations of literary "theology." These voices, like the gnostic voices recovered at Nag Hammadi, are only now being heard in chorus; and Pagels' study of "the gnostic feminism" (as the *New York Review of*

Books labeled it) helps to illuminate some aspects of a cultural authority predicated on the suppression or domination of other voices.

Reconsidering patristic writings in light of the contemporary gnostic writings, Pagels argues that claims for exclusive authority made by the self-styled orthodoxy of the early Christian Church depended upon a mystification of history: the church fathers, in order to establish privileged texts, claimed that Jesus himself had invested the spiritual authority of the Church in certain individuals, who in turn passed this power on to their chosen successors. Their claim to a privileged spiritual authority rested upon the interpretation of the Resurrection as a historical event witnessed by the eleven remaining disciples. By this interpretation, all "true" spiritual authority derives from the apostles' witnessing of the literally resurrected Christ—an unrepeatable experience. Remarking the political genius of this doctrine, Pagels outlines its consequences, showing how the restriction of authority to this small band and their chosen successors divided the community into those who had power and those who didn't, privileged authorities and those whom such claims to privilege would dispossess of authority. The interpretation of the Resurrection as a historical event placed its advocates in a position of unchallengeable political dominance: "It legitimized a hierarchy of persons through whose authority all others must approach God" (*GG*, p. 27).

By contrast, the gnostics, interpreting the Resurrection in symbolic terms, resisted the mediating spiritual authority that the "orthodox" sought to institute in the Church. Pagels illustrates this conflict between the orthodox and gnostic positions by analyzing a passage from the gnostic "Gospel of Mary" in which Mary Magdalene comforts the disciples as they mourn after Jesus' death. Mary tells them: " 'Do not weep, and do not grieve, and do not doubt; for his grace will be with you completely, and will protect you.' " Peter then invites Mary, Pagels writes, " 'to tell us the words of the Savior which you remember.' But to Peter's surprise, Mary does not tell anecdotes from the past; instead, she explains that she has just seen the Lord in a vision received through the mind, and she goes on to tell what he revealed to her." Andrew and Peter ridicule Mary's claim that the Lord appeared in her vision, but Levi defends her: " 'Peter, . . . if the Savior made her worthy, who are you to reject her?' . . . Peter, apparently representing the orthodox position, looks to past events, suspicious of those who 'see the Lord' in visions: Mary, representing the gnostic, claims to experience his continuing presence" (*GG*, p. 13).[11]

The gnostic position, then, held that those who had received *gnosis*, that is, self-knowledge as knowledge of divinity,

> had gone beyond the church's teaching and had transcended the authority of its hierarchy. . . . They argued that only one's own experience offers the ultimate criterion of truth, taking precedence over all secondhand testimony and all tradition—even gnostic tra-

dition! They celebrated every form of creative invention as evidence that a person has become spiritually alive. On this theory, the structure of authority can never be fixed into an institutional framework: it must remain spontaneous, charismatic, and open. [*GG*, p. 25]

Pagels' study of "the politics of monotheism" illuminates the fact that the Church's aspirations to "catholicism," or universality, rendered the gnostic and orthodox interpretations of the Resurrection not merely different, nor even antithetical, but mutually exclusive. The coincidence of spiritual and political authority in the Church's self-styled orthodoxy (or "right opinion") made "heretics" of gnostics, defining as politically dangerous those who did not subscribe to the church fathers' mystified historical authority. By contrast, prior to any consideration of the "truth" of their writings, the gnostics neither claimed for themselves nor honored the historically based, absolute authority that the church fathers claimed. It was not, then, a question merely of competing canons, of differing doctrines or guidelines propounded by groups vying for cultural dominance, but of two mutually contradictory stances toward spiritual authority: one defined in such a way as to subsume political power and the other defined in such a way as to preclude the mediation of spiritual authority and, thus, the concept of a transcendentally grounded political authority.

Pagels concludes that the gnostic gospels reopen for our time the central issue of the early Christian controversies—"What is the source of religious authority? . . . What is the relation between the authority of one's own experience and that claimed for the Scriptures, the ritual, and the clergy?" (*GG*, p. 151)—for that issue was formerly settled by fiat, by the violence of political suppression as the cult of orthodoxy, aspiring to *culture*, sought and gained dominance over other cults. In literary culture, the concept of the canon preserves in secularized form some important aspects of the politics of cultural domination which Pagels elucidates in the early Christian Church. As the rediscovery of the repressed gnostic texts casts a new light on the conquests of orthodoxy and the idealization of "one faith" at the cost of many voices, so the entry of marginal texts into the modern literary curriculum not only "opens up" the canon but opens to question the idea of a canon. To explore more fully the workings of canonical authority in a literary context, I will turn now to a passage in *Paradise Lost*—the canonical text par excellence of English literature—which represents the conversion of Eve to orthodoxy. My interest in this passage is not in the dimensions of Milton's views on women as such but in the lines of force already inscribed in the Genesis story that Milton's retelling makes visible.[12]

2. The Invention of Eve and Adam

Eve's story of her first waking in book 4 of *Paradise Lost* is an archetypal scene of canonical instruction. Nowhere are the designs of orthodoxy

more vividly displayed than in this passage in which Eve herself utters
the words which consign her authority to Adam, and through him to
Milton's God, and thence to Milton's poem, and through the poem to
the ancient patriarchal tradition.[13] Eve opens her narrative with an apostrophe to Adam—

> O thou for whom
> And from whom I was form'd flesh of thy flesh,
> And without whom am to no end, my Guide
> And Head
> [4.440–43]

—which shows that she has already absorbed the wisdom of her teachers,
for she echoes Adam's naming of her (see 8.494–97) adapted from Genesis
2:23. She repeats this gesture of self-subordination at the end of her
own reminiscences. In the space between, however, Eve remembers an
origin innocent of patriarchal indoctrination, one whose resonances the
covering trope of narcissism does not entirely suffice to control. Recalling
her first waking "Under a shade on flow'rs," Eve remembers that she
heard a "murmuring sound / Of Waters issu'd from a Cave," which led
her to a "green bank" where she lay down to "look into the clear / Smooth
Lake, that to me seem'd another Sky" (4.451–59). But it is not, of course,
only "another Sky" that Eve sees reflected in the pool; she also sees what
she does not yet understand to be her own image:

> A Shape within the wat'ry gleam appear'd
> Bending to look on me, I started back,
> It started back, but pleas'd I soon return'd,
> Pleas'd it return'd as soon with answering looks
> Of sympathy and love; there I had fixt
> Mine eyes till now, and pin'd with vain desire,
> Had not a voice thus warned me, What thou seest,
> What there thou seest fair Creature is thyself,
> With thee it came and goes; but follow me,
> And I will bring thee where no shadow stays
> Thy coming, and thy soft imbraces, hee
> Whose image thou art, him thou shalt enjoy
> Inseparably thine, to him shalt bear
> Multitudes like thyself, and thence be call'd
> Mother of human Race
> [4.461–75]

This scenario imputes to the newborn Eve as her first desire a "vain"
narcissism, against which her gently accomplished conversion to the wiser
purposes of Adam and God seems a fortunate rise. But the master plot
in which the untutored Eve plays the role of doomed narcissist only
partially obscures the actual terms of her conversion, which require that

she abandon not merely her image in the pool but her very self—a self subtly discounted by the explaining "voice," which *equates* it with the insubstantial image in the pool: "What there thou seest . . . is thyself." The reflection is not *of* Eve: according to the voice, it *is* Eve. As the voice interprets her to herself, Eve is not a self, a subject, at all; she is rather a substanceless image, a mere "shadow" without object until the voice unites her to Adam—"hee / Whose image thou art"—much as Wendy stitches Peter Pan to his shadow.

Having reproduced the voice's call, Eve continues in her own voice with a rhetorical question that gestures toward repressed alternatives:

> what could I do,
> But follow straight, invisibly thus led?
> Till I espi'd thee, fair indeed and tall,
> Under a Platan, yet methought less fair,
> Less winning soft, less amiably mild,
> Than that smooth wat'ry image; back I turn'd,
> Thou following cri'd'st aloud, Return fair *Eve*,
> Whom fli'st thou? whom thou fli'st, of him thou art,
> His flesh, his bone; to give thee being I lent
> Out of my side to thee, nearest my heart
> Substantial Life, to have thee by my side
> Henceforth an individual solace dear;
> Part of my Soul I seek thee, and thee claim
> My other half: with that thy gentle hand
> Seiz'd mine, I yielded, and from that time see
> How beauty is excell'd by manly grace
> And wisdom, which alone is truly fair.
>
> [4.475–91]

As the benefits or "graces" of conversion promised by the voice—sexual pleasure and "Multitudes like thyself"—begin to materialize in Adam, the still autonomous Eve repeals the bargain, for the advertised original does not equal in interest the self she has been called upon to renounce. As she turns away to follow her own desire, Adam himself takes over from the voice the burden of educating Eve to her secondariness, recounting the "history" of her derivation from his rib. This tale informs Eve of an ontological debt she has unwittingly incurred to the generous lender of her "Substantial Life"—not that she might exist to, for, and from herself but rather that he might "have thee by my side / . . . an individual [inseparable] solace dear." Eve is "Part" of Adam's whole, his "other half," to which he lays "claim" by an oxymoronic gentle seizure; her debt to him, as he represents it, is such that she can repay it only by ceding to him her very self.

Eve's relation to Adam as mirror and shadow is the paradigmatic relation which canonical authority institutes between itself and its believers in converting them from the authority of their own experience to a "higher" authority. It also illustrates the way in which patriarchal culture at large imprints itself upon the minds of women and men. Eve's indoctrination into her own "identity" is complete at the point at which her imagination is so successfully colonized by patriarchal authority that she literally becomes its voice. As her narrative shows, she has internalized the voices and values of her mentors: her speech reproduces the words of the "voice" and of Adam and concludes with an assurance that she has indeed been successfully taught to "see" for herself the superiority of Adam's virtues to her own, limited as far as she knows to the "beauty" briefly glimpsed in the pool. In this way she becomes a "Part" not only of Adam but of the cultural economy which inscribes itself in her speech— or, more accurately, which takes over her speech: Eve does not speak patriarchal discourse; it speaks her.[14] The outer limits of her speech are given by the possibilities of this discourse. So long as she does not go beyond those limits her "credit" in the patriarchal system is ensured. It is not simply, then, that Eve accepts Milton's cultural currency at "face value." Rather, as the nativity story in which she traces her transformation from newborn innocent—tabula rasa—to patriarchal woman suggests, she *is* its face value. It is her image that appears on its bills of credit, the image of the idealized and objectified woman whose belief in her role underwrites patriarchal power.

The cultural economy erected upon Eve's credence exists on condition that Eve can "read" the world in only one way, by making herself the mirror of the patriarchal authority of Adam, Milton's God, Milton himself, and Western culture that the voice tells her she is. Indeed, the poem's master plot is designed precisely to discourage any "Eve" from reading this authority in any other way. As Diana Hume George points out, it is not primarily narcissism to which the beautiful talking serpent tempts Eve but *knowledge:* to cease respecting the authority fetish of an invisible power and to see the world for herself.[15] That *Paradise Lost*, the story of the Fall, is a violent parable of *gnosis* punished attests to the threat that Eve's desire for experienced rather than mediated knowledge poses to an authority which defines and proves itself chiefly in the successful prohibition of all other authorities.

To question the "face value" of Milton's cultural currency from within the poem, as Milton's Eve does, is to be blasted by the cultural and poetic authority that controls its plot and representation. But a gnostic "Eve," reading outside the bounds of that authority and not crediting the imagery that Milton would make a universal currency, disrupts that economy by a regard which makes visible what can work only so long as it remains hidden—the power moving Eve's conversion, that is, the power of Milton's God. In Eve's nativity scene, this power is imaged in the disembodied "voice"; and it is precisely the *invisibility* of this voice and of the "history"— originating in Adam's dream (see 8.287–484)—by which Adam attributes to Eve her secondary status that strikingly links this imagery to the church fathers' mystified history of the Resurrection, that invisible past invoked to justify their claims to privileged spiritual authority. The invisible voice that guides Eve away from the visible image of herself in the world to him whose image she is allegorizes what is literally the *secret* not only of spiritual and literary authority in Milton's poem but of cultural authority as such. The mystified authority of Christian doctrine underwrites the voice's injunctions, as it does the church fathers' claims to "right opinion." In both literatures, invisibility is a *definitive* attribute of authority: the power of the voice and of the church fathers, like that of the Wizard of Oz, resides in and depends upon invisibility.[16]

The dynamics of visibility and invisibility in Eve's and Adam's nativities uncover the hidden operations of power in Milton's text, which elaborately exfoliates the cultural text it draws upon. Their autobiographical narratives reveal a powerful subtext, at once literary and cultural, that works to associate Eve with visibility and Adam with invisibility from their first moments. As Maureen Quilligan observes, the relation of Eve's nativity imagery to Adam's replicates the relation between Eve and Adam themselves; for when Adam woke, "Straight toward Heav'n my wond'ring Eyes I turn'd, / And gaz'd a while the ample Sky," requesting it and the "enlighten'd Earth" to "Tell, if ye saw, how came I thus, how here?" (8.257–58, 274, 277). "Where Adam looks up at the true sky and then springs up, immediately to intuit his maker," Quilligan writes, "Eve bends down to look into 'another sky'—a secondary, mediated, reflective sky: a mirror, in more ways than one, of her own being."[17]

Adam's leaping upright to apostrophize a transcendent sky while Eve, supine, gazes into a "sky" that is to Adam's as her knowledge is to his—not the thing itself but a watery reflection—indeed supports the ontological hierarchy so crucial to Milton's purposes in *Paradise Lost*. But these images also intimate—or betray—the deep structure of that hierarchy: a defense against the apparent ascendancy of *Eve's* power. Eve's first act is to move toward the maternally murmuring pool that returns an image of herself in the visible world. Her "father" is out of sight and out of mind, but the reflecting face of the maternal waters gives back an image of her visible self. Adam, by contrast, is a motherless child. He sees with joy the "Hill, Dale, and shady Woods, and sunny Plains, / And liquid Lapse of murmuring Streams," but he does not identify with earthly bodies—not even his own (8.262–63). Adam "perus[es]" himself "Limb by Limb" (8.267), but like Emerson concludes that his body is "Not-Him." The sight of it only inspires him with questions that presuppose not the maternal life source from which bodies come but a father:

> Tell, if ye saw, how came I thus, how here?
> Not of myself; by some great Maker then,
> In goodness and in power preëminent;

Tell me, how may I know him, how adore,
From whom I have that thus I move and live
[8.277–81]

Adam projects a specifically male Creator, subordinating body and earth—
all that Adam can see—to an invisible father.
While it might seem that in these two scenes Milton is simply setting
up intimations of Adam's intrinsic spiritual superiority to Eve, Adam's
nativity offers another reading of his orientation toward transcendence.
Adam's turn to "higher" things can also be read as alienation from his
body and the visible world, an alienation which his God and the establishment of a hierarchical relation to Eve are designed to heal. Apostro-
phizing a sky and earth which give back no self-image, Adam finds none
until he succeeds in turning Eve into his reflection: "Whom fli'st thou?
whom thou fli'st, of him thou art." In this relation, Eve's visible, earth-
identified being is subordinated to Adam's intangible spiritual being.
Thus Eve can tell Adam that it is she who enjoys "So far the happier
Lot, enjoying thee / Preëminent by so much odds, while thou / Like
consort to thyself canst nowhere find" (4.446–48) and that he has taught
her to "see / How beauty is excell'd by manly grace / And wisdom, which
alone is truly fair" (4.489–91). The visible "beauty" of Eve's image bows
to the invisible fairness of "manly grace / And wisdom" in a contest which
appears to originate in Adam's need to make the visible world reflect
himself.
    Adam's need to possess Eve is usually understood as complemented
by her need for his guidance, but Milton's text suggests a more subtle
and more compelling source for this need: Adam's sense of inadequacy
in face of what he sees as Eve's perfection. The apparent self-sufficiency
glimpsed in her nativity account ("back I turn'd," interestingly misrep-
resented by Adam in book 8, lines 500–510) is amplified by Adam in
talking with Raphael. When he first saw Eve, Adam recalls, "what seem'd
fair in all the World, seem'd now / Mean, or in her summ'd up, in her
contain'd" (8.472–73), and he cannot reconcile her apparent perfection
with God's assurance of his own superiority. He worries about whether:

        Nature fail'd in mee, and left some part
        Not proof enough such Object to sustain,
        Or from my side subducting, took perhaps
        More than enough; . . .
        . . . .
                    [for] when I approach
        Her loveliness, so absolute she seems
        And in herself complete, so well to know
        Her own, that what she wills to do or say,
        Seems wisest, virtuousest, discreetest, best;
        All higher knowledge in her presence falls

> Degraded, Wisdom in discourse with her
> Loses discount'nanc't, and like folly shows;
> Authority and Reason on her wait,
> As one intended first, not after made
> Occasionally; and to consummate all,
> Greatness of mind and nobleness thir seat
> Build in her loveliest, and create an awe
> About her, as a guard Angel plac't.
>   [8.534–59]

What is interesting about Adam's representation of his own sense of inadequacy with respect to Eve is that it focuses on the body—specifically, *on the rib* which, he fancies, God took from his body to make Eve. That Adam's anxiety should take this particular form suggests that the "completeness" he fears in Eve and lacks in himself attaches to the function Adam associates with his rib: the power to create a human being. Adam's dream of Eve's creation from his rib fulfills his wish for an organ that performs the life-creating function of Eve's womb. The initial difference between Adam and Eve, then, is not Adam's inner superiority but simply sexual difference; Adam's fantasy of Eve's subordinate creation dramatizes an archetypal womb envy as constitutive of male identity.[18]

Considered in this Light, the God that Adam projects in his nativity appears designed to institute a hierarchy to compensate for the disparity he feels between himself and Eve. It is not that Adam is an imperfect image of his God, rather, his God is a *perfected* image of Adam: an all-powerful *male* Creator who soothes Adam's fears of female power by Himself claiming credit for the original creation of the world and, further, by bestowing upon Adam "Dominion" over the fruits of this creation through authorizing him to name the animals *and Eve*. The naming ritual enables Adam to translate his fantasy of power from the realm of desire to history and the world, instituting male dominance over language, nature, and woman. The perfection Adam attributes to the God who authorizes his "Dominion" counters the power he perceives in Eve. As Eve seems to him "absolute . . . / And in herself complete" so must his God possess these qualities in order to compete with her. Milton's curious elaboration of Genesis 2:18 makes a point of God's perfection in contrast to Adam's imperfection without Eve: God baits Adam after he requests a companion, saying in effect, "I'm alone; don't you think I'm happy?" and Adam replies, "Thou in thyself art perfet, and in thee / Is no deficience found; not so is Man" (8.415–16). Adam's "perfet" God enables him to contend with the self-sufficiency he sees and fears in Eve, precisely by authorizing Adam's possession of her. Through the dream of the rib Adam both enacts a parody of birth and gains possession of the womb by claiming credit for woman herself. In this way he himself becomes as "perfet" as he can, appropriating in indirect and symbolic but consequential ways the creative power and self-sufficiency he attributes to Eve and to his God.

The shadow of the repressed mother, then, falls as tangibly over Adam's nativity scene as it does upon Eve's. Necessitated by Adam's awe of Eve's life-giving body and his wish to incorporate her power in himself, this repression mutely signals that patriarchal power is not simply one attribute among others of Adam's God but its primary motive and constituent. As the nativity scene represents Him, Adam's God is a personification of patriarchal power, created in the image of and in competition with the maternal power that Adam perceives in Eve. The overt hierarchy of God over Adam and Adam over Eve which is the text's "argument" is underlain (and undermined) by a more ancient *perceived* hierarchy of Eve over Adam, still apparent in the "ghostlier demarcations" of Adam's transumptive myth. In the power dynamics of Adam's nativity scene, the self-sufficient Eve and the compensatory God that Adam projects out of his fear are the true rivals, as Christ's jealous rebuke to Adam after the Fall confirms:

> Was shee thy God, that her thou didst obey
> Before his voice, or was shee made thy guide,
> Superior, or but equal, that to her
> Thou didst resign thy Manhood, and the Place
> Wherein God set thee above her
> [10.145–49]

The nativities of Adam and Eve in Milton's poem bear out the archetypal association of maleness with invisibility and of femaleness with visibility that some theorists argue is given in male and female relations to childbirth and, through childbirth, to the world and the future. In *Moses and Monotheism*, Freud celebrates civilization as the triumph of invisibility over visibility. Freud links what he labels "the progress in spirituality" in Western culture to three tropes of invisibility: the triumph of Moses' unrepresentable God over idols, "which means the compulsion to worship an invisible God"; the evolution of symbolic language, through which abstract thinking assumed priority over "lower psychical activity which concerned itself with the immediate perceptions of the sense organs"; and "the turning from the mother to the father," from matriarchy to patriarchy, which, says Freud, "signifies above all a victory of spirituality over the senses . . . since maternity is proved by the senses whereas paternity is a surmise."[19] Following Dorothy Dinnerstein, Jonathan Culler shifts the priorities of Freud's reading of human history. The establishment of patriarchal power, he suggests, is not merely an instance, along with the preference for an invisible God, of the triumph of spirituality; rather, "when we consider that the invisible, omnipotent God is God the Father, not to say God of the Patriarchs, we may well wonder whether, on the contrary, the promotion of the invisible over the visible ... is not a consequence or effect of the establishment of paternal authority."[20] Dinnerstein and other feminists go further, interpreting hierarchical dualism not as a "consequence or effect" but as the *means* of establishing paternal authority, a *compensatory* effort on the part of the male to control a natural world to which he is bound in relatively remote and mediated ways.[21] Freud himself runs significantly aground on the question of what motivates the hierarchy of the invisible over the visible: "The world of the senses becomes gradually mastered by spirituality, and . . . man feels proud and uplifted by each such step in progress. One does not know, however, why this should be so" (*MM*, p. 151). In fact, a few pages earlier, he argues that the *invisibility* of Moses' divine patriarch aroused in the minds of believers "a much more grandiose idea of their God" and that this august invisible god endowed believers themselves with grandeur by association: "Whoever believed in this God took part in his greatness, so to speak, might feel uplifted himself" (*MM*, pp. 143). So Adam's first colloquy with his God raises him above the earth to literalized heights, the mount of Paradise:

> *Adam*, rise,
> . . . .
> . . . he took me rais'd,
> . . . .
> . . . led me up
> A woody Mountain; whose high top . . .
> [was so beautifully planted], that what I saw
> Of Earth before scarce pleasant seem'd.
> [8.296–306]

Adam's God enables him to transcend earthly being and in so doing to gain a power he hungers for, as his "sudden appetite / To pluck and eat" the fruits of paradise implies (8.308–9).

Returning now to Eve's nativity narrative, we can see that her story allegorizes Freud's analysis of the "triumph" of invisibility. The God that Adam sees is invisible to her; she, too, progresses from a "lowly" absorption in images of the senses to more grandiose "conceptions"; and she turns away from the maternal waters in which she finds her reflected image to identify with a patriarchy whose power is specifically *not* visible, prevailing even though it is to all *appearances* "less fair, / Less winning sôft, less amiably mild, / Than that smooth wat'ry image" of herself in the world. The fable of Eve's conversion from her own visible being in the world to invisible patriarchal authority traces a conversion from being in and for herself to serving a "higher" power—from the authority of her own experience to the hidden authority symbolized in the prohibited Tree of Knowledge.

Yet this power is not transcendent; it must be authorized by Eve's belief—a belief enlisted through the invisible voice's claim that it *already* exists and, further, through its equally strategic representation of Eve as a mere "shadow" or image that has and can have no value except for what patriarchal authority attaches to her. Eve's value is created by the patriarchy whose discourse she becomes. Her narrative proves the "triumph" of her education or colonization; she has received the imprimatur of the realm, has *become* its text, image, and token of value. Assuring her own power within the terms it offers her, she also assures its literal power: her discourse makes its invisible power visible *as herself*. Her passive role in the patriarchal cultural economy—"what could I do, / But follow straight invisibly thus led?"—resembles that of the paper on which monetary value is inscribed.²² The imprinting of patriarchal authority upon Eve, like the printing of paper money, transforms intrinsically worthless material into pure value. Any object chosen to be the medium of trade must, of course, be worth less than its exchange value; otherwise, it is soon de-idealized, reverting from an image of value to an object of value.²³ Similarly, in order for her to serve as the idealized currency of patriarchal culture, Eve's intrinsic value must be denied; her self, her subjectivity, must be *devalued* to resemble the worthless paper on which the inscription designating money, or credit, is stamped. Eve's subjectivity, her being-for-herself, is the "paper" upon which patriarchal authority imprints its own valuation, thereby "uplifting" her allegedly worthless being ("shadow," reflection, "image") to pure value.

Gubar observes that numerous images of women in texts by male authors suggest that "the female body has been feared for its power to articulate itself."²⁴ Milton's Eve brings the threat of woman's self-articulation into focus: it is the danger posed by her speaking from her body, from an experience that exists outside patriarchal authority, as did the untutored, self-reflective consciousness Milton represents as narcissistic. Such speech threatens the very basis of the cultural currency. As woman begins to speak a discourse no longer defined and limited by the patriarchal inscription, Eve's voice recovers its intrinsic value. Just as paper would no longer be available to serve as a medium of exchange were its use-value to exceed its exchange-value, so it no longer profits Eve to hand over the "blank pages" of her subjectivity to the patriarchal imprint. At this point, the patriarchal currency fails: to overturn a cliché, it is no longer worth the paper it's printed on.

What the failure of its currency means for the patriarchal economy is not that we no longer read its texts but that we read them in a different way, using interpretive strategies that mark a shift from a sacred to a secular interpretive model, from an economy of invisible transactions to one of *visible* exchange. Concluding *A Room of One's Own*, Woolf refers to *Paradise Lost* as "Milton's bogey."²⁵ From a gnostic vantage point, *Paradise Lost* loses its power as "bogey" or scarecrow and becomes, instead, a cultural artifact situated in history, its power analyzable as that of an ancient and deeply ingrained pattern in Western thought, reinvented to serve the interests of modern society and realized in language of un-surpassed subtlety and *explicable* sublimity. Read in such a way that the invisible becomes visible; the transcendent, historical; the sacred icon, a cultural image; the "bogey," old clothes upon a stick, Milton's poem becomes as powerful an instrument for the undoing of the cultural economy inscribed in it as it was for its institution—more powerful, indeed, than less "pure" forms of patriarchal currency.

The critique of patriarchal / canonical authority assumes that literary authority is a mode of social authority and that literary value is inseparable from ideology. The "Eves" no longer crediting their image in Milton's poem value his literary achievement no less than do such proponents of canon-making ideologies as Harold Bloom; but the poem no longer shuts out the view. Precisely because of the ways in which our own history is implicated in the poem, we continue to hear the other voices which Milton's literary and cultural history making dominates and which, pre-senting different models of literary / social authority, disrupt the canonical economy of Milton's text as the gnostic voices disrupted the economy of Christian orthodoxy. To explore some implications of this disruption, I will turn now to compare the representation of poetic authority in *Paradise Lost* with that of Isak Dinesen's short story "The Blank Page," a text Susan Gubar recently brought to wide attention. This story about woman's body and spirit relates itself dialectically to the biblical patriarchal tradition which Milton deepens and extends. Existing both inside and outside that tradition, it exemplifies Eve's speech as it breaks through the limits of patriarchal discourse. By comparing the connections drawn between sex-uality and authority in these works, I wish to suggest that Milton's patriarchal epic and Dinesen's very short story about women's speaking silence are, in important ways, complementary forms in our literary culture.[26]

3. Counter-Currencies: Milton and "The Blank Page"

"I can conceive," wrote Woolf of *Paradise Lost*, "that this is the essence, of which almost all other poetry is the dilution."[27] Woolf echoes innumerable readers, but the hypothetical cast of her remark unhinges the judgment just enough to expose its presumption of a particular idea of poetry. Her speculative judgment is also a definition, a tautology: *Paradise Lost* is the essence of poetry / the essence of poetry is *Paradise Lost*. In context, the judgment reflects a rather uncomfortable acquiescence to a certain ideal of poetic greatness. Milton, Woolf says, gives her "no help in judging life; I scarcely feel that Milton lived or knew men and women"; yet beside his sublime depth of style, even Shakespeare seems "a little troubled. personal, hot and imperfect," and this sublime, impersonal perfection she names "poetry."[28]

We may wonder, however, how far the Miltonic sublime derives not from sheer linguistic virtuosity but from thematic resonances that history has proved all but invisible to mortal sight. Milton's nativity scenes, I have argued, reveal that the repression of the mother is the genesis of Genesis. As Milton unveils his Muse in the first of his four invocations, the repression that shapes his epic story is found to mirror a similar repression in the representation of his poetic authority. The Muse of book 1 is a protean figure. Opening *Paradise Lost*, Milton invokes what seems at first a perfectly conventional "Heav'nly Muse"—identified by Merritt Hughes with the Urania of book 7 and the Celestial Patroness of book 9—to tell the story of "man's first disobedience" redeemed by "one greater Man" in order to "justify the ways of God to men" (1.6, 1, 4, 26). At line 7, this figure is particularized as Moses' Muse, the Muse of Genesis through whose inspiration Moses "first taught the chosen Seed, / In the Beginning how the Heav'ns and Earth / Rose out of *Chaos*" (1.8–10). At line 17, the Muse undergoes another, more startling, translation, from *witness* of Creation to *Creator*:

> And chiefly Thou O Spirit, that dost prefer
> Before all Temples th'upright heart and pure,
> Instruct me, for Thou know'st; Thou from the first
> Wast present, and with mighty wings outspread
> Dove-like satst brooding on the vast Abyss
> And mad'st it pregnant
>
> [1.17–22]

It is finally this imagined author of Creation that Milton asks to tell the story of Creation (see 1.27–30).

The invocation of the Creator as Muse is surprising; it is rather as though Homer has invoked not Calliope but Zeus to tell the story of the Trojan War. What is at stake in Milton's construction of his Muse is, of course, his own poetic authority. Milton moves past the sublimated social authority of the Homeric Muse to invoke his God directly, thereby creating an image of a poetic authority that mediates between his conception of the absolute and the "nation" for whom he meant his poem to be "example." Like the orthodox doctrine of the Resurrection as historical event upon which the church fathers based their claims for authority, Milton's Muse underwrites his claims to a specific kind of poetic authority, a power grounded in priority of witness to human history—in *having been there* where his hearers were not. Milton's Muse is at once a model for and a projection of his own ambitious poetic authority, which he seeks to ground in first and highest things. Its authority for the creation of song is based on its authority for the Creation itself. In the role of Milton's Muse this "Spirit" becomes the Logos, the Word that calls all things into being. As such, it is a figure for the cultural authority to which Milton aspires as creator and poet, the absolute authority for history that only one who is both creator and namer can claim. Like Moses' invisible God and like Eve's invisible voice, the God / Muse that Milton projects "uplifts" him from the human to the sublime, from blindness to vision, from the limitations of the visible to invisible power. It meets Milton's prayer:

> What in me is dark
> Illumine, what is low raise and support;
> That to the highth of this great Argument
> I may assert Eternal Providence,
> And justify the ways of God to men.
>
> [1.22–26]

As Milton transforms his Muse into his God, an attendant change occurs: the apparently conventional, presumably female, "Heav'nly Muse" is "transsexualized" even as it is elevated, precisely at the point at which Milton has most at stake in establishing his epic authority. That this is no accident of iconographic tradition is clear from Milton's embellishment of the verse "The earth was without form and void, and darkness was upon the face of the deep; and the Spirit of God was moving over the face of the waters" (Gen. 1:2). Milton's apostrophe, "[Thou who] with mighty wings outspread / Dove-like satst brooding on the vast Abyss / And mad'st it pregnant," transforms his Muse not just into a Creator-figure but into that powerful, self-sufficient *male* Creator so crucial to Adam in his relations with Eve. Milton's image heightens the procreative "hovering" or "brooding" of the Hebrew text but in such a way as to annihilate its female aspect: the maternal—and *material*—life-giving waters of Genesis 1:2 become, in Milton, darkness and silence, an "Abyss," whereas the male impregnator, "Spirit" and divine voice, is addressed as the author of both the Creation and the creation story which Milton tells.

Milton's silencing and voiding of female creativity recall the anxiety about female independence allegorized in the nativities, and his invocation brings all the elements of Freud's "progress in spirituality" into play. The male Logos called upon to articulate the cosmos against an abyss of female silence overcomes the anxieties generated by the tension between visible maternity and invisible paternity by appropriating female power to itself in a parody of parthenogenesis. Milton's image of creation is an archetypally patriarchal image, imagining as it does an absolutely original and self-sufficient paternal act, prior to and unthreatened by all others, from which issues the visible world. His image of epic authority thus depicts in small the "genesis" of the patriarchal authority which is the basis of Milton's cultural power and of his epic theme. Milton's emphatic suppression of the female in his transformation of Genesis is integral to his authority in patriarchal culture, preenacting the silencing of Eve and the Fall which follows upon her violation of the orthodox prohibition of knowledge.[29]

Yet the cost of such authority is the repression of another kind of knowledge, that *human* knowledge the absence of which Woolf remarked. In the famous invocation to book 3, Milton writes of his literal blindness in terms which do not represent the invisible power of the sublime as a simple triumph over the visible, or spiritual power as satisfactory compensation for loss of the visible world:

> Thus with the Year
> Seasons return, but not to me returns
> Day, or the sweet approach of Ev'n or Morn,
> . . . .
> . . . or human face divine;
> . . . .
> . . . from the cheerful ways of men
> Cut off, and for the Book of knowledge fair
> Presented with a Universal blanc
> Of Nature's works to me expung'd and ras'd,
> And wisdom at one entrance quite shut out.
> So much the rather thou Celestial Light
> Shine inward, . . .
> . . . .
> . . . that I may see and tell
> Of things invisible to mortal sight.
>
> [3.40–55]

These invocations, which play out in small the sexual dynamics of *Paradise Lost*, suggest that the story of the epic enterprise, the victory of invisibility and the compensations of "Celestial Light," has not yet been fully told. If the epic tradition has in a very real sense been built upon female silence, then the patriarchal authority Milton establishes in *Paradise Lost* is not mere precondition for his story; it *is* that story.

If *Paradise Lost* issues from an epic authority founded upon women's silence, Dinesen's "Blank Page" is the voice of that silence. Dinesen's storyteller compares the power of speaking silence specifically to the Miltonic tradition of "highest inspiration":

"Where the story-teller is loyal, eternally and unswervingly loyal to the story, there, in the end, silence will speak. Where the story has been betrayed, silence is but emptiness. But we, the faithful, when we have spoken our last word, will hear the voice of silence . . ."

"Who then," she continues, "tells a finer tale than any of us? Silence does. And where does one read a deeper tale than upon the most perfectly printed page of the most precious book? Upon the blank page. When a royal and gallant pen, in the moment of its highest inspiration, has written down its tale with the rarest ink of all—where, then, may one read a still deeper, sweeter, merrier, and more cruel tale than that? Upon the blank page."[30]

Here is the inverted image of the rivalry between female and male creativity found in Milton's imagery of creative power, and here too the contest is obscurely won. In what sense can the story of the "blank page" be understood to triumph over Milton's high inspiration? It would seem that this triumph must be construed as the feat of showing that silence does speak, that Milton's words cannot possess the *absolute* authority claimed in the image of the Muse as Logos. The speaking silence of the blank page undermines the authority of Milton's scriptures in the same way that Eve's untutored speech does. Its story cannot be told within—yet is the suppressed condition of—patriarchal discourse.

Though less than six pages long, "The Blank Page" begins with a leisurely prologue in which Dinesen's storyteller, like Milton, marks out the terms of her authority. As in *Paradise Lost*, her prologue and her story mirror each other; but whereas Milton's imagery of epic authority privileges the Father and the "Spirit," her authority and her story come through her mothers and belong to the *material* world. The story opens with a frame narrator who sets the scene, a nameless ancient city in which the telling of stores is the sustenance of bodies: "By the ancient city gate sat an old coffee-brown, black-veiled woman who made her living telling stories. . . . Now if she is well paid and in good spirits, she will go on" ("BP," pp. 99, 100). Where Milton's poetic ambition fixes upon invisible highest things, the storyteller's are less grand, concerned first with biological economy. Like Milton, she defines her authority in historical terms, but while he obliterates human forebears—even Moses—"soaring above" to unmediated communion with his "Muse," the storyteller literally *embodies* the teaching of a chain of mother's mothers, all better storytellers than she yet now merged with her as she carries on their "work": "They and I have become one" ("BP," p. 99).

That work is itself bound up with the experience of the female body, for the teller is a Scheherazade whose tales defer death at the hand of patriarchal authority. It is not justification of the ways of God to men but woman's life that is at stake in her craft. Her tale defends not against the literal death that threatens Scheherazade but against a death of the spirit imaged in the tales which the storyteller heard in her youth from young men: "I have told many tales, one more than a thousand, since that time when I first let young men tell me, myself, tales of a red rose, two smooth lily buds, and four silky, supple, deadly, entwining snakes" ("BP," p. 99). The young men's tales allegorize a metaphorical death of woman in patriarchal culture, a "deadly" break between the female body and a speaking subject who disappears into silence upon reaching sexual maturity. The disjunction between the fertile female body and speech is exemplified by her grandmother's two bodies—in youth the dancer's, "often-embraced," and in age the storyteller's, a wrinkled apple ("BP," p. 99). As a child in her grandmother's hard school, the storyteller was unable to understand the "loyal[ty] to the story" through which silence is made to speak: having not yet become a woman, she could not distinguish between speaking silence and empty silence nor feel loyalty to the story at once of female sexuality and female creativity in patriarchal culture ("BP," p. 100). The female body in history is not only the story proper of "The Blank Page" but quite directly its source, inspiration, and authority.

The authority of the female storytellers is not circumscribed by patriarchal tradition; yet it is informed by it. Recounting the history of the convent where flax is cultivated and made into the finest "flower-white" linen of Portugal, the storyteller explains that the first seed for the flax was brought by a Portuguese crusader from the Holy Land. The story of the flax seed is also the story of her own tale: "Diligence . . . is a good thing, and religion is a good thing, but the very first germ of a story will come from some mystical place outside the story itself" ("BP," p. 102). These seed images echo many others in the story: the Annunciation scene, pictured as the Virgin gathering eggs in her mother's poultry yard while Gabriel descends from heaven; the sisters' seeding of the flax fields in the spring; and the imagery of impregnation on the marked "pages" of linen framed and hung in the convent. What is interesting about the superposition of linseed and story-germ is that both picture a remote and indirect fertilization of female production and creation. Though the storyteller cannot read, her grandmother's grandmother learned from an old rabbi and passed her knowledge on, and she cites the Book of Joshua (see Josh. 15:17–19) in describing how the flax seed came from the holy lands of Lecha and Maresha. These lands were made fertile by Achsah's demand that her father Caleb "Give me a blessing!" through which she received "the upper springs and the nether springs" to water her land ("BP," p. 102). The storyteller knows the Bible only as she knows her tales, through oral tradition, in this case "seeded" by the old rabbi. Yet in making her own story continuous with it, she augments biblical authority even as she acknowledges its own in her story and in the sisters' flax and linen.

In tracing the linseed back to Achsah's demand, the storyteller simultaneously allegorizes the history of her own authority and of the story that both takes shape within patriarchal culture and escapes it. Achsah's demand of her father for "the blessing of springs of water," the means of creativity, is the creative speech from which the story of the blank page and the industry of the Convento Velho grow ("BP," p. 102). In this economy of female creativity, women use the father's gift to create their own blessings, outside the fatal authority of patriarchy. They invest their patrimony in a new culture which subverts the ancient, deeply engrained mythology of the war between the sexes: woman as scapegoat; the "fallen" state of the body and labor; and the fetishizing of woman as sexual object, virgin, mother, and property.

The Annunciation image, then, is the paradigm for convent and story, representing the seed which comes to woman from "somewhere outside." The convent society is not entirely independent of patriarchal values: it is in concept a kind of harem of "brides of Christ," and its "first privilege" is to supply the matrimonial sheets ceremoniously displayed in proof of noble brides' virginity, "before the morning gift had yet been handed over" ("BP," p. 102). But within the convent walls exists a world in which the concept of a Fall appears to have no meaning. The nuns are "a blithe and active sisterhood. They take much pleasure in their holy meditations, and will busy themselves joyfully" with their work ("BP," p. 101). Nowhere is their independence of the fallen world of hard toil at the accursed ground more evident than in the joy the sisters take in their labor:

> The long field below the convent is plowed with gentle-eyed, milk-white bullocks, and the seed is skillfully sown out by labor-hardened virginal hands with mold under the nails. At the time when the flax field flowers, the whole valley becomes air-blue, the very color of the apron which the blessed virgin put on to go out and collect eggs. . . . During this month the villagers many miles round raise their eyes to the flax field and ask one another: "Has the convent been lifted into heaven? Or have our good little sisters succeeded in pulling down heaven to them?" ["BP," p. 101]

The sisters create a "heaven" in which the visible world and the work of hands coincide with joy of thought. The story celebrates their female economy as innocent of the dichotomies between visibility and invisibility, body and spirit, the human face and divinity, earth and heaven, which in patriarchal culture attach to gender in such a way as to put enmity between woman's seed and man's, imaged and disowned in the phallic serpent. The "blank page" of linen in the convent's gallery tells the story of escape from the patriarchal sexual economy with its fetish of virgin blood on matrimonial sheets, not only in the specific instance it memorializes but in the many which echo it in the story—Achsah, the Virgin Mary, the sisterhood, the storyteller, and the spinster who makes the "sacred and secretly gay" pilgrimage to the convent to view the blank page, pausing like a gnostic Eve on her way up into the mountains "to see the view widen to all sides" ("BP," pp. 103, 104). The indeterminate text of the blank page gestures beyond a sexual economy which makes woman's body the symbol of patriarchal authority—credit or goods—toward body and spirit no longer divided and no longer inscribed with the designs of an external mastery.

To the Adam-and-Eve-like pair who are her audience, the storyteller says that the old women who tell stories "know the story of the blank page. But we are somewhat averse to telling it, for it might well, among the uninitiated, weaken our own credit. All the same . . . my sweet and pretty lady and gentlemen of the generous hearts[,] I shall tell it to you" ("BP," p. 100). As Milton's orthodox story of the Fall is one in which all are initiated and which many still credit, the gnostic "Blank Page" is a riddle, a "counter-currency" of unfamiliar inscription and authority. But cultural authority, like money, is a social convention underwritten by common belief. Within the gender distinctions instituted by patriarchy, epic authority is "male" and the authority of "The Blank Page," which seeks not to dominate other voices but to let silence speak, is "female." But this "pregnant" juxtaposition points beyond static dichotomies to active rereadings of the texts that have shaped our traditions alongside those that have been repressed and toward questioning and reimagining the structures of authority for a world in which authority need no longer be "male" and coercive nor silence "female" and subversive, in which, in other words, speech and silence are no longer tied to an archetypal— and arbitrary—hierarchy of gender.

The problem of revising the ways in which the literary academy deploys its culture-making power is obviously too large to address here. But the feminist (or antipatriarchal) challenge to the ideal of "the literary canon" points to the need to transform a pedagogy which conceives "Great Books" on the model of sacred texts into one which calls into question the unexamined hierarchies invoked by the Arnoldian ideal, "the acquainting ourselves with the best that has been thought and said in the world." A recent exponent of this ideal, Harry Levin, has written that it must not be laid aside, for "without this, we will lose our most valued patrimony, our collective memory."[31] But there can be no hope for a "community of ideas," or for anything like the consensus a "canon" requires, based on a heritage in which domination and hierarchy are the very ground for literary and social authority—a "patrimony" accumulated at the expense of silencing woman's culture-making power in "matrimony." Yet, if the "collective memory" held in the traditional canon of Western literature is a danger to the future so long as it is propagated by a "Great Books" pedagogy in the traditional curriculum, it also has powerful possibilities, read from a critical perspective, as an instrument for change. Few of us can free ourselves completely from the power ideologies inscribed in the idea of the canon and in many of its texts merely by not reading "canonical" texts, because we have been reading the patriarchal "arche-text" all our lives. But we can, through strategies of rereading that expose the deeper structures of authority and through interplay with texts of a different stamp, pursue a kind of collective psychoanalysis, transforming "bogeys" that hide invisible power into investments both visible and alterable. In doing so, we approach traditional texts not as the mystifying (and self-limiting) "best" that has been thought and said in the world but as a *visible* past against which we can teach our students to imagine a different future. Because its skeptical regard of the past is informed by responsibility to that future, feminist theory is a powerful tool with which to replace Arnold's outworn dictum. As women begin to come into a share of the "patrimony," we can begin to imagine a redistribution of "credit" that will undo the invisible power of the literary tradition and make for a richer world.

1. Virginia Woolf, *Jacob's Room* (1922; New York, 1978), pp. 40–41.

2. Since the male-female relationship is the archetypal hierarchy in Western culture, "woman" has become a fashionable image for analysts of cultural politics, notably in deconstructive theory and practice. The dangers of this appropriation to the interests of actual women have been discussed by Nancy K. Miller in "The Text's Heroine: A Feminist Critic and Her Fictions," *Diacritics* 12 (Summer 1982): 48–53. She argues for combining a post-humanistic theory which throws center, periphery, and subject into question with a critical practice that does not lose sight of the *literally* marginal and precarious position female authors and teachers now hold in the academy. While it is manifestly not true that the "canonical" and "gnostic" stances toward authority that I explore in this essay belong in any simple way to actual men and women, respectively, history—and literary history—render these alignments no more heuristic than descriptive.

3. Elaine Showalter, "Women and the Literary Curriculum," *College English* 32 (May 1971): 855.

4. See Judith Fetterley, *The Resisting Reader: A Feminist Approach to American Fiction* (Bloomington, Ind., 1978).

5. This "opening" was propounded from Third World, feminist, and Marxist points of view in the collection of essays that appeared in the wake of the sixties' questioning of authority, *The Politics of Literature: Dissenting Essays on the Teaching of Literature,* ed. Louis Kampf and Paul Lauter (New York, 1972), and later in *English Literature: Opening Up the Canon,* ed. Leslie A. Fiedler and Houston A. Baker, Jr., Selected Papers from the English Institute, 1979, n.s. 4 (Baltimore, 1981).

In order to situate the issues of my argument, it is useful to recall here Ernst Robert Curtius' description of the intellectual economy that he considered to have replaced the concept of the canon in the twentieth century. Citing Valery Larbaud, he distinguishes between "la carte politique et la carte intellectuelle du monde." The anachronistic French model of national canons competing for the colonization of intellectual territories has ceded, he says, to literary cosmopolitanism, "a politics of mind which has left behind all pretensions to hegemony, and is concerned only with facilitating and accelerating the exchange of intellectual merchandise" (*European Literature and the Latin Middle Ages,* trans. Willard R. Trask [1948; Princeton, N.J., 1973], pp. 271, 272). In Curtius' account, which posits the transformation of cultural imperialism into a world market in which intellectual "goods" are freely exchanged, not only the concept of a closed canon but the canonizing stance itself becomes obsolescent along with the hegemonic and universal (or "catholic") pretensions of parochial cultures—Judeo-Christian, national, or European. The evangelical projects of ethnocentric beliefs are presumed dead or defunct, and belief in the supremacy of a single cultural authority gives way to diverse and mutually translatable cultural "currencies." These admit of equation and free exchange in a global economy governed not by transcendent and hegemonic conceptions of value but by *translatability*—of sensibility as well as language. Curtius' idealized image of a free-market cultural economy usefully distinguishes the cultural issues of the twentieth century from those of earlier periods, but his wishful depoliticization of this economy can be understood only in the context of nationalist politics in the first half of the century. In fact, the "intellectual free market" has the defects of its economic analogue, and both are, in any case, virtually male monopolies.

6. See, for example, Florence Howe, "Those We Still Don't Read," *College English* 43 (Jan. 1981): 16.

7. Fetterley, *The Resisting Reader,* p. xx.

8. Elaine Pagels, *The Gnostic Gospels* (New York, 1979), p. xxii; all further references to this work, abbreviated *GG*, will be included parenthetically in the text. Critics who object that Pagels gives scant attention to the diversity of voices within Christian orthodoxy err in supposing her discussion to concern unity and diversity as such rather than the politics implicit in orthodox and gnostic stances toward spiritual authority. The gnostic position as she describes it leads logically not to political anarchy but rather to a demystification of the political sphere.

9. J. Hillis Miller, "The Function of Rhetorical Study at the Present Time," *The State of the Discipline, 1970s–1980s, ADE Bulletin* 62 (Sept.-Nov. 1979): 12; cited by Sandra Gilbert, "What Do Feminist Critics Want? or, A Postcard from the Volcano," *ADE Bulletin* 66 (Winter 1980): 20. Miller acknowledges the "strongly preservative or conservative" character of his pronouncement (p. 12).

10. Susan Gubar, " 'The Blank Page' and the Issues of Female Creativity," *Writing and Sexual Difference, Critical Inquiry* 8 (Winter 1981): 261, 262.

11. For the complete text, see "The Gospel of Mary," in *The Nag Hammadi Library in English*, ed. James N. Robinson, trans. Members of the Coptic Gnostic Library Project of the Institute for Antiquity and Christianity (New York, 1977), pp. 471–74.

12. John Milton's sexual politics has become an issue of increasing importance in Milton criticism in the last decade; among many illuminating studies are Marcia Landy, "Kinship and the Role of Women in *Paradise Lost*," *Milton Studies* 4 (1972): 3–18, and " 'A Free and Open Encounter': Milton and the Modern Reader," *Milton Studies* 9 (1976): 3–36; Barbara K. Lewalski, "Milton on Women—Yet Once More," *Milton Studies* 6 (1974): 3–20; Diane McColley, " 'Daughter of God and Man': The Subordination of Milton's Eve," in *Familiar Colloquy: Essays Presented to Arthur Edward Barker*, ed. Patricia Bruckmann (Ottawa, 1978), pp. 196–208; Joan Malory Webber, "The Politics of Poetry: Feminism and *Paradise Lost*," *Milton Studies* 14 (1980): 3–24; Northrop Frye, "The Revelation to Eve," in *"Paradise Lost": A Tercentenary Tribute*, ed. Balachandra Rajan (Toronto, 1969), pp. 18–47; and Marilyn R. Farwell, "Eve, the Separation Scene, and the Renaissance Idea of Androgyny," *Milton Studies* 16 (1982): 3–20.

13. See Milton, *Paradise Lost, Complete Poems and Major Prose*, ed. Merritt Y. Hughes (Indianapolis, 1957), bk. 4; all further references to this work will be included in the text, with book and line numbers in parentheses.

Milton draws his account of the creation of Adam and Eve mainly from that by the [Jahwist] scribe (Gen. 2:4–3:20, ninth–tenth century B.C.), rather than from the P[riestly] scribe's account (Gen. 1:26–27, fifth–sixth century B.C.). In the P scribe's text, female and male are co-originary. But, for a discussion of the exaggeration of patriarchal values in the J scribe's Hebrew text by the translators of the English texts, see Casey Miller and Kate Swift, *Words and Women: New Language in New Times* (New York, 1978), pp. 15–16, citing Phyllis Trible's "Depatriarchalizing in Biblical Interpretation," *Journal of the American Academy of Religion* 41 (Mar. 1973): 35–42.

14. The limits of Eve's discourse in her nativity story illustrate the interest of the concept of authority as reframed by Michel Foucault: " 'What are the modes of existence of this discourse?' 'Where does it come from; how is it circulated; who controls it?' " ("What Is an Author?," *Language, Counter-Memory, Practice: Selected Essays and Interviews*, ed. Donald F. Bouchard, trans. Bouchard and Sherry Simon [Ithaca, N.Y., 1977], p. 138).

15. See Diana Hume George, "Stumbling on Melons: Sexual Dialectics and Discrimination in English Departments," in *English Literature: Opening Up the Canon*, pp. 120–26.

16. Foucault theorizes that invisibility is inherent in and necessary to the workings of power: "Power is tolerable only on condition that it mask a substantial part of itself. Its success is proportional to its ability to hide its own mechanisms. . . . For it, secrecy is not in the nature of an abuse; it is indispensable to its operation" (*The History of Sexuality: Volume I, an Introduction*, trans. Robert Hurley [New York, 1980], p. 86).

17. Maureen Quilligan, *Milton's Spenser: The Politics of Reading* (Ithaca, N.Y., 1983), pp. 227–28. Quilligan pursues a different line of argument, reevaluating Eve's centrality

in the poem read as integrally concerned with instituting "a new kind of family structure concurrent with the 'rises' of protestantism and of capitalism with its free market ideologies" (p. 177).

18. Milton develops with subtlety and precision the motive of womb envy already strikingly apparent in the J scribe's creation story (Gen. 2:4–3:20). The motive of compensation in Adam's appropriation of the power of naming—language—is illuminated by his naming the woman Eve (*Hawwah*), derived from the Hebrew root *havah* ("to live"). Other details contribute to this interpretation of the rib fantasy, not least Eve's impressive birth announcement in Genesis 4:1: " 'I have acquired a man with the help of Yahweh.' " Such a reading suggests that the cultural conditions that conduce to the malaise of penis envy are "erected" on a prior malaise of womb envy; and, indeed, so patriarchal a historian as Amaury de Riencourt writes that our "original" creation story "was taken wholesale" from a *more* original Sumerian mythology centered not on patriarchal namers but on female fertility gods (*Sex and Power in History* [New York, 1974], p. 37; see also pp. 36–38). On this last point, see Wolfgang Lederer, "Envy and Loathing—The Patriarchal Revolt," *The Fear of Women* (New York, 1968), pp. 153–68. See also Virginia R. Mollenkott, n. 29 below.

19. Sigmund Freud, *Moses and Monotheism*, trans. Katherine Jones (New York, 1967), pp. 142, 144, 145–46; all further references to this work, abbreviated *MM*, will be included parenthetically in the text.

20. Jonathan Culler, *On Deconstruction: Theory and Criticism after Structuralism* (Ithaca, N.Y., 1982), p. 59; see also pp. 58–60.

21. The most extensive exploration of this theme, linking the structures of individual psychology in Western society to those of its cultural institutions, is Dorothy Dinnerstein, *The Mermaid and the Minotaur: Sexual Arrangements and Human Malaise* (New York, 1976).

22. Feminist theorists have drawn upon Marxist anthropologists' analyses of women as objects of exchange in kinship systems to analyze women as the "goods" through which patriarchal power passes; see, for example, Gayle Rubin, "The Traffic in Women: Notes on the 'Political Economy' of Sex," *Toward an Anthropology of Women*, ed. Rayna R. Reiter (New York, 1975), pp. 157–210, and Luce Irigaray, "Des Marchandises entre elles" [When the goods get together], *Ce sexe qui n'en est pas un* [This sex which isn't one] (Paris, 1977), pp. 189–93, trans. Claudia Reeder in *New French Feminisms: An Anthology*, ed. Elaine Marks and Isabelle de Courtivron (New York, 1981), pp. 107–10. I am conceiving the issue of cultural authority in terms of credit rather than barter or coins in order to analyze the workings of patriarchal authority, but my argument has some parallels to Irigaray's discussion of the disruption of the patriarchal sexual economy effected by women's removing themselves from this market.

23. Ideally, the medium of trade should be intrinsically worthless; Gresham's law that "bad" money (coins of baser metals) drives out "good" money (gold or silver coins) points to the advantage of the almost "pure" credit embodied in paper money. Gold and silver coins are money conceived as portable stores of value rather than as credit.

24. Gubar, " 'The Blank Page' and the Issues of Female Creativity," p. 246.

25. Woolf, *A Room of One's Own* (1928; New York, 1957), p. 118. Woolf says that women will write "if we . . . see human beings . . . and the sky, too, and the trees or whatever it may be in themselves; if we look past Milton's bogey, for no human being should shut out the view" (p. 118). Gilbert takes up the image in "Milton's Bogey: Patriarchal Poetry and Women Readers," Gilbert and Gubar, *The Madwoman in the Attic: The Woman Writer and the Nineteenth-Century Literary Imagination* (New Haven, Conn., 1979), pp. 187–212. Gilbert identifies women writers with Eve and Satan, all "resisting readers," but, I think, does not fully rescue their gnostic readings from the patriarchal framework within which they are damned.

26. See Myra Jehlen, "Archimedes and the Paradox of Feminist Criticism," *Signs* 6 (Summer 1981): 575–601, and Coppélia Kahn, "Excavating 'Those Dim Minoan Regions': Maternal Subtexts in Patriarchal Literature," *Diacritics* 12 (Summer 1982): 32–41. Both address "the gender of genre" with respect to the bourgeois novel and Shakespearean tragedy.

27. Woolf, *A Writer's Diary*, ed. Leonard Woolf (New York, 1954), p. 6.

28. Ibid., pp. 5, 6.

29. For a different reading of the sexual ambiguity of Milton's Muse, see Mollenkott, "Some Implications of Milton's Androgynous Muse," *Bucknell Review* 24 (Spring 1978): 27–36. Mollenkott sees the Muse as androgynous and as "beautifully symboli[zing] the womb envy that is so deeply repressed in the human male" (p. 32); however, she does not acknowledge the *appropriation* of female power by the male in Milton's image of his Muse. See also Farwell, n. 12 above.

30. Isak Dinesen, "The Blank Page," *Last Tales* (New York, 1957), p. 100; all further references to this work, abbreviated "BP," will be included parenthetically in the text. I am indebted to Susan Gubar's insightful and suggestive reading of this story; see no. 10 above.

31. Harry Levin, "Core, Canon, Curriculum," *College English* 43 (Apr. 1981): 362.

Wrestling with the Angel:
Paradise Lost and Feminist Criticism

William Shullenberger

I

Generations of readers have testified to the terror and amazement of reading *Paradise Lost*, and many who have written in the wake of Milton and under his power have found that they must risk everything, and wrestle like Jacob with an angel for the equivocal blessing of life and identity. Keats put the matter most succinctly as he put aside his great fragment of Miltonic grandeur, *Hyperion*: "Life to him would be death to me" (212). To read Milton well becomes a trial of identity for the reader, and a trial of the integrity and flexibility of the reader's critical process. For even as Milton's text changes for each generation of readers, so does the text put each reader's assumptions under challenge, so that she may emerge from a reading with everything she has come to know and believe complicated, enriched, enlarged, and sometimes transfigured utterly.[1]

Such a challenge and such a promise offer themselves to women readers as well as men. This belief comes not only from my local and personal experience as a fledgling teacher of Milton at a largely women's college, but from the evidence of the last half century of Milton criticism, the very best of which has included work by Rosemond Tuve, Helen Gardner, Irene Samuel, Isabel MacCaffrey, Anne Ferry, Joan Webber, Barbara Lewalski, Kathleen Swaim, Virginia Mollenkott, Stella Revard, Mary Ann Radzinowicz, and Diane McOlley. A fundamental assertion of feminist criticism of Milton's poetry is that it "constructs its gods and

its speech on the bedrock of woman's silence" (Froula, "Pechter's spectre" 178) and yet the tradition of strong women readers of Milton seems to indicate that the promise of authority and identity, the possible blessing of imaginative life, offered by the poetry, is not gender-bound. The feminist criticism which has emerged in the last fifteen years has sharpened attention to the sexual politics of Milton's poetry, to his epic transcription of the religious and familial institutions of Puritanism, and to his influence on women readers and writers. Feminist critics have insisted on Milton's centrality as a writer for women to study, but the unquestioned assumption about that study is that it is bound to be antithetical, as if the only woman's response to poetry with the kind of claims which Milton makes is to be a resisting reader, to anatomize the terror and refuse the amazement, to dismiss the possibility of blessing as if it could only be given to a son. What, then, of the "traditional" women critics of Milton? Have they purchased their interpretive authority by sacrificing the authority of their experience as women? This seems to be the appropriate feminist response. And yet, what if there is something in *Paradise Lost* which survives and challenges the developing feminist critique of Milton, because its site is the very blind spot of the critics, and its voice is the unacknowledged undersong of their own critical and human hopes?

Sandra Gilbert, expatiating on Virginia Woolf's image of "Milton's Bogey" eclipsing her vision, suggests that Milton, in his central poem, "cuts women off from the spaciousness of possibility" (188). Gilbert's criticism in particular, and feminist criticism at large, may accomplish that of which it accuses Milton: it may cut women readers off from the "spaciousness of possibility" afforded by the poet. Anyone approaching Milton through the perspective afforded by Gilbert in her influential book, *The Madwoman in the Attic*, might well be persuaded not to bother. Gilbert and her colleague Susan Gubar stress Milton's immense presence to the imaginations of the Brontes, Austen, George Eliot, Dickinson, Mary Shelley and others, yet their explication of his centrality is a polemic which develops within, and never questions, its very first offhand remark about Milton's "undeniable, misogyny" (21). Would not a young woman reader, vaguely unsure about the value of "canonical" literature to begin with, and uneasy about Milton's imposing reputation, assume that Gilbert can be trusted to articulate the women's position on Milton:

> A prophet or priestly bard and therefore a guardian of the sacred mysteries of patriarchy, he serenely proposes to justify the ways of God to men, calls upon subservient female muses for the assistance that is his due (and in real life upon slavish daughters for the same sort of assistance), and at the same time wars upon women with a barrage of angry words, just as God wars on Satan. (210)

Ergo, women, why waste your time? Virtually every phrase in Gilbert's remark is worth a patient refutation.[2] It is to the credit of other feminist critics that they either have denied the charge of "undeniable misogyny" which Gilbert bases on dubious biographical sources,[3] or demonstrate its irrelevance to the study of Milton's typicality as a Puritan poet, and his imaginative placement of woman in the Puritan cosmos. But the damage has already been done, the view cut off: undergraduate readers are more likely to have their impressions of Milton formed by Gilbert's blockbuster than by Lewalski's or Webber's careful defense of the poet in *Milton Studies*, or Diane McColley's rich scholarly celebration of Milton's Eve.[4]

It would be fruitless to argue that Milton was not

a poet of his age, or that his poetry is not consequently and explicitly patriarchal. He could not be a feminist in any way in which we understand the term, for the way of feminist thinking was at best obscure and marginal in the seventeenth century.[1] However, just as Raphael's baffling disquisition to Adam on astronomy in Book VIII of *Paradise Lost* seems to include the cosmos of Einstein as a possibility of thought, so does Milton include and encourage the possibility of feminist thinking in his representations of identity, relationship, and freedom. Joan Webber has said,

> Milton's sense of the direction in which humanity has to move is generally one which prepares the way for feminist thinking. When he did raise issues involving women's importance and women's rights, he was awkwardly and imperfectly breaking ground. ("Politics" 5–6)[5]

I would say more than this: the subtext of *Paradise Lost* encourages and supports feminist reading. Equating patriarchy with misogyny, feminist critics to this point have neglected or obscured the elements in this subtext, because the prospect of finding their own critical idealism confirmed and encouraged by so powerful a patriarchal text would be embarrassing.

One of the dynamic elements of Milton's poem is its radical self-criticism, an impulse which most of us, whatever our persuasion, male or female, would just as soon ignore or avoid. Believing the Bible to be the source of all our thinking about the divine and the human condition, Milton was bound to the representation of God as Father, and of a created order fashioned by and in God's image. Is it possible for a patriarchal order of being to be liberating rather than oppressive? Satan's answer to the problem of divine authority is revolt, self-assertion, the will to power. His *non serviam* seems to provide feminist criticism a ready and easy, yet tragically self-defeating, way to intellectual freedom. Rejecting the "feminine" servitude of Heaven, Satan provides us insight not into the psychology of liberation *from* patriarchy, but into the narcissistic sado-masochism of so-called male heroism. In the empire he raises, he provides the archetype of totalitarian culture, the culture which

the masculine mystique raises in homage to its own
failure to love. In Satan, then, Milton offers a
deliberate critique of the ghost of oppression which
haunts patriarchal thinking. But in his representation of Heaven and of the possibilities of earth,
he suggests the openness and energy of a *provisional*
patriarchy which is in process toward a time
beyond time when God shall be all in all (III.
274–341). As Webber remarked, "it is unusual for
the patriarch to surrender his power voluntarily,
foreseeing the end of all rule" ("Politics" 9).
  Milton thus consciously explores the prob-
lematics of patriarchal politics, psychology, and
poetry. His conception of the creative process as
it unfolds in time and in the time of his poem is
as firmly and fluidly androgynous as Woolf or
Carolyn Heilbrun could wish for.[6] His representation of true heroism, embodied in the gracious actions of Christ and of Eve, anticipates what
feminist psychologists and social historians describe
as "women's values" (Heilbrun; Gilligan). He
dignifies Eve by assigning her coinheritance with
Adam of the divine patrimony of "Truth, Wisdom,
Sanctitude severe and pure, / Severe, but in true
filial freedom plac't," (IV. 293–94) wherein human
being most truly reflects and honors its origin and
end. He isolates and exposes anti-feminist thinking by concentrating it explicitly in the litany of
fallen Adam's diatribes against Eve. (X. 897–908)
And he diagnoses and purges the aberrations of
unbalanced masculine "virtue" in the Romantically
heroic figure of Satan. Milton's best critics have
been effectively stating these points, but their fundamentally defensive strategy has seemed only to
sharpen and harden the battle lines, and to leave
untouched feminism's deepest skepticism about
Milton's liberating power. We thus seem to be
trapped in a set of Blake's unyielding negations
rather than progressing by contraries. The feminist
questions have been put to Milton, and the questions have been powerful and serious. But if, as I
am suggesting, Milton was asking those questions
himself in composing *Paradise Lost*, then an in-
vestigation of the poem in terms of those questions
may yield a feminist reading which encourages
women readers to read Milton as seriously and
sympathetically as he is reading them.

II

  Let the following summary of central feminist
arguments about *Paradise Lost* provide us a map
for exploring the poem:

1. Milton's God, "patriarch of patriarchs,"
institutes a rule of masculine authority
which is static, closed, and oppressive,
especially to women, who are "excluded
from heaven" and subordinated on earth
(Gilbert, Landy).

2. The structure of the bourgeois family
determines Milton's representation of
Adam and Eve's roles in Paradise. The
security of Eden depends upon the
bourgeois values of sexual restraint, a male-
dominated gender hierarchy, and absolute
submissiveness to the will of the Father
(Landy, Di Salvo, Quilligan).

3. Eve, archetypal woman, is necessarily
devalued by such a system. Her potentially
sinister sexuality is domesticated by the institution of marriage, and her creativity, her
voice, is silenced as she is impressed with
the need to submit to and articulate the imperatives of the patriarchal voice (Landy;
Froula, "When Eve Reads Milton").

4. Since Eve's creative energies and identity are neutralized by the order of the
Father, her deepest sympathies are with the
revolutionary artist and Romantic hero of
the poem, Satan. Satan provides women an
example of an energetic, defiant, self-created
identity and assertive sexuality (Gilbert
204).

  Not all feminist critics would assent to all of these
points, but they do indicate a set of central concerns which imply and support each other. *Paradise
Lost* incarnates "father consciousness" in virtually
pure form (Bly), and thus provides women the opportunity to diagnose the ways in which that
presiding consciousness dictates their destiny. To
question the poem deeply in terms of these issues
is to find it engaged, in a way more rich and complicated than feminist criticism has thus far been

willing to imagine, with all that concerns us most in our search for identity, our cultivation of creativity, and our concern for relationships. Let us reconsider, then, what responses the poem suggests to feminist questions about Milton's God, his placement of Eve in the hierarchies of earth and heaven, and his representation of Satan.

Milton's God. Of Milton's God we need to remember that, except for what God permits humanity to know, he is an unknowable absolute, beyond representation, hence beyond the categories and accidents of our cultural existence. Since, in his theological treatise, Milton insists that God is not only invisible but silent, it seems reasonable to speculate that God exceeds the oppositions of gender identity. Nevertheless, according to the theory of accommodation by which medieval and Renaissance theologians accounted for the validity of any representation of God

> Our safest way is to form in our minds such a conception of God, as shall correspond with his own delineation of himself in the sacred writings. For granted that both in the literal and figurative description of God, he is exhibited not as he really is, but in such a manner as may be within the scope of our comprehensions, yet we ought to maintain such a conception of him as he, in condescending to accommodate himself to our capacity, has shown that he desires we should conceive. (*DDC*, 31–33)

God as "Father," then, is a "figurative description," not as he really is; but insofar as it is a description privileged by the "sacred writings" of Scripture, it is bound to have priority, for Milton, over other possible representations. Milton's theology and his poetry are thus necessarily and nominally patriarchal. Feminist criticism provokes the question whether the poetry is consequently *repressively* patriarchal. Does Milton acknowledge the provisionality of his own governing metaphor, or does he insist on the divine privilege of the metaphor as a way of shoring up the authority of fathers in family, economy, and state, and as a way of rendering mothers submissive "slaves to the species" (Gilbert 197; Landy 11; Quilligan 224).

One of Milton's hardest tasks in the epic is to represent as a dramatic character a divine figure who is essentially unrepresentable. The line of criticism of Milton's God as stuffy and cruel Godfather runs from Dr. Johnson through C. S. Lewis and William Empson to feminist critics. Jackie Di Salvo characterizes the Father as a "divine overseer spying upon his children," a "sort of domestic cop" who "speaks in the clearly distinguishable tones of the self-righteous English bourgeois pouring scorn on the heads of those they have ruined" (Di Salvo 158, 175); he is, in short, the Puritan patriarch writ large (23). Joan Webber's defense of Milton's sexual politics begins with explicit agreement that Milton's God is "self-justifying, dictatorial, and judgmental"; she proceeds to argue that Milton does not accept him as is, nor is this Father satisfied with himself. He is himself in process toward full realization of the higher state projected in the images of light which illuminate Book III of *Paradise Lost*. For Webber, the dictatorial Father of Old Testament theology, the God whose power is challenged by Satan, foresees the voluntary surrender of all authority to his Son, who embodies the more "feminine" qualities of love and mercy associated with the New Testament God, and the ultimate distribution of the power and divine energy throughout all creation, so that "God shall be all in all" (III. 341; Webber 8–9).

Webber's own theological premises about an Old Testament God of wrath and a New Testament God of mercy may be questionable, but she makes powerful sense of the anomaly of a patriarch who surrenders his power voluntarily, foreseeing the end of all rule. What this astonishing image might suggest to feminist and Marxist critics of Milton is a position which outflanks their own: a God of history who does not dictate history but so responds to history as to foresee his own self-sacrificial identification with it provides a model of authority by which all claims to temporal authority and power may be measured. Such a God is not reactionary, validating claims of kings, prime ministers, premiers or fathers to authority over others, but revolutionary, calling into question all authority which makes its claims at the expense of human liberty and dignity. To be an image of God is to empower and to enfranchise others—in Puritan terms, to make their salvation possible—not to restrain or deny them their liberty. And to be an image of God is to be like the Son, who represents the divine concern for love and mercy in a dialogue with a Father who enunciates, not without pathos and sympathy, the divine concern for justice.[7]

Yet to understand the Son as a being separate from the Father and morally or poetically more palatable than the Father is to misconstrue the dynamics of identity figured forth in their dialogue. The Father addresses the Son as "My word, my wisdom, and effectual might," who speaks his very thoughts (III. 170-71). The poet amplifies the intimate concord of will between Father and Son in referring to the Son's "substantial expression" of divine compassion, love, and grace (III. 139-42); and the heavenly hosts laud him as "Divine Similitude, / In whose conspicuous count'nance, / Without cloud / Made visible, th'Almightie Father shines, / Whom else no creature can behold" (III. 384-87). As image of God, the Son makes God visible to other orders of being. As word of God, when the Son speaks in the poem, he is amplifying the thought of the Father. As God's "effectual might," when he acts, he demonstrates the power of the Father. Yet when he chooses, he chooses freely, as a being whom the Father has dignified with will and the power to act upon it.

To understand the Son, then, is to understand something of the Father's deepest nature, in particular, the qualities of "Divine compassion," "Love without end, and without measure Grace." Does not the Son thus embody, in the master plot of the poem, the archetypal patterns of what feminist philosopher Sarah Ruddick describes as "maternal thought": a loving, self-giving concern with relationship that overcomes death itself? Milton, in his representation of the Deity, accepts the biblical imagery of Father and Son but not at the expense of values conventionally considered "feminine." If Sonship is proposed as the model of human identity in the poem, that identity is no more determined by or bound to human gender than is Milton's maternal image of the Son. To be identified as "Son of God" is not to be male-identified, but to be God-identified, to stand in a certain creative and reflective relation of creature to Creator, wherein one chooses to live in relation

to others motivated by love, compassion, and grace. Recent research by Carol Gilligan, asserting that women's ethical decisions distinguish themselves from men's by being made according to values of relationship rather than principle, might encourage us to speculate that it will be easier for women to enter Milton's vision of Heaven than it will be for men.

Eve and the Hierarchies of Earth and Heaven. But does Milton include the values of the feminine in Heaven at the expense of women's authority and creativity on earth? As Marcia Landy expresses it, "in his portrayal of Eve, Milton has captured central aspects of a myth which is being seriously questioned today" (Landy 5). This myth involves Milton's commitment to "the centrality of marriage, to the designated roles of the man as creator and provider and of woman as procreator, submissive to her husband's natural authority" (Landy 5). The feminist portrait of Milton's Eve is thus a hypostasis of the Puritan housewife. Eve admittedly fills the outline, but does the outline contain her? To begin with, in honoring Eve Milton asserts the dignity of what is called women's work, and he locates the field of action of his poem in what Elizabeth Janeway has characterized as "woman's place." *Paradise Lost* is an epic of domestic heroism, and its cosmic reach and eschatological resonance center on a woman and a man in a garden plot enjoying the fruits and making the difficult choices of daily existence, the choices upon which their very being in the universe and in history depend.[8] According to Adrienne Rich, "We would be rightly skeptical of a feminism which denied the value and dignity of traditional woman's work in the home" (262). To take Rich at her word is to be rightly skeptical of a feminist criticism which repudiates a male poet who honors such work above all human activity. Eve and Adam's gardening is strenuous labor of cultivation and harvesting, a metaphor for the rigors of imaginative life, not the leisure pursuit of suburbanites in the nude or the passive self-gratification of infants on the body of their mother earth.[9]

Seen in this light, the archangel Raphael's warning to Adam, "be lowly wise: / Think only what concerns thee and thy being" (VIII., 173-74), directs Adam's attention to the existential fullness and immediacy which we have been led, by the eighth book of the poem, to associate with Eve. Her food preparation is an art of earth more dignified in its spirituality than Adam's fruitless and quizzical astronomical speculation. To find in Eve's food preparation something demeaning requires a neglect of Milton's careful associations of her with the generative vitality of the earth, with the sweet abundance of Eden, and with the great goddesses of fruition and childbirth and the hearth which Milton had received from classical myth. Eve *is* Eden, and the poetry of pristine astonishment appropriate to that paradisal place is hers.[10] In this place where labor is not divided from love, and the body is not bruised to pleasure soul, food preparation has the dignity of ritual, and the simple, sensuous, and passionate completeness of art.

In a review of a recent book about American women poets, Susan Gubar writes

> women poets turn . . . to the domestic or natural world with which women have traditionally been associated. From Bradstreet's praise of Queen Elizabeth I to Miss Rich's essays on both Bradstreet and Dickinson, all three writers celebrate female models of creativity. Similarly, from Bradstreet's guilty attachment to earthly existence, to Dickinson's pleasure in cooking and gardening and Miss Rich's affirmation of ordinary scenes of lovemaking, all three validate the commonplace realities of domestic life. In their reverence for generativity, friendship and home, these poets substitute nurturance and mutuality for masculine modes of domination.
>
> (Gubar 26)

In short, these poets follow the way of Eve as archetypal woman poet, and of Milton in giving her imaginative life. The values honored here are the values of Milton's Eden: earthly existence, cooking, gardening, "ordinary scenes of lovemaking," nurturance, generativity, mutuality. But what is valued in the poetry of Bradstreet, Dickinson, and Rich is condemned in the poetry of Milton. No feminist critic has yet seen fit to complicate or challenge the assertion by Gubar's colleague Sandra Gilbert that Milton "wars upon women with a barrage of angry words" (Gilbert 210).

If this apparent double standard is not the result of gender blindness on the part of the critics, then it is most likely a matter of the critics as modern readers coping with Milton's paradoxical principle of subordination. As Raphael's sublime disquisition reveals (V. 469-505), Milton's universe is an ordered plenitude, and the structure of that order is flexibly hierarchical. The seal of freedom and integrity is to know and to affirm one's proper place, to acknowledge one's responsibility to superior beings through respect and obedience and one's responsibility to inferior beings through protective stewardship. There is no arguing away from the textual fact, central to the feminist critique of *Paradise Lost*, that the matrimonial structure of Eden is the human embodiment of this pattern. Eve is subordinate to Adam. God asserts it, Raphael insists on it, Adam accepts it (not without anxiety), and Eve herself affirms it:

> My Author and Disposer, what thou bidd'st
> Unargu'd I obey; so God ordains,
> God is thy Law, thou mine: to know no more
> Is woman's happiest knowledge and her praise.
> (IV. 635-38)

The evidence of Eve's acknowledged dependence on Adam suggests to feminist critics that woman's subjection and silence is the necessary condition for the whole edifice of Puritan politics, theology, and poetry. The poem's repeated and occasionally strident insistence on that condition suggests that Milton, like his Adam, anxious about Eve's potent and uncanny otherness, "projects his 'perfect' god out of his fearful beholding of Eve, body, and the power of birth" (Froula, "Pechter's Spectre" 173). From this need to justify the authority of the invisible male God by the subjection of the natural woman, Milton makes the efficient cause of the Fall Eve's foolish assertion of her independence; the Fall forces her to learn and accept, once and for all, her inferior status.

On these grounds, the feminist critique of Milton appears strongest. The doctrine of woman's subordination is explicit in the text, and the historical context makes clear that even among radical thinkers this doctrine was taken for granted. But why does Milton so grate upon his readers by giving the doctrine such prominence? Perhaps he wishes us to reflect on the very complexity of the idea of subordination in the universe he imagines. If we do so, we find a creative tension between the idea abstracted and the idea enacted. Removed from context, the stresses on Eve's "inferior charms" could certainly fill a misogynist's handbill. Restored to context, they may mean something very different. Consider, for instance, one of the poem's most emphatic devaluations of Eve, Raphael's chastisement of Adam for potential uxoriousness (VIII. 561–94). Adam has just described the divine colloquy in which God challenges and encourages him to articulate his need for a partner. God disguises his intention in order to encourage Adam to imagine clearly, to understand himself. May not Raphael's rebuke perform a similar task: not to demean Eve, but to challenge Adam to clarify and defend his love for her? Adam's forthright response, which honors Eve's "thousand decencies that daily flow / From all her words and actions," (VIII. 601–02), indicates that Raphael's apparent demeaning of Eve has served to exalt Adam's understanding of her.

"Superiority" and "inferiority" are thus not static but processive and relational concepts, terrifically complicated in the poem by at least four factors: rhetorical context, as I've just suggested; the dynamics of human relationship; the Puritan understanding that all rational beings are equal in their responsibilities to God; and the Gospel paradox that the last shall be first, which turns all conventional thinking about hierarchy on its head. Diane McColley may be understating the point when she succinctly declares, "in *Paradise Lost* subordination is not inferiority" (35).

A close reading of Milton's initial description of Adam and Eve in their pristine dignity provides a sense of how the text performs its complications and reversals of the principle of subordination. The division of experience imagined here seems to support the feminist diagnosis of Milton's patriarchal bias:

Two of far nobler shape erect and tall,
Godlike erect, with native Honor clad
In naked Majesty seem'd Lords of all,
And worthy seem'd, for in thir looks Divine
The image of thir glorious Maker shone,

Truth, Wisdom, Sanctitude, severe and pure,
Severe, but in true filial freedom plac't;
Whence true autority in men; though both
Not equal, as thir sex not equal seem'd;
For contemplation hee and valor form'd,
For softness shee and sweet attractive Grace,
Hee for God only, shee for God in him:
His fair large Front and Eye sublime declar'd
Absolute rule; and Hyacinthine Locks
Round from his parted forelock manly hung
Clust'ring, but not beneath his shoulders broad:
Shee as a veil down to the slender waist
Her unadorned golden tresses wore
Dishevell'd, but in wanton ringlets wav'd
As the Vine curls her tendrils, which impli'd
Subjection, but requir'd with gentle sway,
And by her yielded, by him best receiv'd,
Yielded with coy submission, modest pride,
And sweet reluctant amorous delay.
(IV. 288–311)

Yet there are few passages in which Milton's apparent marked difference from us and his apparent simplicity of assertion so challenge us to re-examine our own assumptions about maleness and femaleness, about reciprocity and the distribution of power in relationship, about the way in which identity is disclosed through the subtle negotiations of love. Do we apply a double standard to Milton for his explicit assertion of gender differences — masculine rationality and attention to principle, feminine attention to natural process and the sustenance of relationship — which we either covertly assume as bases for personal or sexual pride, or more explicitly describe, as in works of archetypal criticism, feminist psychology or social history? If recent feminist work in other disciplines supports the description of gender differences, of woman's having a different kind of being in the world from man, might it not be worthwhile for feminist critics to study rather than to condemn Milton's representation of such differences?

Before we consider the division of experience imagined by Milton, we need to note how closely the archetypal human parents are bound by those qualities which make the image of God. "Godlike erect, with native honor clad," they share in "Truth, Wisdom, Sanctitude severe and pure."

"Male and female created he them": Milton initially establishes how much Adam and Eve share, how gloriously distinct they are from all other creatures, how fully each participates in the majesty of what Blake would call the Human Form Divine. But it is easy to miss this and be arrested by the Pauline assertion of their difference, and of Eve's subordination to Adam: "though both / Not equal, as thir sex not equal seem'd; / For contemplation hee and valor form'd, / For softness shee and sweet attractive grace, / Hee for God only, she for God in him." The complex relationship of filiality, freedom and authority has already established that human identity is a relational structure, not a matter of the intact and absolute self; in this complex all human beings, men and women, discover freedom and authority through fidelity, filiality, the recognition of one's dependence on the ground of one's being. This should prepare us to read the emphatic "not equal" in the distinction of the sexes as a sign more of Eve's significant difference from Adam than of her inherent inferiority to him.[11] In the intricate enactment of their relationship we can see Milton complicating what feminist readers wish to describe as straightforward "masculine modes of domination" by an explicit "reverence for generativity, friendship and home."

Thus we need to proceed very carefully in assessing Milton's description of gender differences. First we need to recognize that if contemplation and valor are fundamentally masculine values, and if softness and grace are feminine values, either set is essentially inadequate in the absence of the other. Milton reminds us that human identity consists in the mutual dignity of the couple—the androgynous pair, if you will—which is, in the book of Genesis from which he draws his material, the adequate divine image: "God created man in his own image, in his own image created he him; male and female created he them" (Genesis 1: 27; KJV). Adam's contemplation and valor bereft of Eve's humanizing sensitivity to the sweetness of Eden would be arid and empty; Eve's softness and sweetness in the absence of Adam's spiritual rigor could become, like Eden left uncultivated, a wilderness choking on its own waste fertility.

Second, we need to attend to the ways in which the key words of gender designation are not local-

ly restricted to the characters of Adam and Eve, but participate in the larger networks of value and meaning which the poet has been suggesting from the first line of the poem. We need to recall that the prototype of all that a man could ask for in the exhibition of contemplation and valor has been Satan, so that there is nothing inherently dignified about these so-called "masculine" virtues. Eve's "grace," however, opens into another order of language altogether. The full epiphany of "attractive grace" in the poem is the self-giving Son who declares:

> man shall find grace,
> And shall grace not find means,that finds her way,
> The speediest of thy winged messengers,
> To visit all thy creatures, and to all
> Comes unprevented, unimplor'd, unsought?
>
> (III. 227-31)

Grace, then, personified as feminine yet demonstrated by the Son, is the dynamic energy that gives the poem—and gives humanity—life by breaking our love affair with death. By characterizing Eve as graceful, Milton is testifying to a quality he considers divine, not marking Eve with a gender-based weakness.[12] He also foreshadows the first gracious human action after the Fall, when Eve breaks the grip of self-hatred and mutual accusation by subordinating herself, by pleading for Adam's forgiveness, and by offering her own life as a sacrifice out of her love for Adam, even as the Son had offered his in the heavenly council scene (X. 909-46; cf. III. 236-65).

Third, we need to recall that even Milton's source for the clear-cut utterance, "He for God only, shee for God in him," Paul's first epistle to the Corinthians, is not a scriptural occasion for the suppression of women, but a description of mutual dependence and help founded on the filial relation to the Creator:

> But I would have you know, that the head of every man is Christ; and the head of the woman is the man; and the head of Christ is God. . . . For a man indeed ought not to cover his head, forasmuch as he is the image and glory of God: But the woman is the glory of the man. For the man is not of the

woman; but the woman of the man. Neither was the man created for the woman, but the woman for the man. For this cause ought the woman to have power on her head because of the angels. Nevertheless neither is the man without the woman, neither the woman without the man, in the Lord. For as the woman is of the man, even so is the man also by the woman; but all things of God.

(I Corinthians 11: 3, 7-12)

The assertion of male superiority yields in the last two sentences to the assertion of divine superiority upon which all human relationship depends.[13] Milton subtly and consistently revises our attitudes toward relationship by placing human relationship in its appropriate divine context. McColley notes of the passage which is such a stumbling block for the contemporary reader:

The conclusion Renaissance ears are likely to have expected is not "shee for God in him" but simply "shee for him." And this distinction is so vital that Milton's whole characterization of Eve may be referred to it. She is in the right so long as she serves not just Adam but "God in him" and much that she has been blamed for may be regarded as a way of avoiding a mutually narcissistic or enslaving condition of servitude to something less in him than God (42).

The radical responsibility involved in Eve's relationship to God *through* Adam leads to the fourth point that can be made about Milton's gender distinctions. The apparent superiority and authority of man over woman, the clean distinction between genders asserted as a matter of political power—"His fair large Front and Eye sublime declar'd / Absolute rule"[14]—is complicated on the one hand by the primary relation of each to God, before whom both stand as responsive children, and on the other hand by the subtle demands of human love which transforms hierarchical thinking continually. Eve's "subjection" is "requir'd with gentle sway, / And by her yielded, by him best receiv'd, / Yielded with coy submission, modest pride, / And sweet reluctant amorous delay" (IV.

307-11). By the end of this delicate erotic exchange, what has become of the declaration of Adam's "absolute rule"? Eve's "subjection" requires of Adam a "gentle sway" not predictable from the clarities of "absolute rule"; Eve's "sweet attractive grace" has a persuasive and transfiguring effect on him whom she addresses as her "author and disposer." The language of power is inadequate to account for the reciprocities of love, and subordination is displayed as an act of dignified love, not servitude.

As if to anticipate our prurient astonishment at and fascination with this first description of unfallen sexual bliss, Milton follows his description with a castigation of our debased versions of sexuality (IV. 312-18), where honor is sterilized as either hypocritical fraud or frozen prudery, and mutual desire is always contaminated by some measure of the will to power. As Adam and Eve pass "naked on, nor shunn'd the sight / Of God or Angel, for they thought no ill" (IV. 319-20), we're reminded that our angle of vision into Paradise is shared with Satan (Kermode 113-14), who saw "undelighted all delight," and in the torment of whose self-vexing desire pleasure can come only in destruction. The poem thus exposes our own remoteness from the human possibility embodied in Adam and Eve. To indict Milton for genderal rigidity is to project on him our own frustration with the diminished possibilities that the fallen world we inhabit seems to afford the sexual life which Milton says, throughout the poem, animates the world.[15] Perhaps the sexual hierarchy which Milton represents in Eden is a time-bound and gender-bound conception. But perhaps we are much more bound by our inability to explore Adam and Eve as archetypal possibilities. For the questions raised in *Paradise Lost* about how hierarchy is established and lived out persist in the private and the collective arrangements which we try to create for ourselves. Do we delude ourselves to believe that the complex and largely unstated negotiations and agreements over power, the demonstrations of particular strengths and limitations, the possibilities of mutual help and of desire and of the dignity of selflessness, have become any less the sources of potential problems and of potential creativity for us than they were in Milton's Eden? Milton, by the time he completed *Paradise*

Lost, was no utopian poet. No political program could compensate for the strenuous exercise of the imaginative liberty and the psychological self-scrutiny and the willingness to sacrifice which he called faith. More than most of us are able to do, Milton shows us in Adam and Eve a relationship which depoliticizes itself through love and work, a possibility of what human life might be when labor does not mean one thing for a man and another for a woman because labor is not divided from love; when each partner enriches the life of the other because imagination and feeling, reason and desire, the life of spirit and the life of the senses, are not categorically isolated according to gender; when identity is not other than community; and when the distributions of domestic power are conditioned by the greater informing power of unselfish love. Perhaps for this reason, more actively politically radical in a more dangerous period than any of us would dare to be, Milton remains a scandal and a threat to politically-based criticism.

Satan as hero. Milton's stress upon identity as a non-self-centered, relational structure means that, on earth as in heaven, to be is to be an image of an other, and especially of the unconditioned Other who is the source and security of all being. Adam and Eve's relationship is the fluid human achievement of this model of identity. All that is Edenic argues against the feminist embrace of Satan as the covert hero of the poem and Eve's model for a self-assertive identity. There are three interrelated elements to the implicit or explicit feminist admiration of Satan. An "aristocratic egalitarian," he incarnates the spirit of heroic resistance and revolt which can inspire a feminist response to a male-dominated culture (Gilbert 201). Asserting the existential will of a being who declares himself "self-begot, self-raised / By our own quick'ning power" (V. 860–61), Satan provides a type of independent identity which women must learn to forge in their desire to create themselves in terms of "authority of their own experience" (Froula, "When Eve Reads" 334). Finally, as "the incarnation of worldly male sexuality," according to Sandra Gilbert, Satan is "enormously attractive to women" (206). Of Satan's sexual appeal to women readers and writers I will hazard no comment other than that it seems perilous to think that the arche-

typal model for seduction and betrayal is a figure to whom women can entrust their fate. Gilbert's remarks about Satan's sexual electricity seem to me as profound an aberration of feminist intention as Karl Keller's "Notes on Sleeping with Emily Dickinson," which appears in a recent collection of feminist essays on Dickinson. The assertion of Satan's libertarian politics and Romantic identity requires a more exacting response.

Satan is, like other charismatic dictators, a master of the rhetoric of liberation and collective identity. A glance at the mass rally of fallen angels assembling off the burning lake (I. 531 ff.) provides a classic insight into the semiotics of fascism. The effect is thrilling; the reader is moved by the assertion of heroic dignity in the face of unutterable and infinite pain. But anyone who has seen Riefenstahl's *Triumph of the Will* will recognize the totalitarian paraphernalia—ensigns and trumpets, the sobering monotony of military music, the choreography of vast numbers of identitiless individuals into the expression of a single seemingly indomitable will. That Satan's championing of hard liberty before the yoke of servile pomp is a strategy which consolidates his own power is a point of which the poet reminds us continually.[16] That the strategy of Satan's warfare against God in the poem is a primordial act of terrorism—the execution of revenge through the maiming of that which the enemy loves most—ought to dim some of his heroic lustre. Nevertheless, Gilbert claims that Satan affords women the prospect of the envisioning of "more sublime alternate lives," and "his rebellious visionary politics have often been used by women as metaphoric disguises for sexual politics" (205).

In her envisioning of Satan as revolutionary hero, Gilbert acknowledges her own links to the Promethean reading of *Paradise Lost* in Blake's *The Marriage of Heaven and Hell*, Shelley's *A Defense of Poetry*, and Mary Shelley's *Frankenstein*. Yet she does not follow the Romantic course of response to Satan, which parallels the Romantic response to the liberating possibilities of the French Revolution, and recognize that Satan may be the type of a tragic hero but not an image of political and personal liberation: Blake's Jesus and Shelley's Prometheus and Asia transform reality by means of self-sacrificial love and forgiveness rather than by the aggressive defiance of Satan, which only succeeds by imposing ever more monstrous versions of tyranny. The feminist response to *Paradise Lost* ought to make a similar shift in its attention and study Eve's genuine links with the Son of God as true hero rather than her profoundly ironic and contrasting parallels to Satan. Social historian Joan Ringelheim has studied the responses of Jewish death camp prisoners in Nazi Germany and has tentatively concluded that the responses were gender-specific. Women pair-bonded, created surrogate families for nurturance, protection, sharing; the collective response made an endurance possible in the face of conditions which were bound to destroy the isolate and independent ego. Men apparently were generally incapable of this kind of interdependence. Ringelheim proposes that we need to revise our ideas of heroism, to replace the image of defiant self-assertion with the thousand daily acts of self-sacrifice and sharing which permitted the community of victims to endure until the shadow of death lifted. In response to the original holocaust, that catastrophe of human will which brought death into the world and all our woe, Milton imagines the Son standing before the ruined parents of humanity,

pitying how they stood
Before him naked to the air, that now
Must suffer change, disdain'd not to begin
Thenceforth the form of servant to assume,
As when he wash'd his servants' feet, so now
As Father of his Family he clad
Thir nakedness with Skins of Beasts, or slain,
Or as the Snake with youthful coat repaid;
And thought not much to clothe his Enemies:
Nor hee thir outward only with the Skins
Of Beasts, but inward nakedness, much more
Opprobrious, with his Robe of righteousness,
Arraying cover'd from his Father's sight.
(X. 211-23)

This kind of heroism, a familial and selfless identification with those who suffer, is unimaginable to a hero like Satan, as is Eve's first gesture to restore the shattered human community, searching past guilt, self-assertion and self-justification, and terror to a restored interdependence with Adam. Modern readers might be disappointed by the im-

age of a revolutionary selflessness, preferring the easier, more recognizable grandeur of a self-proclaimed freedom fighter. Yet the true heroes of *Paradise Lost*, like the heroes of the death camps, might as well be nameless, for it is not the heroic assertion of self which the poem honors, but what Milton calls "the better fortitude / Of Patience and Heroic Martyrdom" (IX. 31-32).

The question of identity in *Paradise Lost* is perhaps even more difficult for the modern reader than the political question. Once Satan is demythologized, exposed as impotent dictator and terrorist, it's difficult to sustain the delusion of his grandeur. Yet his assertion of identity seems very close to the way in which we conceive ourselves. Here perhaps we are most at odds with Milton, for the assumption of a central, independent, experientially-based "self" on which feminist readings are founded is exposed by the poet as, in the cases of Adam and Eve, naive, and in the case of Satan, demonic. Milton presents Satan as the disintegrated, self-absorbed, and creativity-hating being which Adam and Eve might become if the work of love and imagination were not ultimately more powerful in the restitution of human identity than the self-loving hatred of Satan is in threatening it.

For Gilbert, Satan's Romantic self-assertion provides Eve the only alternative to existence as domestic drudge (203 ff.). Christine Froula, analyzing Eve's "nativity scene" (IV. 449-91), suggests how rapidly Eve, in turning from her own beautiful image in the water to Adam, is converted from "the authority of her own experience" to "the hidden authority symbolized in the prohibited Tree of Knowledge" (When Eve Reads" 334). Froula spends an enormous amount of intelligence in circumventing the obvious here. What would have happened to the plot—and to the human race—if Eve had returned to what Froula calls "being in and for herself" and spent her life playing hide-and-seek with her own reflection? Eve at this point in the poem *has* no experience, and it is the movement from self-absorbed primary narcissism to a recognition of the self as an image of an other that Milton here explores with lyric and psychological economy. The traumatic passage from isolate and self-absorbed being to a being for and with and in relation to others involves for Milton, as for the Freudian psychoanalyst Jacques Lacan, a movement from a "mirror stage" in which others stand only as mirrors of one's self to a symbolic stage in which identity is a relational structure, a differential structure which works like a metaphor: we find out who we are by discovering what we are like in the presence of others who matter most to us. We need only compare Satan's amnesia to Eve's and Adam's hallowed retrieval of their moments of wakening consciousness to discover the radically different ideas of selfhood which Milton is exploring. Satan appeals to the vanishing point of consciousness, the point of time when we are unaware of our own existence, as negative evidence for his own position of independence:

> We know no time when we were not as now;
> Know none before us, self-begot, self-rais'd
> By our own quick'ning power, when fatal course
> Had circl'd his full Orb, the birth mature
> Of this our native Heav'n, Ethereal Sons.
> (V. 859–63)

Satan's version of self-sufficiency is involved with organicist fatality and depends on a continual state of amnesia about the origins and evidence of his own being. For if he denies all the evidence of a connection with a power of life which generated and sustains him, in effect he denies himself a history and an identity – and, of course, a future, because he is bound in a maze of repetitive compulsion, which can only lead to a perpetual re-enactment of the moment of his having chosen to be cast out from the presence of others which, in return for service, for relation, confers selfhood. Adam and Eve, in what Froula beautifully calls their "nativity scenes," recollect those moments of apprehension of their connectedness to all being, and of their identities not as separate selves but as relational structures, a being for others. Their memory is related to their faith, which is the form of their identity; their faith becomes a kind of remembering forward – the imagination of a future as laden with promise as the past has been. And their own distinctive remembrances of birth are bound to the archangel Raphael's narrative, in Book VII, of the great verbal event of creation, that occasion of mystery and disclosure of creative

power which many moments in the poem have referred to as the very matrix of generativity, the fertile marriage between form and substance, between the contrary yet fluid principles of male and female, by which all individual creations may be measured. Milton's God, we learn, is the only being who has the possibility of self-closure, yet he chooses the vitality and the peril of a creativity which allows otherness, and ultimately, through the substantial expression of his Son, renews that choice by sacrificing himself for the redemption of human otherness, true human identity. The self-closure of Satan is a life-denying and a knowledge-denying posture, but the whole movement of the epic suggests that knowledge isn't private or self-conscious; it's open, public, shared and cumulative, as is identity.

III

The various themes in *Paradise Lost* traced by feminist critics – the authority of the God-father, the Puritan domestication of women's experience, the revolutionary clarion-call of Satan – all seem to converge in the question of identity. The dynamics of identity in the poem are considerably more complicated than feminist criticism has yet acknowledged: so complicated, indeed, as to challenge feminist critics to re-examine their own psychological premises. For the model of an ego-centric self, whose horizons of knowledge are contained by the authority of that self's experience, is at best naive and narcissistic, and at worst the destructive parody of identity which Milton presents us in Satan. Identity, as *Paradise Lost* instructs us, can only be discovered in relationship. To love another is, in the terms of the poem, to become the image of the other. Eve, turning away from her "smooth, watery" self-image, discovers identity in relation to one who honors her as "Best Image of myself and dearer half" (V. 95). To become an image of an other is to give that other visible, palpable, significant presence in the world, to provide symbolic form to the other's self. Eve thus stands in the same identifying relation to Adam as the Son stands in relation to the Father. Insofar as the Son is the "greater Man" who is the poem's true hero and even its true form (Fish, "Discovery as Form"), the analogy does no indignity to Eve. Identity itself becomes a way of presence which is neither narcissistic nor possessive. In the absence of this work of imagination and love, identity becomes self-absorbed and, as we can see in Satan's distorted reflections in the allegoric figures of Sin and Death, the work of imaging forth becomes monstrous. We are a long way from Eden and from Heaven, where it is impossible to love another without loving one's self. But it seems worthwhile to ask what this idea of identity as imaging forth—giving imaginative body to the self of the other—might mean for the feminist criticism of Milton. It would mean making present in the critical text the dynamic elements of the Miltonic text which have been previously obscured or repressed. Feminist critics have been doing this by way of their attention to the image of Eve and their description of the patriarchal code of Puritanism which generates the text of *Paradise Lost*. The text is thus not in danger of suffering feminist neglect. Froula has called it "the canonical text par excellence" ("When Eve Reads" 326), and Jackie Di Salvo has testified to its centrality to feminist criticism in even stronger language:

> Milton becomes the key to all human history and human consciousness because it was the seventeenth-century English bourgeoisie that first wrapped history in a ball and rolled it toward the overwhelming questions of human development. . . . Milton gave otherwise invisible and unconscious ideological assumptions and psychological experiences a concrete form, and thus resembles the prophet Los who, in *Jerusalem*, gives "a body to Falshood that it may be cast off forever." (144-45)

The image of Milton which emerges from feminist reading is thus both powerful and monstrous. Milton becomes a patriarchal shibboleth, a jealous angel of authority with whom, as Satan remarks about God the Father,

> Peace is despair'd
> For who can think submission? War then, War
> Open or understood, must be resolv'd.
> (I. 660-62)

We might see, in the vehemence of such essays as Gilbert's and Di Salvo's, the hyperbolic valuation of the poet as a symptom of a distorted form of critical love. In any case, eternal enmity, as we can see in the archetypal misreader, Satan, can only impoverish the imagination's life. If the feminist image of Milton is distorted thus far, it is due to the repression or willed ignorance of those powerful currents of imagination, radical love, and self-criticism by which Milton continually tests and complicates an apparent ideology of male superiority. If we can, following Sandra Gilbert's appropriation of Woolf, "see beyond Milton's bogey"—the bogey, that is, invented by feminist criticism—we might rediscover the challenging yet affirmative precursor honored by Margaret Fuller:

> [Milton] is the purity of Puritanism. He understood the nature of liberty, of justice—what is required for the unimpeded action of conscience—what constitutes true marriage, and the scope of a manly education. He is one of the Fathers of the Age, of that new Idea which agitates the sleep of Europe, and of which America, if awake to the design of Heaven and her own duty, would become the principal exponent. But the Father is still far beyond the understanding of his child. (38-39)

My hope is that this essay makes possible a feminist re-vision of Milton, and that the countercurrents of thought which surface here will disrupt the present caricature of Milton so that the next wave of feminist criticism might image forth a figure no less strange and imposing, but more a possible source of life, health, strength, and self-knowledge.

Sarah Lawrence College

NOTES

[1] The modern commentator who insists most forcefully and studies most clearly the affective pressure of Milton's poetry is Stanley Fish, especially in *Surprised By Sin*. Maureen Quilligan adapts Fish's procedures in her examination of the placement of the woman reader of *Paradise Lost*. Quilligan reaches the provocative conclu-

sion that for a woman, the price of a rewarding reading of the poem is the perspective of submission and obedience; but she shies away from the proposal that "the fit female reader—she who chooses obedience and submission—is a paradigm for the fit reader of the poem" (242). I would like to reopen that question by exploring the way in which Milton challenges every reader to think through what we mean by submission, subordination, identity and freedom. In this sense, what Quilligan explores as a particular demand upon women readers is rather a demand upon everyone who enters the poem from a fallen (or even unfallen) perspective.

² Philip Gallagher effectively anatomizes Gilbert's logical and rhetorical strategies in his letter to PMLA; the journal includes a rebuttal of Gallagher's analysis by Gilbert.

³ Gilbert's sole "biographical" resource for her assertions about Milton's domestic tyranny is Robert Graves's vitriolic *Wife to Mr. Milton*. Here Gilbert's invocation of the principle of critical "misprision" allows for a fundamental dishonesty at the center of her argument. At this point Gilbert's procedures open themselves not just to interpretive differences but to basic questions about the ethics of scholarship.

⁴ Other important responses to the feminist critique of *Paradise Lost* include those by Mollenkott and Peczenik. Both provide useful discussions of the idea of hierarchy; Peczenik's study of marital reciprocity is consonant with my point of view here, and Mollenkott explores the problem of mediating Milton's text to modern students.

⁵ Hill briefly describes the limits of thinking about marriage and the place of women among the radical sectarians of the English Revolution (117–21). Hilda Smith roots the origins of modern feminist thought in the lives and writing of several seventeenth-century women of landed, aristocratic origin and monarchist sympathies. If Smith is right in detecting here the first wave of feminism in England, she implies the paradox of feminism's original linkage with an essentially conservative and anti-democratic ideology which Milton opposed all of his mature life.

⁶ See especially Mollenkott's "Some Implications of Milton's Androgynous Muse." Woolf's powerful speculations about the androgynous temper of the artist can be found in *A Room of One's Own* (170–71) and provide a great deal of the comic energy of *Orlando*. Although not focussing on the androgynous complexity of Milton's muse and the poet's relation to her, Marilyn Farwell examines the limits of the application of the Renaissance

idea of androgyny to *Paradise Lost*. Farwell describes the gradual feminist disaffection with the idea of androgyny as a disguised version of male superiority and usefully indicates the limits of describing Adam and Eve's marriage in terms of the paradigm of androgyny. She explains that Eve's intelligence, independence and responsibility as a character prevent a too easy absorption of her into an androgynous unit in which "masculine" qualities of reason would dominate "feminine" qualities of passion.

⁷ The sense of *pathos* in the speech of a Father who is frequently treated as impervious to human suffering was eloquently expressed by Barbara Lewalski in her reading of the "ingrate" speech (III, 97 ff.) included in her lecture on the celestial colloquy at the Le Moyne College Forum on Religion and Literature. Although Lewalski's discussion has subsequently been printed, the tonalities of speech, especially divine speech, tend to get lost on the page. When she read from the Father's speech, Lewalski registered beneath the outrage a deep undertone of grief.

⁸ Quilligan explains the importance of the domestic dimension of the epic in the social and historical context of seventeenth-century Protestantism: "If each believer had become his own priest, and was no longer a member of an institutionally visible church, this priest found his congregation shrunk to the literal foundation upon which Paul had based his metaphoric description of Christ's relationship to his church: the love of a husband for his wife" (224). Quilligan argues that the dissolution of other structures of patriarchal authority necessitated Milton's embedding that authority firmly and inflexibly, according to divine sanction, in the nuclear family.

⁹ Barbara Lewalski explores the metaphor of gardening in "Innocence and Experience in Milton's Eden." "Suburbanites in the nude" is Northrop Frye's charming epithet in *The Return of Eden* (66). Jackie Di Salvo describes Adam and Eve's paradisal condition as infantile in "Blake Encountering Milton" (164).

¹⁰ Kathleen Swaim explores the association of Eve with Eden. For Eve's associations with nature and with classical myths of the great goddess see Frye, "The Revelation to Eve." Stephanie Demetrakopoulos parodies the association of Eve with Eden: "Milton continually tightens this sinister relationship between Eve and the garden.... The feminine forces of the garden finally overwhelm Adam: the frail and lonely embodiment of the masculine principle in Eden.... Without Adam she is incapable of withstanding Satan's wiles; she thinks

herself ready for any test, but her intelligence is allied to the vegetative, earthly forces that surround her. Not only does she look like a flower, she thinks like one" (100). Dematrakopoulos thus veers in two directions in her witty reconstruction of Eve: on the one hand, she is a "stupid woman," on the other, she is an embodiment of sinister wisdom, "cosmically castrating, the original, archetypal *vagina dentata*" (106). This schizophrenic portrait anticipates Sandra Gilbert's not only in its conclusion that Eve's deepest links are with Satan, but in its procedure of ignoring the contexts which require the reader to work out the *differences* between Eve and her sinister classical and Renaissance precedents. The feminist bipolar Eve – stupid woman and seductress – closely corresponds to the patterns of clerical misogyny from which Milton attempted to rescue her as McColley has amply demonstrated. Froula and Quilligan discern a more complicated character structure in Eve and explore rather the anxiety about sexuality, authority, and inspiration she provokes as a potentially independent being.

[11] In an otherwise attentive reading, Quilligan accepts at face value the subordination and consequent devaluation of Eve as one to whom divinity must be mediated (224). Compare McColley's challenging questions: "Are Adam and Eve 'not equal' in all ways or only in regard to sex? Does inequality imply disparity of merit, or only distinction of qualities? Do their bodily forms limit Adam to contemplation and valor and Eve to softness and grace, or are these talents to be shared? If he is for God only, is he not for God in her? these questions can be answered only by watching Adam and Eve unfold in response to experience and to each other" (41).

[12] Eve's "grace" is related to the Renaissance art theorists' pairing of "beauty" and "grace" by Harinder Marjara. Milton complicates my wish to stress Eve's association with "grace" by Eve's own confession of her discovery that "beauty is excelld by manly grace / And wisdom, which alone is truly fair" (IV. 490-91).

[13] Veselin Kesich's radical reconsideration of Paul's attitude toward women should be read by anyone who is troubled by the assertion of Paul's antifeminism. Kesich's detailed analysis of Paul's exhortation to the Corinthians has enriched my understanding of Milton, and in particular of *Paradise Lost* IV. 288-311.

[14] Note that "Absolute rule" may refer to Adam's decreed dominion over the other creatures of the earth rather than to his domestic authority.

[15] Milton's representation of unfallen sexuality is itself theologically radical; that creation is originally and con-

tinually conceived as a process of sexual generation is evident from the initial invocation (I. 19-22), and especially pronounced in the account of creation in Book VII.

[16] Although the phrase about "hard liberty" is Mammon's (ll. 256-57), the position is ostensibly Satan's; each of the pandemoniac speeches represents an aspect of the despairing fallen imagination which is fully embodied in Satan.

WORKS CITED

Bly, Robert. "I Came Out of the Mother Naked." *Sleepers Joining Hands*. New York: Harper and Row, 1973.

Demetrakopoulos, Stephanie A. "Eve as a Circean and Courtly Fatal Woman." *Milton Quarterly* 9 (1975): 99-107.

Di Salvo, Jackie. "Blake Encountering Milton: Politics and the Family in *Paradise Lost* and *The Four Zoas*." *Milton and the Line of Vision*. Ed. Joseph Anthony Wittreich, Jr. Madison: U of Wisconsin P, 1975. 143-84.

Farwell, Marilyn R. "Eve, the Separation Scene, and the Renaissance Idea of Androgyny." *Milton Studies* 16 (1982): 3-20.

Fish, Stanley. "Discovery as Form in *Paradise Lost*." *New Essays on Paradise Lost*. Ed. Thomas Kranidas. Berkeley: U of California P, 1971. 1-14.

———. *Surprised by Sin: The Reader in Paradise Lost*. New York: St. Martin's, 1967.

Froula, Christine. "Pechter's Specter: Milton's Bogey Writ Small; or Why is He Afraid of Virginia Woolf?" *Critical Inquiry* 11 (1984): 171-78.

———. "When Eve Reads Milton: Undoing the Canonical Economy." *Critical Inquiry* 10 (1983): 321-47.

Frye, Northrop. *The Return of Eden: Five Essays on Milton's Epics*. Toronto: U of Toronto P, 1965.

———. "The Revelation to Eve." *Paradise Lost: A Tercentenary Tribute*. Ed. Balachandra Rajan. Toronto: U of Toronto P, 1969. 18-47.

Fuller, Margaret. "The Prose Works of Milton." *Papers on Literature and Art*. New York: Wiley and Putnam, 1846.

Gallagher, Philip. "Milton's Bogey." *PMLA* 94 (1979): 319-21.

Gilbert, Sandra, and Susan Gubar. *The Madwoman in the Attic: The Woman Writer and the Nineteenth-Century Literary Imagination.* New Haven: Yale UP, 1979.

Gilligan, Carol. *In a Different Voice: Psychological Theory and Women's Development.* Cambridge: Harvard UP, 1982.

Gubar, Susan. "When Eve Needed an Alias." *New York Times Book Review* 19 February 1984: 26.

Graves, Robert. *Wife to Mr. Milton: The Story of Marie Powell.* New York: Creative Age, 1944.

Heilbrun, Carolyn. *Toward a Recognition of Androgyny.* New York: Alfred A. Knopf, 1973.

Hill, Christopher. *Milton and the English Revolution.* New York: Penguin, 1979.

Janeway, Elizabeth. *Man's World, Woman's Place: A Study in Social Mythology.* New York: Morrow, 1971.

Keats, John. *The Letters of John Keats, 1814–1821.* Ed. Hyder Edward Rollins. Vol. 2. Cambridge: Harvard UP, 1958.

Keller, Karl. "Notes on Sleeping with Emily Dickinson." *Feminist Critics Read Emily Dickinson.* Ed. Suzanne Juhasz. Bloomington: U of Indiana P, 1983. 67–79.

Kermode, Frank. "Adam Unparadised." *The Living Milton.* Ed. Frank Kermode. London: Routledge and Kegan Paul, 1963. 85–123.

Kesich, Veselin. "St. Paul: Anti-Feminist or Liberator?" *St. Vladimir's Theological Quarterly* 21 (1977): 1–25.

Lacan, Jacques. "The function and field of speech and language in psychoanalysis." *Ecrits: A Selection.* Ed. and trans. Alan Sheridan. New York: Norton, 1977. 30–113.

———. "The mirror stage as formative of the function of the I." *Ecrits.* 1–7.

Landy, Marcia. "Kinship and the Role of Women in *Paradise Lost.*" *Milton Studies* 4 (1972): 3–18.

Lewalski, Barbara. "Innocence and Experience in Milton's Eden." *New Essays on Paradise Lost.* Ed. Thomas Kranidas. Berkeley: U of California P, 1971. 86–117.

———. "Milton on Women—Yet Once More." *Milton Studies* 6 (1974): 3–20.

———. "Milton's Literary God: The Uses of Generic Multiplicity." Lecture at the Le Moyne College Forum on Religion and Literature. 22 October 1983. Rpt. in Paradise Lost *and the Rhetoric of Literary Forms.* Princeton UP, 1985.

MacCaffrey, Isabel. "The Theme of *Paradise Lost,* Book III." *New Essays on* Paradise Lost. Ed. Thomas Kranidas. Berkeley: U of California P, 1971. 58–85.

McColley, Diane Kelsey. *Milton's Eve.* Urbana: U of Illinois P, 1983.

Marjara, Harinder. "'Beauty' and 'Grace' in *Paradise Lost.*" *Milton Quarterly* 18 (1984): 50–52.

Milton, John. *John Milton: Complete Poems and Major Prose.* Ed. Merritt Y. Hughes. New York: Odyssey, 1957.

———. *The Works of John Milton.* Ed. Frank Allen Patterson et. al. 16 vols. New York: Columbia UP, 1933. Vol. 14. (Cited as DDC).

Mollenkott, Virginia. "Milton and Women's Liberation: A Note on Teaching Method." *Milton Quarterly* 7 (1973): 99–103.

———. "Some Implications of Milton's Androgynous Muse." *Bucknell Review* 24 (1978): 27–36.

Peczenik, F. "Fit Help: The Egalitarian Marriage in *Paradise Lost.*" *Mosaic* 17 (1984): 29–48.

Pechter, Edward. "When Pechter Reads Froula Pretending She's Eve Reading Milton; or, New Feminist is But Old Priest Writ Large." *Critical Inquiry* 11 (1984): 163–70.

Quilligan, Maureen. *Milton's Spenser: The Politics of Reading.* Ithaca: Cornell UP, 1983.

Rich, Adrienne. *On Lies, Secrets and Silence: Selected Prose, 1966–78.* New York: Norton, 1978.

Ringelheim, Joan. "Women and the Holocaust." Sarah Lawrence Women's Studies Lecture. 15 February 1984.

Ruddick, Sarah. "Maternal Thinking." *Feminist Studies* 6 (1980): 342–67.

Smith, Hilda L. *Reason's Disciples: Seventeenth-Century English Feminists.* Urbana: U of Illinois P, 1982.

Swaim, Kathleen. "Flowers, Fruit, and Seed: A Reading of *Paradise Lost.*" *Milton Studies* 5 (1973): 155–76.

Webber, Joan Malory. "The Politics of Poetry: Feminism and *Paradise Lost.*" *Milton Studies* 14 (1980): 3–24.

———. "Walking on Water: Milton, Stevens, and Contemporary American Poetry." *Milton and the Line of Vision.* Ed. Joseph Anthony Wittreich, Jr. Madison: U of Wisconsin P, 1975. 231-68.

Woolf, Virginia. *A Room of One's Own.* New York: Harcourt, 1929.

——————

THE PROBLEM OF SATAN

"SATAN", wrote Sir Walter Raleigh, "unavoidably reminds us of Prometheus, and although there are essential differences, we are not made to feel them essential. His very situation as the fearless antagonist of Omnipotence makes him either a fool or a hero, and Milton is far indeed from permitting us to think him a fool."[1] Raleigh's conclusion reflects very fairly the trend of opinion in the preceding century, which, while not always insisting that Satan was a hero,[2] invariably endowed him with his share of heroic qualities. It is only recently that critics have become audible who prefer the less noble of the opposed alternatives. Charles Williams, the first of them, in a brief but thought-provoking introduction to Milton's poetry, spoke ominously of Satan's "solemn antics".[3] C. S. Lewis then took the hint up and developed it more aggressively. Satan became for him "a personified self-contradiction", a being ultimately farcical, a creature who could not be brought into contact with the real without laughter arising "just as steam *must* when water meets fire".[4] So challenging a formulation could naturally not pass unchallenged and Professor Stoll, backed by the resources of nineteenth century criticism, demanded at some length that the devil be given his due.[5] Mr. Rostrevor Hamilton, using Raleigh's antithesis for a title, insisted that the poet had his reasons of which the Puritan knew nothing, and that the Satan created by Milton's imagination was nobler and more admirable than the devil conceived by his intellect.[6] The controversy died away except for occasional salvoes in learned periodicals,[7] but the issues it raised are sufficiently important to be discussed again in somewhat different surroundings.

Now when a problem of this kind is presented to us the first

287

thing we need to ask about is the adequacy of the vocabulary in which it is formulated. That "hero or fool?" is a leading question is not in itself regrettable. What is regrettable is that it is the sort of leading question which is bound to result in a misleading answer. Given certain ethical systems Satan is ultimately heroic and given others he is ultimately farcical. But what we are concerned with is poetry rather than ethics and Satan considered as a poetic force is different from Satan as a cosmic principle. For when that principle becomes dramatically real, when it comes alive in the radius of human experience, you cannot bring to its poetic deployment the simple emotions of mirth or admiration. Your response to it must not be unconditional. You have to see it as an element in a concerted whole, a single fact in a poetic process. Therefore to understand its nature and function you need to relate it to the pattern it fulfils and the background of belief against which it is presented.

It is when we undertake this reconsideration that critical differences of shading begin to emerge. Our response to Satan is, I imagine, one of cautious interest. We think of him either as an abstract conception or else, more immediately, as someone in whom evil is mixed with good but who is doomed to destruction by the flaw of self-love. But with Milton's contemporaries the response was predominantly one of fear. If like Calvin they thought of Satan as "an enemie that is in courage most hardie, in strength most mightie, in policies most subtle, in diligence and celeritie unweariable, with all sorts of engins plenteously furnishd, in skill of warre most readie",[8] that was only so that they could stand guard more vigilantly against their relentless opponent. If like Defoe they saw him as "a mighty, a terrible, an immortal Being; infinitely superior to man, as well in the dignity of his nature, as in the dreadful powers he retains still about him",[9] the vision served to remind them inescapably that it was only by God's grace that they could hope to overcome the enormous forces against which they were contending. When Milton's great figure is silhouetted against this background the effect must be as Addison points out "to raise and terrify our imagina-

THE PROBLEM OF SATAN

tions".[10] So the heroic qualities which Satan brings to his mission, the fortitude, the steadfast hate, the implacable resolution which is founded on despair are qualities not to be imitated or admired. They are defiled by the evil to which they are consecrated. If Milton dwells upon them it is because he knows that you will put them in their context, that you will see Satan's virtues as perverted by their end and darkening therefore to their inevitable eclipse, corroded and eaten out by the nemesis beyond them. The moral condemnation is never explicitly, or even poetically, denied. Touched on repeatedly in parenthesis, it is also always there as an undertone to the imagery. Words like Memphis and Alcairo may be nothing more than brilliant names to us. To Milton's contemporaries they were darkened with contempt. When Satan was described to them as a "great Sultan" the phrase would have reminded them of tyranny rather than splendour. When the fallen angels were likened to the cavalry of Egypt, a plague of locusts and a barbarian invasion, they would have given full weight to the mounting disapproval which lies behind the simile. As for the great Satanic defiances, they would have admired them for their strength and deplored them for their perversity. To quote Addison once more, Satan's sentiments "are every way answerable to his character, and suitable to a created Being of the most exalted and most depraved nature. . . . Amidst the impieties which this enraged Spirit utters . . . the author has taken care to introduce none that is not big with absurdity and incapable of shocking a religious reader".[11] The sympathy for Satan which the poetry imposes, the admiration it compels for his Promethean qualities, are meant to be controlled by this sort of moral reaction. And the same sense of proportion should cover his intellectual argument. When Satan appeals to "just right and the fixt laws of Heav'n", when he grounds his mandate on the ultimate nature of things, and when, in betraying overtones, he couples God's "tyranny" with "the excess of joy", you are not supposed to take these statements at their face value. Other politicians have made claims somewhat similar, and Satan's assertions as the champion of liberty would amuse, rather than perplex, those who were brought up to think of him as the first liar.

But to set aside the problem at this point is to leave its most interesting elements unstated. It is right to insist that Milton's Satan is not presented in a moral vacuum, that there is a background of unremitting hostility against which his poetic presence must be built up. But though the system within which he exists is never questioned, though it is seldom ignored and frequently remembered, its immediate implications are progressively subdued. We know, and even Satan knows, that the God against whom he is contending is omnipotent. But against the settled strength of his heroism, against the desperate and deliberate valour of Hell, that fact dies down to an abstract and distant necessity. When the weight of the poetry is thus thrown in on Satan's side, the effect must be to equalize in our imaginations the relative magnitude of the contending forces. We see Satan so clearly that we can hardly see anything else, and though conscious, we are not always or inescapably conscious, of the strength and authority of the forces which control him. The conflict, then, is neither Promethean or farcical. It is dramatically real in proportion as you assent to the illusion of equality which the poem communicates.

That illusion, however, is not intended to last. In our first glimpse of the solemnities of heaven, in the deliberations of the celestial council, in the love and mercy which are poured into the Son's sacrifice, the stature of the whole infernal enterprise is meant to be implicitly reduced. But Milton's verse is not equal to the occasion. His reliance on biblical phrasing undoubtedly meant far more to his contemporaries than it can ever mean to us, but even when every allowance has been made for this difference in impact, the drab legalities of Milton's celestial style are too curt and chill to be poetically successful. It is only in the speech on Mount Niphates, when the external magnificence surrounding Satan is stripped away, that we find his stature visibly reduced and his heroic grandeur battered and corroded by the endless siege of contraries within him.

THE PROBLEM OF SATAN

> . . . horror and doubt distract
> His troubl'd thoughts, and from the bottom stirr
> The Hell within him, for within him Hell
> He brings, and round about him, nor from Hell
> One step no more then from himself can fly
> By change of place.

Pinned on this torment he is driven from concession to concession. He admits that God is omnipotent and his own revolt unjustified. He wishes that he were ordained an "inferiour Angel", only to realize that if he were less exalted he would not be less evil. He curses God's love but ends by cursing himself. He thinks of submission but his pride rejects it; then, as desperation forces him to consider the idea, he finds that the breach between him and God is so great that no atonement could possibly heal it and that, in the last analysis, he has not even the power to atone. When we are brought up in this manner against Satan's inner helplessness, his sheer inability to be other than he is, the splendour of his presence starts to crumble. It is one of the functions of the Niphates speech to effect this reduction in scale for by doing so it helps to link two conceptions of Satan which might otherwise be harassingly opposed. On the one hand we have the "apostate Angel", the leader of all but unconquerable armies, the antagonist to God in the theatre of world history. On the other hand we need to have someone whose characteristic qualities are cunning and subtlety rather than heroic valour, someone sufficiently small to be met and conquered by Adam and Eve in the arena of their original righteousness. One hastens to add that the two conceptions are not contradictory and are in fact meant to be imaginatively reconciled in a true understanding of the nature of evil. Jeremy Taylor achieves the synthesis memorably in prose:

His [God's] mercies make contemptible means instrumental to great purposes, and a small herb the remedy of the greatest diseases; he impedes the Devil's rage and infatuates his counsels, he diverts his malice, and defeats his purposes, he bindes him in the chaine of darknesse and gives him no power over the children of light; he suffers him to walk in solitary places and yet

291

fetters him that he cannot disturb the sleep of a childe; he hath given him mighty power and yet a young maiden that resists him shall make him flee away; he hath given him a vast knowledge and yet an ignorant man can confute him with the twelve articles of his creed, he gave him power over the winds and made him Prince of the air and yet the breath of a holy prayer can drive him as far as the utmost sea;[12]

The same contrast is realized poetically by Milton. Satan's omnipotence against the background of evil blends into his impotence in the presence of good. The transition from one state to the other probably begins with his deception of Uriel but it is felt most inescapably in that devouring inner chaos which is revealed to us in the Niphates soliloquy. When we see Satan transfixed upon the rocks of his hatred, confirmed in evil as the servant of his selfhood, able only to do as his inner logic demands, we see him, in his limitations, more clearly as our antagonist and know ourselves sufficient to stand against him. The imagery accordingly becomes more and more homilectical; it is addressed to Everyman in the familiar traditions of the pulpit, in figures whose content is plain and unmistakable and whose moral meaning is insistently asserted. Thus Satan appearing before Uriel as a stripling Cherub, may remind us of Burton's claim that the Devil sometimes "transforms himself into an angel of light, and is so cunning that he is able, if it were possible, to deceive the very elect".[13] But Milton makes sure that we will draw the necessary inference by using the occasion for a sermon on hypocrisy. Again when Satan descends from Mount Niphates, smoothing his perturbations "with outward calme" the preacher's voice informs us that he was the first "that practisd falshood under saintly shew". When the fiend leaps into Paradise Milton begins by appealing to his audience in the country:

> As when a prowling Wolfe,
> Whom hunger drives to seek new haunt for prey,
> Watching where Shepherds pen thir Flocks at eeve
> In hurdl'd Cotes amid the field secure,
> Leaps o're the fence with ease into the Fould:

THE PROBLEM OF SATAN

But to make condemnation doubly sure this is followed by a simile for Everyman in Bread Street:

> Or as a Thief bent to unhoord the cash
> Of some rich Burgher, whose substantial dores
> Cross-barrd and bolted fast, fear no assault,
> In at the window climbs, or o're the tiles;
> So clomb this first grand Thief into God's Fould.

And the pamphleteer in Milton cannot resist the afterthought:

> So since into his Church lewd Hirelings climbe.

After about two hundred lines of the fourth book this homely didacticism begins to have its way. Satan's dimensions are reduced so effectively that we hardly notice how, in the process, his titles lose their lustre, how the "Archfiend" of the first book becomes "the Fiend" or the "arch-fellon" and how for the first time he begins to be "the Devil". It is fitting that this new being should sit like a cormorant on the tree of life, and even his malicious leering at the happiness of Eve and Adam is well in keeping with the Satan of popular sentiment. Protestants had long opposed the exaltation of the single above the married state, thinking of it, in Ames's words as "a diabolical presumption".[14] It is only a step from this, and not a large one poetically, to make the Devil jealous of wedded love. But even before this Satan has begun to posture and protest, according to the conventions of his villainy. His pity for Adam and Eve is eventually only an elaborate form of self-pity:

> Ah gentle pair, yee little think how nigh
> Your change approaches, when all these delights
> Will vanish and deliver ye to woe,
> More woe, the more your taste is now of joy;
> Happie, but for so happy ill secur'd
> Long to continue, and this high seat your Heav'n
> Ill fenc't for Heav'n to keep out such a foe
> As now is entered; yet no purpos'd foe
> To you whom I could pittie thus forlorne
> Though I unpittied: League with you I seek,
> And mutual amitie so streight, so close,

PARADISE LOST

That I with you must dwell, or you with me
Henceforth; my dwelling haply may not please
Like this fair Paradise, your sense, yet such
Accept your Makers work; he gave it me,
Which I as freely give; Hell shall unfould
To entertain you two, her widest Gates
And send forth all her Kings; there will be room,
Not like these narrow limits, to receive
Your numerous offspring; if no better place,
Thank him who puts me loath to this revenge
On you who wrong me not for him who wrongd.

No more impressive evidence of Satan's degeneration could be cited. The lamentations mingled with the macabre gloating, the horrific irony seasoned with complaint are all confessions of his inner emptiness. And this vacancy is reflected in the texture of the verse. Lines like "That I with you must dwell, or you with me" are symptomatically lacking in any sense of direction. Their tiredness stands in unmistakable contrast to the rock-like assurance of the Archangel's words in Hell:

Fall'n Cherube, to be weak is miserable
Doing or Suffering: but of this be sure,
To do ought good never will be our task,
But ever to do ill our sole delight,
As being the contrary to his high will
Whom we resist. If then his Providence
Out of our evil seek to bring forth good,
Our labour must be to pervert that end,
And out of good still to find means of evil;

Even the invocation here is meaningful and moving. It has about it the strength of native courtesy, the condescension of intrinsic merit, the responsibility mingled with protective guidance which, in a great leader, is noblest in defeat. How different it all is from the crocodile condolences of the Devil inspecting Paradise. And how different are the threatenings of the passage in Book IV, the palpable attempt to make your flesh creep, from the strange force of poetic concentration which settles implacably on that one word *pervert*. The words

THE PROBLEM OF SATAN

in the first book are steadfast and impregnable with the long stressed monosyllables aiding and buttressing their massive resolution. They preach perversion without apology or comment, and for the moment you feel that perversion absolute, unalterable as a fact in nature, an element in the geography of Hell. By contrast, the passage from the fourth book is forced and undecided. The level monosyllables are listless rather than militant. The being who speaks these words, torn and transfixed by self-interrogation, is one who invites this scornful comment of Zephon:

> Think not, revolted Spirit, thy shape the same,
> Or undiminisht brightness, to be known
> As when thou stoodst in Heav'n upright and pure;
> That Glorie then, when thou no more wast good
> Departed from thee, and thou resembl'st now
> Thy sin and place of doom obscure and foule.

And Satan himself is forced to accept this verdict

> ... abasht the Devil stood
> And felt how awful goodness is, and saw
> Vertue in her shape how lovly, saw, and pin'd
> His loss; but chiefly to find here observd
> His lustre visibly impar'd; yet seemed
> Undaunted.

The form of the ruined Archangel is inexorably losing its brightness. Once indeed, under the lash of Gabriel's comments it flares into a reminiscence of its former splendour. But the "allarm'd" Satan dilated "like *Teneriff* or *Atlas*" is never quite as impressive as the "Unterrifi'd" Satan who challenges Death at the outset of his journey through Chaos. He is too concerned with winning verbal victories, with shifty deceits and elaborate evasions. He accepts (as one cannot imagine the earlier Satan accepting) the symbolic verdict of the scales suspended in Heaven. The implication plainly is that the heroic in Satan is yielding to the perverted, and that the passions which led him to war with his creator are beginning to recoil on the intelligence which released them.

In the fifth book we revert to a Satan who, chronologically, ought to be at his noblest. Instead, we find only a professional politician, a propagandist who, like all propagandists, is an ardent champion of the Rights of Man and is therefore able to be generously indignant about the despotic tendencies of government in Heaven. It is a Satan notably different from the Archangel of the first books, and those who feel this discrepancy are compelled either to assume that Milton changed his mind about Satan as he drew him, or else find ways of making the difference acceptable. One way of dealing with the evidence is to assume that Satan is chiefly what the occasion makes him. What he is, depends on what he does. The intruder in Eden is not quite the explorer of Chaos and both of them differ from the "false Archangel" whom Abdiel conquers in "debate of truth". The battle in Heaven is, we should remember, part of a Sermon preached to Adam; it is intended to warn him against an opponent who may conquer him by force of persuasion but cannot conquer him by force of arms. So the qualities stressed are Satan's specious plausibility in argument and, side by side with this, his very real ineptness when he is faced with the weapons of reason and the right. I have dealt in an earlier chapter with Satan's complaints and suggested that Milton's contemporaries could hardly have taken them seriously. But even if they were inclined to do so they would have been set right by the evidence of the Niphates soliloquy, with its betraying confession that God's service was never onerous, and that ambition, not altruism, drove Satan to revolt. The other half of Milton's poetic intention is to suggest Satan's tawdriness and triviality when he is measured against the values of Heaven. It is a tawdriness first felt in the Devil's encounter with Gabriel but confirmed now by a style which can be fantastically complicated, by speeches which bristle with the equipment of the orator, with jaunty sarcasm and irrelevant puns.

> That we were formd then saist thou? and the work
> Of secondarie hands, by task transferd
> From Father to his Son? Strange point and new!
> Doctrin which we would know whence learnt: who saw
> When this creation was? rememberst thou

THE PROBLEM OF SATAN

Thy making, while the Maker gave thee being?
We know no time when we were not as now;
Know none before us, self-begot, self-rais'd
By our own quick'ning power, when fatal course
Had circl'd his full Orbe, the birth mature
Of this our native Heav'n, Ethereal Sons.
Our puissance is our own, our own right hand
Shall teach us highest deeds, by proof to try
Who is our equal: then thou shall behold
Whether by supplication we intend
Address, and to begirt th'Almighty Throne,
Beseeching or besieging.

The spectacle of the arch-heretic accusing the saints of
heresy (Milton frequently calls the loyal angels saints)[15] is one
which would certainly have encouraged the violent dislike
which every saint felt for Satan. And their feelings would not
have been moderated by Satan's extraordinary arguments,
his perverse insolence in calling Abdiel seditious, and his
uncouth explanations of how he was "self-begot". Such
behaviour for them would have justified Abdiel's verdict:
"Thyself not free but to thyself enthrall'd." In Satan's utter
incomprehension of the joyous obedience which binds man to
right reason, in his persistent confusion of servitude with
service, they would have seen the flaws in the rhetoric Abdiel
mastered, and the diabolic persuasions which they too must
subdue, within themselves, on the field of Christian warfare.

When we next see Satan his fortunes have sunk much
lower. He has had to journey in darkness seven times round
the earth to avoid the vigilance of the angels guarding Paradise. Now, having entered the garden by an underground
river at midnight, he pours his "bursting passion" into
"plaints" that invite comparison with his earlier soliloquy.
This time he addresses the earth instead of the sun and, just
as the sun once reminded him of the glory he had lost, the
earth now suggests to him the glory he is to recover. It is a
glory which at most can be only a shadow of his former
brightness, but Satan is now so much the victim of his eloquence that he convinces himself that Earth is superior to

297

Heaven.[16] The creature who finds ease "onely in destroying"
is the embodiment of the evil he accepted as his good. Unable
to alleviate his misery he finds solace only in making others
as miserable as he is. His mind is diseased with the obsession
of revenge. He talks of man as the "Favorite of Heav'n" and
of the creation as an act of spite. He envies, only less than
God, the "gentle pair" whom he once said he could pity. If
he is good it is because he is "stupidly good" in a momentary,
bewildered abstraction from himself. Yet even in this depth
of degradation he can still rise to what the occasion makes
him. The classics come, as so often, to his rescue, the proper
names glitter to suit his serpentine stratagems and, mounting
on the pedestal of an occasional simile, he becomes as lovely
as temptation is to the tempted. Admittedly when the deed
has been done, he slinks away to escape the judgment of God
but, despite the implications of this incident, he is allowed to
masquerade as an "Angel bright" and to strut through Chaos
with his diabolic progeny. Meeting the infernal council in
surroundings suitably Turkish, he can still outshine the stars
in "permissive glory". He addresses them on the great enterprise and on his own heroism in making the adventure
successful. He alludes (quite falsely) to the fierce opposition
which he encountered from Night and from Chaos. He claims
with catastrophic foolishness to have purchased a Universe
with a bruise and an apple, and having held God up as an
object for laughter he is greeted appropriately with a "universal hiss". The punishment which descends is terrible but
justified. As we leave the humiliated powers of Hell, tormented by the fruits of their imagined victory, the contrast
makes more reassuring the repentance of Adam and Eve and
their reconciliation to the good which Satan denies.

During these last few paragraphs I have tried to suggest
that what Satan is depends on his circumstances, and how
his behaviour and implied stature are determined by his
functions. I hope I have not suggested that he is nothing more
than a collection of abstract properties, properties which can
be irresponsibly shuffled to meet the demands of varying
situations. But, if he is more than this, he is also more than a

THE PROBLEM OF SATAN

theological exercise, or a means of illustrating a preconceived theory of evil. He is, in short, a poetic representation, and Milton's special problem is to take those qualities which the general imagination associates with Satan and work them into a stable poetic whole. Those qualities are by no means interdependent and in juxtaposition may often seem contradictory. They can be brought together in poetry, or poetic prose, in the emotions kindled by antithesis and paradox. But, in the more spacious economy of a narrative poem, such lyrical insights are neither proper nor possible. The truth must be revealed in action, not reflection, and so the qualities which the poem portrays are most convincing when they are made to emerge from the situations in which they are presented. If Satan is heroic, he should be heroic in Hell. If he is melodramatic, he is best so in the serene peace of Eden. If he combines weakness in understanding with subtlety in debate, that combination is best revealed in circumstances which Milton's contemporaries would associate with Christian warfare. The qualities, then, are harmonized by their relationship to a fable which is constructed to imply them. They can be brought together still more closely by the disposition of that fable, that is by the divergence between the chronological and the reading order. Chronologically Satan's deterioration is neither continual nor consistent: before his fall from Heaven he is far less impressive than he is immediately after it. But the difference (made unavoidable by Satan's function in Heaven) is one submerged in the unity which the reading order stipulates, the inexorable law of Satan's degeneration which is exercised so evenly from the first books to the last.

Satan's history therefore is meant to be read poetically. You may bring to it (and indeed it is essential that you should bring to it) the preconceptions of an established moral outlook. But such preconceptions are no more than an equipment, an accepted means of reacting to the poem. They are what Milton assumes rather than what he demonstrates. Given the organization of sensibility they imply, the function of the poem is to play upon it, to use it as far as possible as a medium through which its own character is created and known. To vary the metaphor a little, the poem imposes its perspective on your feelings. The great figure of Satan and its inexorable decline confirms and yet insensibly rearranges the mass of beliefs and sentiments which you bring to it. You see it as a sermon on the weakness of evil and you learn more clearly than you can from any philosophy that evil must die by the logic of its being. But it is also a sermon on the strength of evil; because you see Satan created as he is, huge in the magnificence with which the first books surround him, you are compelled to know him as the Prince of Darkness and to admit his dominion over the forces of history. When two facts so apparently opposed are reconciled in one figure a poetic synthesis has been effected. Add to that synthesis the emotions which it orders, fear of the marauder and contempt for the liar, with wary admiration of the orator's resources, add to these the dramatic insights of soliloquy, and the result must make Satan symbolically alive within the universe which Milton's epic operates. In defining or interpreting this life, "hero" and "fool" are inadequate alternatives. They are descriptions, not so much of the poetry, as of the moral system which the poetry is said to recommend, or else of the intellectual convictions which Milton's imagination is taken to deny.

In opposition I have tried to maintain that Milton's heart was not at war with his head and that his Satan is on the whole what he intended to make him. Here and there Milton's execution may falter. But if we look at his picture through seventeenth century eyes, if we try not to impose upon it the deceptions of our own historic and personal perspectives, its implications should be plain and unmistakable. The failure lies not in the depiction of Satan but in that of the heavenly values which should subdue him. Those values are only imperfectly realized. So, though one half of the picture may be painted convincingly, the other half is sketched rather than painted. Milton's God is what his Satan never is, a collection of abstract properties, or, in his greatest moments, a treatise on free-will. The Son moves us more deeply, particularly in

THE PROBLEM OF SATAN

the quiet, firm monosyllables in which he announces his sacrifice. But the spare precision of the language Milton gives him is lit only seldom by the ardour which should inform it. Clothed in the language of Ezekiel's vision his triumph over Satan must have its moments of majesty, but it remains a moral rather than a poetic victory.

It is I think the barrenness of this victory which makes some misunderstanding of Satan's function inevitable. His regression faces us with a sort of vacuum and though the values which triumph over him are everywhere announced they are never brought to the foreground of our assent. Milton can describe pride, and in doing so condemn it; but love is to him never much more than loyalty, and humility teaches him only to "stand and wait". He may justify God's ways but he does not celebrate them. His sense of responsibility is too contractual, too persistently concerned with the mechanics of crime and punishment, for goodness or mercy to come into being within it. Because such goodness is so seldom real within the limits of Milton's poetry it becomes possible to claim that the poet was interested predominantly in evil, or even that evil was unconsciously his good. Such conclusions are to my mind untenable. Milton knows his Satan well enough to reject him and to make that rejection a poetic fact. If that dismissal is never stabilized in its transformation by a higher poetic acceptance, the failure should not blind us to the poverty of the values Milton condemns or to the reality and force of his depiction of evil.

THE POET AND SATAN IN
PARADISE LOST

William G. Riggs

Realizing that the desire to achieve "Things unattempted yet
in Prose or Rhyme" offers a potential for sin, Milton employs
parallels between the narrator of *Paradise Lost* and Satan to indicate his awareness that great endeavors, even his own, may be
pridefully motivated. But he defines carefully the difference
between his "advent'rous" singing and satanic overreaching.
The sharp contrast between the narrator's dependence on
divine guidance and Satan's claims of self-sufficiency is repeatedly asserted within the context of striking similarities: both
poet and Devil undertake great adventures; both, dwelling in
hostile darkness, soar toward light; both, in need of direction,
seek guidance from light (holy Light, Uriel) and primal sources
of hexaemeral knowledge (Urania, Uriel). Milton supports
such general parallels by the repetition of specific details and
by numerous verbal echoes. But Satan lies to Uriel, curses the
sun, and, inverting the poet's creative impulse, invokes his
proper muse in Chaos. The devils can sing; they pursue the
philosophical issues with which *Paradise Lost* is concerned;
they build "Monument[s] / Of merit high." These satanic
perversions of good mean more than that the devils are bad;
they mean that man may be beguiled by some "fair appearing
good." A Solomon may fall "To Idols foul." A poet exploring
"things invisible to mortal sight" must humbly hope that he is
not deluded, that all *is* "Hers who brings it nightly to [his]
Ear."

I

A FAMILIAR GROUP of Milton's readers have not shared Adam's confidence that "Evil into the mind of God or Man / May come and
go, so unapprov'd, and leave / No spot or blame behind" (V, 117–19);[1]

they have instead assumed, less charitably, that the impact of Satan's character in *Paradise Lost* implies an uncomprehended diabolical complicity on the part of the poet. Such readings have been vigorously rebutted,[2] but they manage to persist because they respond with appealing directness to what can hardly be missed: Satan is impressive. He impresses not just the romantic imagination and its offshoots; in seventeenth-century England the appeal of his heroics would have touched any admirer of Achilles or Hector or Aeneas. Of course most of Milton's first audience would have been willing, ultimately, to accept the poet's stated assessment of Satan's heroism, whereas Shelley, for instance, was not. But precisely because Milton's early readers knew the Devil was bad and did not, like C. S. Lewis, have to prove it, they could respond more openly to his admirable qualities, to his suffering fortitude and constancy of purpose. Much post-Romantic criticism has lost this sense of balance and has viewed *Paradise Lost* partially. Milton clearly intends to condemn Satan (who could doubt it?), but he just as clearly provides materials for the Satanist critique—a critique which offers us valuable intuitions: "Milton . . . was a true poet and of the Devil's party without knowing it."[3] Blake's notorious claim not only helps to suggest the complexity of Milton's struggle with evil; it also serves to isolate an important dimension of *Paradise Lost* by insisting that Milton's relationship as poet to the structure he created is a primary concern and that, in particular, the relationship of the poet to Satan is crucial. These are important considerations, but they remain distorted in Blake and those who subsequently have shared his attitude toward the place of Satan in Milton's poem. The reason for this distortion is plain: the Satanists, almost without exception, presume to know more than Milton about the workings of the creative imagination. I will be arguing that to so presume is usually to ignore the information Milton offers us concerning his own creative process. In his characterization of Satan, Milton leaves us little room for second-guessing about his unconscious sympathies. His poem demonstrates an acute sensitivity to both the appeals and the dangers of Satanism; his imagination is not covertly inflamed by fallen grandeur. In short, Milton knew exactly to what extent he was "of the Devil's party." In his epic he anticipates the Satanist response by repeatedly asking us to compare his portrait of the poet with his portrait of Satan. The similarities are not hidden; the differences are consciously and carefully defined.

That the description of the poet in *Paradise Lost* contributes significantly to the epic's total design has become a commonplace of recent commentary on Milton's poetry.[4] Milton, it is argued, presents the poet as a character within his own poem, a character whose fallen circumstances and aspirations to the knowledge of God mirror in several ways concerns central to the "argument" pursued in the epic's narrative. This sense of the poet's allusive participation in his own narrative has emerged from a view of the poem's structure which suggests analogical complexity as a principle of design. Since 1930 when E. M. W. Tillyard presented his first full-length study of Milton,[5] critics have been emphasizing that in *Paradise Lost* events in Heaven, on Earth, and in Hell correspond to each other by means of continually reverberating motifs. The poem repeatedly echoes itself, and the echoes serve to transform the chronologically transient occurrences of ordinary narrative into eternal paradigms. Milton, in this view, consistently unifies his narrative materials (and his ontology) by explicit comparisons between the divine, the human, and the infernal. While Adam's disobedience seems in part the result of Satan's fall, it is also an echo of Satan's sin. The Son's missions of creation are played against the backdrop of Satan's circumstantially similar voyages of destruction. The first council in Heaven pointedly recalls the consult in Pandaemonium. Heavenly paternity is parodied by Satan and his hellish offspring. To Milton's modern critics, the range of such analogies has appeared vastly extendible and has recently been seen to circumscribe the reader as well as the poet.[6] Milton's rhetoric may well be intended to draw the reader into an analogical participation in the story of the fall, but it seems to me that such participation, if it is to begin, begins at second hand with a view of the poet, a character clearly placed within *Paradise Lost* as an extended and concrete example of the relevance of Milton's cosmic drama to fallen man. My concern here, to consider the poet and Satan together, presents only a partial view of this relevance, but it is a good place to begin. Certainly for Milton the choices typical of Satan constituted the most radical agonies of our fallen world.

II

Denis Saurat has told us that "Milton had Satan in him and wanted to drive him out."[7] This is a blunt way to put things, but

Saurat would be close to the truth if he did not also insist that Milton was unaware of his potential Satanism—in particular that he was unaware of the potentially Satanic aspect of his aspiration to so great a work as *Paradise Lost*. When in Book II we discover Satan poised on the brink of Hell contemplating his flight into Chaos, his "thoughts inflamed of Highest design" (II, 630), or when we are told that Satan, "Thus high uplifted beyond hope, aspires / Beyond thus high" (II, 7–8), we should not shy away from recalling the poet at the outset desiring "with no middle flight . . . to soar / Above th' *Aonian* Mount" (I, 14–15). Or again, when in Book I we hear Satan's prideful self-justification, "till then who knew / The force of those dire Arms?" (I, 93–94), and later find him once more willing to face an "unknown Region . . ./ Unknown dangers" (II, 443–44), we should not, in supposed deference to the forgetful poet, refuse to recollect his initial aspiration to try the unknown and achieve "things unattempted yet" (I, 16). We should not, in short, smugly assume that Milton was missing the potential irony of such comparisons. By means of echoes like these he intends us to ask a question, a question he himself was, I think, the first to ask: is the attempt to write *Paradise Lost* presumptuous? Milton answers, "Yes, 'I have presum'd, / An Earthly Guest, and drawn Empyreal Air'" (VII, 13–14); his constant hope, however, is that the risk he runs is not prompted by self-justifying and self-inflating pride.

In the invocation to Book I Milton's poet announces his subject, "Man's First Disobedience" (I, 1), and proceeds directly to exalt its importance—to make clear from the outset the audacity of his attempt to explain to fallen men the justice of God's ways. He calls to a heavenly muse:

> I thence
> Invoke thy aid to my advent'rous Song,
> That with no middle flight intends to soar
> Above th' *Aonian* Mount, while it pursues
> Things unattempted yet in Prose or Rhyme.   (I, 12–16)

There is no quibbling with greatness here. Milton is probably echoing Ariosto, who at the beginning of *Orlando Furioso* had proudly invoked not a heavenly muse but his own mistress.[8] By ranking himself beside the Italian poet, Milton may ultimately intend a contrast: like Adam, Ariosto hearkened to the promptings of a mortal woman;

the poet of *Paradise Lost* looks to higher authority. Initially, however, the allusion serves simply to recall Ariosto's haughty tone ("I make no doubt but I shall have the skill / As much as I have promised to fulfill"),[9] and thereby to emphasize the hint of hubris latent throughout the first prologue to *Paradise Lost*. Less than twenty-five lines after this ambitious beginning Milton's epic voice sings of Satan:

> with all his Host
> Of Rebel Angels, by whose aid aspiring
> To set himself in Glory above his Peers,
> He trusted to have equall'd the most High.
>
> . . . .
>
> Him the Almighty Power
> Hurl'd headlong flaming from th' Ethereal Sky
> With hideous ruin and combustion down
> To bottomless perdition.   (I, 37–40; 44–47)

The immediate juxtaposition of the soaring ascent anticipated by the poet with the precipitous fall of the rebel angels suggests, at least, that Milton saw in his own circumstances as aspiring singer of divine epic the potential consequences of Satan's "ambitious aim." In viewing Satan and his cohorts we shall see this suggestion continually reinforced—for example, in the fall of Mulciber at the end of Book I. Here, specifically, an architect of things divine is cast down for his share in satanic overreaching.[10]

The initial invocation is not, of course, a cry of rebellion but a call for divine assistance:

> What in me is dark
> Illumine, what is low raise and support;
> That to the highth of this great Argument
> I may assert Eternal Providence
> And justify the ways of God to men.   (I, 22–26)

It should be clear that for Milton it is the poet's submission to the voice of his muse, to divine inspiration, which ultimately distinguishes the soaring creation of *Paradise Lost* from an act of blasphemous pride. Milton does not, however, present the invocation of a heavenly muse as his only defense against presuming too much. Throughout the narrative he remains sensitive to the relationship between himself as poet and his subject; he examines every implication of his creative act with a care which suggests a fear of self-delusion. While he insists

on the pious intentions of what he undertakes, he never neglects
to expose the satanic aspect of his poetic posture.

III

The mechanism of the poet's inspiration is based on a paradoxical pattern of outward darkness and inward illumination. In the
prologue to Book III, Milton employs this paradox to express not only
his humble dependence on God's grace but also the weakness and
corresponding audacity of his presumptuous adventure beyond his
own "Diurnal Sphere." Like fallen Satan, throwing round "his balefull
eyes" (I, 56) in Hell, the poet, a fallen man, dwells in darkness:

> but thou [Light]
> Revisit'st not these eyes, that roll in vain
> To find thy piercing ray, and find no dawn;
> So thick a drop serene hath quencht thir Orbs,
> Or dim suffusion veil'd.   (III, 22–26)

To aim high from the depths of such obscurity is to echo Satan's
despairing boast:

> From this descent
> Celestial Virtues rising, will appear
> More glorious and more dread than from no fall.   (II, 14–17)[11]

Throughout his prologues, the poet, "In darkness, and with dangers
compast round" (VII, 27), repeatedly emphasizes the baseness of his
condition; such an emphasis cannot exclude an awareness of the
similarity between the poet's physical circumstances and those of his
epic villain whose dwelling place is measured by its distance from
light.[12] Indeed, in his second invocation Milton insists on this similarity
by placing his narrator in a posture much more broadly reminiscent
of Satan:

> Thee [holy Light] I revisit now with bolder wing
> Escap't the Stygian Pool, though long detain'd
> In that obscure sojourn, while in my flight
> Through utter and through middle darkness borne
> With other notes than to th' *Orphean* Lyre
> I sung of *Chaos* and *Eternal* Night.   (III, 13–18)

This passage follows *directly* the conclusion of Book II—over one
hundred lines describing Satan's escape from Hell and labored flight
up through Chaos. In a sense, of course, the epic narrator must trace

Satan's journey in order to describe it. But to take pains to visualize both the narrator and Satan struggling through "this wild Abyss / The Womb of nature" (II, 910–11)—Satan "Audacious" (II, 931), the poet "with bolder wing"—achieves nothing so much as to suggest an analogy between the two daring voyagers. The analogy is not simply glimpsed; Milton develops it in detail.

Just as the poet in the prologue to Book III has labored out of darkness to win the visionary illumination bestowed by God, so Satan's flight in Book II through the "darksome Desert" of Chaos is directed toward light. As the arch Fiend approaches the Sun, his "visual ray" is

> sharp'n'd . . .
> To Objects distant far, whereby he soon
> Saw within ken a glorious Angel stand
> The same whom *John* saw also in the Sun.   (III, 620–23)

The poet has, at the beginning of this book, applied to holy Light for direction and increased clarity that he might "see and tell / Of things invisible to mortal sight" (III, 54–55). So here Satan, "Alone thus wand'ring" (III, 667), applies to the Regent of the Sun, Uriel, for assistance in his anti-creative task. His formal address to Uriel is an unmistakable, though bombastic, echo of a Miltonic invocation:

> *Uriel*, for thou of those sev'n Spirits that stand
> In sight of God's high Throne, gloriously bright,
> The first art wont his great authentic will
> Interpreter through highest Heav'n to bring,
> Where all his Sons thy Embassy attend;
> And here art likeliest by supreme decree
> Like honor to obtain, and as his Eye
> To visit oft this new Creation round. . . .
> · · · · · · · ·
>   Brightest Seraph, tell
> In which of all these shining Orbs hath Man
> His fixed seat, or fixed seat hath none
> But all these shining Orbs his choice to dwell;
> That I may find him, and with secret gaze,
> Or open admiration him behold.   (III, 654–61; 667–72)

Satan, dissembling, does not simply adopt the supplicating posture of the poet: while his rhetoric is inflated and his periods suspended beyond anything the poet, speaking for himself, attempts, still the

content and syntactic formulas of Satan's speech distinctly recall
the voice of the poet invoking his muse. Satan's request for heavenly
guidance ("Brightest Seraph, tell") is, of course, the keynote of Milton's
first invocation ("Instruct me, for Thou know'st. . . . Say first" [I,
19, 27]). The compound string of eulogistic epithet and description
through which Satan ingratiates himself with Uriel and Satan's cautious offering of alternatives ("In which . . . hath Man / His fixed
seat, or fixed seat hath none / . . . with secret gaze, / Or open admiration") look back to the beginning of Book III and the poet's address
to Light:

> Hail holy Light, offspring of Heav'n first-born
> Or of th' Eternal Coeternal beam
> May I express thee unblam'd? since God is Light,
> And never but in unapproached Light
> Dwelt from Eternity, dwelt then in thee
> Bright effluence of bright essence increat.   (III, 1–6)

Again in Book VII we find a similar suspended list of heavenly
qualities and a similar offering of alternatives which here place Urania,
like Uriel, "In sight of God's high Throne":

> Descend from Heav'n *Urania*, by that name
> If rightly thou art call'd
> . . . .
>   for thou
> Nor of the Muses nine, nor on the top
> Of old *Olympus* dwell'st, but Heav'nly born,
> Before the Hills appear'd, or Fountain flow'd,
> Thou with Eternal Wisdom didst converse,
> Wisdom thy Sister, and with her didst play
> In presence of th' Almighty Father.   (VII, 1–2, 5–11)

Before the powers of heavenly instruction Satan, in his manner, resembles the poet, a humble servant of God—a resemblance good
enough to fool Uriel. The likeness between the two is further suggested by the fact that Uriel, to whom the Devil looks for aid, shares
with the poet's muse ("Thou from the first / Wast present" [I, 19–20])
special knowledge of the Creation: "I saw when at his Word the
formless mass / This world's material mould, came to a heap" (III,
708–09). These multiple similarities do not seem random. That both
Satan and the poet seek, in syntactically echoing passages, assistance
from light and from sources of hexaemeral knowledge should appear

striking. It should make clear that Milton is looking at the poet's situation in terms of Satan's fallen posture and wishes to communicate this perspective. The question, to repeat, is why Milton invites such a comparison, and the answer, again, is that recognizing the audacity of his own high poetic aspirations he wishes to distinguish them clearly from the kind of aspiring he sees as satanic. He is after the contrast, but he does not wish to gain it by slighting the similarities. On the contrary, the more clearly he can see and project the similarities between the poet and Satan, the more sure he can be that he has not been blinded by pride.

The crucial contrast is obvious but significant in that Milton employs it to speak for himself. Satan, unlike the poet, is lying. Uriel is persuaded to think that the Devil's purposes are exactly opposite to what they really are:

> Fair Angel, thy desire which tends to know
> The works of God, thereby to glorify
> The great Work-Master, *leads to no excess*
> *That reaches blame, but rather merits praise*
> *The more it seems excess.*   (III, 694–98; my italics)

The glorification of God is not what Satan has in mind, but it is precisely what the poet sees as the province of his own attempt. For the poet what "seems excess"—the attempt to discover "things invisible to mortal sight"—will, he hopes, "merit praise." Milton here seizes the occasion of the Devil's lie to define his own purposes.

Milton's use of Satan's stance as a foil to the poet's position is perhaps made most explicit at the beginning of Book IV. Here the Fiend, having landed on "Niphates top," turns his gaze toward Heaven and speaks directly to the Sun. The speech is roughly an inversion, perhaps a parody, of Milton's familiar "Hail holy Light":

> O thou that with surpassing Glory crown'd
> Look'st from thy sole Dominion like the God
> Of this new World; at whose sight all the Stars
> Hide thir diminisht heads; to thee I call,
> But with no friendly voice, and add thy name
> O Sun, to tell thee how I hate thy beams
> That bring to my remembrance from what state
> I fell, how glorious once above thy Sphere:
> Till Pride and worse Ambition threw me down. (IV, 32–41)

The poet and the Devil again, in a warped glass, reflect each other, and latent in the fact that Milton's hymn to holy Light can be subjected to satanic parody is the suggestion that hubristic presumption lies close to the surface of the second invocation. But the poet has hesitated: "May I express thee unblamed?" Perhaps he may. In the most obvious sense the comparable addresses to light serve emphatically to demonstrate the difference between the poet and the Apostate. While the poet asks for assistance, humbles himself before holy Light, prays, Satan hurls envious defiance at a lesser luminary.

IV

As I have been suggesting, basic to this comparison of the poet and Satan is Milton's symbolic use of place and posture. The physical circumstances in which Satan and the poet find themselves often have clear moral equivalents. It is nothing new to notice that in *Paradise Lost* physical movement and physical placement frequently suggest moral states. Hell is a place as are Heaven and Eden; to sin is to fall. An aspect of this equation of physical and moral in which recent critics have shown interest is Milton's use of the verb *wander*. Isabel MacCaffrey, for one, documents the fact that "Not only moral values, but the intellectual values on which they depend, can be objectified, in Milton's topography, by the identification of physical and spiritual 'wandering.' *Error* is the linking word."[18] I have already cited Satan describing to Uriel his erratic and malicious voyage through Chaos, "Alone thus wand'ring." MacCaffrey lists additional instances of Milton's use of the verb, such as his description of the wandering pilgrims who sought Christ in Golgotha (III, 476–77), Adam's warning against "wand'ring thoughts, and notions vaine" (VIII, 187), Eve's recognition of loss ("From thee / How shall I part, and wither wander down / Into a lower World" [XI, 281–83]), and the poignant "wand'ring steps and slow," which completes Milton's picture of our fallen parents. Clearly *wander* is one of the several words in *Paradise Lost* to which the reader becomes sensitized through repetition. Recently Stanley Fish has added to MacCaffrey's list and has warned us against the attempt to read *wander* the same way in different contexts.[14] The relevance of context to meaning is, of course, crucial, but with a word used as Milton uses *wander*, repetition tends—as I think Fish would agree—to encourage a comparison of the very contexts within which the word appears. Discriminations, such as can be made, are the result of these comparisons.

What interests me here about *wander* is that it serves to relate the poet of the prologues to the characters of Milton's narrative. What we learn of the word in the poem proper lends a sense of human helplessness to the lyrical lines:

> Yet not the more
> Cease I to wander where the Muses haunt
> Clear Spring, or shady Grove, or Sunny Hill,
> Smit with the love of sacred Song.   (III, 26–29)[15]

Everywhere in the prologues Milton's description of the poet's creative song is seen metaphorically as a journey—a dark descent, a soaring flight. This spatial sense of human activity is, of course, informed by the Puritan preachers' favorite image of the Christian life: the wayfaring pilgrim, seeking Heaven, directed by light. As the pilgrims "stray'd so farr . . . / In Golgotha" remind us, such wayfaring was full of perils for frail humanity. In the prologue to Book VII Milton repeats the word *wander* to relate these perils specifically to the poet whose journey passes dangerously near the abyss of satanic aspiration:

> Up led by thee [Urania]
> Into the Heav'n of Heav'ns I have presum'd
> An Earthly Guest, and drawn Empyreal Air,
> Thy temp'ring; with like safety guided down
> Return me to my Native Element:
> Lest from this flying Steed unrein'd, (as once
> *Bellerophon*, though from a lower Clime)
> Dismounted on th' *Aeleian* Field I fall
> Erroneous there to wander and forlorn.   (VII, 12–20)

Here Milton's poet wishes to avoid the erroneous wandering of a Bellerophon (a type of Satan) by means of celestial assistance.[16] He asks Urania that he be "led" and "guided" in his epic wayfaring. The request parallels Satan's plea for assistance during his wandering flight through Chaos:

> Ye Powers
> And Spirits of this nethermost Abyss
> *Chaos* and *ancient Night*, I come no Spy,
> With purpose to explore or to disturb

> The secrets of your Realm, but by constraint
> Wand'ring this darksome Desert, as my way
> Lies through your spacious Empire up to light,
> Alone, and without guide, half lost, I seek
> What rediest path leads where your gloomy bounds
> Confine with Heav'n; or if some other place
> From your Dominion won, th' Ethereal King
> Possesses lately, thither to arrive
> I travel this profound, direct my course.   (II, 968–80)

These passages, taken together, serve again to emphasize explicitly the difference between Satan's mission to falsify God's ways to man and Milton's task. In his attempt at ordered poetic creation Milton's epic voice directs its request to Heaven, the ultimate source of all creation; Satan, on the other hand, intending to destroy, to "Erect the Standard . . . of *ancient Night*" (II, 986) where God has built, applies for guidance to disorder itself.

It should by now be clear that in depicting Satan's effort to subvert God's providential ways Milton continually reminds us of the poet's own activity. In the description related by the epic voice, Satan's intention of beguiling mankind initially appears—not just to the devils—as an immense undertaking "Of hazard" (II, 453, 455). To the infernal host Satan's destructive journey is "th' adventure" (II, 474), Satan "their great adventurer" (X, 440); and when the Devil himself describes his "adventure hard" (X, 468) we are surely meant to recall that the poet's own voyaging in Hell and Heaven is "advent'rous" (I, 13). Yet here, so the poet hopes, the similarity ends. "Whom shall we find / Sufficient" (II, 403–04), Beëlzebub asks, and Satan answers, "this enterprise / None shall partake with me" (II, 465–66). The Devil deludes himself about his own self-sufficiency continually; in action he hopes to succeed through individual "strength," "art," and "evasion" (II, 410–11). The poet, by contrast, is weak ("fall'n on evil days / On evil days though fall'n, and evil tongues" [VII, 25–26]), artless ("my unpremeditated Verse" [IX, 24]), and completely open concerning the possibilities, dangers, and intentions of his song. While the poet aspires to "no middle flight," he is ultimately dependent for support on divine inspiration; the Devil, attempting "solitary flight" (II, 632), benightedly convinces himself that he is "self-begot, self-rais'd" (V, 860). In describing Mammon's proposal to found an empire in Hell after the pattern of Heaven the epic voice gives us the phrase which exactly describes the kind of comparison Milton is attempting between poet and devil: "emulation opposite" (II, 298).

V

The ways in which the poet of *Paradise Lost* "emulates" the devils may at first glance appear puzzling. Take, for example, a small detail from Book I—Satan's rousing of his troops from the burning lake:

> Yet to thir General's Voice they soon obey'd
> Innumerable. As when the potent Rod
> Of *Amram's* Son in *Egypt's* evil day
> Wav'd round the Coast, up call'd a pitchy cloud
> Of *Locusts*, warping on the Eastern Wind,
> That o'er the Realm of impious *Pharaoh* hung
> Like Night, and darken'd all the Land of *Nile*.   (I, 337–43)

In the standard Christian typology which controls most of *Paradise Lost*, Satan is placed at the head of a list of villains which prominently includes Pharaoh, not his opposite, Moses. But here it is primarily "*Amram's* Son" with whom Satan is compared—"That Shepherd, who first taught the chosen Seed, / In the Beginning how the Heav'ns and Earth / Rose out of Chaos" (I, 8–10)—that shepherd with whom Milton has compared the poet at the beginning of Book I. It should appear initially odd that Milton employs the figure of Moses to describe both the poet and the Devil. It should appear odd, that is, until it becomes clear that Milton is consistently laboring to place poet and devil in comparable contexts. For Milton the shape of good and evil could be paradoxically similar; both Moses *and* Pharaoh could, superficially, resemble Satan, as they do in this passage if we look at it closely. Not only does Satan, in summoning his fallen cohorts, appear as Moses calling forth the plague of locusts; he also resembles here his proper type, Pharaoh, in that the plague he calls forth, while it descends on a land of captivity, descends at the same time on his own land. The devils are both slaves and masters, both seraphic lords and locusts (a standard analogy);[17] they are their own Hell. This doubleness of reference with respect to Satan and the devils is picked up within a few lines and emphasized:

Till, as a signal giv'n, th' uplifted Spear
Of thir great Sultan waving to direct
Thir course, in even balance down they light.   (I, 347–49)

While the uplifted spear of Satan continues to resemble the "potent
Rod / Of *Amram's* Son," the appellation "great Sultan" simultaneously
identifies the Devil with Moses' enemy, Pharaoh. The complexity of
Milton's use of allusion here corresponds to his attitude toward the
infernal host. The devils are not simply monstrous. They incorporate
and reflect (and, of course, pervert) the world's magnificence, even,
in shadowing the chosen seed, its blessedness.

William Empson has provided some lively commentary on the
similarity between diabolical attitudes and the attitudes of men of
virtue as Milton saw them. Empson quotes Satan's address to the
rebel forces in Book V:

Thrones, Dominations, Princedoms, Virtues, Powers,
If these magnific Titles yet remain
Not merely titular. . . .

. . . .

Will ye submit your necks, and choose to bend
The supple knee? ye will not, if I trust
To know ye right, or if ye know yourselves
Natives and Sons of Heav'n possest before
By none, and if not equal all yet free,
Equally free; for Orders and Degrees
Jar not with liberty, but well consist.
Who can in reason then or right assume
Monarchy over such as live by right
His equals, if in power and splendor less,
In freedom equal? or can introduce
Law and Edict on us, who without law
Err not? Much less for this to be our Lord,
And look for adoration to th' abuse
Of those Imperial Titles which assert
Our being ordain'd to govern, not to serve? (V, 772–74, 787–802)

It is startling to come to this passage directly from a reading of
Milton's prose controversy. Not only does Satan argue, like the
republican Milton, from a position which couples native liberty with
an insistence on degree and discipline; in writing this speech Milton
could hardly have escaped hearing the accents of his own voice:

Is it such an unspeakable joy to serve, such felicity to wear a yoke, to clink our shackles looked on by pretended law of subjection, more intolerable and hopeless to be ever shaken off than those which are knocked on by illegal injury and violence?[18]

. . . .

I find both in our own and foreign story, that dukes, earls, and marquises were at first not hereditary, not empty and vain titles, but names of trust and office; and with the office ceasing, as induces me to be of opinion that every worthy man in parliament . . . might for the public good be thought a fit peer and judge of the king. . . .Whence doubtless our ancestors, who were not ignorant with what rights either nature or ancient constitution had endowed them . . . thought it no way illegal to depose and put to death their tyrannous kings.[19]

Empson's estimate of the effect of Satan's republicanism on Milton's contemporaries should make any fair-minded reader pause:

Surely the first readers must have found this intriguing; the only good writer who had defended the regicide was ascribing to the devils the sentiments still firmly held by himself and his proscribed party. They would not find the speech particularly dull and cooked-up, as Mr. Eliot did; and they would not be at all sure how far the author meant the devil's remarks to be wrong.[20]

Empson is not concerned so much with the inconsistency of Milton's politics (they are not inconsistent here) as with the unattractiveness of his theology. He quite clearly sees the trouble with Satan's rebellion, which is, of course, that Satan is not simply opposing a "King anointed" (V, 777), an absolute monarch "upheld by old repute, / Consent or custom" (I, 639–40); he is rebelling against God, the source of all degree, a non-authoritarian, immanent deity.[21] What is interesting about Empson's exposition is that he displays broadly what no reader should miss: the subject of *Paradise Lost* is rebellion, rebellion faulted by an author who himself was for his own and subsequent ages the prime spokesman for "the good old Cause." Typically, Milton did not attempt to disguise this seeming paradox. Schooled in rebellion, he openly granted the Devil the advantage of what he had learned in defense of liberty. I am not as sure as Empson that Milton's contemporaries would have been confused as to "how far the author meant the devil's remarks to be wrong," but I think it undeniable that the politics of Hell are an instance of Milton's concern to demonstrate, both to his readers and to himself, how close in fact he was to a satanic position.

Other instances of the poet's proximity to satanism occur in Book
II—particularly in the passage describing Hell's Olympian games:

> Others more milde,
> Retreated in a silent valley, sing
> With notes Angelical to many a Harp
> Thir own Heroic deeds and hapless Fall
> By doom of Battel; and complain that Fate
> Free Vertue should enthrall to Force or Chance.
>
> . . . .
>
> Others apart sat on a Hill retir'd,
> In thoughts more elevate, and reason'd high
> Of Providence, Foreknowledge, Will and Fate,
> Fixt Fate, Free will, Foreknowledge absolute,
> And found no end in wandring mazes lost.
> Of good and evil much they argu'd then,
> Of happiness and final misery.   (II, 546–51; 557–63)

Dennis Burden is the most recent critic to observe that "this intellectual and poetic Hell is something with which the poem is deeply
concerned."[22] The poets of Hell sing epic ("Thir own Heroic deeds")
and tragedy ("complain that Fate / Free Vertue should enthrall to
Force or Chance");[23] the infernal philosophers reason "high / Of
Providence, Foreknowledge, Will and Fate"; and the song of the poet-
philosopher, Milton, is crucially involved in all of this. While he
aspires to sing Christian heroism, "argument / Not less but more
Heroic than the wrath / Of stern Achilles" (IX, 13–15); while his
tragic notes (IX, 6) are tempered by Providence, not ruled by
Chance; and while his explanation of "Free will" and "Foreknowledge
absolute" is not, like the devils' speculation, cut off from God; still
his consignment of the pagan precedents for his song to Hell argues
for his willingness to expose how close his hoped-for light is to darkness. Burden's sense of Milton's mind is, I think, correct: Milton's
experience in controversy made him instinctively seize upon the
counterargument. He wished to encompass his adversary, not ignore
him, and his encompassment of Satan made him fully aware of the
seductions the satanic posture had for a mind such as his own.

VI

Just as Milton allows the devils to engage in something like his
own poetic activity, so too he is willing to lay bare the dangers latent

in the fundamental source of this activity, his inspiration. The essential message of Milton's epic invocations is, to repeat, that everything, for the poet, depends upon his muse. The muse is both his support and his justification. Such support, such justification is not commanded by the poet; rather it is sought by prayer, the efficacy of which must remain in doubt. Milton's final prologue in *Paradise Lost* ends with the fear that "all [may] be mine / Not Hers who brings it nightly to my Ear" (IX, 46–47). This tenuousness as to the sources and effectiveness of the poet's inspiration is often implicit in the poem's "argument," and one place in which such an implication can be found is in Milton's treatment of topography.

.Inspiration in *Paradise Lost* is almost inevitably associated with a physical setting. Milton's sense of place in this is traditional: he selects mountains and neighboring woods and waters as the sites of inspirational vision. His classical precedents for such settings, which he names outright or suggests by description, are the haunts of the Homeric muses: "th' *Aonian* Mount" (I, 15), "th' *Olympian* Hill" (VII, 3), and the Castalian Spring on Mount Parnassus (III, 28). Yet while he does not cease "to wander where the Muses haunt / Clear Spring, or shady Grove, or Sunny Hill" (III, 27–28), he wishes to soar above "th' *Olympian* Hill" and therefore prefers the biblical counterparts to these places of inspiration. He calls the Mosaic Muse "Of *Oreb*, or of *Sinai*" (I, 7) and the spirit dwelling in "*Sion* and th' flowery Brooks beneath" (III, 30).

"*Sion* Hill / . . . and *Siloa's* Brook" (I, 10–11) represent for Milton and his Christian contemporaries archetypal settings for the manifestations of God's grace. In Book III Satan views "Direct against" the magnificent stairs which Jacob will see ascending to Heaven

> A passage down to th' Earth, a passage wide,
> Wider by far than that of after-times
> Over Mount *Sion*, and, though that were large,
> Over the Promis'd land to God so dear,
> By which, to visit oft those happy Tribes,
> On high behests his Angels to and fro
> Pass'd frequent. (III, 528–34)

As these lines suggest, Sion Hill, on which David built his altar, Solomon, the Temple, constituted in Milton's traditional thought a focal point of communication between man and God. Milton's translation of Psalm lxxxiv puts it this way:

> 1 How lovely are thy dwellings fair!
>   O Lord of Hosts, how dear
>   The *pleasant* Tabernacles are
>   Where thou dost dwell so near!
>
>   . . . .
>
> 4 Happy who in thy house reside
>   Where thee they ever praise,
> 5 Happy whose strength in thee doth bide,
>   And in their hearts thy ways!
> 6 They pass through Baca's *thirsty* Vale,
>   *That dry and barren ground*
>   As through a fruitful wat'ry Dale
>   Where Springs and Show'rs abound.
> 7 They journey on from strength to strength
>   With joy and gladsome cheer,
>   *Till* all before *our* God *at length*
>   In Sion do appear.
>
> (1–4; 17–28; Milton's italics indicating his additions.)

This psalm displays the typological dimension of Sion, the first among God's "dwellings fair." In *Paradise Lost* we frequently see types of Sion Hill: Mount Sinai is clearly one; in respect to inspiration Milton seems to have considered Olympus and Parnassus pagan shadows of God's holy hill; Michael, descending from Heaven to instruct fallen Adam,

>   on a Hill made halt
>   A glorious Apparition, had not doubt
>   And carnal fear that day dimm'd *Adam's* eye.
>   Not that more glorious, when the Angels met
>   *Jacob* in *Mahanaim*, where he saw
>   The field Pavilion'd with his Guardians bright;
>   Nor that which on the flaming Mount appear'd
>   In *Dothan*, cover'd with a Camp of Fire
>   Against the Syrian King.   (XI, 210–18)

To administer Adam's vision of the future, the archangel ascends with our first father "a Hill / Of Paradise the highest" (XI, 377–78), and Raphael, sent by God to instruct unfallen man, alights upon "th' Eastern cliff of Paradise" (V, 275), itself a promontory from which our fallen parents must "wander down / Into a lower World" (XI, 282–83).

Paradise, of course, is not simply one of the fair dwelling places of God. It is also the site of Satan's fatal deception. Similarly the mount of speculation on which Adam learns from Michael "the sum / Of wisdom" (XII, 575–76) is compared by Milton to a place of Satanic temptation:

> Not higher that Hill nor wider looking round,
> Whereon for different cause the Tempter set
> Our second *Adam* in the Wilderness,
> To show him all the Earth's kingdoms and thir Glory.
>
> (XI, 381–84)

If we look back at the roll call of devils in Book I, it becomes clear that this double aspect—sacred and profane—consistently characterizes Milton's conception of the places of inspiration. In such settings men have heard infernal as well as heavenly voices:

> The chief were those who from the Pit of Hell
> Roaming to seek thir prey on earth, durst fix
> Thir Seats long after next the Seat of God,
> Thir Altars by his Altar, Gods ador'd
> Among the Nations round, and durst abide
> *Jehovah* thund'ring out of *Sion*, thron'd
> Between the Cherubim; yea, often plac'd
> Within his Sanctuary itself thir Shrines,
> Abominations; and with cursed things
> His holy Rites, and solemn Feasts profan'd
> And with thir darkness durst affront his light.   (I, 381–91)

From Sion Hill itself, a dwelling place of the poet's muse, Milton moves to its environs and in so doing continues to convey the impression that divine inspiration can be confused with abomination by the unwary:

> Nor content with such
> Audacious neighborhood, the wisest heart
> Of *Solomon* he [Moloch] led by fraud to build
> His Temple right against the Temple of God
> On that opprobrious Hill, and made his Grove
> The pleasant Valley of *Hinnom, Tophet* thence
> And black *Gehenna* call'd, the Type of Hell.   (I, 399–405)

Here "that opprobrious Hill," which appears twice more in the following fifty lines as "that Hill of scandal" (I, 416) and "th' offensive
Mountain" (I, 443), is, strictly considered, Mount Olivetti and
represents, like Sion Hill, a frequently profaned site of God's condescension to men. (The "Hill of scandal" could in one sense actually
be called Sion Hill since, for Milton, all Jerusalem's hills were the
hills of Sion.)[24] The settings Milton associates with his Christian muse
are further recalled in this passage by "the Type of Hell." A reader
familiar with the geography of the Holy Land would notice that this
same "pleasant Valley of *Hinnom*" is, as described by Jerome,
"watered by the fountains of Siloam" (*In Jeremiam*, vii, 31)—by the
"*Siloa's* Brook" of Milton's initial invocation.[25] There is no real need
to spend more time looking at a map of the Holy Land. My point is
this: in the catalogue of devils Milton locates the fallen angels, emerged
from Hell, in landmarks similar or identical to the places of inspiration
mentioned by the poet at the beginning of *Paradise Lost,* and this
placement suggests the dangers of hearkening to a voice speaking
out of Sion. The poet runs a risk. Even the classical muses whom he
refuses to ignore out of hand (III, 27–28; his debt to former epic is,
he realizes, immense) are here emphatically consigned to Hell (I,
508–21).

It is, of course, true that Milton did not invent the geography of
his infernal roll call, that his purpose was not simply to provide a
contrasting echo to the landmarks of his first invocation. Nevertheless
in his continued emphasis on the fact that the worship of God can be
twisted and perverted into the adoration of Satan, he could hardly
have missed the implication that the holiest of men must constantly
be wary lest, blinded, their devotions degenerate to fume. The Devil
was, in Milton's mind, constantly ready to deceive the proud man,
and in this passage describing Sion's descent to idolatry, Milton's
primary example of a man so deceived is Solomon "whose heart
though large / Beguil'd by fair Idolatresses, fell / To Idols foul"
(I, 444–46). I would like to suggest that the figure of Solomon had a
particular exemplary significance for Milton. Solomon's name was, of
course, associated with divine poetry, and Milton clearly saw himself
as writing in the tradition of Sion's singers. At the same time Solomon's
uxoriousness certainly represented for Milton—as both his life and
his great epic testify—a crucial source of human error. But most

significantly, I think, Solomon had built, under the guidance of God, the greatest religious monument of the Mosaic world, the Temple— a structure which, in medieval and Renaissance theories of artistic creation, constituted the ultimate model for all artistic endeavor.[26] Solomon, building after the divinely revealed fabric of God's world in "Measure, Number, and Weight" (Wisdom of Solomon xi, 21), had served for ages since Augustine as the archetypal example of the human artist working in imitation of God's creative act. Milton and his readers would not have missed the implication that, as a divinely inspired work, *Paradise Lost* was obviously comparable both to the Temple and to the world itself. Marvell, in his dedicatory poem, assumes these analogies to be commonplace:

> Thy verse created like thy theme sublime
> In Number, Weight, and Measure needs not Rime.

Milton seems to be underscoring this connection between Solomon and the poet when he emphasizes by repetition that it was Solomon's "heart though large," his "wisest heart" which was "led by fraud to build / His [Moloch's] Temple right against the Temple of God." The emphasis recalls the poet of the first invocation whose Muse prefers "Before all Temples th' upright heart and pure" (I, 18). While the poet is praying that his own heart will not be deceived, "led by fraud," that he will not build an idolatrous temple, the example of Solomon remains before him as a warning that those once confident of God's blessing can still fall from grace.

While the example of Solomon's idolatrous building casts a warning shadow over Milton's own "advent'rous" (I, 13) attempt at a poetic monument to God, it also serves as a mundane type of Hell's infernal arts—of Pandaemonium, "Built like a Temple" (I, 713) which far surpasses the world's "greatest Monuments of Fame, / And Strength and Art" (I, 695–96), and of the "Advent'rous work" (X, 255) undertaken by Sin and Death, the causeway from Hell, "a Monument / Of merit high" (X, 258–59) which, like all infernal creations, parodies God's own building in Chaos. In the case of Solomon's idolatrous works, we are dealing with an instance of human history reflecting the play of forces and events in the cosmos at large. Such a view of history was orthodox, and, as many have recognized, such a view is central to the unity of Milton's epic. In *Paradise Lost*

Milton repeatedly exploits cosmic polarity to project on a grand scale the predicament of man and the choices available to him: man should, as one of the multitude of God's servants, obey the Almighty and magnify Him through works; like a devil man may disobey God and fall, his life and works then becoming dross for the hellhound Death. The cosmic tensions of *Paradise Lost* reflect in particular the situation of the poet who, as a member of a fallen race, precariously attempts to counter the potential pride of his artistic aspirations with the humility of selfless intentions and dependence on God. Viewed with reference to the poet's own artistic predicament, the examples of negative creativity which extend from Pandaemonium to the song which ravishes Hell (II, 546–55) seem continually to suggest that the infernal aping of heavenly artistry is dangerously similar to Milton's effort in *Paradise Lost* to build, like Solomon, in imitation of the divine creative acts. My argument has been that the explicit comparison of poet and devil in *Paradise Lost* are intended by Milton to demonstrate an undeluded recognition of the satanic potential of his poetic act. Within the epic, ambition and presumption dog the poet in the form of satanic resemblances to his attempt to understand and give poetic shape to the pattern of God's ways with men. But, by the very act of objectifying such resemblances in infernal analogies to the poet's aspiring flight, Milton is able to keep differences clearly in sight. When in Hell the devils ask, "As he our darkness, cannot we his Light / Imitate when we please?" (II, 269–70), an analogy to the poet's own undertaking is clearly in view. At the same time, however, the difference between poet and devil is here equally plain. The poet cannot imitate God's light *at will*. Like the earthly and heavenly opposites of sin—the prophets, the angels, the Son—Milton labors to express God's will, not his own. He rejects satanic self-sufficiency; he invokes the muse.

Boston University

NOTES

1. All citations of Milton's poems refer to *John Milton: Complete Poems and Major Prose,* ed. Merritt Y. Hughes (New York, 1957).

2. Prominent voices here are C. S. Lewis, *A Preface to "Paradise Lost"* (London, 1942) and Douglas Bush, *"Paradise Lost" in Our Time* (New York, 1948).

3. William Blake, *The Marriage of Heaven and Hell* in *The Complete Writings of William Blake*, ed. Geoffrey Keynes (Oxford, 1966), p. 150.

4. See in particular Anne Davidson Ferry, *Milton's Epic Voice* (Cambridge, Mass., 1963); Isabel Gamble MacCaffrey, *"Paradise Lost" as "Myth"* (Cambridge, Mass., 1959); Jackson I. Cope, *The Metaphoric Structure of "Paradise Lost"* (Baltimore, 1962); Joseph H. Summers, *The Muse's Method* (Cambridge, Mass., 1962); Louis L. Martz, *The Paradise Within* (New Haven, 1964); Dennis H. Burden, *The Logical Epic* (Cambridge, Mass., 1967).

5. E. M. W. Tillyard, *Milton* (London, 1930).

6. See Stanley Eugene Fish, *Surprised by Sin* (New York, 1967) and Jon S. Lawry, *The Shadow of Heaven* (Ithaca, N. Y., 1968).

7. Denis Saurat, *Milton, Man and Thinker* (New York, 1925), p. 220.

8. The "things unattempted yet" topos has a long history, for a summary of which see Ernst Robert Curtius, *European Literature and the Latin Middle Ages*, trans. Willard Trask (New York, 1953), pp. 85–86. Milton was surely aware of this tradition, as he was also undoubtedly aware that his most recent significant predecessor in the use of this topos was Ariosto. See Hughes' note to I, 16 and IX, 29–31 of *Paradise Lost*.

9. Harington's translation.

10. For a discussion of satanic artistry see pp. 79–80.

11. This also imitates the pattern of paradox inherent in the fortunate fall. Milton continually shows us that the shape of good can be imitated by evil.

12. Note Sin's description of Hell: "With terrors and with clamors compasst round" (II, 862). In addition to being "In darkness, and with dangers compast round" (VII, 27), the poet is plagued by "the barbarous dissonance / Of Bacchus and his Revellers" (VII, 32–33).

13. *"Paradise Lost" as "Myth,"* p. 190.

14. *Surprised by Sin,* pp. 130–41.

15. For a similar comment on these lines see Ferry, *Milton's Epic Voice,* p. 41.

16. See J. B. Broadbent, *Some Graver Subject: An Essay on "Paradise Lost"* (London, 1960), p. 235: ". . . but why Bellerophon? It can only be because the invocation intrudes into the poem's structure the poet's anxiety about the presumptuous heroics of Book VI and the cosmography of Books VII and VIII. Bellerophon insures Milton against the sin of Adam and Eve, curiosity." See also Summers, *The Muse's Method,* p. 137: "The poet contrasts his own presumption in composing what we have read thus far with Satan's; but he faces the possibility that he may fall, to wander in madness like Bellerophon, if divine wisdom does not attend him in his descent to our 'Native Element.'"

17. The analogy is based on Revelation ix, 1–6.

18. *The Tenure of Kings and Magistrates* (Columbia edition, V, 25).

19. *The Ready and Easy Way to Establish a Free Commonwealth* (Columbia edition, VI, 136).

20. William Empson, *Milton's God* (London, 1961), p. 82.

21. Ibid., p. 75.

22. *The Logical Epic,* p. 58.

23. See Howard Schultz, *Milton and Forbidden Knowledge* (New York, 1955), p. 90. In a discussion of this passage similar to Burden's, Schultz assures

us that Milton is referring to tragedy here by comparing lines 550–51 with *Paradise Regained* IV, 261–66.

24. See, for evidence of this, Milton's version of Psalm lxxxvii.

25. See Allan H. Gilbert, *A Geographical Dictionary of Milton* (New Haven, 1919), p. 145. Gilbert believes that Milton's description of the valley as "pleasant" depends on Jerome.

26. For discussions of the relevance of Solomon's Temple to medieval and Renaissance theories of art see, in addition to Curtius, Rudolf Wittkower, *Architectural Principles in the Age of Humanism* (London, 1952) and Otto von Simson, *The Gothic Cathedral* (New York, 1954).

STEPHEN M. FALLON

Milton's Sin and Death:
The Ontology of Allegory in Paradise Lost

WITH characteristic bluntness, Samuel Johnson wrote that "Milton's allegory of Sin and Death is undoubtedly faulty," largely because it "shock[s] the mind by ascribing effects to nonentity."[1] Johnson's reservations have been shared by many before and since: what are these insubstantial beings, these abstractions, doing in *Paradise Lost*? why this extended allegory in an otherwise non-allegorical epic? The diametric opposition between recent discussions of Milton's allegory by Philip J. Gallagher and Maureen Quilligan demonstrates the persistence of these questions. Gallagher posits Milton's belief in the literal truth of his narrative and argues that the allegory does not violate ontological consistency for the simple reason that Sin and Death are "consistently real (i.e., physical and historical) throughout Milton's major epic, their allegorical onomastics notwithstanding."[2] Conversely, Quilligan asserts that in Sin and Death Satan "has authored something less than pure *res*. He can't do the real thing."[3] The allegorical episodes, Quilligan argues, are self-consciously fictional "brackets" with which Milton simultaneously reminds the reader of the fictionality of the entire epic and emphasizes the "intimate truth" of the bracketed material. I will argue that a proper perspective lies between these opposed ones, or rather that it contains elements of each. Gallagher is right to emphasize the literal truth of Milton's narrative, and Quilligan the unreality of Sin and Death. These apparently contradictory positions can be reconciled with an understanding of the poet's ontology. In what follows I will

1. Johnson, *Lives of the English Poets* (1783), I, 258. For a survey of eighteenth-century objections to Milton's allegory, see Joseph H. Summers, *The Muse's Method: An Introduction to "Paradise Lost"* (Cambridge, Mass., 1962), pp. 32–39.

2. Gallagher, "'Real or Allegoric': The Ontology of Sin and Death in *Paradise Lost*," *English Literary Renaissance*, 6 (1976), 317.

3. Quilligan, *Milton's Spenser: The Politics of Reading* (Ithaca, N.Y., 1983), p. 126.

demonstrate that the nature of Sin and Death is consistent with Milton's Augustinian ontology of evil, and that Milton naturally turns to the "lesser reality" of allegory to present characters who are the negation rather than the expression of substance.[4]

I: Milton's Augustinian Ontology of Evil

St. Augustine denies ontological status to evil, insisting that evil is not an entity but privation (*privatio*) of entity. All created things are essentially good, but free creatures can turn away from their own perfections and from God. Evil lies in this free turning, not in the creature's substance. Since evil is the privation, or corruption, of a good nature, it requires the good for its derivative existence. In the *City of God* (XIV, xi) Augustine writes that "evil in truth cannot exist without good, since the natures in which evil exists, in so far as they are natures, are certainly good," and in the *Confessions* (III, vii) that "evil is nothing except the privation of good until that good is gone altogether."[5] What remains after the "good is gone altogether"? The question is the key to the ontology of Sin and Death; the answer is, in a word, nothing: "Thus if things are deprived of all good, they become altogether nothing: accordingly, as long as they are, they are good. Therefore, *wheresoever things are, they are good, and evil,* the origin of which I was seeking, *is not a substance,* because if it were a substance, it would be good" (*Confessions* VII, xii; my italics). In metaphysical, as opposed to moral, terms, evil is nonentity, the negation rather than the expression of being. In examining Milton's allegory, we will have reason to remember Augustine's formula in the *City of God* (XII, iii): "solely good things can somewhere exist, solely evil things nowhere."[6]

Given his *a priori* belief in free will, Milton would naturally be attracted to an argument that finds the origin of evil in the creature's choice. Furthermore, Milton shares the two-edged imperative that leads

4. That Milton's ontology of evil is Augustinian is not a new point. C. S. Lewis noted the similarity in *A Preface to "Paradise Lost"* (1942; rpt. London, 1961), pp. 66–72; he has been seconded recently by Peter A. Fiore's *Milton and Augustine: Patterns of Augustinian Thought in "Paradise Lost"* (University Park, Pa., 1981), pp. 12–22. Because the reader's familiarity with the shared ontology is essential for my argument concerning the allegory, I outline the evidence briefly at the outset.

5. Here and elsewhere, I translate from the Latin text of the Bibliothèque Augustinienne's *Oeuvres de Saint Augustin;* the passage from *De Civitate Dei* appear in vol. XXXV (Bruges, 1959) and the passages from the *Confessions* in vols. XIII and XIV (Bruges, 1962). References to these works will be made by book and chapter number in the text.

6. The transplantation of this concept from Augustine's Neoplatonic theology to Aquinas' Aristotelean one indicates its vitality in the Christian tradition; for Aquinas on evil as privation see the *Summa Theologica* I, Q.48, art. 1.

Augustine to his ontology of evil: the fear of Manicheism on the one hand and of the imputation of evil to God on the other.[7] For these reasons it is not surprising to hear Milton echo Augustine in his own *Christian Doctrine:* "Nothing is neither good nor any kind of thing at all. All entity is good: nonentity, not good (*Ens omne est bonum, non ens non bonum*)."[8] The inescapable converse, true for Milton as for Augustine, is that evil has no ontological status; it is not an entity but the privation of entity.[9] This much can be inferred from the collation of the just-cited passage with one from the *Art of Logic: "habitus . . . est ens, privatio non ens"* (*Works* XI, 148). *"Habitus"* Milton defines as that in a subject "to which the affirmative by its very nature belongs" (*CP* VIII, 267). *"Habitus,"* being *"ens,"* is therefore *"bonum"; "privatio,"* being *"non ens,"* is therefore *"non bonum."*[10] Metaphysical evil for both Augustine and Milton is the loss or privation of entity; it is the measure of the negative distance between created perfection and willed corruption.

Augustine and Milton distinguish between metaphysical and moral evil, which, as I hope to demonstrate, are embodied in Sin and Death and Satan respectively. Metaphysical evil is the negative distance between created perfection and willed corruption; moral evil is the diseased will of the corrupt creature. But for Augustine and Milton, even moral evil lies ultimately not in action, but in deficiency or privation. Augustine writes in the *City of God* (XII,vii): "Let no one seek, therefore, for an

7. And if James Holly Hanford's reading of the Commonplace Book is correct, then Milton consulted the *City of God* in 1657 or 1658, important years for both the *Christian Doctrine* and *Paradise Lost;* see "The Chronology of Milton's Private Studies," in *John Milton: Poet and Humanist* (Cleveland, O., 1966), p. 101. Unlike Milton, Augustine considered the privative nature of evil to be inseparable from *creatio ex nihilo* (*City of God* XIV, xiii); Milton violates Augustine's rule and separates these doctrines.

8. Bk. I, Ch. vii: this passage can be found in the *Complete Prose Works of John Milton,* ed. Don M. Wolfe and others (8 vols.; New Haven, 1953–1982), VI, 310, and in *The Works of John Milton,* ed. Frank A. Patterson and others (18 vols.; New York, 1930–1938), XV, 26. Here and elsewhere I use the Yale edition (cited in the text as *CP*) for translations of Milton's prose, and the Columbia edition (cited in the text as *Works*) for the Latin original.

9. For the law of reciprocity assuring this conclusion, see the *Art of Logic* (*CP* VIII, 297, 312, and 315).

10. Milton seems to contradict the Augustinian position of the *Christian Doctrine* when he writes in the *Art of Logic* that "I would not also call sin a privation" (*CP* VIII, 268). But in his denial that sin is privation, Milton refers to a morally evil action and not to metaphysical evil. Sumner's translation makes this more clear than Carey's: "I should not say that a sin is a privation" (*Works* XI, 149). That Sumner's "a sin" (clearly referring to a morally evil action) is a better translation than Carey's "sin" is discernible from the clause that follows: "because it this or that is a sin it is not a privation" (*CP* VIII, 268). It is the 'thisness' or thatness' of a sin that makes it not a privation. In *Christian Doctrine* Milton describes the *action* of a sin not as sin itself but as "the essence or element in which [sin] exists" (*CP* VI, 391).

efficient cause of the evil will; for it is not efficient but deficient, because the will is not a doing of something, but a failing to do something." Milton parallels this idea in his discussion of "actual sin" or "the evil action or crime itself" in the *Christian Doctrine*: "It is called 'actual' not because sin is really an action, on the contrary it is a deficiency (*privatio*), but because it usually exists in some action. For every action is intrinsically good; it is only its misdirection or deviation from the set course of law which can properly be called evil. So action is not the material out of which sin is made, but only the ὑποκείμενον, the essence or element in which it exists" (*CP* VI, 391). Thus the gulf of nonentity can be seen yawning even behind moral evil.

In the Augustinian conception of evil as the privation of entity lies the ontological rationale for Milton's use of allegory. If Sin and Death embody metaphysical evil, then their "lesser reality" as allegorical characters fits Milton's ontology of evil. The embodiment is illusory and paradoxical, for metaphysical evil does not exist. But to avoid begging the question of the reality of allegorical characters, I turn now to the nature of allegory and its changing status in the seventeenth century.

II: Allegory and Ontology

Coleridge defines personification allegory, the type of allegory with which this essay is concerned, as the use of "one set of agents and images" to represent "moral qualities or conceptions of the mind that are not in themselves objects of the senses."[11] By the late seventeenth century this important literary mode had, after a late flowering in the work of Spenser and his literary heirs, ceased to answer to the ontological assumptions of the educated audience, and had retreated into the strictly circumscribed refuge of Bunyanesque Baptist literature. The reasons for allegory's decline are twofold and interrelated. First, by its nature personification allegory involves characters of a different order of reality from those of mimetic narrative. Second, by the light of the seventeenth century's new, and increasingly empirical, standards of truth, which depend on the gradual displacement of realism by nominalism, the different reality of abstractions is demoted to a lesser reality and in some minds to non-reality.

11. *Miscellaneous Criticism*, ed. T. M. Raysor (London, 1936), p. 30. The arguments of this essay are not meant to apply to what Angus Fletcher calls the allegory of "topical allusion," in which poets write of contemporaries under the veil of invented names; see *Allegory: The Theory of a Symbolic Mode* (Ithaca, N.Y., 1964), p. 26.

Allegory does not represent real human beings; rather, it personifies the qualities, or abstractions, that inhere in human beings. Angus Fletcher's description of allegorical characters as "daemonic agents" illuminates their relationship to substantial existence. Fletcher suggests a similarity between allegorical agents and the daemons, or intermediate spirits, of Roman religion.[12] These daemons, whose name derives from the term "to divide," share control of men, each directing one function or part of the body.[13] In the same way allegorical agents represent parts of a divided whole. An allegorical character's excessive singleness of purpose parallels the phenomenon of daemonic possession. If an allegorical character were to appear in our midst, we would be struck by his "absolutely one-track mind"; we would perceive that "he did not control his own destiny, but appeared to be controlled by some foreign force, something outside the sphere of his own ego."[14] This singleness of purpose results from a splintering of personality; an aspect is separated from the whole and embodied. Leaving aside the question of psychotic possession, this description accounts for the existence of mimetic and allegorical characters on separate ontological planes.

It is important to note with Fletcher that elaborate physical description does not change an allegorical character into a mimetic one. Allegorical agents reveal by their actions not internal psychologies but the abstractions (often as complex as psychologies in sophisticated allegory) that lie behind them. However much surface detail is added to an allegorical character like Guyon, he does not become a mimetic one like Jude Fawley. Fletcher demonstrates that the "naturalist detail" of some allegory does not serve a "journalistic function"; instead it points rhetorically to the daemonic attributes of the character.[15]

While medieval allegorists recognized the difference between the ontological status of persons represented by mimetic characters and the abstractions represented by allegorical characters, they nevertheless saw the latter as essentially real. Owen Barfield describes the assumptions behind allegory: "For us, the characters in an allegory are 'personified abstractions,' but for the man of the Middle Ages Grammar or Rhetoric, Mercy or 'Daunger,' were real to begin with, simply *because* they were

12. Fletcher, pp. 43–46; for another discussion of the affinity between allegory and Roman religion, see C. S. Lewis, *The Allegory of Love: A Study in Medieval Tradition* (London, 1936), pp. 48–66.

13. Fletcher, pp. 59–60.

14. Fletcher, pp. 40–41.

15. Fletcher, pp. 198–99.

'names.'"[16] Barfield here invokes the now familiar connection between allegory and Platonist-Aristotelean realism, which, contrary to modern realism, posits that what we call "abstractions" have real existence.[17] The "ideas" or "universals" of this classical/medieval realism lie behind allegorical agents. Not surprisingly, the great age of allegory was a realist age.[18]

Some defining of terms is in order here, since I will be speaking of allegorical agents as representing simultaneously universals and accidents, and some readers might be accustomed to thinking of the former as general and essential and the latter as particular and inessential. In Platonic and Aristotelean terms, accident is a variety of predicate, along with attribute. Any concrete subject has predicates or qualities, which if essential are attributes and if inessential accidents. If one were to say that Solomon was a just rational animal and king, one would be naming accidents (just and king) and attributes (rational animal) of the man Solomon. Justice is a universal or idea, but since it is not necessarily predicated of any particular man (as are rationality and animality), it is accidental in whomever it exists. For Plato, the predicates are the unchanging universals, since one can change a subject by changing its predicates, but one cannot change a predicate by changing its subject: thus an unjust John Doe is different from a just John Doe, but the justice of a just Richard Roe is the same justice. The essential rationality and the accidental justice of any particular man participate in the ideas of rationality and justice. Since subjects (the particular) are mutable and predicates (the universals) immutable, Plato granted ontological status to the latter but not to the former. Aristotle diverged from Plato by granting ontological status to concrete subject as well as to immaterial predicate.[19]

16. *Saving the Appearances: A Study in Idolatry* (New York. [1965]), p. 86.

17. See, e.g., Thomas P. Roche, Jr., *The Kindly Flame: A Study of the Third and Fourth Books of Spenser's "Faerie Queene"* (Princeton, N.J., 1964), p. 4, and Isabel MacCaffrey, *"Paradise Lost" as Myth* (Cambridge, Mass., 1959), p. 82.

18. Despite the perennial challenge to realism from nominalism, represented most visibly by Roscellinus and William of Ockham, nominalism remained a minority reaction to realist orthodoxy. Of course medieval realism was far from univocal, as Meyrick Carré points out in his *Realists and Nominalists* (London, 1946), an excellent introduction to this topic. It accommodated a variety of positions from Augustine's Neoplatonic extreme realism, through Abelard's and Aquinas' moderate realism, to the very attenuated realism sometimes advanced by the usually nominalist Ockham.

19. This account is necessarily simplified, especially for Aristotle, who divides predicate into four types (genus, definition, property, and accident), but the necessary simplification does not distort the point in question, since the first three types are divisions of attribute. For Plato on

Milton's understanding of accident accords with the model presented here. In the *Art of Logic* he uses the terms "subject" and "adjunct" (*subjectum* and *adjunctum*) for subject and accident, and cites Aristotle as his principal authority.[20] Milton gives as examples of adjuncts or accidents such universals as health, strength, beauty, and honor, along with more external accidents such as riches and clothing (*CP* VIII, 243). For Milton, as for Plato and Aristotle, accidents are inessential only in the strict logical and metaphysical senses (as in the case of Solomon's justice). Milton explicitly denies that they are necessarily negligible or "fortuitous" qualities: "Whatever happens extrinsically to any subject, whether fortuitously or not, is that subject's adjunct. What are called the goods and evils of the spirit, of the body and of the whole man are adjuncts of the spirit, the body and the man" (*CP* VIII, 245).

Allegory's vitality owed much to the realist belief in the actual existence of universals outlined above. But the Middle Ages witnessed a progressive moderation of extreme Platonist realism, precipitated by the criticism of the nominalist minority, who denied the existence of universals. The universals, from their privileged status in Plato's realm of Ideas (universals exist as separate entities), moved under the influence of Aristotle into things (universals exist, but only within things), and finally retreated into mind (universals exist as modes of thought). One can chart the course of medieval realism by contrasting its early exponent, Augustine, its greatest poet, Dante, and its Renaissance heir, René Descartes. While Augustine places the universals in the mind of the biblical God, he otherwise remains entirely consistent with Plato in granting them ontological priority over the concrete subjects in which they manifest themselves. The position given to the universals by Dante is less exalted, as we see in a passage from the *Vita Nuova* (xxv) of particular significance to my argument in its connection of metaphysics and allegory: "It may be that someone worthy of having every doubt cleared up could be puzzled at my speaking of Love as if it were a thing in itself, as if it were not only an intellectual substance, but also a bodily substance. This is patently false, for Love *does not exist in itself as a substance, but is an accident in a substance*."[21] The extreme realists Plato and Augustine would have said that accidents are universals that exist in themselves as well as in

accident, see the *Sophist* 247b. ff., and the *Republic* 5.454; for Aristotle on accident, see *Topics* I, ch. iv-v, and *Metaphysics* VI, ch. iii.

20. *CP* VIII, 242–249, and *Work*, XI, 79–99; the citation of Aristotle appears in *CP* VIII, 245.

21. *Dante's Vita Nuova*, tr. Mark Musa (Bloomington, Ind., 1973), p. 54.

particular subjects, and moreover that this former existence is more real than the existence of the subjects. In his Third Meditation, employing the scholastic terminology for which Hobbes criticized him, Descartes goes further in reducing the ontological pretensions of the universals: "Undoubtedly, the ideas which represent substances to me amount to something more and, so to speak, contain within themselves more objective reality (i.e. participate by representation in a higher degree of being or perfection) than the ideas which merely represent modes or accidents."[22] Descartes makes explicit what seems implicit in Dante. Both of these moderate realists recognize the reality of accidents, which as universals are the stuff of allegorical characterization, but Dante perhaps and Descartes surely assign to them a reality derivative from and lesser than that which they acknowledge in substance, whether corporeal or intellectual. For Augustine, the extreme realist, universals have a greater reality than things, for Dante at least a different reality, and for Descartes a lesser reality.

The implications for allegory of this philosophical trend are ominous. If the universals or accidents lose ontological weight, then so do the allegorical agents who represent them. Paraphrasing Descartes, we may say that *characters* representing substantial beings (i.e., mimetic characters) contain more reality than those representing accidents in substances. It is in this sense that I speak of the "lesser reality" of allegorical characters in Milton's century. The term reflects new seventeenth-century assumptions about the nature of reality; it is not meant to account in a reductive manner for the experience of allegory in the more thoroughly realist Middle Ages.

Even greater damage to the ontological claims of allegory came at the hands of the nominalists. In his "Objections" to the *Meditations,* the arch-nominalist Hobbes calls Descartes to task for the passage quoted above: "M. Descartes should consider afresh what 'more reality' means. Does reality admit of more and less?"[23] For the nominalist there are only things, and the layering of reality upon which allegory depends is eliminated. We can underestimate the strength of seventeenth-century nominalism by reviewing the chorus of vituperative abuse heaped on the "monster of Malmesbury" by his contemporaries.[24] But the depth of

22. *The Philosophical Writings of Descartes,* tr. John Cottingham, Robert Stoothoff, and Dugald Murdoch (Cambridge, Eng., 1984–1985), II, 28. The passage in parentheses was added in the 1647 French translation approved by Descartes; it may or may not be from his hand.

23. *The Philosophical Writings of Descartes,* II, 71.

24. For the best exposition and analysis of the replies to Hobbes, see Samuel I. Mintz, *The*

passionate response is itself implicit evidence of the perception of a real threat on the part of the realists. A more direct if still implicit indication of the strength of nominalism is the explosive growth of the new science, the empiricist epistemology of which is based on nominalist ontology. By denying the existence of universals, nominalism led to the method of arriving at general principles by observation of particular sensible things.

While the Cambridge Platonists did advocate an extreme realism, theirs was a rearguard action. The mainstream debate in mid-seventeenth-century England was between moderate realism and nominalism; the former lessened the reality of universals and the latter rejected universals altogether. We would expect to find then a decline in the status of the literary mode that depends on universals. And, indeed, there is a reaction against allegory in the seventeenth century.[25] Despite the interest in allegory evident in his *Wisdom of the Ancients,* Sir Francis Bacon reveals some reservations in the second book of the *Advancement of Learning.* Allegory, or "Allusive or Parabollical narration," was formerly necessary "to express any point of reason which was more sharp or subtile than the vulgar in that manner; because men in those times wanted both variety of examples and subtilty of conceit."[26] In Bacon's eyes this type of allegory at least springs from the limitations, since outgrown, of artist and audience, and not from the nature of unseen reality. He retains the old rhetorical justification for allegory, but without the cosmological and metaphysical sanctions that made it vital.

Appropriately, we find evidence of the decline of allegory in the seventeenth century's response to the giant of allegory on its threshold, Edmund Spenser. It is tempting to speculate that his choice of a self-consciously archaic diction finds a complement in a choice of a self-consciously archaic mode. In any event, the seventeenth century admires Spenser's descriptive and narrative powers but deprecates his allegory. In his *Discourse upon Gondibert* (1650) William D'Avenant compares the allegory first to feverish dreams and then to painted scenery that detracts from solid dramatic action. He laments that Spenser's great talents were wasted on allegory instead of "upon matter of a more natural, and

Hunting of Leviathan: Seventeenth-Century Reactions to the Materialism and Moral Philosophy of Thomas Hobbes (Cambridge, Eng., 1969).

25. For a perspective on the decline of allegory after Spenser different from the one I offer here, see the chapter on "The End of Allegory" in Michael Murrin's _The Veil of Allegory: Some Notes Toward a Theory of Allegorical Rhetoric in the English Renaissance_ (Chicago, Ill., 1969), pp. 167–98.

26. _Advancement of Learning,_ in vol. III of the _Works,_ ed. James Spedding, Robert Leslie Ellis, and Douglas Denon Heath (New York, 1968), p. 344.

therefore of a more usefull kind."[27] According to Thomas Rymer in 1674, Spenser was misled by the Italian Ariosto; he remarks that "It was the vice of those Times to affect superstitiously the *Allegory*; and nothing would then be current without a mystical meaning. We must blame the Italians for debauching great *Spencer's* judgement."[28] In *An Account of the Greatest English Poets* (1694), Joseph Addison praises Spenser's descriptions but charges that the poet's story "amus'd a Barb'rous Age; / . . . uncultivate and rude":

> But now the Mystick Tale, that pleas'd of Yore,
> Can charm an understanding Age no more;
> The long-spun Allegories fulsom grow,
> While the dull Moral lyes too plain below.[29]

The dichtomy between rude and cultured ages echoes Bacon's; the fact that a mere one hundred years separate Spenser and Addison underlines the seventeenth century's growing confidence in its progress on the road to the possession of a new truth.

Fundamental changes are usually gradual, and allegories were written in the seventeenth century. One main current flows from the influence of Spenser, but it dies out with the generation of such Spenserians as the Fletchers and Henry More. A later current is mechanick Puritan allegory, dominated by Bunyan.[30] Yet however sophisticated the moral psychology of these allegories, they are written by and for a philosophically illiterate segment of the population. These allegories ignore questions of ontology confronted by Milton (as I hope to demonstrate) in his allegory of Sin and Death.

Moreover, evidence of the instability of allegory can be gathered even from allegorists themselves. With surprising frequency in the seventeenth century, poets mix allegorical and mimetic characterization and narration. This error, with which Johnson charged Milton, may almost be called conventional. Giles Fletcher's *Christs Victorie and Triumph* (1610)

27. Excerpted in *Spenser: The Critical Heritage*, ed. R. M. Cummings (New York, 1971), p. 188.
28. Cummings, p. 207.
29. Cummings, p. 224.
30. And of course allegories of sorts appear after the seventeenth century. Pope's *Dunciad*, for example, might be regarded as a personifying allegory, but the one extended personification is Dullness, the offspring of the liminal nothingness of Chaos (1.10–16; see below, Section V). Dullness is associated with the triumph of word over substance or meaning (4.149–60), a relationship made possible by the decline of realism. Pope's other characters are not abstractions, but flesh and blood contemporaries. Art, Philosophy, Physic, Metaphysic, Mystery, Mathematics, Religion, and Morality appear briefly at the end of the poem, but only as shorthand for action which has taken place on another plane throughout the poem.

is a curious mixture of the life of Christ and clashes of abstractions in the tradition of Prudentius. Time, Truth, Justice, and Mercy play active roles in Thomas Peyton's fascinatingly paranoid *The Glasse of Time* (1620 and 1623). The uncertainty as to whether Mercy and Justice are aspects of God, independent entities in a realist universe, personal created angelic beings, or mere poetic abstractions exemplifies Peyton's confusion or carelessness about ontology. Richard Crashaw faithfully translates Marino's addition of Cruelty to the three Furies in his *Sospetto d'Herode* (1646). Joseph Beaumont presents Lust as the tutor of Circe in the first canto of *Psyche* (1648). Two final examples are of special interest. In the midst of its versification of the Bible and treatises on the branches of knowledge, Sylvester's du Bartas, a favorite book of the young Milton, contains two allegorical excursions, one of Sleep and another on the Palace of Envy.[31] An allegorical character finds its way even into the *Davideis* of Abraham Cowley (1638–?, pub. 1656), later the poet of the Royal Society. These lines form a small part of Cowley's description of Envy:

> Her garments were deep stain'd in human gore,
> And torn by her own hands, in which she bore
> A knotted whip, and bowl, that to the brim
> Did with green gall, and juice of wormwood swim.[32]

Envy seems to belong more to Spenserian allegory than to Cowley's mimetic epic. And she is not one of those characters of whom Johnson approves, who are "suffered only to do their natural office and retire";[33] she is given "real employment" by Cowley.

These examples reveal that Milton's mixture of allegorical and non-allegorical characters, even if not defensible on grounds of the poet's ontology, would have ample contemporary precedent. More important, they reveal an uncertainty about ontology among the poets. Medieval allegorists, as well as Spenser and Bunyan, are confident in the reality of the abstractions they personify, and are aware that that reality is different in kind from material reality. The mixing of categories in much of seventeenth-century allegory betrays an uncertainty over the realm of reality occupied by accidents-in-substances. A few committed philosophical realists continued to write allegories (e.g., Henry More and his

---

31. *Divine Weekes*, II,iii,1 and II,iii,3; the passages referred to are faithful translations of du Bartas, and not Sylvester's interpolations.
32. *Poems*, ed. A. R. Waller (Cambridge, Eng., 1905), p. 246.
33. Johnson, I, 257.

Platonick Song of the Soul, 1646), but the intellectual environment was no longer as receptive to allegory, which in an earlier age had been, in Lewis' phrase, the "dominant form."

III: Milton and Allegory

Putting aside for the moment the large and difficult question of Milton's attitude toward the philosophical trends leading to the decline of allegory, one can infer his attitude toward the use of allegory from his poetic practice. We all know that Milton told Dryden that "Spenser was his original," yet he does not follow Spenser in choosing the allegorical mode for his epic.[34] Allegorical characters do appear in his earlier poetry, but sparingly even there. "Tragaedia," "Elegeia," and "Fama" have circumscribed roles in the first, second, and fourth elegies respectively. Milton wonders in "Fair Infant" if his niece was truly "sweet smiling Youth" or "sage white-robed Truth."[35] A Vergilian mob of personifications crowds the gates of hell in "In Quintum Novembris" (lines 139–55); Milton, however, does not place a similar group at the gates of his epic hell (Vergil's group is de-allegorized and dispersed throughout Books 11 and 12). Nature, Peace, Truth, and Justice appear as mutes in the "Nativity Ode." Even the allegory-charged *Masque* does not rely on personifying allegory, although the Elder Brother does discourse on the habits of Wisdom, Solitude, and Contemplation (lines 375–81).

Of course the best implicit evidence for Milton's increasing dissatisfaction with the allegorical mode, or at least with the mixing of allegorical and mimetic characters, is the metamorphosis of his early plans for his masterpiece. Milton winnows out allegorical personifications in the successive drafts for a drama on the fall in the Trinity manuscript (*CP* VIII, 554–60). The original draft projects Heavenly Love, Conscience, Death, Faith, Hope and Charity as speaking characters, and Labor, Sicknesse, Discontent, Ignorance "with others" as mutes. The second draft adds Justice, Mercie, and Wisdome to the speakers, and transforms Fear and Death into mutes. In both drafts the

34. In a very recent essay, "From Allegory to Dialectic: Imagining Error in Spenser and Milton," *PMLA*, 101 (1986), 9–23, Gordon Teskey addresses this curious fact; he rehearses the distinction between epic and romance, and argues that Milton disdains the oblique approach to truth that is the hallmark of allegory. Surprisingly, Teskey does not address the allegory of Sin and Death; it will be clear to the reader that I will disagree with his assertion that there is in *Paradise Lost* "no indication that we should read [the allegorical tropes] in any sense but the literal" (p. 19).

35. *John Milton: Complete Poems and Major Prose,* ed. Merritt Y. Hughes (New York, 1957), p. 36. All subsequent references to the poetry are from this edition.

personifications share the stage with men and angels. In a more articulated third draft, now titled "Paradise Lost," Milton specifies that Justice, Mercie, and Wisdome will debate "what should become of man if he fall," and that Faith, Hope, and Charity will "comfort him and instruct him" (*CP* VIII, 554–55). In the still more elaborate fourth draft, headed "Adam unparadiz'd," almost all of the personifications disappear. The debate of Justice, Mercie, and Wisdome is gone; instead, Justice and Mercy speak with Adam after his fall (the debate of Justice and Mercy is subsumed in the dialogue of Father and Son in the eventual fulfillment of these early drafts).

In an essay appearing with the Trinity drafts James Holly Hanford argues that the personifications disappear because "the whole design has moved somewhat away from the Italianate conception guiding the earlier drafts."[36] There is an element of truth here; Rymer, as we have seen, blamed Spenser's allegory on the Italians. But we should not forget that the mixing of allegorical and mimetic characters was quite popular in England. The debate of Justice and Mercy itself appears in Giles Fletcher's *Christs Victorie,* his brother Phineas' *Purple Island* (ca. 1610, pub. 1633), and Thomas Peyton's *Glasse of Time.*[37] It may be partly true, as Hanford also suggests, that the change results from Milton's "working out" the Biblical themes;[38] it is certainly true that by the time he comes to write his epic he has worked out a new role for allegory.

One part of allegory's role in the epic has already been established, most notably in Anne Ferry's *Milton's Epic Voice*: Milton's allegory expresses fallen epistemology, the perverse refusal of Satan and his devils to acknowledge the unity of a monist universe.[39] As Ferry demonstrates, from the poem's mythic point of view, allegory represents a descent into a sterile and illusory division of inner and outer phenomena, of the spiritual and physical. Quilligan's observation that Ferry's "mechanistic definition of allegory" causes her to "miss much of Spenser's power" is accurate,[40] but it does not disqualify Ferry's thesis. As we have seen, Milton's contemporaries shared this definition of allegory and underes-

36. "Notes on Milton's *Paradise Lost* and Other Biblical Scenarios," in *CP* VIII, 587.

37. C. A. Patrides discusses the tradition (based on Psalms 85:10), explains its popularity among Protestant writers, and relates it to Milton's third book in *Milton and the Christian Tradition* (Oxford, 1966), pp. 130–42.

38. Hanford, "Notes," p. 587.

39. *Milton's Epic Voice: The Narrator in "Paradise Lost"* (Cambridge, Mass., 1963), pp. 116–46; see also Arnold Stein, *Answerable Style: Essays on "Paradise Lost"* (Minneapolis, Minn., 1953), pp. 157–158, and MacCaffrey, p. 197.

40. Quilligan, p. 92.

timation of Spenser. An intellectual environment fostering a supple and
organic response to allegory disappeared along with confidence in the
reality of universals, or at least with consensus on their nature. Already
present in the seventeenth century is the misunderstanding of and consequent prejudice against allegory that was to culminate in William
Hazlitt's famous assurance that if Spenser's readers "do not meddle with
the allegory, it will not meddle with them."[41]

My thesis on Milton's allegory is meant to complement Ferry's. By
Milton's time allegory was an ideal vehicle for presenting deficient
ontology as well a deficient epistemology. To the extent that Sin and
Death are not merely morally evil characters but rather embodiments of
metaphysical evil (and this remains to be demonstrated), they are not
additional beings in a monist universe, but the privation of being itself.
Milton's genius is to have reserved allegory, the reality of whose characters was more than suspect, for these non-beings.

Milton's eventual choice of a prophetic and mythic narrative is
reflected in the transformation of allegory's role between outline drafts
and completed epic. Mediated truth is rejected in favor of direct truth.
William Kerrigan argues forcefully for the epic's radical claim to truth:
"The epic is offered as another Testament. . . . Milton assumes divine
authority for every word, every event in *Paradise Lost* that does not
appear in Scripture."[42] From the Father to "Parsimonious Emmet"
(7.485), substantial beings inhabit the poem. The reality of wisdom or
mercy is of a different order. Milton does not wish to compromise the
radical claim for the reality of his actors by intermixing with them
characters of a "lesser reality." The gulf between substantial and
mimetic characters and unreal and allegorical characters is unmediated
by real accidents in substances.

IV: The Ontology of Sin and Death

Gallagher's claim that Sin and Death are "real and historical" characters is at variance with the consensus of centuries of readers. Addison
speaks for most when he calls Sin and Death "two Actors of a shadowy
and fictitious Nature,"[43] as does Joseph Summers when he terms them

---

41. "On Chaucer and Spenser," excerpted in *The Prince of Poets: Essays on Edmund Spenser,* ed.
John R. Elliot (New York, 1968), pp. 24–25.

42. *The Prophetic Milton* (Charlottesville, Va., 1974), p. 264.

43. *Spectator,* No. 273, reprinted in *Milton: The Critical Heritage,* ed. John T. Shawcross (London,
1970), p. 152.

"real nonetities."[44] When linked with an awareness of Milton's ontology of evil, a close examination of the allegory in *Paradise Lost* reveals precisely how and why Addison and Summers are correct.

One important clue to the nature of Sin and Death has not received enough notice. Sin's narration of the fall in the second book differs dramatically from Raphael's in the fifth. In Raphael's long account of Satan's summons to the North, his speech to his followers, and their fall, there is no room for Sin's spectacular cephalogenesis (5.616–710, 743–802). In her own account of the fall Sin is particular about both place and time scheme; she sprang from Satan's head "In Heav'n, *when* at th'Assembly, and in sight / Of all the Seraphim with thee combin'd / In bold conspiracy against Heav'n's King" (2.749–51; my italics). She again points to the time after the horrible incest:

> such joy thou took'st
> With me in secret, that my womb conceiv'd
> A growing burden. *Meanwhile* War arose,
> And fields were fought in Heav'n. (2.765–68; my italics)

The monstrous birth and copulation do not occur *after* Satan's tempting speech and *before* the War in Heaven, but *over the same time*. The temporal adverbs make unmistakable that what we have here is an alternative vision of the fall, and not merely an event unfolding within the context of the fall narrated by Raphael. These alternative visions cannot occupy the same ontological space. Sin and Death are not substances; they are "accidents in a substance," and that substance is Satan and his devils.

The character Sin *is* the allegorical embodiment of Satan's turning from God; Death embodies the result of that turning, impairment of the reason and acquired physical grossness. In the *City of God* (XII,vii) Augustine comments that "defection from that which is in the highest degree, to that which is less, this is to begin to have an evil will." Sin and Death are this defection. While Satan is morally evil, Sin and Death are metaphysical evil itself, which is the privation of entity. Their actions, as Sin's narration of the fall suggests, unfold within Satan and other fallen creatures; as such they are unique in the poem's monist universe in which internal condition and external action are not otherwise separated.

---

44. *The Muse's Method*, p. 39. Summers' term is not self-contradictory; one definition of entity is "Something that has a real existence; an ENS, as distinguished from a mere function, attribute, relation, etc." (*OED* 3). In the first part of this definition, incidentally, one finds the modern prejudice against the reality of abstraction, which in the seventeenth century militated against allegory.

Another way of saying all this is that Sin and Death are the measure of
the negative ontological distance between Lucifer and Satan. To borrow
mathematical terms, they function as negative numbers in a universe
created with positives only. We have already seen that Milton connects
sin with privation of entity; he does the same with death when discussing
the first two of its four degrees in the *Christian Doctrine* (I,xii). The first
degree of death entails "the loss of divine protection and favor, which
results in the lessening of the majesty of the human countenance, and the
degradation of the mind" (*CP* VI, 394). Under the rubric of "spiritual
death" come "the loss (*privatio*) of that divine grace and innate righteousness by which, in the beginning, man lived with God," the "loss (*privatio*)
or at least the extensive darkening of that right reason, whose function it
was to discern the chief good," and the "extinction of righteousness and
of the liberty to do good" (*CP* VI, 394–95). Death in these senses is an
accident in Satan's substance. All of these deficiencies can be found in
him; the examples are too well known to require detailed rehearsal. The
darkening of Satan's reason is evident in such moments as his assertion of
self-creation and his deluded and sophistical addresses to his followers.
His loss of righteousness and ability to do good is pathetically clear in his
necessarily abortive gestures toward repentance. Zephon bears witness
to the loss of majestic countenance in particular and his spiritual decay in
general:

> Think not, revolted Spirit, thy shape the same,
> Or undiminisht brightness, to be known
> As when thou stood'st in Heav'n upright and pure;
> That Glory then, when thou no more wast good,
> Departed from thee, and thou resembl'st now
> Thy sin and place of doom obscure and foul. (4.835–40)

The change in "shape" or body (*OED* 5.b) entails in a monist universe
nothing less than a change in essence. By the death resulting from sin,
Satan is reduced; he suffers a loss of goodness, which is by definition
being.

In a phenomenon that negatively mirrors Christian liberty, evil kicks
creatures free on the ontological ladder. This ladder might be described
anachronistically as an up escalator: God makes men and angels perfect
in their own ways, and both are offered greater perfection through
obedience. Raphael suggests as much to Adam and Eve in his speech on
the scale of nature (5.493–503). Abdiel provides a glimpse of a similar
improvement for angels; he explains to Satan that God has no thought

"To make us less, bent rather to exalt / Our happy state under one Head more near / United" (5.829–31).[45] Through evil, the creature jumps off the escalator and is free to fashion his own diminished being. This is the ironic truth behind Satan's specious claim of self-creation. Sin and Death, the real nonentities, measure the distance between Lucifer and Satan, as well as that between man "Improv'd by tract of time" (5.498) and the vicious, diseased men populating the dismal chronicle of the epic's final books.

That Sin and Death are indeed paradoxical embodiments of privative, metaphysical evil is clear from their ontological distance from the poem's most morally evil substantial character. Peter A. Fiore points out that Satan's *nature* is good; "This, of course, is not to assert that Satan and the fallen angels are morally good. It simply means that, in an ontological realm, that which exists is good and that which has fallen from existence is evil."[46] Like all other substances, Satan is metaphysically good. Sin and Death embody "that which has fallen from existence." Satan is no "Less than Arch-Angel ruin'd" (1.593); his "form had not yet lost / All her Original brightness" (1.591–92). Without the remnants of created perfection, romantic readings of Satan as hero would be not only wrong but inexplicable. Even evil actions, as we have seen, are essentially good action misdirected, and Satan at times reveals a capacity for good, even if dormant and ineffectual:

> That space the Evil one abstracted stood
> From his own evil, and for the time remain'd
> Stupidly good, of enmity disarm'd,
> Of guile, of hate, of envy, of revenge. (9.463–66)[47]

As a substantial creature Satan retains shreds of goodness. It is inconceivable, on the other hand, that Sin and Death could be "stupidly good" or "abstracted from their own evil." The latter would involve literal abstraction from themselves, which is, unlike figurative abstraction, metaphysically impossible.

It is not only their difference from the morally evil Satan that identifies Sin and Death as metaphysical evil or nonentity. Their ontological status, or rather lack thereof, can be inferred from their appearance and their genesis. Sin is given the specious, rhetorical substantiality

45. For an interesting discussion of this passage, see Albert C. Labriola, "'Thy Humiliation Shall Exalt': The Christology of *Paradise Lost*," *Milton Studies*, 15 (1981), 29–42.
46. Fiore, p. 16; Augustine makes the same point in the *City of God* XIX, xiii.
47. See also 1.604–09; 2.482–83; 4.42–48, 846–49.

typical of allegorical characterization. Gallagher, who takes this substantiality at face value, would have done well to heed Fletcher's warning on the function of naturalist detail in allegory. Sin's body is a collection of emblems, a mismatched assortment of parts created not by God but by a creature's perverse imagination. Her role as mirror for Satan's narcissism (2.764) points to her indeterminate mutability of form and to her insubstantiality as an aspect of Satanic pyschology. And if Sin's substantiality is specious, her son's is palpably illusory:

> The other shape
> If shape it might be call'd that shape had none
> Distinguishable in member, joint, or limb,
> Or substance might be call'd that shadow seem'd,
> For each seem'd either; black it stood as Night,
> Fierce as ten Furies, terrible as Hell,
> And shook a dreadful Dart; what seem'd his head
> The likeness of a Kingly Crown had on. (2.666–73)

This is not the angels' "soft / And uncompounded . . . Essence pure" (1.424–25). Angels are tenuous substances; Death only "seems" to be a substance, and then only at times.

The manifest insubstantiality of Death has ramifications for Sin. Death would appear to have inherited insubstantiality (and thus nonentity) from Sin. This paradoxical genetic speculation follows from Milton's Augustinian ontology of evil. Milton shares this sentiment from the *Confessions* (VII, xii): "Thus it was revealed and made visible to me that everything you [God] have made is good, and that there are no substances at all that you have not made." When we remember that Milton's angels do not reproduce (one angelological heresy that Milton does not share), we can be sure that to grant Sin and Death independent substantial existence would be to confer divine creativity on Satan. The same dilemma does not arise when we realize that Sin and Death are not substantial creatures but the measure of deficiency in creatures.

Any argument concerning the ontology of Sin and Death must make sense of the crucial passage on their arrival in paradise:

> Meanwhile in Paradise the hellish pair
> Too soon arrived, *Sin* there in power before,
> Once actual, now in body, and to dwell
> Habitual habitant; behind her *Death*
> Close following pace for pace. (10.585–89)

Gallagher interprets these lines to support his contention that Sin is substantial: "She occupies the space in three distinct ways: 'in power' (i.e., potentially, before the fall, because of Adam's and Eve's fallibility); 'actual[ly]' (i.e., spiritually, upon the completion of original sin, which in Adam's case was also an actual sin); and 'in body' (i.e., physically, when she and Death arrive bodily there). These distinctions are unintelligible unless one admits Sin's literal ontology."[48] These distinctions are, however, quite intelligible without any such admission. Gallagher confuses "actual sin," or the commission of crime, with the spiritual death resulting from sin; in other words, he mixes cause and effect. Sin is potential through human fallibility ("in power"), it is actually committed ("actual"), and it affects the sinner by depriving him of grace, righteousness, freedom, beauty, and other perfections ("in body"). Sin and Death are "in body" because they become accidents *in* man's substance after the fall; they have no existence outside the fallen creature, only in his turning from God and the resulting spiritual deficiency and physical mortality.

Evidence of Sin's and Death's material activity turns out in every case to be questionable. They open the massive gates of Hell for Satan, but Satan is in fact allowed to leave Hell not by them but by the same "will / And high permission of all ruling Heaven" that allows him to escape the burning lake (1.211–12). The spontaneous self-opening of Heaven's gates (7.205–07) casts further doubt on the apparent material agency of Sin and Death in opening their gates. The bridge they build across Chaos seems to be substantial. But MacCaffrey rightly suggests that "it is impossible to accept the bridge from Hell quite as unreservedly as 'real,' as the cosmography of Book III."[49] The numerological and iconographic description at 2.643–48 points beyond the bridge to its abstract meaning.[50] Milton seems to ascribe real material agency to Sin and Death when he notes that at their passing "the blasted Stars lookt wan, / And Planets, Planet-strook, real Eclipse / Then suffer'd" (10.412–14). But we learn shortly afterward that the stellar and terrestrial changes that follow man's fall are effected by God and his angels (10.692–94) and not by Sin and Death, as Quilligan acutely observes.[51] The allegorical characters express rather than cause these changes. As nonentities, Sin and Death cannot create or move anything; at most they measure the degree to which free creatures undo created perfection. Thus Milton does not

48. Gallagher, p. 324.
49. MacCaffrey, p. 199.
50. Ferry, p. 122.
51. Quilligan, p. 126.

"give them any real employment, or ascribe to them any material agency" as Johnson complains,[52] and as other poets do with their allegorical characters. Milton clearly divides the derivative and deficient ontological realm of Sin and Death from the main plane of reality in *Paradise Lost.*

V: Additional Allegory—Chaos and the Limbo of Vanity

I have explained the propriety of Milton's allegorization of Sin and Death in terms of their ontological deficiency. I would like to suggest briefly the ways in which other instances of Milton's allegory confirm my argument. The "horror Plum'd" (4.989) that sits on Satan's crest and the "Victory . . . Eagle-wing'd" (6.762–63) in the Son's chariot are no more than rhetorical flourishes; they have allusive and figurative weight but they are not characters. The court of Chaos and the Limbo of Vanity are more important exercises in allegory, and both, although in ways different from Sin and Death, are "less real" than other characters and places in the epic.

The character Chaos, inseparable from the realm he personifies, is surrounded by a Hesiodic mythic-allegoric court of Night, Orcus, Ades, Demogorgon, Rumor, Chance, Tumult, Confusion, and Discord (2.959–67). Being material, Chaos is not metaphysical evil.[53] But there is another way in which he is "less real" than creation and creatures. In his non-world, form and matter are not combined; without stabilizing form, qualities are fluid and "things" cannot sustain themselves: "For hot, cold, moist, and dry, four Champions fierce / Strive here for Maistry, and to Battle bring / Thir embryon Atoms" (2.898–900). In creation, Milton writes in the *Christian Doctrine,* God adds to prime matter forms, "which, incidentally, are themselves material" (*CP* VI, 308). As the state of matter before the addition of forms, Chaos is less real than created substance. Metaphysical evil is the negation of substance; Chaos is the state of matter before substance *as we experience it* comes into being. Thus Milton describes it in terms associated with gestation:

> The Womb of nature and perhaps her Grave,
> Of neither Sea, nor Shore, nor Aire, nor Fire,
> But all these in their pregnant causes mixt
> Confus'dly. (2.911–14)

Satan, with his characteristic perversity, refers to Chaos as "abortive" (2.441). Chaos is more real than Sin and Death (because it is material),

52. Johnson, I, 258.
53. Nor is he even morally evil. We should note that, despite his apparent eagerness to aid Satan, Chaos speaks *only* with Satan. This ineffectual and pliable figure does respond immediately to the word of the Son at creation.

but less real than creation (because it lacks forms). The character and his realm exist on the border between being and not-being. Again, Milton echoes Augustine, who describes the first matter in the *Confessions* (XII,viii) as "almost nothing." Satan calls Chaos "unreal" (10.471), although of course we must take his observations with a grain of salt. In any event, the unformed matter of Chaos represents a different order of reality than does creation, and again Milton uses the allegorical mode to signal the difference.

The Limbo of Vanity, significantly, borders on Chaos, and as a "windy Sea of Land" it shares Chaos' confusion of elements (3.440). The keynote to this anti-Catholic set-piece is dissolution. "Fools float to Limbo dissolved into Aereal vapors" (3.445). Limbo attracts those who turn to emptiness rather than to God's perfection, and who are punished not with Hell but with ignominious disintegration (there is an interesting parallel between Limbo and Dante's vestibule of hell):

> All th'unaccomplisht works of Nature's hand,
> Abortive, monstrous, or unkindly mixt,
> Dissolv'd on Earth, fleet hither, and in vain,
> Till final dissolution, wander here. (3.455–58)

Limbo is a *figurative* counterpart to Chaos, receiving creatures who fall back into nothingness. In its essential figurativeness Limbo is unique in *Paradise Lost* and does not after all require a defense of its allegorical presentation. Unlike Sin and Death and the realm of Chaos, the Limbo of Vanity is not an object of Milton's belief. If this marvelous flight of fancy requires any rationale, it can be found in the poet's delight in the flight of Ariosto's Astolfo to the moon and in the pamphleteer's savage and polemical wit.

I have outlined a causal relationship between a movement from realism to nominalism and a decline in the status of allegory, and argued that Milton's use of allegory reflects this decline. My argument does not depend on viewing Milton as a nominalist, which he emphatically is not. The author of *Areopagitica* could never assent to Hobbes' proposition that "the first truths were arbitrarily made by those that first of all imposed names upon things."[54] Nevertheless, even the moderate realism of the seventeenth century, as represented by Descartes, assigns a "lesser reality" to universals. I leave open the large question of the precise degree of Milton's realism, for my argument does not depend on its answer. Milton is certainly interested in the questions of ontology that

54. *De Corpore*, in *The English Works of Thomas Hobbes*, ed. William Molesworth (London, 1839–1845), I, 36.

occupied his contemporaries; his idiosyncratic and consistent monist solution tells us that. It is also certain that he participates in the movement of his century by assigning a smaller and smaller role to allegory. In this essay I have proposed that the response of the realist Milton to the decline in the status of universals and the concomitant decline in the status of allegorical characters was to use allegory to present an accident that truly has no ontological weight. Evil is the ultimate accident. While mercy, justice, wisdom, etc., are accidents in particular men, to a Christian realist they are universal entities created by God and essential to creation as a whole. Evil, on the other hand, is radically accidental, essential neither to any creature nor to God's creation. If his contemporaries doubted the reality of the universals represented by allegorical agents, Milton would give them allegorical agents that represented the unreal. They paradoxically embody the nothingness of evil, and not the universals that inhere in creatures.

Thus Milton's allegory of Sin and Death is not haphazard; it corresponds to his Augustinian ontology of evil and comments on the fate of allegory itself. My argument maintains, like Gallagher's, that Milton is firmly in control of the ontology of his characters, but without the impossible assertion that Milton places in his true epic physical creatures named Sin and Death. My argument recognizes, like Quilligan's, the radical non-reality of Sin and Death, but avoids the cumbersome explanatory machinery of overtly fictional allegorical brackets that emphasize by contrast the inner truthfulness of the enclosed fictional material. Ockham's Razor can be usefully applied here, for Milton's plan is ingeniously simpler. Rejecting the promiscuous use of allegory authorized by contemporary precedent, and with which he himself experimented in the Trinity manuscript, Milton uses allegory in his mimetic epic to point to the ontological deficiency of evil. He reserves allegorical status for the paradoxical embodiments of metaphysical evil, which is the negation rather than the expression of substance. Johnson and the rest were right to recognize ontological and generic inconsistency in *Paradise Lost*. What they did not recognize is that the contrast between the mimetic and allegorical modes is itself consistent with the ontological gulf between the goodness of entity and the nonentity of evil.[55]

UNIVERSITY OF NOTRE DAME

55. This essay has benefited from the advice and comments of William Kerrigan and Owen Barfield, and particularly of Philip J. Gallagher, whose recent death has deprived Milton studies of one of its most passionate and articulate voices.

Milton's Defensive God: A Reappraisal

By Gary D. Hamilton *

C. S. Lewis' well-known contention that " A God, theologically speaking, much worse than Milton's would escape criticism if only He had been made sufficiently awful, mysterious and vague " seems to invite the conclusion that there is little connection between the theology which God the Father advocates in Book III of *Paradise Lost* and Milton's artistic decisions regarding the presentation of God.[1] Such a conclusion is misleading, however, and only complicates the modern reader's difficult task of appreciating what Milton was trying to accomplish in this much-criticized section of the poem. It is my contention that the best place to begin understanding Milton's handling of Book III is with the theology it presents, for in the theology we discover the kind of God which Milton's treatment was designed to reinforce. The brand of theology in Book III has generally been recognized as Arminian.[2] But more than the mere application of an appropriate label is needed to illuminate the relationship between meaning and method. Milton's creation of a God " not mysterious " is related to the effort to make him " un-Calvinistic," and the way that God speaks has much to do with whom he is speaking against.

It is now commonplace to question the wisdom of Milton's decision to allow God to speak on his own behalf; and those critics appear to be in the majority who dislike what they interpret as the defensive

* I would like to acknowledge a grant from the General Research Board, University of Maryland, College Park, Maryland, which assisted me in my research on this topic.

[1] C. S. Lewis, *A Preface to Paradise Lost* (London, 1947), p. 126.
[2] Maurice Kelley, "The Theological Dogma of *Paradise Lost*, III, 173-202," *PMLA*, LII (1937), 75-9, presents a clear account of the Arminianism of Book III.

tone of the Father's speeches.[3] For some critics this defensive tone is most readily explained by speculating about doubts in the mind of Milton himself. A. J. Waldock, noting how anxious Milton is to prove God does not cause the Fall, claims that "Never to the end of the poem does he succeed in living down this particular worry" and that the poet, in presenting God's arguments, conveys an impression of "nervousness, insecurity and doubt."[4] William Empson, who amusingly labors to prove the traditional God of Christianity "very wicked," discovers Milton's redeeming feature in his struggle "to make his God appear less wicked." "That this searching goes on in *Paradise Lost*," says Empson, "is the chief source of its fascination and poignancy."[5] Also using the poem to explore Milton's shifting feelings toward God, Arthur Sewell maintains, "*Paradise Lost* is the poem of a man whose mind is troubled and changing."[6] The efforts to make God appear "less wicked" and the proofs that God does not cause the Fall are elements in the poem which need to be reckoned with. Yet they will be more fully understood if approached not as expressions of Milton's personal problems, but as problems of the times, to which Milton was addressing himself in the limited way that the demands of epic form allowed.

I.

What many have called the defensive tone of Book III can best be accounted for by the fact that the poem was written at a time when the Arminian-Calvinist controversy, centering on the doctrine of absolute predestination, was still very much alive in many circles in England. One needs only to read a modest number of available mid-

---

[3] In addition to Lewis, other significant statements of disapproval are found in J. B. Broadbent, *Some Graver Subject: An Essay on Paradise Lost* (London, 1960), pp. 144 ff.; Northrop Frye, *The Return of Eden: Five Essays on Milton's Epics* (Toronto, 1965), pp. 99 ff.; Herbert Grierson, *Milton and Wordsworth* (New York, 1937), p. 106; John Peter, *A Critique of Paradise Lost* (New York, 1960), pp. 11 ff.; and A. J. A. Waldock, *Paradise Lost and its Critics* (London and New York, 1947), pp. 98 ff.

[4] Waldock, pp. 104, 103.

[5] *Milton's God* (London, 1961), pp. 10, 11.

[6] *A Study of Milton's Christian Doctrine* (London, 1939), p. 157. Sewell mistakenly attributes the "severe" manner of God in Book III to Milton's lingering Calvinism.

seventeenth century theological treatises to become aware that this issue ranks, along with the question of church polity, among the most important theological problems of the age. The debate over the extent of God's role in determining man's destiny, which became most intense in England in the 1650's, had been growing ever since the Dutch theologian Arminius, at the turn of the century, challenged the Calvinist position and declared that it did, in fact, make God rather than man the author of sin.[7] Milton reflects in God's defense of himself the restlessness of an age that had come to have doubts about the goodness of its Calvinist God. In Book III God is defending himself against Calvinism, that theological system which had so dominated the hearts and minds of Milton's generation. God's defense is not directed against the whole system, of course, but against those aspects which Milton and many others were finding inconsistent with their understanding of God's goodness.

The issues involved in the Arminian-Calvinist controversy were complex ones which do not lend themselves to short, easy explanations. But beneath the complexity of the arguments, which were to leave even Milton's devils "in wandring mazes lost,"[8] there lay a readily discernible motivating spirit permeating the position of each

[7] Arminius (*The Writings of James Arminius*, tr. James Nichols, W. R. Bagnall [Grand Rapids, 1956], I, 229) asserts that if God has denied to man "such a portion of grace as is sufficient and necessary to enable him to avoid sin," then we must conclude "God really sins . . . God is the only sinner." Thomas Pierce, *The Christians Rescue from the Grand Error of the Heathen* (London, 1658), in his collection of tracts discusses and enlarges upon Arminius' charge. Other important treatments of the theological controversy include: Pierre du Moulin, *The Anatomy of Arminianisme* (London, 1620); William Prynne, *Anti-Arminianisme* (London, 1630); William Twisse, *Vindiciae Gratiae, Potestatis ac Providentiae Dei* (Amsterdam, 1632; 1648), and *The Riches of God's Love . . . Consistent with His Absolute Hatred* (London, 1653); [Samuel Hoard], *God's Love to Mankind* (London, 1633); John Owen, *A Display of Arminianism* (London, 1642) and *The Doctrine of the Saints' Perseverance Explained and Confirmed* (London, 1654); John Goodwin, *Redemption Redeemed* (London, 1652), and *The Agreement and Distance of Brethren* (London, 1653). Helpful secondary accounts are James Nichols, *Calvinism and Arminianism Compared* (London, 1824); and Thomas Jackson, *The Life of John Goodwin* (London, 1822).

[8] See *Paradise Lost*, II, 558-61. All quotations from the poem are from *John Milton: Complete Poems and Major Prose*, ed. Merritt Y. Hughes (New York, 1957). Further citations are all from Book III and will be indicated by line number in the text.

party in the debate. Perhaps what most significantly distinguished the Arminians from the Calvinists was the way in which they worded their description of the nature of God. Instead of a Calvinist God of power the Arminians insisted upon portraying, above all else, a God of love. Their argumentative weapon was John iii: 16, " For God so loved the world that he gave his only begotten son, that whosoever believeth in him, shall not perish but have everlasting life." [9] This scriptural passage was a source of embarrassment for the Calvinists and challenged them to call forth their most ingenious exegetical skills. In the first phrase, " For God so loved the world," " world " had to be interpreted as meaning " the elect," for Christ did not die for all men, only the elect, those whom God had chosen from all eternity. Likewise, " whosoever believeth in him shall not perish " had to be taken to mean " whosoever God causes to believe," for saving faith was only given to those whom God had chosen to save. The Calvinist objection to the Arminians was that they undermined the sovereignty of God's grace. Indeed, the cornerstone of the Calvinist doctrine of predestination was the sovereignty of grace. If man could choose whether or not he would accept God's grace, then it was man, not God, who received the glory for aiding in his own salvation. But if salvation was truly a free act of grace, it could not be dependent upon man's will acting independently of that grace. Furthermore, if God was all-powerful, his grace had to be irresistible.

The obvious corollary, spelled out clearly by Calvin, but given even more emphasis by his followers, was that God showed forth his glory, that is, his power, by arbitrarily saving some men and damning others.[10] He made the decision of who goes where, not on

---

[9] Anthony Farindon, ed., *Golden Remains of the Ever Memorable Mr. John Hales* (London, 1688), dedicatory letter, attributes Hales's " good-night " to Calvin to a moving exposition of John iii: 16 by Episcopius. For confirmation of the centrality of this verse, see Arminius, *Writings*, I, 232 ff. and Goodwin, *Redemption Redeemed*, pp. 74-85. Milton, *The Christian Doctrine*, in *Works of John Milton*, gen. ed. Frank Patterson (New York, 1931-8), XV, 319-21, indicates the absurdity of Calvinist manipulation of this verse. For a Calvinist interpretation see Twisse, *Riches of God's Love*, pp. 108 ff.

[10] John Calvin, *Institutes of the Christian Religion* [Bk. III, Ch. XXIV, Sec. 14], ed. John T. McNeill (Philadelphia, 1960), II, 981, states that the wicked " have been given over to this depravity because they have been raised up by the just but inscrutable judgment of God to display his glory in their condemnation."

the basis of the individual's merits—this would be the heretical doctrine of justification by works—but solely because it pleased him. The long, complicated dissertations on God which seventeenth century Calvinists produced often echo the arguments that Duns Scotus presented against Aquinas' theology when he explained how absurd it was to seek a necessary reason for what was not necessary. Scotus had concluded that "the divine will wills because it wills, and no reason can be given."[11] For Calvinists, too, God's justice was inexplicable. Calvin himself had said, "If then we cannot determine a reason why he vouchsafes mercy to his own, except it so pleases him, neither shall we have reason for rejecting others, other than his will."[12] The Arminians, however, were not willing to tolerate an apparently unreasonable God. Benjamin Whichcote, countering the idea that God's mysterious ways cannot be understood, sums up their position: "God does not, because of his Omnipotency, deal Arbitrarily with us; but according to Right, and Reason: and whatever he does, is therefore Accountable; because Reasonable."[13]

That the Calvinist theology was the dominant one in England as Milton probably began writing *Paradise Lost* is most clearly illustrated by the fact that the Commission of Triers and Ejectors, set up by Cromwell in the 1650's to examine the orthodoxy of all ministers, refused to allow anyone to preach who would not publicly denounce Arminian views.[14] The official rejection of Arminianism did not, of course, eliminate the problems which many honest men continued to have with the apparently irrational actions of their Calvinist God. Discussing the reasons for his conversion to Arminianism in the mid-1640's, John Goodwin recalls the preachers who taught him "that there are some reprobates, and these not a few neither, towards whom

---

[11] Frederick Copleston, *A History of Philosophy* (Westminster, Md., 1957), II, 531.

[12] *Institutes* [Bk. III, Ch. XXII, Sec. 11], II, 947.

[13] *Moral and Religious Aphorisms* (London, 1930), p. 48.

[14] Richard Baxter, *Reliquiae Baxterianae* (London, 1696), Part first, 72, explains that the Commission of Triers was "severe against all Arminians." Bitter attacks on and descriptions of the proceedings of the commission can be found in Anthony Sadler, *Inquisitio Anglicana* (London, 1654); and Laurence Womack, *An Examination of Tilenus Before the Triers* (1658), reprinted in Nichols, *Calvinism and Arminianism Compared*, pp. 8-90.

God sheweth no patience or long sufferance at all, imagining that many infants of days, yea and many immediately from the womb, are sent to the lake that burneth with fire and brimstone for evermore. . . . My soul hath once been in the secret of these men: but let it never enter thereinto more."[15] The Calvinist doctrine presented in such vivid terms was bound to create some doubts about God's goodness. Richard Baxter, who tried to devise a compromise between Calvinism and Arminianism, found it necessary to write a tract called "God's Goodness Vindicated." His first publisher, in 1671, laments to his readers that it is "too well known, how much this amiable Divine Goodness is denied or doubted of. What cavils are raised against it by men of corrupt minds! What secret prejudice lies against it, and how deeply rooted in our depraved nature! Yea, with how fearful suggestions and apprehensions are some godly Christians . . . sometimes perplexed about it! And even such as are grounded and settled in it, are liable to be assaulted, and many sometimes stagger and stumble at it."[16] Baxter himself explains that his purpose was to "help all such persons out of the snare of this dangerous and troublesome temptation." "Who can love him whom he believeth to be bad, and so unlovely?" asks Baxter.[17] In this respect Milton's Book III may not be unlike Baxter's tract. Perhaps Milton also had those "unlovely" aspects of Calvinism very much in mind when he set out to "assert Eternal Providence, and justify the ways of God."

II.

Those who are embarrassed by the presence of theology in Book III are free to find solace in the suggestion that Milton meant the dialogue between the Father and Son to be read as drama rather than dogma.[18] However, it is unlikely that the embarrassment would have been shared by Milton's first readers; they would have been much better able to accept the dialogue for what it often is—a well-organized

[15] *Exposition of the Ninth Chapter to the Romans* (London, 1653), p. 265.
[16] *The Practical Works of the Rev. Richard Baxter*, ed. William Orme (London, 1830), VIII, 509.
[17] Baxter, VIII, 511, 532.
[18] Irene Samuel, "The Dialogue in Heaven: A Reconsideration of *Paradise Lost*, III, 1-417," *PMLA*, LXXII (1957), 601.

and carefully planned lesson in theology, aimed at bolstering the Englishman's faith in the goodness of God by showing him how to avoid the pitfalls which the Calvinist theologians were setting in the way of appreciating divine benevolence. While the lesson might understandably be offensive today, Milton no doubt regarded it as a most necessary part of his effort to produce a work which was "doctrinal and exemplary to a nation." The modern reader may find the manner of Milton's God less puzzling, and thus perhaps less offensive, by imagining him conducting a debate with a high Calvinist God with whom he is sharing a speaker's platform. Having exerted this effort, the reader may even be able to admire the Father's strategy, which is designed to concentrate on divine goodness and, above all, divine reasonableness.

The Father's first speech is an elaborate and explicit denial of the charge for which Arminius and his followers had shown the Calvinists liable—that they make God the author of sin. This theological issue had been introduced in an amusing way in Book II, when Milton had Sin indirectly deny the charge by revealing that her author is Satan, out of whose head she sprang. Now in Book III, God, after announcing that man will give in to temptation, very seriously proclaims,

> I made him just and right
> Sufficient to have stood, though free to fall.
> Such I created all th' Ethereal Powers
> And Spirits, both them who stood and them who fail'd:
> Freely they stood who stood, and fell who fell. (98-102)

And a few lines later:

> They therefore as to right belong'd,
> So were created, nor can justly accuse
> Thir maker, or thir making, or thir Fate. (111-3)

Then after making a traditional distinction between predestination and foreknowledge (114-9), which had been denied by the Calvinists, Milton, as if to make absolutely sure that his readers grasp the important theological lesson, has God again explain:

> They trespass, Authors to themselves in all
> Both what they judge and what they choose; for so
> I form'd them free, and free they must remain,

Till they enthrall themselves: I else must change
Thir nature, and revoke the high Decree
Unchangeable, Eternal, which ordain'd
Thir freedom: they themselves ordain'd thir fall. (122-18)

A seventeenth century reader coming across these last lines would
not fail to notice how Milton was manipulating current theological
jargon. One of the arguments usually evoked to refute the Arminian
substitution of conditional decrees for absolute decrees was an appeal
to God's immutability. Thomas Whitfeld, launching one of the many
Calvinist attacks on the Arminian assertion that God wills a man's
salvation upon condition that he will believe, explains,

That which is absolutely Eternal, hath neither beginning nor end: but the doctrine
of the conditional decree fastens an end, and so soon as that takes place, this is
expired . . . so that by this means, Election must needs be in time, and not before
all time . . . the doctrine of the conditional will and decree, makes these [divine
counsels] to be mutable and changeable.[19]

For the Calvinists the "high Decree/Unchangeable, Eternal" was
the irrevokable decree, proclaimed from all eternity, that some men
would be saved and some men would be damned. Whitfeld's master,
William Twisse, the interlocutor of the Assembly of Divines and the
most frequently cited spokesman for supralapsarian Calvinism in
Milton's day, had carefully shown that the Fall itself must be regarded as ordained by God.[20] But Milton's God says "the high
Decree/Unchangeable" is that man shall be free, the very point
which Twisse and his followers were unable to explain. When God
states he "ordain'd/Thir freedom, they themselves ordain'd thir fall,"

---

[19] *A Vindication of the Doctrine of God's Absolute Decree* (London, 1657), p. 4.
[20] The significance of William Twisse's *Vindiciae Gratiae*, which first appeared in
1632, lies in the clear-cut distinction it made between supralapsarian and sublapsarian Calvinism. Placing the object of God's absolute decree in a "mass not-yet-
created," Twisse criticizes Calvinist Pierre du Moulin's attempt to deny God as the
author of sin by asserting the object of the decree in a "mass of sinners." This
sublapsarian position, according to Twisse, diminished God's glory, was inconsistent,
and did not escape the Arminian charge. Denying that reprobation be without the
consideration of sin, Twisse nevertheless asserts that the Fall was ordained by God
as part of His original plan, which was to culminate in the mercy bestowed on the
elect. See *Vindiciae Gratiae* (1648), Lib. 1, par. 1, sect. 4, digr. 3-6, pp. 70-96.
Supralapsarians are sometimes called high Calvinists and sublapsarians moderate
Calvinists. I shall hereafter use the terms interchangeably.

he is skillfully using customary high Calvinist language to deny high Calvinist conclusions.[21]

The note on which God ends his first speech is often overlooked by critics predisposed to view Milton's God as a tyrant. The Father concludes by announcing, " Mercy first and last shall brightest shine " (134). God is again playing with current theological terminology when he explains his reasons for this decision:

> The first sort by thir own suggestion fell,
> Self-tempted, self-deprav'd: Man therefore shall find grace,
> The other none: in Mercy and Justice both,
> Through Heav'n and Earth, so shall my glory excel. (129-33)

These lines, often puzzled over by those who want to reconcile them with treatments of Satan and his followers elsewhere in the poem, will seem less enigmatic when examined against the background of Calvinism. Milton's first readers would immediately have recognized that God is employing an interesting variation on the doctrine of double predestination. To share their recognition we need only to recall that the Calvinist God *arbitrarily* chose some men to be saved and others to be damned in order to show forth his glory through his mercy and his justice. Milton's God, too, is saying that his glory shall excel " in Mercy and Justice both," but there is nothing arbitrary about the manner in which this glory is to be manifested. He shall show forth his justice by condemning the devils, and he shall show forth his mercy by offering salvation to man. Those who feel that God is still wicked for condemning the poor devils need only compare Milton's formula to the Calvinist solution. They should also compare Milton's final line, " But Mercy first and last shall brightest shine," with some of the Calvinist pronouncements that the vast majority of mankind have been damned and the elect are few.

The Son's role in his first response to the Father is that of clarifier. His speech should not be labeled "suasive, as if he has to work on God to prevent him from changing his mind and delivering a sterner sentence."[22] The Father's future course of action has already been

---

[21] Cf. Peter, *A Critique of Paradise Lost*, pp. 11-2, who uses the reference to the " Unchangeable " decrees as evidence that God is prone to " self-exoneration."

[22] Peter, p. 12.

firmly declared, and the Son now seeks to spell out the significance of this declaration in the context of other less praiseworthy alternatives. Focussing on the bleaker options which the Father might have chosen, the Son leads up to a statement which can only be fully understood in the context of the Arminian-Calvinist controversy: " So should thy goodness, and thy greatness both/Be question'd and blasphem'd without defense" (165-6). For the Arminians God's goodness could not be defended if He were viewed as arbitrarily excluding some men from His grace. For the Calvinists, on the other hand, God's greatness could not be defended if men could thwart His will by refusing the salvation intended for them. In refuting an Arminian objection Twisse leaves no doubt about which of the two attributes he wanted his God to possess: " Yet ask I pray any man of judgment, which is the chiefer attribute of a King, and more glorious of the two, his prerogative or his clemency? Clemency is a very vulgar vertue, but the royall prerogative is peculiar to one." [23] The Son, however, would want Twisse's question answered quite differently, for his words imply the Arminian position that God's goodness constitutes his greatness. God's best defense, according to the Son, is that his " Mercy first and last shall brightest shine."

If the Father's first speech removes the barriers which the high Calvinists had thrown in the way of praising God's goodness, his second speech removes the blocks which even the moderate Calvinists had set up. God begins his second speech where his first speech left off, with the subject of mercy. Now, however, he goes on to define more precisely the scope of his mercy. While the sublapsarians did not believe, as the supralapsarians did, that God had ordained the Fall in order that he might fulfill his decree to save the elect, they nevertheless confirmed that God, after the Fall, bestowed his mercy on some men and withheld it from others according to his pleasure. To the poor sinner concerned about his spiritual status, the uncertainty as to whether God had predestined him to eternal salvation or damnation could understandably hinder his full appreciation of God's goodness. The Father dispels all anxieties, however, by declaring the Arminian view of general redemption: " man shall not quite be lost,

---

[23] Twisse, *Riches of God's Love*, p. 123.

but sav'd who will" (173). What made this Arminian view so controversial was, as we have noted, the suspicion that this proposition shifts the emphasis from God's grace to man's corrupted will as the determining element in man's salvation. In *Of True Religion* Milton was to explain that the Arminian is "condemn'd for setting up free will against free grace; but that Imputation he disclaims in all his writings and grounds himself largly upon Scripture only."[24] In the next line of the Father's speech Milton shows his awareness of the possible tendency in his readers toward condemnation, by the kind of word-play he uses to counter their suspicion: "Yet not of will in him, but grace in me/Freely voutsaf't." The stress which the previous phrase, "sav'd who will," had put on man's role is immediately qualified and replaced by emphasis on God's role, carried out in this speech through the repetition of the pronoun "me." "Grace in me" is followed by "Upheld by me," "By me upheld," and "to me owe/All his deliv'rance, and to none but me." The repetition is necessary in order to impress upon the reader that acceptance of the conditional predestination of those who believe is no more a threat to the sovereignty of God's grace than is the doctrine of absolute predestination.[25]

Next come the lines which have confused many who ponder the Arminianism of Book III: "Some I have chosen of peculiar grace/Elect above the rest; so is my will" (183-4). First of all, these words must be approached from the rhetorical point of view. Milton's reference to "peculiar grace" serves the same function as the repetition of the pronoun "me" in the preceding lines. It disarms the readers who are predisposed against God's Arminianism and informs them that it does not do violence to God's sovereignty. From the theological point of view the lines are consistent with Milton's own position in the *Christian Doctrine* and thus not inconsistent with his Arminianism, rightly understood. In his theological treatise Milton says that the doctrine of general redemption does not mean that God's will must be confined so that all men must receive grace in equal measure: "That an equal portion of grace should not be extended to all, is attributable to the supreme will alone; that there are none

[24] *Works*, VI, 169.
[25] Cf. Peter, p. 13, who feels repetition of "me" smacks of self-aggrandizement.

to whom he does not vouchsafe grace sufficient for their salvation is attributable to his justice." [26] Motivating this statement is Milton's refusal to impose limits upon God unnecessarily. The Calvinists unnecessarily limited the scope of God's mercy to a few; Milton will not limit God by refusing to permit Him to give special grace to a few. Milton's views correspond in part with those of Baxter, who explains, "And if besides all the mercy that God sheweth to others, he do antecedently and positively elect certain persons, by an absolute decree, to overcome all their resistances of his Spirit . . . what is there in this that is injurious to any others? . . . . Is this any detraction from, or diminution of his universal grace? Or rather a higher demonstration of his goodness? As it is no wrong to man that God maketh angels more holy, immutable and happy." [27] Milton surely would have objected to the reference to "an absolute decree" but would undoubtedly have agreed with the argument that "peculiar grace" does not detract from or diminish universal grace. Indeed, had Milton's God failed to mention "peculiar grace," he may have neglected "a higher demonstration of his goodness."

Appreciation for the goodness of God would not have been undermined for Milton's first readers by the final part of the Father's second speech, where he delivers the famous line, "Die hee or Justice must" (280). The call for "rigid satisfaction, death for death" was part of a widely held theory of atonement accepted by Arminians and Calvinists alike. [28] Although Milton apparently felt no compulsion to abandon this legalism, he does not in *Paradise Lost* stress the severity of God's justice; God calls for satisfaction after the proposition that mercy shall shine brightest has been thoroughly discussed. The main function of God's demand is the dramatic one of providing an opportunity for Christ to respond freely. Besides offering a parallel to the voluntary mission undertaken by Satan, Milton reinforces the Arminianism of Book III by showing that even Christ has the choice

[26] *Works*, XIV, 147-9. Cf. Kelley, *PMLA*, LII, 79, who makes a rather strained effort to show the Arminianism of lines 183-4.
[27] "God's Goodness Vindicated," *Works*, VIII, 529.
[28] My research confirms the findings of C. A. Patrides, "Milton and the Protestant Theory of Atonement," *PMLA*, LXIV (1959), 7-13. Goodwin, *Redemption Redeemed*, p. 18, gives one of the strongest statements of this position when he insists, "the death of Christ is soveraignly necessary."

of whether or not to carry out God's will. The exaltation of the Son, the dramatic culmination of the previous speeches, is handled so that it reinforces the central theological message of the book. The Son's voluntary response opens with the subject which closed the Father's first speech, "Man shall find grace." The theme of the Son's speech and the Father's answer to it is that the Son will do for man what man cannot do for himself. The appropriate reply for the reader, who hopefully is now purged of doubts about God's goodness acquired through a Calvinist upbringing, is announced in the hymn of praise sung by the Heavenly Choir: "Father of Mercy and Grace, thou didst not doom/So strictly, but much more to pity incline" (401-2).

Against the background of this angelic hymn of praise it is hard not to contrast the harsher modern sounds of condemnation—condemnation because Milton, by making God into a lawyer who argues his own case, destroys the mystery which modern man living in a scientific age so desperately needs. Perhaps the appropriate answer to the modern reader who is disgusted with Milton's presentation of God is that one man's God is another man's Devil. What Milton's first readers needed was not so much a mysterious God as a reasonable God. To an audience concerned with God's arbitrary, apparently irrational distribution of justice and mercy, Milton presents a God who has reasons for what he does. He creates man free so that his obedience will have a meaning; he grants man grace and not the devils because man was not self-tempted; he demands satisfaction for man's disobedience because his justice must be fulfilled; and he will save those who do not scorn his mercy.

For Milton, then, the risks of making God do the talking were never so great or so apparent as they have been to Waldock, or to Lewis. This is not to say, however, that Milton would have felt unchallenged by the task of presenting God. For Milton the real artistic challenge was to present a reasonable God who at the same time sounded like a god. His challenge was to find for God a suitable voice, one which had to be as unlike Adam's as it would be unlike Satan's. It had, in short, to be an unanthropomorphic voice, passionless, impersonal. The extent to which Milton succeeded in finding a suitable voice is a necessary and proper issue for the literary critic to explore. Yet each critic's verdict is bound to reflect what he imagines Milton's purpose to have been. For those who read God's defense as that of a guilty or angry parent, the issue is already settled; he is too anthropomorphic. But if we can hear in this defense the words of the Divine Teacher, proclaiming truths that needed to be proclaimed, the voice may sound more like the voice of authority which Milton intended it to be.[29]

University of Maryland

[29] Stanley Fish, *Surprised by Sin* (London, 1967), pp. 77, 65, admirably defends the rightness of God's " pedagogical stance," and recognizes that God's question, " Whose fault? " (96) is part of the method of exposition rather than an emotional outburst. Irene Samuel, *PMLA*, LXXII, 603, acknowledges the "toneless voice of moral law " set up as a deliberate contrast to Satan's " ringing utterances."

"UNCLOISTER'D VIRTUE":
ADAM AND EVE IN MILTON'S PARADISE

Thomas H. Blackburn

Milton, following Genesis, dates man's Fall from his eating the fruit of the "Tree of the Knowledge of Good and Evil," yet in *Paradise Lost* Adam and Eve know evil before they disobey God's command. Set forth in part in Raphael's instructive discourses and acknowledged in the speeches of Adam and Eve themselves, this prelapsarian knowledge is conceptual. It makes Adam and Eve free and responsible moral agents, but is not therefore incompatible with innocence: they may "see, and know, and yet abstain." The series of choices they survive in innocence proves them "sufficient to have stood," yet also foreshadows their corruption by manifesting potentialities which make them "free to fall." By eating the fruit they for the first time actualize evil in their own existence, and the "event" for which the tree is named is this new and catastrophic knowledge of evil as an experienced actuality. The Fall is neither the inexplicable ruin of an ignorant bliss nor the inevitable result of a flawed creation. Milton's conception of a knowledgeable, yet sinless, innocence not only is congruent with his analysis of virtue in *Areopagitica,* but also makes possible a narrative rendering of the Fall which is coherent, credible, and dramatic.

I F T H E innocence of Adam and Eve in *Paradise Lost* is, or should have been, a condition very like that "cloister'd virtue" which Milton "cannot praise" in *Areopagitica,* then the integrity of the poet and his epic may be seriously questioned. Either Milton has chosen a subject which requires him to present a static and ignorant bliss as the highest human happiness, or to avoid that aesthetic and psychological pitfall, has undercut the dramatic and doctrinal center of his poem by enduing Adam and Eve before the Fall with some of the failings of fallen mankind. Were their innocence truly "cloister'd" Adam and Eve would be not only sinless, but also incapable of sin— moral, as it were, by default. They could neither "see" nor "know" what "vice promises," and thus would not face that choice between vice and virtue which is for Milton the very essence of reason.[1] Possessing no true freedom of the will they could not will their own corruption, nor could they be justly held responsible for so doing. The alternate assumption, that they were created impure from the beginning, is equally as destructive to Milton's argument for the justice of God's ways to men. The punishment of Adam and Eve for a disobedience they could neither will nor avoid in either case would be a monstrous injustice, and the promise of redemption through Christ would become a cynical farce. The literary consequences would be no less drastic: a flawed innocence would destroy the premise of drama in the Fall, and an incorruptible innocence would preclude any credible epic plot.

Of those critics who find the innocence depicted in Genesis incompatible with any credible shift to a fallen state, Millicent Bell's views are typical: "The transition between Man and Woman incorrupt and mankind corrupted is simply to be accepted as having happened. Yet the mind cannot accept the fact that perfection was capable of corruption without denying the absoluteness of perfection."[2] A most cloistered virtue, bearing within itself no potentiality for change and immune to external influence, is suggested by "the absoluteness of perfection." Like E. M. W. Tillyard, Miss Bell sees an Adam and Eve innocent in this definition as impossible characters in a narrative which requires, to use Aristotle's terms, a "probable or necessary" sequence of events. With Tillyard, she suggests that for this reason, "in one way or another it was necessary to create an Eve liable to temptation and so to remove the threshold of her transition to sin to some indefinite moment in the past."[3] Tillyard fixes this point in Eve's dream (V, 28–94), but one can easily enough find traces of what he calls "feelings which though nominally felt in the state of innocence are actually not compatible with it" as early as Eve's first inclination to prefer her own reflected image to Adam, or Adam's initial self-assertion in his petition to his creator for a mate.[4] Once innocence is equated with Miss Bell's "absoluteness of perfection" it becomes impossible to find that Adam and Eve were ever innocent. The corollary is inevitable, and as drawn by A. J. A. Waldock and others it becomes an argument for the view that God's ways to men cannot be defended: if Adam and Eve were never innocent, then God must have created them flawed, and thus punishes their defection under false pretenses.[5]

Bell and Tillyard agree that Milton did not, or could not, portray innocence as they believe Genesis requires, either because no successful epic narrative could incorporate such a state, or because the poet's sympathies were secretly with the "wayfaring Christian" of the fallen world.[6] Basil Willey, however, thinks that Milton did achieve the required portrait of perfection (and here he is in the company of Dr. Johnson), but that to do so involved not only a fault in the poem, but also a paradoxical betrayal of his deep humanist belief in rational freedom:

> Genesis, to which Milton must needs adhere, represented the Fall as due to, or consisting of, the acquisition by Man of that very knowledge, the Knowledge of good and evil, by the possession of which alone Milton the humanist believed man could be truly virtuous. Here indeed was a strange situation: Milton, believing, as we have seen, in "Knowledge," and in "Reason" as choice of good by a free agent cognisant of evil, selects as the subject of his greatest poem a fable which represents the acquisition of these very things as the source of all our woe. It may be said that it is only in a fallen state that moral knowledge has become essential . . . ; that, in a word, innocence would have been better than morality. But Milton does not really believe this, as is clearly shown by his failure to convince us that the prelapsarian life of Adam and Eve in the "happy garden" was genuinely happy. "Assuredly we bring not innocence into the world, we bring impurity much rather": this is what Milton knew and believed; yet his adherence to Genesis involved him in the necessity of representing man's true and primal happiness as the innocence of Eden.[7]

The assumption that innocence and morality are not compatible shows Willey to understand "innocence" as "absolute perfection." And, it must be admitted, if Milton either believed in or represented the state of innocence to be so perfect or immutable as Willey and others suppose, the coherence of his narrative, the integrity of his belief in free will, and his "proof" of God's justice would all be suspect.

The possibility of such damaging conclusions arises in part from an ambiguity inherent in our notions of *innocence*. We use the word, on one hand, to characterize the naive purity of an infant, not only untouched by evil, but also ignorant of its very existence and unmoved by the passions which may draw men from righteousness. On the other hand, we also use the word as the antonym of *guilty*, signifying neither ignorance of evil nor the lack of any capability or inclination to indulge in it, but merely that no particular evil or sinful act has at that point been committed. The former idea of innocence is too often that presumed to be implied by Genesis and used by Milton in his epic. The latter idea, however, may well be closer to Milton's conception of man's unfallen state. The *OED* notes that the restriction of the word *innocence* to mean "unacquainted with evil" is essentially a modern usage specialized from the general sense "doing no evil: free from moral wrong, sin or guilt." An innocence fitting the latter sense is suggested, to take a very early example, by the characterization of Adam and Eve in the Caedmonian Genesis: "Young were they both, in beauty fashioned / By God's own power to grace the earth. / They knew not *enduring* nor *doing* of evil" (italics mine).[8] But the test of Milton's meaning is neither Caedmon nor a dictionary. We must turn to *Paradise Lost* and the poet's other works for a defining context. Though Milton in his epic "must needs adhere" to Genesis, his poem expands vastly on the spare biblical story. In the tradition of the exegetes (whose works he knew well), and by virtue of his own Protestant faith in responsible individual interpretation of the Scriptures, he explicates according to his own best lights the meaning of the events he takes as a framework for his poem.[9]

In *Paradise Lost* Milton does not alter the central fact of the Genesis version of the Fall: Adam and Eve fall from innocence by eating the fruit of "the Tree of the Knowledge of Good and Evil." In Genesis this act of disobedience to the explicit will of God *is* "simply to be accepted as having happened." We do not learn enough about Adam and Eve in the few verses between their creation and fall to understand any motivation or discover any cause for the act in antecedent circumstances. The eating of the fruit accounts for the entry of evil into the world of mankind and is the cause of all his subsequent miseries, but unless one accepts aetiological arguments which make the result into a cause, the Fall is essentially causeless. The narrative in Genesis is history, not poetry, according to Aristotle's distinction in the *Poetics* between an account of "what has happened" and "the sort of thing which might happen, the possible according to probability or necessity."[10] In Milton's poem, on the other hand, from Book IV to the middle of Book IX we are with the unfallen Adam and Eve in the Garden. They converse with each other and with their angelic visitor, Raphael. Together they hear Raphael's account of war in heaven and Adam learns of creation; their actions are described to us, and the narrator reflects on their state. In Book III, before they actually appear in the poem, God expounds their nature and previews for the Son (and the reader) the foreknown course of their life. By the time they actually eat the fruit we are quite fully acquainted with their nature and their situation. We are thus informed of the anteced-ent circumstances which must be known if there is to be a chance that the Fall may be seen as the climax of a possible or necessary sequence of events.

Among the circumstances concerning Adam and Eve which are revealed in this expanded narrative is one paradoxical fact of central importance to a proper understanding of innocence and the Fall: long before our first parents in turn taste the fruit, they already possess what we must in some sense call a "knowledge of good and evil."[11] On many occasions before the Fall they both hear and use the words *good* and *evil*, first heard when God announced to Adam the con-dition of life in the garden. They do not, as they did when Adam spoke of "death," wonder what the words might mean. Even before Raphael descends to warn them and educate them further in the history and ways of evil and the power of good, Adam shows not only that he knows what evil is, but also that he is aware of some of its ways and its current relation to Eve and him. Without such knowledge he could scarcely have responded as he does to Eve's satanically inspired dream, misliking it because "of evil sprung," wondering "yet evil whence," and assuring Eve that "Evil into the mind of God or Man / May come and go, so unapprov'd, and leave / No spot or blame behind" (V, 117–19). Calmed and comforted by Adam's words, Eve joins him in a morning hymn asking the continuance of good and the avoidance of evil:

> Hail Universal Lord, be bounteous still
> To give us only good: and if the night
> Have gathered aught of evil, or conceal'd,
> Disperse it, as now light dispels the dark.   (V, 205–08)

A knowledge of good and evil is surely demonstrated by speeches such as these; yet, at the conclusion of the hymn, the narrator notes that they "pray'd innocent" (V, 209).

Raphael, sent by God to warn Adam and Eve of Satan's plot

(though not of all its details), in his two discourses—on the War in Heaven and the Creation—provides further lessons in the unfallen knowledge of good and evil.[12] The story of Satan's revolt tells of the origin of evil as Michael addresses the Apostate as "Author of Evil, unknown till thy revolt" (VI, 262), and the deeds and fate of Satan are concrete examples of what evil is, of anger, pain, hypocrisy, and alienation from God. Evil is known, through Raphael's narrative, in the person of Satan and his followers, and Adam and Eve thereby know *of* evil (though it is not until their Fall that they know evil in the same sense as Satan does). The tale of the Creation has as its keynote the bountiful goodness of God, "whose wisdom had ordained / Good out of evil to create," and his works (VII, 187–88). In the eager strains of their hymns of praise Adam and Eve demonstrate their immediate and unforced perception of this goodness (IV, 720–35; V, 153–209). The contrast between the pain and disorder of revolt in Heaven and the blissful variety and marvelous order of the new creation puts the difference between good and evil in terms unmistakable even to one who has never himself felt the effects of that difference.

Unless one is willing to deny that knowledge may be acquired by a combination of direct admonition and concrete narrative example such as that which Raphael provides, and unless one refuses to accept as evidence of understanding the correct use of the words *good* and *evil* by Adam and Eve in their own speeches, it must be admitted that they already possess a "knowledge of good and evil" before they violate the tree which bears that name. Informed and sophisticated rather than naive or childlike, their innocence consists not of no acquaintance with evil but of no taint by it, of sinlessness rather than ignorance of sin.

A "knowledge of evil" and an awareness of the possibility of corruption are clearly not inconsistent with innocence as Milton conceives it: what then is to be understood by "the Tree of the Knowledge of Good and Evil"? If Adam and Eve already know evil, what sort of knowledge, if any, do they acquire as a result of violating God's prohibition regarding the tree? Milton preserves the name of the tree as it is given in Genesis, but in attempting to understand what the tree and the action around it signify in Milton's thought and in his epic, we face a situation rather like that with regard to his muse,

Urania: we should look to "the meaning, not the name." The "event"—
that is, the result for Adam and Eve of eating the fruit—reveals a
meaning which appears to be in conflict with the simple name.

In Book XI of *Paradise Lost*, announcing his decree that Adam
and Eve should be driven out of Paradise, God begins by describing
the effects of the forbidden fruit:

> O Sons, Like one of us Man is become
> To know both Good and Evil, since his taste
> Of that defended Fruit; but let him boast
> His knowledge of Good lost, and Evil got,
> Happier, had it sufficed him to have known
> Good by itself, and Evil not at all.   (XI, 84–89)

Adam, reviling Eve in Book IX after the fires of their first fallen lust
have been quenched, describes the effect of the tree in similar terms:

> our Eyes
> Op'n'd we find indeed, and find we know
> Both Good and Evil, Good lost and Evil got,
> Bad fruit of Knowledge, if this be to know,
> Which leaves us naked thus.   (IX, 1070–74)

In *Areopagitica* and *The Christian Doctrine* Milton emphasizes that
as a result of the Fall good is no longer known by itself but only in
contrast or opposition to evil:

It was from out the rind of one apple tasted that the knowledge of good and
evil, as two twins cleaving together leaped forth into the world. And perhaps this is the doom which Adam fell into of knowing good and evil,
that is to say, of knowing good by evil.[13]

It was called the tree of the knowledge of good and evil from the event;
for since Adam tasted it, we not only know evil, but we know good only
by means of evil.[14]

All of these assertions about the tree and its effects make it difficult
to take as the meaning of the tree the plain sense which its name seems
to invite. Milton, furthermore, denies explicitly that there is anything
magical or even sacramental about the tree or its fruit: "The tree of
the knowledge of good and evil was not a sacrament; for a sacrament
is a thing to be used, not abstained from: but a pledge, as it were,
and memorial of obedience."[15] Only Satan in *Paradise Lost* promises
a magical transformation, that the tree will give "Life / To knowledge"

(IX, 686–87). When Adam and Eve eat the fruit, however, their intellectual powers are diminished, not heightened; their reason becomes "reasoning" as they spend the "fruitless hours" debating the blame for their change and mooting between themselves alternatives as futile as those we remember from the debate in Hell (IX, 1067–1189; X, 719–1006). Their love turns to lust, their honor to shame, and their innocence to guilt. Disobedience of God's express command, not any power intrinsic in the fruit, wreaks these changes.

That the Fall does not consist of an access of knowledge, as we usually conceive of it, but of a shift in the mode of man's knowledge of good and evil is shown by these changes. In the state of innocence, Adam and Eve live a total *experience* of good; their knowledge of evil, on the other hand, is conceptual. They know the word *evil*, what it has meant when the state so named has been actualized elsewhere, and what act could cause it to be actualized in their own existence. But so long as they remain faithful to God's command, evil remains only a potentiality in their lives: good alone is known as actual and innocence is preserved. When Adam and Eve fall, however, this actual-potential polarity is destroyed. By their disobedience evil is actualized as a part of their direct personal experience. The state of bliss in Paradise, a unique totality of good, is irrecoverably lost, so far as their unaided human capacity to recover it is concerned. Adam and Eve no longer may "know" evil in the guiltless way they did before the Fall. Their doom is not so severe as that of Satan and his rebellious cohorts for whom evil is not only the sole actual state but also their sole potentiality throughout eternity; good, by the grace of God, remains a potentiality for man, yet the actuality of evil predominates so much that good is known only by evil and in the midst of evil.

The mixed state of good and evil which man is to endure is defined concretely by Michael in the vision and narrative through which he prepares Adam for his entry with Eve into the post-Edenic world. The structure of his revelations contrasts markedly with that of the instruction offered Adam by Raphael before the Fall.[16] In Raphael's accounts the exemplification of evil in Satan's rebellion and the glorification of good in the Creation each had its separate place and was not mixed with the other (though the reader may note allusions to or foreshadowings of opposing things to come in each). One account supplies Adam with the conceptual knowledge of evil he needs to avoid falling into the experience of it; the other deepens his understanding of the experience he now enjoys. In Michael's account of man's future, on the other hand, in both vision and narrative good and evil are "as two twins cleaving together." The stories of the few "just men" are intermixed with the proliferating tales of disease, war, and tyranny, and Adam, as the responsive human audience, has great difficulty in sorting the good from the evil. He rejoices erroneously as the "sons of God" enjoy themselves with music, women, and feasting, and despairs prematurely when Christ is persecuted. The effects of the Fall are seen both in the events themselves and in Adam's inability to evaluate them clearly without Michael's guidance. For man the evil which was once a potentiality, localized, as in Raphael's narrative, in Satan and his followers, has now become the actuality described by Michael. The good that flowed through unfallen creation as a totality has become a more distant potentiality, preserved as possible through the promise of redemption in Christ and exemplified in those few "just men" who are his "shadowy types," but no longer that joyful actuality hymned by Raphael.

Michael's account of the future of man, as well as the painful and degrading immediate effects of the Fall on Adam and Eve, defines the "knowledge" acquired in the Fall as experiential knowledge of an actuality, rather than any intellectual enlightenment or increase in moral acuteness. In the face of the evidence that Adam and Eve knew evil before they fell, God's assertion that while unfallen they knew "good by itself, and Evil not at all" makes sense only if this interpretation is accepted. "Knowledge" in this sense is also the only sort which when acquired could lead to a diminution of man's freedom as a moral being. Having sinned, it is no longer possible for Adam and Eve to choose to remain sinless. They go not from ignorance to enlightenment or from naiveté to mature liberty, but from innocence to guilt. In the act of eating the fruit that evil which might otherwise "into the mind of God, or Man / . . . come and go" is "approv'd" in action and leaves, therefore, an indelible "spot or blame." The "meaning" of "knowledge" in the Genesis formula "the Tree of the Knowledge of Good and Evil" as Milton sees it in *Paradise Lost* is clearly closer to "being" or "becoming" than to what we would ordinarily call "knowing."

Such a definition of *knowledge* in this context, moreover, is not simply a result of Milton's idiosyncratic interpretation of Genesis: in connection with the prohibited tree "knowledge" retains some of the sense familiar to us in the biblical usage "carnal knowledge" (in this connection the number of metaphors of sexual violation surrounding the Fall in *Paradise Lost* should be noted). Other interpreters of Genesis have also found that "knowledge" in that context requires special treatment. O. A. Piper in *The Interpreter's Dictionary of the Bible*, under *Knowledge*, writes as follows:

> For the Hebrews "to know" does not simply mean to be aware of the existence or nature of a particular object. Knowledge implies also the awareness of the specific relationship in which the individual stands with the object, or of the significance the object has for him.
>
> The "tree of the knowledge of good and evil" (Gen. 2:17) is not to provide scientific or theosophic knowledge, or a purely theoretical knowledge of moral values. Rather, as the forbidden tree it will disclose the difference between good and evil to the first couple through their very act of eating the fruit. It is through trespassing God's prohibition that one will "know" what the wrong is like—viz. a *quality of one's own self in action*.[17] (italics mine)

Knowledge is no less complex a word in English than in Hebrew: the English word combines in itself two historical senses, that of knowing through sensuous perception (OE *kan*) and of knowing by the mind (Lat. *scire*). According to the *OED*, until 1896 a strong sense of the word was current, signifying "to have personal experience of (something) as affecting oneself, to have experienced, met with, felt or undergone." When "naming" the tree, as we have seen, Milton puts it in a context which focuses its meaning on this strong sense of "knowledge by experience" inherent in the Hebrew name and still current for him in the English.

This reading of "knowledge" as the "event" for which the tree is named also provides a clue to the understanding of God's ironic pronouncement that when Adam falls he "Like one of us . . . is become / To know both Good and Evil" (XI, 84–85). Adam, of course, has not become godlike by eating the fruit; the act lowers, rather than raises, him in the hierarchy of being. Yet, if the knowledge he acquires is the same as that possessed by the gods, must they not also be fallen? That the gods do in fact know good and evil is no less based on experienced actuality than that knowledge is among fallen men; evil, as is apparent in Michael's address to Satan quoted earlier, was "unknown" in Heaven before the revolt. But, though the faithful angels have seen evil actualized and have even suffered some of its effects during the War in Heaven, they themselves have not disobeyed God. Evil could be actualized in Heaven and yet leave the majority of angels untainted by it. On earth, however, Adam and Eve, because they were the only beings enjoying reason and free will, were the only beings capable of actualizing evil. Once Adam joins Eve in eating the fruit the possibility no longer exists that any portion of mankind could know evil as actual without sharing through their descent the guilt for having actualized it.

We must also remember that "actuality" in Heaven and the experience of it are modified by the perspective of eternity and divine omniscience. In this respect the difference between man and the heavenly beings is like that pointed out by Raphael between the intuitive reason of the angels and man's discursive reason (V, 486–90); man's experience, as well as his reasoning, is a temporal process—one experience, one actuality, succeeds another in the passage of time. In the temporal universe the potentiality for evil which is implicit in the possession of free will becomes actualized through man's choice. Through God's grace and Christ's redemptive act the potential for good is restored, but the actualization of that new bliss will not occur until the centuries pass to the end of time. Man endures the actuality of evil in his temporal existence and can only seek comfort in the potentiality for ultimate good revealed in the eschatological promises of Scripture and typified by Christ. From God's "prospect high / In which past, present, future he beholds," this progression is reduced to a single moment; from that perspective, evil in its very moment of actualization has already been turned to good. In Heaven, then, the "knowledge of good and evil" is constantly and instantaneously resolved to good alone. Through revelation and by reason and faith, man may perceive and believe in the time when and the way in which this resolution will also take place for him, and thus achieve a "paradise within," but unlike the heavenly beings he must live outwardly and die in the actuality of his moment in time. Because he himself has actualized evil in the world, his experience cannot be of good *or* evil, but is of good *and* evil, or as Michael puts it, of "supernal Grace contending / With sinfulness of Men" (XI, 359–60). Both gods

and men "know" evil because it has been actualized in their experience, but only for the unfallen gods is the contention between
good and evil ended in its beginning and an experience made possible
in which the actuality of evil does not preclude an uncorrupted
eternity of good.

God's ironic statement reflects on the delusion fostered by Satan
that man could know good and evil in the way the gods in Heaven do.
Neither before nor after the Fall is this possible for Adam and Eve,
yet the knowledge of evil they do possess in their innocence is essential
to their status as free and responsible moral beings before the Fall.
"Uncloister'd" by their possession of that knowledge, they are also
dramatically exposed to choice by other aspects of their situation and
character. Though Paradise is a high place, palisaded by groves and
patrolled by God's angels, the author of evil is permitted easy entry;
throughout Books IV to IX we are constantly reminded of his lurking,
leering presence. The physical barriers of groves and guards can lock
out evil no more effectively than censorship, as Milton asserts in
Areopagitica, can remove "the matter of sin."[18] Adam and Eve not
only know evil and face an occasion for choice in God's command
regarding the tree, but are also further involved in a necessity for
action by the presence of a protagonist for the wrong choice.

The active moral status of the unfallen Adam and Eve is confirmed by the "passions within" with which they were created. In
Paradise Lost the difference between the state of innocence and the
life of fallen man is not one between passionless and passionate
existence, but between passions "rightly tempered" and "high
passions," between "sensual appetite" legitimately satisfied and that
"sensual Appetite, who from beneath / Usurping over sovran Reason
claim'd / Superior sway" (IX, 1129–31). Milton goes to lengths unprecedented in hexaemeral literature to make clear his belief that
Adam and Eve were created with a full complement of human appetites. He turns his back on all interpretations of Genesis which hurry
Adam and Eve out of the Garden before they have a chance to
consummate their match, or which attribute to the Fall the existence
of human sexuality. Adam and Eve hunger and thirst, eat and drink;
Eve takes pains to make their diet not merely nutritious but pleasing
as well, "Taste after taste upheld with kindliest change" (V, 336).
Both of them feel the attraction of physical beauty in each other and

the Garden around them. Among the passions they possess must be reckoned those of the mind as well as the senses. They are eager for knowledge of themselves and the creation which they rule; they even show signs of incipient egotism.[19] None of these passions, however, is of itself incompatible with innocence: "rightly tempered," that is, exercised according to the dictates of reason and not "sovran" over it, the passions are the "very ingredients" of that virtue which defines innocence. When Eve turns from her own reflection to acknowledge the superior attractions of Adam's "manly grace / And Wisdom," she has chosen to direct her passion toward the greater good recognized by reason rather than remain entranced by the real but lesser good which is her own soft beauty (IV, 477–91). Though her passions are momentarily distempered by the dream which Satan insinuates into her fancy, she rejects those promptings and accepts Adam's reasonable counsel. If, when she remains adamant in her decision to labor away from Adam for a morning, she does choose a lesser good over a greater, it is to be known as such only by the outcome (which was not necessitated by her choice to leave), and she departs forewarned by Adam's last "reasoning words" (IX, 379). Adam passes the first test of his rational freedom when he petitions God for a fit mate to match his stature as a reasonable being instead of seeking mere sensual gratification with a lower creature. Raphael's counsel persuades him to refrain from speculation on "matters hid," and convinces him that "to know / That which before us lies in daily life / Is the prime Wisdom" (VIII, 192–94). When Adam lets Eve go on the fatal morning, he neither forces her obedience nor yields his reason to her beauty:

> Go: for thy stay, not free, absents thee more;
> Go in thy native innocence, rely
> On what thou hast of virtue, summon all,
> For God towards thee hath done his part, do thine. (IX, 372–75)

Innocence here is clearly no bar to morality but its support, and Adam's acquiescence in this instance is very different from that at the Fall, when he is "fondly overcome with femal charm" (IX, 999). Each of the passions felt by Adam and Eve is indeed involved in their fall— Satan and then the fallen Eve appeal not only to the sensual appetites of hunger and sex, but also to the mental "appetites" of curiosity and selfish egotism—but until the fruit is actually tasted these same passions, held in proper bounds, are the sources not of woe but of bliss.

Adam and Eve make a number of choices before the Fall; what distinguishes the decision which is the Fall is not that it is the first time they had a choice to make, but that it is the first time that they allowed passion to take the sway from reason in directing the will. That their passions do appear and that Adam and Eve recognize the difference between good and evil objects of passion are evidence that their freedom of the will is a genuine freedom. The strength of their passions also makes their choice not to be ruled by them a positive exercise of moral virtue. True freedom of the will could not exist or be demonstrated in the absence of that "liability to fall" with which Adam and Eve were created, but it is equally as manifest in a refusal to succumb to temptation as in acquiescence to Satan's blandishments.[20] The series of choices Adam and Eve make before the Fall in fact shows a series of victories over what Albert W. Fields calls "the darker side of self."[21] Had they not been created with a "darker side" as well as a self like God, they could not have been truly free. When they eat the fruit they pass not from a cloistered and immutable perfection to undeserved corruption, though corruption of their moral being is one of the results of the Fall, but from a free and joyous innocence to the straitened misery of guilt.[22]

To insist then, as many have, that man becomes faced with moral questions only when he is fallen, and thus lives an interesting and dramatic life only then, is to misunderstand not only the conception of innocence in *Paradise Lost*, but also the ideal of virtuous freedom and morality so eloquently set forth in *Areopagitica*. Defending the liberty of printing and reading, Milton never asserts that true moral choice requires the actual personal experience of evil: indeed, the opposite is the case. Through uncensored reading one may escape the confines of "cloister'd virtue" and "know the utmost which vice promises to her followers"; yet, because this knowledge is acquired without the necessity of actually partaking of vice, the reader may, like the unfallen gods, remain untainted, though not untested. The ideal is "to see and know and yet abstain."[23] In *Paradise Lost* the account of Satan's rebellion is in many respects the equivalent for Adam and Eve of a book which shows what "vice promises"; Eve's dream provides an even more striking example of a knowledge of vice acquired without corruption by it. The unfallen Adam and Eve, in fact, are held up in *Areopagitica* as a model of morality for fallen man. Though the treatise is directed to man "in the field of this world," in arguing the futility of laws which seek to shelter man from the matter of or occasion for sin, Milton describes Adam in terms which rule out any notion of naive or cloistered innocence; any such notion would, of course, make Adam's example irrelevant for fallen man:

Many there be that complain of divine providence for suffering Adam to transgress, foolish tongues! when God gave him reason, he gave him freedom to choose, for reason is but choosing; he had been else a mere artificial Adam, such an Adam as he is in the motions. We ourselves esteem not of that obedience, or love, or gift, which is of force: God therefore left him free, set before him a provoking object, ever almost in his eyes; herein consisted his merit, herein the right of his reward, the praise of his abstinence. Wherefore did he create passions within us, pleasures round about us, but that these rightly tempered are the very ingredients of virtue?[24]

In *Paradise Lost*, as we have seen, Adam and Eve before the Fall are no more like "Adam as he is in the motions" than is the Adam described in *Areopagitica*.

Far from describing what Milton's Adam and Eve should be but are not in the state of innocence, Willey's definition of the exercise of reason as "the choice of good by a free agent cognisant of evil" fits precisely the behavior of unfallen man in the epic. This aspect of man's primal nature is summarized by God in Book III in lines which echo Milton's description of Adam in *Areopagitica*:

> I made him just and right,
> Sufficient to have stood, though free to fall.
> Such I created all th'ethereal Powers
> And Spirits, both them who stood and them who fail'd:
> Freely they stood who stood, and fell who fell.
> Not free, what proof could they have giv'n sincere
> Of true allegiance, constant Faith or Love,
> Where only what they needs must do, appear'd,
> Not what they would? what praise could they receive?
> What pleasure I from such obedience paid,
> When Will and Reason (Reason also is choice)
> Useless and vain, of freedom both despoil'd,
> Made passive both, had serv'd necessity,
> Not mee. (98–111)

In addition, Raphael, just before the Fall, admonishes Adam that "to stand or fall / Free in thine own arbitrement it lies" (VIII, 640–41). Adam earlier admits to Raphael that he knows himself "to be both will and deed created free" (V, 549), and belief in the responsible freedom to choose their own fate underlies Adam's arguments to dissuade Eve from separate work in the garden, and is finally the reason why he lets her go. In their freedom Adam and Eve constantly face the possibility of sin. This freedom, with the "passions within" and the "provoking object" without making it a truly moral state, is seen by Milton as the glory of man's creation, and with the gift of reason, as the fundamental source of man's preeminent dignity among the creatures of the earth.

Milton's conception of life before the Fall, as I have attempted to outline it here, not only is satisfying as it endues Adam and Eve with a real freedom which is nonetheless consistent with innocence, but also as it makes possible a narrative rendering of the Fall which is coherent, credible, and dramatic. The change from innocence to corruption is no less sudden than it is in Genesis, no less a cataclysmic moment in history, but it is, as it is not in Genesis, the culmination of a clearly motivated and fully probable dramatic action. When Adam and Eve fall in *Paradise Lost* we need not merely "accept it as having happened": the history of Genesis is transmuted into the plot of *Paradise Lost*. In developing this plot Milton does not resort to "faking" or to delineating an Adam and Eve corrupt before the Fall; in the state of innocence they do not possess "some of the failings of the fallen."[25] They never actualize those failings, though they plentifully demonstrate a potential to do so. As the moment of the Fall draws closer through Books IV to IX of the epic, we as readers, through the hindsight of history, directed by the epic flashbacks in the poem's complex chronology, become increasingly aware that possibility is shading into probability, that potential is about to become actualized, but until the fruit is eaten, probability involves no necessity. The historical fact of the Fall, known by the reader and foreknown by God from his "prospect high" is what makes the Fall seem inevitable to us. This sense of the historical inevitability of the disobedience of Adam and Eve should not be confused with the possibilities and probabilities which operate in the narrative itself. Milton regularly reminds us that right up to the actual eating of the fruit Adam and Eve are "yet sinless." In the formula "sufficient to have stood, though free to fall," he sums up the potentialities with which man was created. Time and time again before the Fall Adam and Eve manifest the potentialities which prove them truly "free to fall"; yet, as H. V. S. Ogden has noted, were it not for the fact that they did fall, one would take such incidents as Eve's dream or Adam's rebuke by Raphael for uxorious tendencies as contributions to their sufficiency rather than portents of their fall.[26]

To understand the crucial relation between potential and actuality in the life of Adam and Eve, one must read *Paradise Lost* simultaneously from both eternal and temporal perspectives. The chronology of the narrative itself and the achronological structure viewed by God and the narrator must both be given full attention.[27] To focus only on the certainties foreknown by God is to ignore the genuine moral freedom enjoyed by Adam and Eve before they fall; to focus only on the human drama of Adam and Eve is to ignore the context which gives meaning to that drama. From the moment of their creation Adam and Eve are not puppets, nor, conversely, are they ever isolated individual egos adrift in an existential void. Both before and after the Fall they are thinking, knowing, feeling beings, endued with free will and faced by crucial choices in a world which has value and meaning. Milton in *Paradise Lost* is true both to his art and to his humanist ethos. The Fall of Adam and Eve is as truly dramatic and genuinely moral an action as that involving a "wayfaring [warfaring] Christian" in the fallen world or any hero of secular epic or tragedy.

Swarthmore College

NOTES

1. *Areopagitica,* in *John Milton: Complete Poems and Major Prose,* ed. Merritt Y. Hughes (New York, 1957), p. 733; *Paradise Lost* III, 108 "(Reason also is choice)." All references to *Areopagitica* and *Paradise Lost* are to Hughes' edition; further citations of *Paradise Lost* are in the text by book and line.

2. Millicent Bell, "The Fallacy of the Fall in *Paradise Lost,*" *PMLA,* LXVIII (1953), 863. Miss Bell's essay gave rise to several responses: see Wayne Shumaker's reply in *PMLA,* LXX (1955), 1185 ff., and also H. V. S. Ogden, "The Crisis of *Paradise Lost* Reconsidered," *PQ,* XXXVI (1957), 1–19. For an argument with some similarities to mine, see Joseph H. Summers, *The Muse's Method* (London, 1962), pp. 149–50.

3. Bell, "The Fallacy of the Fall," p. 864.

4. E. M. W. Tillyard, "The Crisis of *Paradise Lost*," in his *Studies in Milton* (London, 1951), p. 11.

5. A. J. A. Waldock, *"Paradise Lost" and Its Critics* (Cambridge, Eng., 1947), pp. 18–24, 42, and passim: "What, after all, has Milton—the Milton of the great famous sayings in the prose works, the Milton who could not praise a fugitive and cloistered virtue unexercised and unbreathed—to do with the effortless innocence, the 'blank' virtue of prelapsarian man?" (p. 22). For a more strident extrapolation of the argument, see William Empson, *Milton's God*, rev. ed. (London, 1965).

6. To suggest the dual aspects of pilgrimage and struggle in Milton's idea of the Christian life one is tempted to conflate into one reading the "wayfaring" of the first edition of *Areopagitica* and the "warfaring" of subsequent editions.

7. *The Seventeenth Century Background* (1934; reprint, New York, 1955), p. 244. Cf. Samuel Johnson, "Milton," in *Lives of the English Poets*.

8. Watson Kirkconnell, ed. and trans., *The Celestial Cycle*, "The Caedmonian *Genesis*" (Toronto, 1952), p. 24.

9. See Arnold Williams, *The Common Expositor* (Chapel Hill, 1948), C. A. Patrides, *Milton and the Christian Tradition* (Oxford, 1966), and J. M. Evans, *"Paradise Lost" and the Genesis Tradition* (Oxford, 1968). Evans notes thoroughly the debt Milton owed to earlier interpretations of Genesis, but he also concludes that Milton "revolutionized the traditional view of Eden and pre-lapsarian Man" (p. 269).

10. *Poetics*, IX, 1451a.

11. Evans notes that a number of writers, including Philo Judaeus, loath to conceive of man created without moral prudence, assert that he possessed knowledge of good and evil before the Fall. These writers, however, then either posit some scientific rather than ethical knowledge as the fruit of the tree, or place the Fall elsewhere (p. 72).

12. For an extended analysis of these discourses as "tutorial narrative," see Jon S. Lawry, *The Shadow of Heaven* (Ithaca, 1968), pp. 183 ff.

13. Hughes, *John Milton*, p. 728.

14. *The Christian Doctrine*, ch. X, in *The Student's Milton*, rev. ed., ed. F. A. Patterson (New York, 1957), p. 986.

15. Ibid. Dennis H. Burden, in *The Logical Epic* (Cambridge, Mass., 1967), pp. 97–123, argues that the forbidden knowledge is of astronomy. Were this so, however, God (and Milton) could be justly accused by Satan of a capricious prohibition.

16. Lawry notes the parallel between Michael's mission and Raphael's which I develop here: "These books (V–VIII) concentrate the effort to define for man the essence of Paradise under the aegis of choice, balancing the post-lapsarian definition of man and the world in Books XI–XII" (*Shadow of Heaven*, p. 183).

17. G. A. Buttrick, ed. (New York, 1962). Among the patristic and scholastic interpretations of the tree collected by Evans, two are of special relevance here: St. Augustine, *De Gen. Con. Man.* II. ix–xi, "the sin of the heart will bring its own punishment, for by *experience* it will learn the difference between the good it has forsaken and the evil into which it has fallen. And this will be to that soul the tasting of the fruit of the tree of the discernment of good and evil" (quoted in Evans, *"Paradise Lost" and the Genesis Tradition*, p. 75); Peter Comestor, *Hist. Schol., Lib. Gen.* xiii, "the tree of knowledge was named from

the event which followed the tasting of it. Before that man did not know what was evil, as he had not *experienced* it" (quoted in ibid., p. 170, all italics mine).

18. Hughes, *John Milton*, p. 733.

19. Eve's momentary narcissism at her first awakening, her dream when the guard of reason is down, the sexuality of her relations with Adam, and her desire to prove herself in solitary labor among the groves of Paradise, are all evidence of "passions within" and a lively sense of pleasures "round about." Adam's request for a proper mate, his curiosity about the heavens, and his tendency toward passionate overvaluation of Eve all attest to the presence within him of desires which could possibly catch the sway of his will from reason.

20. Milton's assertion that Adam and Eve were created with a "liability to fall" is found in *The Christian Doctrine*, ch. XI, in *The Student's Milton*, ed. F. A. Patterson, p. 997.

21. Albert W. Fields, "Milton and Self-knowledge," *PMLA*, LXXXIII (1968), p. 394.

22. Though I find Evans' argument in most respects compatible with mine, if different in emphasis, I cannot agree that "the difference between unfallen and fallen Man is simply the difference between a well and a badly tended Garden. It is a difference of degree, not of kind. That is why Paradise can be regained" (*"Paradise Lost" and the Genesis Tradition*, p. 271). This view ignores the guilt which must be atoned for if a Paradise both external and internal is to be restored. No matter how well a man may tend his spiritual and moral garden and with faith achieve a "paradise within," mankind must still live in the midst of "all our woe" until primal bliss is returned in "new Heaven and new earth" at the end of time.

23. Hughes, *John Milton*, p. 729.

24. Ibid., p. 733. Burden, *The Logical Epic*, pp. 125 ff., argues that Milton in the epic could not logically allow the tree to be provocative. I argue that it must be so if the logic of Adam and Eve's freedom is to hold.

25. Tillyard, "The Crisis of *Paradise Lost*," p. 10, accuses Milton of resorting to "some faking, perfectly legitimate in a poem, yet faking nevertheless," in order to make his narrative work.

26. Ogden, "The Crisis of *Paradise Lost* Reconsidered," p. 3: "The subsequent event determines our perspective, . . . experience could have strengthened innocence and confirmed rectitude as readily as in the event it destroyed them."

27. Lawry, in suggesting the proper "stance" for a reader of *Paradise Lost*, states neatly one-half of the dual focus I see as necessary: "Much of our difficulty with *Paradise Lost* arises from our failure to view lateral human history from this ultimately eternal stance. We usually isolate only one or another segment of time and event and rest all of our sense of God's meaning within it. We should instead utilize the stance of Book III in order that we place any particular segment within the perspective of Heaven, which is also that of epic" (*Shadow of Heaven*, p. 155). I suggest that the "perspective of Heaven" is one of the perspectives from which the poem should be read, but that the epic makes "lateral human history" equally important. The paradoxical relation of time to eternity, of man's perceptions to God's, is central to both the art and the theology of the poem.

Copyright Acknowledgments

Gordon Campbell, "The Mortalist Heresy in *Paradise Lost*" *Milton Quarterly* 13 (1979): 33–36. Copyright © Roy C. Flannagan and the Johns Hopkins University Press. Reprinted by permission of the Johns Hopkins University Press.

Millicent Bell, "The Fallacy of the Fall in *Paradise Lost*" *Publications of the Modern Language Association* 68 (1953) 863–883. Reprinted with the permission of the Modern Language Association.

Virginia R. Mollenkott, "Milton's Rejection of the Fortunate Fall" *Milton Quarterly* 6 (1972) 1–5. Copyright © Roy C. Flannagan and the Johns Hopkins University Press. Reprinted by permission of the Johns Hopkins University Press.

Paul Stevens, "*Paradise Lost* and the Colonial Imperative" *Milton Studies* 34 (1996) 3–21. From MILTON STUDIES XXXIV, Albert C. Labriola and Michael Lieb, Guest Editors. Copyright © 1996 by University of Pittsburgh Press. Reprinted by permission of the publisher.

Barbara Kiefer Lewalski, "*Paradise Lost* and Milton's Politics" *Milton Studies* 38 (2000) 141–168. From MILTON STUDIES XXXVIII, Albert C. Labriola and Michael Lieb, Guest Editors. Copyright © 2000 by University of Pittsburgh Press. Reprinted by permission of the publisher.

Christine Froula, "When Eve Reads Milton: Undoing the Canonical Economy" *Critical Inquiry* 10 (1983) 321–347. Reprinted with the permission of the University of Chicago Press, publisher.

William Shullenberger, "Wrestling with the Angel: Paradise Lost and Feminist Criticism" *Milton Quarterly* 20 (1986): 69–85. Copyright © Roy C. Flannagan and the Johns Hopkins University Press. Reprinted by permission of the Johns Hopkins University Press.

Balachandra Rajan, "The Problem of Satan" in *Paradise Lost and the Seventeenth Century Reader*, Chatto, 1962, 93–107. Reprinted with the permission of Chatto and Windus.

William G. Riggs, "The Poet and Satan in *Paradise Lost*" *Milton Studies* 2 (1970) 59–82. From MILTON STUDIES II, Albert C. Labriola and Michael Lieb, Guest Editors. Copyright © 1970 by University of Pittsburgh Press. Reprinted by permission of the publisher.

Stephen M. Fallon, "Milton's Sin and Death: the Ontology of Allegory in *Paradise Lost*" *English Language Research* 17 (1987) 329–350. Reprinted with the permission of University of Birmingham.

Gary D. Hamilton, "Milton's Defensive God: a Reappraisal" *Studies in Philology* 69 (1972): 87–100. Copyright © 1972 by the University of North Carolina Press. Used by permission of the publisher.

Thomas Blackburn, "Uncloister'd Virtue: Adam and Eve in Milton's Paradise" *Milton Studies* 11 (1971) 119–137. From MILTON STUDIES XI, Albert C. Labriola and Michael Lieb, Guest Editors. Copyright © 1971 by University of Pittsburgh Press. Reprinted by permission of the publisher.

www.ingramcontent.com/pod-product-compliance
Ingram Content Group UK Ltd.
Pitfield, Milton Keynes, MK11 3LW, UK
UKHW020856280225
455677UK00006B/64